The expatriate American experimentalist composer Conlon Nancarrow is increasingly recognised as having one of the most innovative musical minds of this century. His music, almost all written for player piano, is the most rhythmically complex ever written, couched in intricate contrapuntal systems using up to twelve different tempos at the same time. Yet despite its complexity, Nancarrow's music drew its early influences from the jazz pianism of Art Tatum and Earl Hines and from the rhythms of Indian music; Nancarrow's whirlwinds of notes are joyously physical in their energy. Composed in almost complete isolation from 1940 on, this music has achieved international fame only in the last few years. Born in 1912, the son of the mayor of Texarkana, Nancarrow fought in the Lincoln Brigade, then fled America to Mexico City to avoid being hounded for his former Communist affiliations. The author travelled to Mexico City to research Nancarrow's music and to discuss it with him. He analyses sixty-five works, virtually the composer's complete output, and includes a biographical chapter containing much information never before published.

Music in the Twentieth Century
GENERAL EDITOR Arnold Whittall

This series offers a wide perspective on music and musical life in the twentieth century.

Books included will range from historical and biographical studies concentrating particularly on the context and circumstances in which composers were writing, to analytical and critical studies concerned with the nature of musical language and questions of compositional process. The importance given to context will also be reflected in studies dealing with, for example, the patronage, publishing, and promotion of new music, and in accounts of the musical life of particular countries.

PUBLISHED TITLES

Robert Orledge *Satie the composer*
Kathryn Bailey *The twelve-note music of Anton Webern*
Silvina Milstein *Arnold Schoenberg: notes, sets, forms*
Christopher Hailey *Franz Schreker, 1878–1934: a cultural biography*
James Pritchett *The music of John Cage*
Joseph N. Straus *The music of Ruth Crawford Seeger*

Music in the Twentieth Century

GENERAL EDITOR ARNOLD WHITTALL

The music of Conlon Nancarrow

Conlon Nancarrow (photo: Philip Makanna; courtesy of Eva Soltes Associates)

The music of
Conlon Nancarrow

KYLE GANN

CAMBRIDGE
UNIVERSITY PRESS

CAMBRIDGE UNIVERSITY PRESS
Cambridge, New York, Melbourne, Madrid, Cape Town, Singapore, São Paulo

Cambridge University Press
The Edinburgh Building, Cambridge CB2 2RU, UK

Published in the United States of America by Cambridge University Press, New York

www.cambridge.org
Information on this title: www.cambridge.org/9780521465342

First published 1995
This digitally printed first paperback version 2006

A catalogue record for this publication is available from the British Library

Library of Congress Cataloguing in Publication data
Gann, Kyle.
The music of Conlon Nancarrow / Kyle Gann.
   p.   cm. – (Music in the twentieth century)
Includes discography and bibliographical references.
ISBN 0 521 46534 6 (hardback)
1. Nancarrow, Conlon, 1912– – Criticism and interpretation.
I. Title. II. Series.
MT92.N36636 1995
786.2' 092 – dc20 94–29969 CIP MN

ISBN-13 978-0-521-46534-2 hardback
ISBN-10 0-521-46534-6 hardback

ISBN-13 978-0-521-02807-3 paperback
ISBN-10 0-521-02807-8 paperback

I dedicate this book to my mother, Mary Katherine Harris Gann. When I was thirteen I asked her why there were no great American twentieth-century composers. She replied that there were: Roy Harris and Charles Ives. From that moment, my path was clear.

Contents

Preface

When I began researching this book, I was often called upon to explain to strangers, relatives, and Mexican cab drivers that I was writing about an eccentric Mexico City composer who wrote music for player piano. That's one way to look at Conlon Nancarrow. Another is that his name must be placed next to those of Ockeghem, Josquin, Bach, Haydn, Webern, and Babbitt as composers who redefined in a technical sense what the act of musical composition can be. Yet another is that he can be counted with Ives, Ruggles, Cowell, Cage, Partch, Harrison, Feldman, Oliveros, Ashley, and Young as one of those outrageously original, challenging minds with which the brief history of American music already seems overly blessed.

In the current, still nascent state of Nancarrow scholarship, it seemed urgent to make this book serve primarily as a groundwork for analysis of Nancarrow's music, and only secondarily as an introduction to his work for the general contemporary music lover. Chapters 1 and 2 should prove of general interest, accessible to anyone curious about this composer with the exorbitant underground reputation. The core of the book, the analyses of the Player Piano Studies, will be most helpful to those who have access to either the recordings or the scores. Those who have the scores may want to number the systems, since system length is the only dependable time unit in many of Nancarrow's studies. In the case of works issued on compact disc, notably Wergo's recording of the complete player piano studies, I have indicated timings of musical events according to the second-counter, in hope that a reader without the scores will get an aural sense of the analysis.

My primary aim has been to give, as much as possible, an account of the complete rhythmic skeleton and form of every piece Nancarrow has written. Many of the later player piano studies are too complex to succumb to a general treatise, and it was all I could do to sketch an outline. I have said less than I would have liked about Nancarrow's contrapuntal criteria, his structural use of register, or his pitch usage in general, especially in the later studies. Tempo structure in Nancarrow's music is systematically developed from study to study, and forms the primary interest; pitch manipulation is largely intuitive and ad hoc, and would require more space to examine work by work.

My first thanks must go to Stuart Smith, who got me started on this project and spent tremendous unrecompensed time reading and offering suggestions. I profusely thank H. Wiley Hitchcock for his help, advice, and encouragement in this project as in so many others. Trimpin became my comrade in Nancarrow scholarship, giving me pages and pages of helpful computerized charts over steins of rich German beer. Peter Garland, Sylvia Smith, and Don Gillespie provided me with scores, James Tenney with the unpublished works and some helpful analytical advice. Charles Amirkhanian smoothed my way to a composer reputed to be difficult to approach. Eva Soltes, Helen Zimbler, William Duckworth, and Carlos Sandoval contributed valuable information. Doug Simmons provided expert editing advice. Penny Souster made the book possible. My wife Nancy Cook, who became a "Nancarrow widow" the way some women become football widows, accepted my *idée fixe* with humor and love. Yoko Seguira, Mrs Nancarrow, was a warm, funny, and helpful informant, and a gracious hostess. And Charles Nancarrow, since departed, treated me to a delightful evening of reminiscence.

Most of all I thank Conlon Nancarrow for cooperating in every possible respect, for his hospitality in Mexico City, for becoming a warm friend, for enduring dozens of answerless questions about music he had written decades earlier, for spending years of his life punching piano rolls with no guarantee that anyone would ever care about their contents, and for having the phenomenal imagination to create a body of music the likes of which no other individual could have ever dreamed up.

Musical extracts are reproduced by kind permission of the following:
Smith Publications–Sonic Art Editions for Examples 1.3 (String Quartet No. 3), 1.8 (String Quartet No. 1), 3.1, 3.2, 3.6, 3.7, 3.9–3.12, 10.2, 10.4–10.7; C. F. Peters Corporation for Examples 1.3 (Sonatina), 1.8 (Sonatina), 3.3, 3.4, 10.13; Boosey and Hawkes Music Publishers Ltd for Examples 10.8–10.12; Schott and Co. Ltd (European-American) for Examples 1.2, 1.3 (Studies)–1.8 (Studies), 1.9, 4.4, 4.8, 5.3–5.9, 5.11–5.17, 5.19, 6.2–6.7, 6.9, 6.17, 6.19, 6.21–6.23, 6.27, 6.30, 7.7, 7.10, 7.17, 7,18, 8.1, 8.3–8.10, 8.13–8.15, 8.19, 8.24, 8.25, 8.27, 8.28, 8.30, 8.32, 8.35–8.37, 8.40, 8.43, 8.46, 8.47, 8.49, 8.51, 8.53–8.55, 8.57, 9.3, 9.4, 9.6, 9.7, 9.9, 9.10, 9.12, 9.13, 9.15, 9.17–9.20, 9.22–9.24, 9.27.

1

The music: general considerations

Compared to the musical traditions of Africa, India, and Indonesia, European classical music has always been rhythmically limited. As soon as American composers broke away from Europe following World War I, they made an aggressive attempt to remedy this deficiency. They found themselves thwarted, however, first by the difficulty of notating extreme rhythmic complexity, then by the greater obstacle of getting performers to execute their rhythms accurately. Henry Cowell (1897–1965), an early ethnomusicologist and the twentieth century's first great theorist of rhythm, invented a new rhythmic notation in an aesthetically revolutionary treatise titled *New Musical Resources*, published in 1930 though written some dozen years earlier. He was interested in superimposing rhythms derived from equal divisions of a common beat: for example, dividing a whole note into five, six, and seven equal parts, and playing the different beats all at once. This exercise would effectively layer three tempos simultaneously, in ratios of 5:6:7. Addressing the problem of execution, he wrote,

> An argument against the development of more diversified rhythms might be their difficulty of performance . . . Some of the rhythms developed through the present acoustical investigation could not be played by any living performer; but these highly engrossing rhythmical complexes could easily be cut on a player-piano roll. This would give a real reason for writing music specially for player-piano, such as music written for it at present does not seem to have.[1]

Later, in a record review, he repeated his suggestion even more forcefully:

> To hear a harmony of several different rhythms played together is fascinating, and gives a curious esthetic pleasure unobtainable from any other source. Such rhythms are played by primitives at times, but our musicians find them almost if not entirely impossible to perform well. Why not hear music from player piano rolls on which have been punched holes giving the ratios of rhythms of the most exquisite subtlety?[2]

Cowell's idea was prophetic, but for once in his life, he left an experiment untried. That task fell to another composer: Conlon Nancarrow from Texarkana, Arkansas.

Nancarrow read *New Musical Resources* in 1939 in New York, as he was preparing to leave for Mexico City to avoid harassment by the American government for his Communist Party connections. Cowell's words fused with a childhood memory – Nancarrow had grown up with a player piano in the home – and sparked one of the strangest careers in the history of music. Like so many other American composers in the 1930s, Nancarrow had been working to extend music's rhythmic vocabulary. Like others, he quickly came to the point at which classical musicians refused to play his music, or at least to play it well. But Nancarrow, self-exiled in Mexico City far from the musical mainstream, took a step few other composers would or could take: he learned to produce his music independently of performers. In 1948, he bought a player piano and embarked on an amazing series of now more than fifty Studies for Player Piano, exploring more aspects of rhythmic superimposition and tempo clash than any other composer had dreamed of doing.

The name Conlon Nancarrow has entered music dictionaries only recently, though he had gained an underground reputation in America by the early sixties. Many contemporary music enthusiasts are unaware of him, let alone general audiences. Where his name *is* found, regularly, is on radical young composers' lists of the musicians who influenced them most. In Europe he is regarded as one of the greatest living composers. In 1981, after finding his recordings in a Paris record store, seminal Hungarian avant-garde composer György Ligeti wrote of Nancarrow, "This music is the greatest discovery since Webern and Ives . . . something great and important for all music history! His music is so utterly original, enjoyable, perfectly constructed, but at the same time emotional . . . for me it's the best music of any composer living today."[3] An obvious part of Nancarrow's obscurity stems from his medium: only those who visit his Mexico City studio have heard the works in their "live" form. Too, printed dissemination of his music has been slow. Between 1977 and 1985, thirty-one of the Studies were published by Peter Garland in his *Soundings* journal from Santa Fe. So far only a handful of analyses have been printed, and those not always accurate. Even musicians aware of Nancarrow by reputation and the few out-of-print recordings do not nearly realize the extent of his compositional achievement. Exploring that achievement will be the purpose of this book.

Overview

Although seventy-five percent of Nancarrow's works are for one instrument, and that an eccentric one, his output is as varied in style, form, and weight as that of any other major composer. He has written light-hearted blues numbers like the Studies for Player Piano Nos. 3, 10, and 45; perfect miniatures like Nos. 4, 6, and 32; contrapuntal tours de force like Nos. 7 and 37; works that independently articulate the concerns of the European avant-garde, like Nos. 20, 23, and 29; formal jewels like Nos. 11, 24, and 36; abstract structuralist sound-patterns like Nos. 5 and 28; virtuoso spectaculars like No. 25; experiments in temporal irrationality like Nos. 33, 40, and 41; one chance piece, No. 44; and, in Nos. 24, 32, 33, 36, 37, 40, 41, 43, and 48, a string of essays exploring different aspects of canon with a thoroughness that rivals Bach's *The Art of Fugue*. Is Nancarrow, like Webern, a painstaking craftsman of elegantly-wrought structures? Yes: listen to Studies Nos. 20, 24, 32, 36. Or is he, like Ives, a wild-eyed eclectic tossing jazz and modernist gestures into crashing cacophonies? Yes again: listen to Studies Nos. 25, 35, 41, 48. One must return to the piano music of Liszt and Busoni to find so many diverse strategies brought to one medium by a single composer.

Although most of Nancarrow's works are very brief (only seven of the Studies run over seven minutes), they do not *sound* brief, largely because of their sheer speed. Within a three-minute study Nancarrow often fits a mass of notes that would have sufficed Liszt for a twenty-five minute sonata. Study No. 36, for example, is under five minutes, but its score is fifty-two pages black with ink. Consequently, the music demands unusually intense listening, not, as in Webern's music, because events are extremely localized, but because so much happens, so many sections go by so quickly. Nancarrow's complete works could be heard in seven hours, but within half that time the listener would be as exhausted as though he had consumed Mahler's ten symphonies in a gulp.

Despite his miniaturization, however, Nancarrow's sense of structure is invariably large-scale. He rarely works as Webern does, mirroring one motive with another (Nos. 7, 35, and 41 are exceptions); instead he is like Stravinsky, with great blocks of material that resist deconstruction. Whereas Beethoven composed long works from short motives, Nancarrow has made brief works from large chunks of melody or rhythm. The fifty-four note melody of the Canon X (Study No. 21), the 120-chord progression of No. 11, the four-page isorhythmic tune of No. 12, the interminably nonrepeating duration-series of No. 20, the twenty chromatic segments of No. 41, the long rhythmic row of No. 45c – these are the irreducible data of Nancarrow analysis; sometimes they can be broken down into subsidiary patterns, elsewhere they seem to have sprung from his head in a protracted flash of inspiration. In fact, his blocks of material are often larger than Stravinsky's, but they do not lead to longer works because they are juxtaposed *simultaneously*, not successively as in *Le sacre du printemps* – a pivotal work, one should keep in mind, in Nancarrow's development as a musician.

Experimentalism

Experimental is a word popularized by John Cage for the new music of the 1950s, though it was used by Nancarrow as early as 1940. Cage's definition of an experimental work was "an act the outcome of which is unknown." The idea of a piece of music being experimental is perhaps drawn from an analogy with science: something never done before is tried in order to gain new knowledge or test a hypothesis. So defined, the term has been controversial, not always welcomed by the composers to whom it has been applied (Varèse and Ashley, for example).

Some of Nancarrow's studies fit the experimental definition better than most of Cage's music does, since outside Nancarrow's work the sheer physical effects of the subtle time relationships he has worked with are completely unknown. Nancarrow often gives the impression that once *he* has heard what an experiment sounds like, there is little need for further attention to it; he has avoided repeating himself to an extent almost unknown among other major figures. With the arguable exception of Study No. 49, there is not a piece in Nancarrow's mature output that does not contain some new idea or twist he had never tried before. The number of compositional ideas he has used only once or twice is astounding. For example (unfamiliar terms on the following list will be fully explained in later chapters):

1. A pitch row split into discrete segments (Study No. 1)
2. A pitch row using internal repetitions of a pitch cell (No. 4)
3. A texture built up from motives that repeat nonsynchronously, i.e., out of phase (also involving every note on the piano without duplication) (No. 5)
4. An isorhythm (repeating rhythmic series) altered by systematic changes of tempo (No. 6)
5. Different isorhythms played at once (No. 7)
6. A piece divided simultaneously into equal-length sections by texture changes, and into a *different* number of equal sections by melodic structure (No. 11)
7. Polyphonic use of isorhythm in which the *color* (pitch row) and *talea* (rhythmic row) are associated differently in each contrapuntal line (No. 20)
8. A canon in which the voices gradually reverse roles (No. 21)
9. A palindromic canon (No. 22)
10. A correspondence between tempo and register (Nos. 23, 37)
11. Rhythmic canon in which the canonic voices have wildly disparate textures (No. 25)
12. Use of a 12-tone row as harmonic determinant for triadic music (No. 25)
13. Accelerating isorhythmic canon (No. 25)
14. A steady beat as a perceptual yardstick for changing tempos (Nos. 27, 28)
15. A "scale" of tempos proportional to a pitch scale (Nos. 28, 37)
16. Interrupted (and resumed) acceleration (No. 29)
17. A tempo canon whose voices theoretically converge *outside* the canon's time frame (No. 31)
18. Isomorphic transformation of a duration pattern to simulate a tempo canon (No. 33, *Two Canons for Ursula*)
19. Tempo changes within layered tempo contrasts (No. 34)
20. An entire movement played at the same time with itself at a different speed (No. 40)
21. An isorhythm accelerated by subtracting from the individual durations (No. 42)
22. Aleatory tempo canon (No. 44)
23. Use of Fibonacci durations to create the same rhythmic motive at different tempos (No. 45)

24   Irrational, unnotatable isorhythm (Nos. 45, 46, 47 – originally one work)
25   Structural acceleration within a tempo canon (No. 48)
26   Tempo canon in which voices are timed to converge *not* all at the same time (String Quartet No. 3)

The list could go on, and it does not even touch the innovations he has returned to repeatedly: irrational tempo relationships, glissandos with selected notes sustained, or the idea of tempo clashes at ratios of 4:5, 24:25, 60:61, and so on. Perhaps it is exactly because Nancarrow was not running around writing orchestra pieces, violin sonatas, song cycles, and commissions like most successful composers that his invariant medium forced so much variety from him. If so, it is a good argument for limitation of medium. Any four of these ideas might have sustained another composer's entire technical vocabulary. Aside from Cage and Stockhausen, what other twentieth-century musical minds have been so fertile?

Nietzsche remarked that Schopenhauer's philosophy was the conception of a young man of twenty-six, and that it forever partook of that period of life's specific qualities. Nancarrow arrived at the preconditions of his music at thirty-five, not twenty-six, but similarly his music has always evoked the young rebel. At eighty-two, he has yet to reach sedate elegance or avuncular predictability. This is partly because of his music's harsh, bristling timbre, in conjunction with the methodical rhythmic wildness that makes his most disciplined structures sound ferocious, untamed. But it is also because of Nancarrow's unremitting experimentalism, his refusal to repeat himself. He is the eternal revolutionary.

Tempos, rhythmic ratios, and the harmonic series

One of Cowell's aims in *New Musical Resources* was to bring to rhythm the same structuring possibilities that had already been applied to pitch, in fact, to draw an analogy between the two (a procedure that Babbitt, Boulez, and Stockhausen would later apply in deriving serialism from twelve-tone technique). The rhythmic theory of Cowell's book was fueled by the insight that pitch intervals and cross-rhythms are manifestations of the same phenomenon, differentiated only by speed. That is, the higher pitch in a purely-tuned interval of a perfect fifth vibrates at a rate one and a half times that of the lower pitch, illustrating a ratio of 3:2. A triplet rhythm over a duple accompaniment, then – three against two – is simply the transfer of the "perfect fifth" idea from the sphere of pitch to that of rhythm.

As the vibrations of a tone are slowed down, the pitch becomes lower, and if the frequency descends lower than a threshold of about sixteen cycles per second, the vibrations are no longer heard as pitch, but as a steady beat. Cowell had a machine invented for him that would keep two sirens tuned at a constant ratio as he slowed them down and sped them up, and he was delighted to hear proof that, as a perfect fifth became slow enough, it turned into a rhythm of three against two. The idea inspired Cowell to hypothesize a system of rhythmic divisions in which each duration is a division of a fundamental duration. *New Musical Resources*

Example 1.1   Diagrams from Henry Cowell's *New Musical Resources*

included diagrams relating simultaneous tempos to triads, based on a fundamental "C-tempo" symbolized by four or eight notes per measure (Example 1.1). Always quick to follow speculation with practice, Cowell wrote a piece, *Quartet Romantic*, about the same time as *New Musical Resources*, in which the four performers play their lines in diverse and ever-changing tempos determined by the pitch ratios in a simple tonal chorale. Unplayable for six decades after its composition, *Quartet Romantic* was first recorded in 1978 by players listening through headphones to a computer clicktrack that provided their tempos.[4]

This was all the theoretical background Nancarrow needed to start experimenting. His first work not written for human hands, the Rhythm Study No. 1, relates all of its rhythms to two different simultaneous tempos, 120 and 210, related by a 4:7 ratio. Four to seven is the ratio of a purely-tuned minor seventh interval, C to a slightly flat B♭. The next explorations were among tempos related by ratios of three, four, and five. From here the chronological progression of Nancarrow's tempo ratios creeps up the harmonic series. The group of seven canonic studies, Nos. 13 through 19, use ratios related to the major or minor triad: expressed as pitch, 3:4 gives the perfect fourth, 4:5 the major third, 3:5 the major sixth, and 12:15:20 a first-inversion minor triad, i.e., G B E. The 5:6:7:8 ratio of Study No. 32 is analogous to an E G B♭ C seventh chord, the 17:18:19:20 of No. 36 to a cluster, C♯ D D♯ E. The 24:25 and 60:61 ratios of Studies Nos. 43 and 48, respectively, represent closely spaced harmonics in the higher octaves. Study No. 33 uses the irrational $\sqrt{2}$:2 ratio of the equal-tempered tritone; Nos. 5 and 50 use the 5:7 ratio that is the smallest integral approximation of a tritone. And in Studies Nos. 40 and 41 Nancarrow went beyond algebraic square roots to the transcendental numbers e and π, whose pitch analogue is irreducible dissonance. In the more recent Study No. 49 Nancarrow has returned to the 4:5:6 ratio of the root-position major triad.

It is worth comment that, although so much of Nancarrow's conception of compositional technique derives from his early contact with *Le sacre du printemps*, the rhythm problems suggested by Cowell pointed to a direction of rhythmic development opposite to that of Stravinsky. One of Stravinsky's feats in *Le sacre* was the extenuation of *additive* rhythm, the grouping of small durational units into irregular meter progressions such as 6/8, 5/8, 9/8, 7/8, 3/8, and so on. Cowell's harmonic-series idea comes from the opposite method of *divisive* rhythm, taking a larger unit (e.g., a whole note) and dividing it simultaneously or successively into equal parts of various lengths. In the middle decades of this century, divisive rhythm was associated with Schoenberg and his followers, additive rhythm with Stravinsky and the neoclassicists. The pairing was somewhat paradoxical: Schoenberg clung to more traditional rhythms partly because his pitch usage was counterintuitive. (This is what Boulez and Stockhausen objected to: they felt a systematic pitch language demanded a systematic rhythmic language.) Stravinsky, on the other hand, stayed closer to the harmonic series in his often-pentatonic melodic language and used rhythm as the radical, counterintuitive element.

The Schoenberg/Stravinsky controversy was one of music's most bitter feuds, and it was raging when Nancarrow began the early studies. Nancarrow has always professed solidarity with the Stravinsky camp, and by the time Schoenberg's followers succeeded in expunging Stravinsky's influence from American compositional practice, Nancarrow had retired to his Mexican isolation. Yet both types of rhythm are found in Nancarrow's music, and it is a kind of watershed in his development when, *notationally*, divisive rhythm wins out over additive, between Studies Nos. 5 and 6. More importantly, however, Nancarrow was the only composer to thoroughly synthesize the two opposing conceptions of rhythm. (Other Americans, notably Roger Sessions and Arthur Berger, wrestled with the contradiction on the pitch front.)

In that respect, Nancarrow's Study No. 1 is prophetic. Paying homage to Cowell's divisive rhythm, Nancarrow notated 4/4 meter in one staff as equal to another's 7/8. His rhythmic groupings within those meters, however, are largely additive, changing between articulations of 3, 4, and 5 beats. Study No. 5, a textbook case, shows how the two rhythmic types intersect. Here the ostinatos group sixteenth notes into repeating duration patterns of 14 7 14 21 7 14 and 15 5

10 5 10 10 20. Nominally these rhythms are additive, but the meter, 35/16, is chosen to integrate beats of 5/16 and 7/16 durations; in short, a 35/16 "hyper-measure" is divided into five equal beats in one voice, seven in another. Like No. 5, Studies 3, 4, 7, 10, 11, and 12 are notated with all voices in the same tempo, organized around an eighth- or sixteenth-note subdivision acting as a common denominator. In No. 6 Nancarrow returns to a large measure divided into three, four, and five in the respective voices. As his tempo ratios increase, notation with a common sixteenth note denominator quickly becomes unwieldy, and he later unites voices via common *multiples*, or hypermeasures,[5] wherever necessary and possible.

Cowell's rhythmic system, especially in his *New Musical Resources* examples and less so in the *Quartet Romantic*, had the limitation of its *periodicity*, the fact that after every few beats all voices re-convene in a simultaneous attack. By retaining additive rhythm within each voice, Nancarrow circumvented that limitation. Once he had marked off tempos across manuscript paper with a template, he no longer needed to draw common barlines to keep voices together, and began to change meters within each tempo. In Study No. 14, the first such instance, the meters fit the accentuation pattern resulting quasi-randomly from a rhythmic process. Starting with No. 24 (one of his most original works on many counts and still his most rhythmically elegant solution), Nancarrow returns to truly additive rhythms occurring in different voices whose tempos effectively divide large hyper-measures into varying numbers of equal beats. Each line considered in itself uses additive rhythm, but the various lines are integrated by an overall divisive rhythmic structure.

The problem with divisive rhythm was its dependence on a too-predictable periodicity. The charge made against additive rhythm was that it had no analogy in pitch, that its use relegated pitch and rhythm to separate structural worlds. (In search of an analogy, Babbitt attempted to bypass additive rhythm in serialism by serializing rhythmic positions within a 6/8 or 12/16 metric grid.) Nancarrow combined the best of both worlds. Beginning with Study No. 24 and continuing with increasing freedom through his most recent studies, he has preserved the energetic, unpredictable feel of additive rhythms within the context of a tempo system related to the pitch relationships of the harmonic series. Inspired by Stravinsky, challenged by Cowell, he is the only composer who completely integrated the microrhythms of one with the macrorhythms of the other, the only one to *solve*, rather than bypass, the Schoenberg/Stravinsky rhythmic dilemma. Nancarrow achieved this feat, of course, at a price few composers would have been willing to pay: he sacrificed the possibility of performance by humans.

Mechanical rhythm

The rhythmic problems broached in Nancarrow's player piano music anticipated many that have arisen in computer music (as well as many more that computer composers have *not* yet worked with). So much has been done now with the electronic sequencing of rhythm that we know much more about mechanically precise rhythm than was known when Nancarrow began punching rolls. Recent studies suggest that absolutely metronomic rhythm is not only humanly impossible, but undesirable from a listening standpoint. The relevant research has been summarized by Jonathan D. Kramer:

> Performers do not render even the simplest of rhythms exactly as notated. For example, we should expect a half note followed by a quarter note to be played in the ratio 2:1 . . . But in fact, the 2:1 ratio is virtually never heard, except when electronically produced. Psychologists Ingmar Bengtsson and Alf Gabrielsson found that, in 38 performances of a Swedish folksong in 3/4 time with most measures containing the half/quarter rhythm, the actual ratio averaged about 1.75:1.[6]

Music meant to be performed, Kramer goes on to say, sounds stiff when mechanically sequenced by a computer, because the ear perceives absolute regularity as awkward and artificial.

What implications do such studies hold for the mechanical perfection of Nancarrow's rhythms? It is true that, in the more "abstract" studies (Nos. 25, 33, 35, 41, and 48, for example), there is little sense of beats falling with the intuitive predictability of a physical gesture. However, in a way Nancarrow's entire output has been a response to that challenge. Like the computer researchers who develop "random deviation" programs to give computerized rhythms a more lifelike feel, Nancarrow has from the very beginning used the player piano to *recreate* rhythmic liberties taken in performance that no notation could convey. In the studies based on the stride piano rhythms of blues (Nos. 3, 4, 10, 45), he has implicitly acknowledged that jazz pianists hardly ever play a dotted rhythm in a 3:1 ratio; instead, Nancarrow often divides his beats into ratios of 3:2, 5:3, or 8:5, all divisions based on the Fibonacci series, related to the intuitively pleasing Golden Section as well as closer to live performance practice. The 4:5 alternation of tempo in the ostinato of Study No. 6, the unevenly divided isorhythms of Nos. 7 and 11, the notes bouncing between tempos in No. 45b, are brilliant models for creating the *appearance* of performance irregularity within regular systems. The player piano has always been for Nancarrow an opportunity to achieve rhythmic deviations Western notation does not easily acknowledge.

Still, as irregularly as Nancarrow may *subdivide* his beats, the beats themselves remain more regular than any pianist would try to play them, and this is a central fact of Nancarrow's tempo conception. Once one has committed himself to working with simultaneous tempos in ratios as close as 14:15:16 (Study No. 24), any interpretive deviation from strictness is out of the question. The slightest *tenuto* or *rubato* in one voice has to be also reflected in the others if the integrity of their relationships is to be maintained; as soon as one robs a note in the 14 tempo of even 1/15th of its value (far less than the 1.75:1 ratio cited by Kramer), it becomes identical to the notes in the 15 tempo, and the point of the exercise has vanished.

What happens, any lover of this music feels, is that the complexity of Nancarrow's tempo relationships compensates for the subconscious, note-to-note complexity lost in the act of mechanical reproduction. (Nancarrow does not even see it as compensation: "When romantic music is played in straight quarter notes and eighth notes," he says, "I find that kind of music boring even *with* the human performance. That's why I don't like romantic music."[7]) Any attempt to hear three lines of contrasting tempo as each keeping its own steady beat focuses the attention so keenly that other perceptual concerns, even those one is more accustomed to, fall by the wayside. As for the desirable ebb and flow of tempo that takes place in performance, this may have been the subconscious motivation behind Nancarrow's acceleration studies (Nos. 8, 21, 22, 23, and 27, plus the finale of the String Quartet No. 3), in which different lines accelerate and ritard not only together, but independently of each other. And the late, unmetered Studies Nos. 41, 45, and 48 approach a chaotic rhythmic energy close to that of free improvisation, as though Nancarrow were still searching to incorporate some kind of "body rhythm" into his mechanical music. As Kramer notes,

> a human performance of one of Nancarrow's more complex studies (if we can imagine the incredible pianist needed to accomplish such a feat) might well be less thrilling than the normal player-piano rendition. The effect of Nancarrow's music thrives not on performance mastery, but on the mechanistic precision of, for example, simultaneous tempos in the ratio of $\sqrt{2}:2$ [Study No. 33]. With such a complex ratio, there is no room for performer nuance. Any deviation from exactitude would sound like an error, not like an expressive interpretation.[8]

Nancarrow also faces the complaint heard by many composers of tape music, that there is no interpretive variety, that the music sounds the same at every performance. As he once put it,

> I am amazed that most people who object to the nonhuman element in computer music or in the player piano have no objection to a Shakespeare sonnet, for example. That sonnet has always remained the same over the centuries. No one suggests it should be changed by a new performance. A painting stays the same forever. The same is true of other works of art. But somehow music is supposed to be different all the time.[9]

The Studies for Player Piano constitute a grab-bag of experiments that perceptual psychologists should have fun with for decades. Nevertheless, in his most recent works for live performers, such as the String Quartet No. 3 and the *Two Canons for Ursula*, Nancarrow (with the help of the Arditti Quartet and Ursula Oppens) has shown that tempo relationships as simple as 3:4:5:6 do leave room for expressive interpretation. Who knows how far future composers and performers will dare to adventure toward even more distant relationships?

Pitch

In 1987 the author interviewed Pierre Boulez, who had only recently been introduced to Nancarrow's music by Elliott Carter and was still excited about the discovery. "For me it was very interesting," Boulez said, "because the rhythmical structure is really very well thought out. Unfortunately, the pitch vocabulary does not follow."

Is Boulez's complaint legitimate? There is a temptation to think of Nancarrow what was once thought of Charles Ives, that he is a revolutionary *naif*, innovative in certain areas, but unsophisticated in respects necessary for greatness. Part of this impression comes, no doubt, from Nancarrow's self-imposed isolation, so parallel to that of Ives. But one must keep in mind that Nancarrow was twenty-eight when he moved to Mexico, and that he had already spent considerable time with some of the best, most advanced musical minds of his era: Henry Cowell (through his book), Nicolas Slonimsky, Roger Sessions, Walter Piston (perhaps even Schoenberg). Traces of twelve-tone thinking crop up in Nancarrow's music from time to time (Study No. 25 uses a twelve-tone row), and the early studies in particular show a sophisticated manipulation of pitch rows. If Nancarrow departed from the chromatic, systemic pitch usage of his contemporaries, it was not because he lacked the technique to manage them, but because he eventually found them inappropriate to what he was doing. One could hardly charge that he found complex pitch systems too much trouble to invent: any composer who would balk at a sizeable expenditure of effort would never have finished punching out even the first five piano rolls.

Whether Nancarrow's pitch thinking has been on the same level as his rhythmic thinking is not a question that can be answered in generalities, because he has made pitch serve so many different purposes. There are studies in which, by Nancarrow's own admission, pitches are little more than an arbitrary string with which to manifest the tempo structure. The fifty-four-note row of Study No. 21 seems makeshift, No. 15 is melodic without being memorable, pitch in No. 22 is a blur, and the recurring seventh chords in No. 33 are far from subtle. One of Nancarrow's departures from the rest of the century's music is his resuscitation of materials that romanticism had rendered banal, such as triads and scales. Always intended to render some rhythmic point more easily audible, they lend an unnerving freshness to his music, though an ear trained to subtle Boulezian sonorities might find them simply awkward.

However, had Nancarrow tried to construct tempo canons from the pitch systems typical of Boulez's *Le marteau sans maître*, he would have defeated his own purposes and become incomprehensible. In the Sonatina and Study No. 1 he goes to ingenious lengths to make inversions and retrogrades invoke the bittersweet intervals of blues. In the other early studies his harmonies authentically recapture a blues style of piano playing. Nancarrow has written catchy, even hummable tunes in Studies Nos. 6, 7, 11, and even 41. The offbeat, never-quite-repeating pitch sequence of No. 4 was a brilliant inspiration. One test of masterful counterpoint should be that no line draws undue attention from the others, and the echoing lines in the softer canons of No. 24 blend as well as anything in Palestrina or Bach. If the purpose of pitch in a canon is to make the canonic structure clear, one could hardly ask for a better melodic subject than that of No. 36, which sweeps the ear into the temporal process. The falling fifths of No. 37 reveal the temporal structure in a way a row could not. And there are many passages where pitch becomes merely a component of timbre, such as the elaborately contoured glissando-arpeggios in Studies Nos. 25, 41, and 48; the filling out may be *analytically* arbitrary (up to a point, after which it is quite systematic), but the ear is satisfied.

In short, one has to answer Boulez both yes and no, and put things in perspective. How sophisticated Nancarrow's pitch systems are depends on what he is trying to achieve. The means are always subservient to the end, a principle even Boulez should go along with.

Harmony

Boulez's complaint may be fair to the extent that harmony is the least developed aspect of Nancarrow's music. In the conventional sense – as simultaneous pitches approached via a confluence of voices – harmony may hardly be said to exist. The striated tempos, the predominantly staccato attacks often mean that exact simultaneities are infrequent and, when they do occur, are too brief to notice. Much of Nancarrow's music moves too quickly for harmony to register. Nevertheless, his use of harmony is perfectly suited to his contrapuntal and rhythmic purposes.

Nancarrow's early harmonies derive from jazz and blues. The ostinatos of Study No. 3, for example, pass repeatedly through C, F, and G, but the change of chord hardly affects what notes lie in the melody, and the same is true of the blues progression that opens No. 10. Rather than color a melody, Nancarrow usually turns blues chords toward a static pandiatonicism. The same is true of the tonal canons, such as Nos. 16 and 19, where Nancarrow aims not for consonance or dissonance, but for a key vaguely defined by the omnipresence of its seven scale steps and blurred by the gradual introduction of foreign pitches. This marks his early Stravinskian influence, similar in method not only to the pandiatonicism of that master's neoclassic music, but to the directionless harmonies of *Le sacre*, which alternate without moving toward perceptible goals. The sense of harmonic *motion* from one set of pitches to another is almost absent in Nancarrow's music, except perhaps in the slowly progressing repeated-note Studies Nos. 20 and 29 and in No. 28's key-rise through the chromatic scale.

In Nancarrow's mature music, especially from Study No. 25 on, but already in Studies Nos. 1, 5, 6, 7, 9, and 12, chords appear not as products of voice-leading or tonal function, but almost always in parallel, as textural extensions of a single line. To reiterate a melody more forcefully, or to highlight it, Nancarrow will articulate it in (to list them in increasing order of emphasis):

1   thirds
2   octaves
3   parallel major triads
4   parallel seventh or ninth chords

Example 1.2   Harmonies from Studies Nos. 25, 33, and 45c

No. 25

No. 33

No. 45

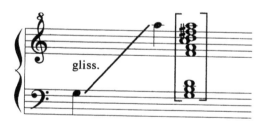

5   larger chords generated from a single interval, or
6   chords which, when condensed within an octave, fill out a contiguous
     diatonic or chromatic scale segment.

To put it another way, it is rare that adjacent chords are functionally differentiated.
Nancarrow's equalizing tendency is most notable in the middle Studies, especially

13

Example 1.3   Pitch motives combining a minor third with a major or minor second

Sonatina

Study No. 3A

No. 3B

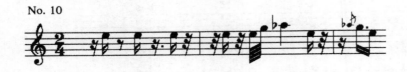

No. 4

No. 10

No. 41

String Quartet No. 3

Example 1.4   Melodies following a rising perfect fourth with a rising minor third

Study No. 8

No. 11

No. 24

No. 35

No. 43

Nos. 24, 25, and 33. Many of the crashing chords of No. 25 comprise every note in a diatonic scale, No. 33 makes its five-note chords both from piling up minor sevenths and major ninths and from spread-out diatonic or whole-tone scale segments, while No. 45c piles up triads polytonally (Example 1.2).

After Study No. 35, Nancarrow largely loses interest in complex individual sonorities, and late studies such as Nos. 41a, 42, 43, 44, 45, 48, 49, and 50 are remarkable for their near-exclusive reliance on the major triad as harmonic material. It is a measure of Nancarrow's independence from his time that, during decades in which all but the most reactionary composers avoided major triads as irretrievably banal and exhausted, he used them in good faith and invested them with a function that carried no shadow of their earlier meaning in tonal music. In the midst of his swirling polyphony, those innocent triads never sound incongruous: each triad expresses its individual root in a way no other chord could. Except where Nancarrow explicitly desires a dense, massive effect (such as in Nos. 25 and 33), his chords invariably lend clarity to the polyphonic structure.

Example 1.5   Melodies turning on a minor third

Study No. 27

No. 31

No. 32

No. 37

Example 1.6   Triad-plus-minor-third motives

Study No. 43

No. 48

Example 1.7   Passages emphasizing a minor third

Study No. 20

No. 23

No. 40

No. 41

No. 42

No. 45

No. 49

Example 1.8   Figures with an ascending major scale and descending minor scale

Sonatina

String Quartet No. 1

Study No. 6

No. 7

No. 35

No. 41

No. 46

Melodic tendencies

Historically, composers have reused forms over and over (sonata form, variations, da capo aria) and varied the melodies within them. Nancarrow's use of certain melodic formulas is so consistent, from the 1941 Sonatina to *Contraption No. 1* of 1993, that he can almost be said to have done the opposite: reuse the melodies over and over and vary the forms around them. Every commentator has noted the importance of the minor third in Nancarrow's melodies, and it appears in many recurring contexts. The prevalent early form is combined with an adjacent half or whole step to build a ubiquitous motive (Example 1.3). Another common form is a rising perfect fourth followed by a rising minor third and often a descending second, in a pattern A–D–F–E or A–D–F–E♭ (Example 1.4). Often the melody turns around minor thirds, as in Example 1.5; or follows a triad with a minor third as in Example 1.6. And, increasingly in the late works, the minor third is stripped down to a mere alternation or obsessive 1–2–3 repetition (Example 1.7). In addition, one of Nancarrow's most characteristic figures is the combination of a major scale segment ascending and a minor scale segment descending (Example 1.8). These figures are so ubiquitous throughout the music that they will be cited in chapters 3 through 10 without special explanation.

Other common figures, such as the superfast glissando or major triad arpeggio, arise in Nancarrow's late music as an enlivening textural trick to which the player piano is well suited. One type of figure, common in Studies Nos. 25, 41, and 48, resists simple description: a figure of extremely fast notes outlining a jagged contour, often filling up a chromatic pitch-space or drawing a tortuous line through the piano's range (Example 1.9). For convenience's sake, this figure has frequently been referred to as simply an "arpeggio" in the following analyses, on the premise that, in a dissonant or atonal context, a jagged chromatic line could serve as the nonlinear arpeggiation of a complex chord. However, Nancarrow takes amusement in having once overheard someone comment at a concert that another composer's work included a "Nancarrow lick." Perhaps there is no better term for the figure than that.

Tempo canon and its formal results

For exploring the problem of several tempos at once, Nancarrow resorted to several forms, some of them prevalent in the 1930s. Arch form, common in Bartók, became a favorite: Study No. 22 is palindromic, No. 1 is nearly so, and the second half of No. 43 runs back through the first half's ideas in reverse order. Studies Nos. 36 and 41 are looser arch forms, with striking asymmetrical features. Half of an arch form can be a linear crescendo: Studies Nos. 5, 28, 29, 42, and 48 increase in speed, texture, or both to a climactic final chord. As an ex-jazz trumpet player, it is natural that Nancarrow used a variation form over an ostinato in Studies Nos. 2, 3, 10, 11, and 45. Studies Nos. 24 and 29 alternate A and B

Example 1.9 Study No. 41b, "Nancarrow lick"

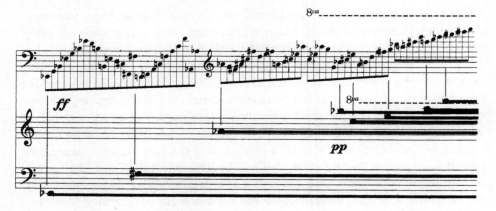

Example 1.10 Tempo canon terminology

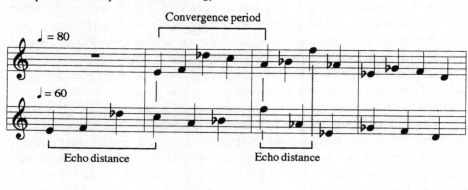

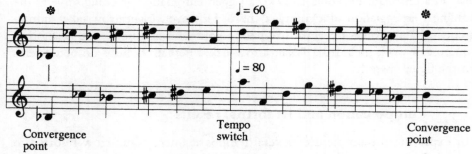

sections, swinging between two processes that interrupt each other. Study No. 7 is the only one that can be construed as a sonata-allegro with first and second themes, and many of Nancarrow's forms are *sui generis*. But the device to which he ultimately devoted the most work and thought was tempo canon: trans- positions of the same melody played in different tempos at the same time.

Nancarrow is not the first composer to write tempo canons, or (as they were called in the Renaissance) mensuration canons – in which two or more voices play the same material at not only different transposition levels but at different tempos as well – but he is the first to write so many different kinds as to necessitate a special terminology. Inherent to the technique of the tempo canon are various events resulting from the canon's structure to determine the overall form. The most central I have chosen to call the *convergence point* (often abbreviated as CP in the analyses), the infinitesimal moment at which all lines have reached identical points in the material they are playing. In the late studies, from No. 24 on, this is usually either the climax or the end of a canon, though occasionally a convergence point will fall inaudibly on a rest, and in a few cases not until *after* the canon is over. Nancarrow's ways of marking the convergence points exhibit astounding ingenuity.

Another major, but less audible, event is the *tempo switch*, a device in which Nancarrow switches the fastest line to the slowest tempo and vice versa, so that the line that has been lagging catches up with the one that has been pulling ahead. By mathematical necessity, the tempo switch always occurs halfway between two convergence points.[10] The perceptual datum by which the ear keeps track of these changes I call the *echo distance* – the temporal gap between an event in one voice and its corresponding recurrence in another. In a tempo canon in which the convergence point is in the middle, for example, the echo distance will grow shorter and shorter as the convergence point is approached, reach zero at the convergence point, then grow progressively longer as it moves away. To calculate echo distance as a precise number of beats requires specifying which voice the relevant beat–unit refers to; for example, in a 4:5 canon an echo distance of five beats with reference to the faster voice equals four beats with reference to the slower. Proportionality between phrase length and echo distance is essential to the compositional technique of the late canons.

In the canons in which meter changes frequently, it sometimes becomes necessary to speak of the *convergence period*, the hypermeasure that exists between (potential) simultaneous attacks in voices moving at different tempos. For example, in a canon at the ratios 14:15:16 (No. 24), one convergence period has fourteen beats in the slowest voice, fifteen in the middle voice, and sixteen in the fastest. Keeping track of convergence periods makes certain calculations easier. For example, in canons based on superparticular ratios (i.e., 4:5, or 9:10), the echo distance will increase (if after the convergence point) or decrease (if before) by one beat per convergence period.[11] In such a case, the echo distance will approximate n beats at a point n convergence periods from a convergence point. In three canons, however – Studies Nos. 33, 40, and 41 – Nancarrow uses irrational tempo relationships, so that, theoretically, no notes in one voice will *ever* coincide with those in another. Under these conditions, the concept of convergence period becomes inapplicable. The greatly simplified example of a hypothetical 3:4 canon in Example 1.10 should fix these essential concepts in mind.

Nancarrow has written more than two dozen canons; no two are alike in structure, and where they differ most importantly is in the number and disposition

Example 1.11 Morphology of Nancarrow's canons

Study No. 16 (not a true canon)

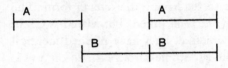

Study No. 14 - Canon 4/5

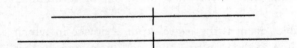

Study No. 19 - Canon 12/15/20

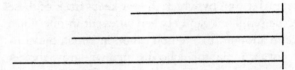

Study No. 15 - Canon 3/4

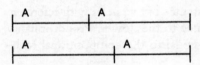

Study No. 17 - Canon 12/15/20

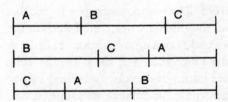

Study No. 18 - Canon 3/4

Study No. 21 - Canon X

Study No. 22 - Canon 1%/1^1/2%/2^1/4%

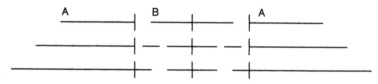

Study No. 24 - Canon 14/15/16

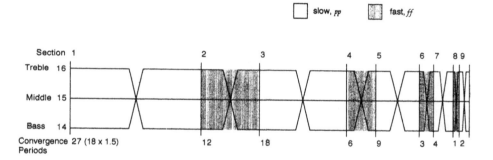

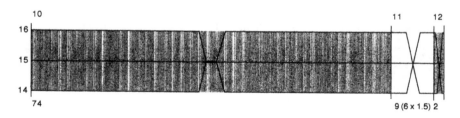

Study No. 26 - Canon 1/1 [/1/1/1/1/1]

Study No. 27 - Canon 5%/6%/8%/11%

Section 1:

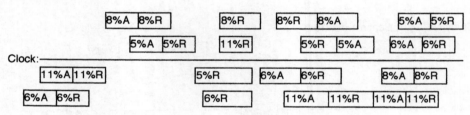

Section 2:   Section 3:   Section 4:

Section 5:   Section 6:   Section 7:   Section 8:

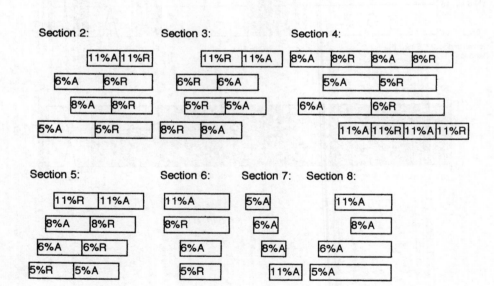

Durations not strictly proportional

24

Study No. 31 - Canon 21/24/25

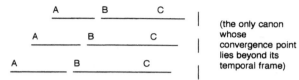

(the only canon whose convergence point lies beyond its temporal frame)

Study No. 32 - Canon 5/6/7/8

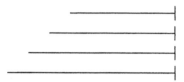

Study No. 33 - Canon (square root of 2)/2

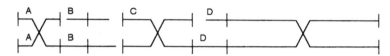

Study No. 34 - Canon $\dfrac{9}{4/5/6}$ / $\dfrac{10}{4/5/6}$ / $\dfrac{11}{4/5/6}$

Study No. 36 - Canon 17/18/19/20

Study No. 37 - Canon 150/160^5/7/168^3/4/180/187^1/2/200/210/225/240/250/262^1/2/281^1/4

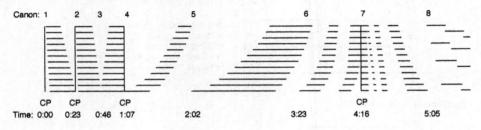

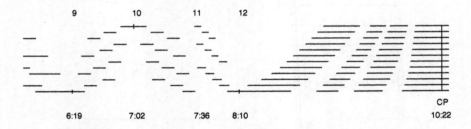

Study No. 44 - Aleatory Round

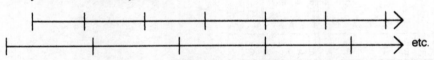

(This canon is playable at any tempo ratio and number of repetitions.)

Study No. 48 - Canon 60/61

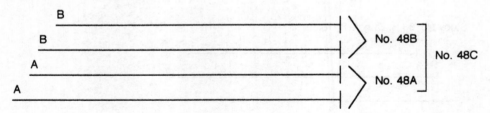

Study No. 49A   No. 49B   No. 49C - Canons 4/5/6

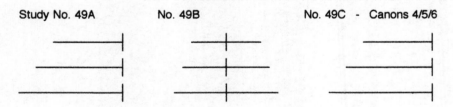

Study No. 50 - Canon $\frac{5/7}{3}$ (Second movement, Piece for Small Orchestra No. 2)

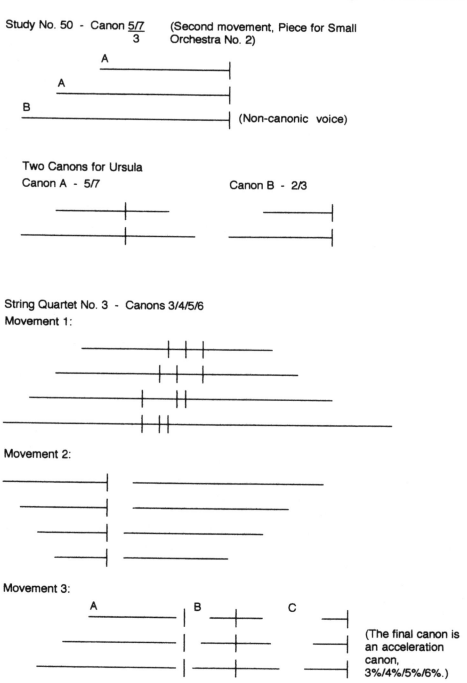

Two Canons for Ursula

Canon A - 5/7   Canon B - 2/3

String Quartet No. 3 - Canons 3/4/5/6
Movement 1:

Movement 2:

Movement 3:

A   B   C

(The final canon is an acceleration canon, 3%/4%/5%/6%.)

of convergence points, the number of voices, and tempo switches. The morpho-
logical outlines of Example 1.11 provide an abstract skeleton of each canon.
Convergence points are marked by vertical lines, tempo switches are marked by
diagonal lines forming an X, and sections of differing material – usually separated
in the music by an extracanonic rest or change of transposition level – are indicated by letter. (Note that the length of each diagram is related to the complexity
of the form, not to its length proportional to the other studies. Lengths within
each diagram are approximately proportionate.)

Nancarrow has far from exhausted the structural possibilities. For instance, he
has never written a canon with a convergence point only at the beginning, nor
one in which the tempo switches are not reciprocal (each moving to the other's
tempo). The first composer to throw the field open, he has left plenty of terrain
for future practitioners. Nevertheless, it seems safe to predict that the ingenuity
that he has applied to finding rhythmic ratios for his tempo canons will not soon
be surpassed.

Timbre

"No recorded image of his compositions ever will reproduce the overwhelming
sensation of raw power and excitement," wrote Charles Amirkhanian in his liner
notes to Nancarrow's 1750 Arch recordings, "generated when sitting 'in the flesh'
in Nancarrow's soundproof studio in Mexico City and listening to his rolls."
Nancarrow disagrees – he felt that Robert Shumaker's pristine tapes played at
New Music America in San Francisco were as glorious a way to experience the
music as any – but the observation is true nonetheless. Crisp, penetrating, electric,
growling – these are weak adjectives for conjuring up the tumult of crashing
chords, five contrapuntal lines at once, figures of hundreds of notes per second
flung out by Nancarrow's modified mechanical pianos.

Of the several player pianos Nancarrow owns and has owned, the two he
writes for and has used to record his works are made by Marshall and Wendell,
and contain Ampico Reproducing Piano mechanisms. Nancarrow has altered the
hammers of both pianos. On one, the wooden hammers have been covered with
steel straps to create a brilliant, piercing sound; the hammers of the other piano are
covered with leather and capped with a metal tack that strikes the strings with a
milder, but still bristly tone. The strident tone that results from these modifications
puts some first-time listeners off, but they make Nancarrow's humble uprights
seem larger and more fierce than a concert grand. It has become apparent, too,
that in composing Nancarrow has increasingly relied on the enhanced ping of his
pianos. At New Music America in New York in 1989 the German composer/
engineer Trimpin played his computer-driven version of Study No. 48 on two
unaltered grand pianos; the sound was muddy, its contrapuntal clarity – so
crystalline in Nancarrow's studio – greatly diminished. The comprehensibility
of the late studies depends on his altered piano hammers.

Another feature peculiar to Nancarrow's pianos should be kept in mind. His Ampico mechanisms play only eighty-three keys of each piano, five fewer than standard, from B_0 to A_7 with the bottom two and top three omitted. (When necessary, I will indicate pitches with the system of the Acoustical Society of America, in which middle C is C_4, the highest C on a normal piano is C_8, the lowest C is C_1, and the note just below C_1 is B_0.) E_4 is thus the central note of Nancarrow's range; many of the studies systematically use all eighty-three notes, and E_4 is a frequent center of symmetry.

The Studies that use two pianos (Nos. 40, 41, and 48) were intended to take advantage of the slight timbre contrast between the two instruments. That contrast can be heard on the 1750 Arch recordings made in 1977, but by 1988 one of the pianos had fallen into disrepair, so the Wergo recordings of these studies are not made "in real time," but by playing each roll on the same piano and overdubbing them in the studio. In 1989, German chemist and player-piano hobbyist Jurgen Hocker sent his protégé, the piano mechanic Jurg Borchardt, to Mexico City to restore Nancarrow's pianos to pristine working condition.

Dynamics

Nancarrow's pianos have the capability of playing crescendos and descrescendos, but he does not use them; like Bach, he says with considerable pride, he belongs to the "terraced dynamic school." At one edge of the piano roll is a place for up to three holes that determine how much air pressure the machine uses, thus how much volume it produces. For whatever reason, these holes are designated 2, 4, and 6. Eight dynamic levels are possible, ranging from no holes to all three. In Nancarrow's punching scores, he notates those levels as (–0–), (–2–), (–4–), (–6–), (4–2), (6–2), (6–4), and (6–4–2). He rarely seems to need all eight levels in one work, however. Study No. 48a contains six dynamic levels, and in the final score Nancarrow notates (6–4–2) and (6–4) as *ff*, (–6–) as *f*, (–4–) as *mf*, (–2–) as *p*, and (–0–) as *pp*. In addition, sustain and soft pedals are available. Nancarrow notates them with dots – (. . .) and (. .) respectively – but hardly ever uses them.

Metronome markings

It is refreshing to realize that the only major composer whose music has been almost entirely mechanically produced is just as wary of precise metronome markings as Beethoven was. Nancarrow's markings are generally rounded off for the sake of arithmetical simplicity, not to be taken literally. If the middle voice in Study No. 24 actually followed a tempo of ♩. = 240, the piece would be over in an all-too-quick 209 seconds, instead of an already ear-dazzling 263; if, however, the marking were changed to a more realistic 191, the other tempo calculations would be needlessly complex. The speed on Nancarrow's pianos is continuously adjustable, from stopped to quite fast, and he has often changed his mind about how fast the studies should run. To the man who insisted on the absolute precision of relative tempos in his music, absolute tempo is an intuitively relative matter.

Between the 1969 Columbia recording and the 1750 Arch recording of 1977, Nancarrow increased the speed of seven studies (by as much as sixteen and a half percent in No. 33), decreased the speed of four, and left only one unchanged. My opinion is that Nancarrow has tended to play his studies too fast, and this is especially true of the 1750 Arch discs. Nancarrow may enjoy the fireworks, or think his listeners enjoy them, but dozens of his best compositional effects could be more clearly heard at slower speeds. More than once I have played a taped study at half-speed to hear exactly what happens. And perhaps Nancarrow has come to agree; the Wergo recordings, released in 1990–91, reveal an average 10.7 percent decrease in the overall tempos of the duplicated studies. Thirty-four of the studies were slowed down by an average of twelve and half percent, some as much as thirty-three (No. 28) and twenty-seven percent (No. 29), with great improvement in comprehensibility. Only four (Nos. 15, 20, 36, and 37) are faster on Wergo, and those by less than five percent.

In addition, as Nancarrow has often noted, as the roll winds around the take-up spindle of his player pianos, the thickness of the column increases and causes a slight speed-up in the music. Philosophically, he sees this acceleration as a natural phenomenon that occurs unconsciously in most musical performance, and points to long African drumming performances as a parallel example.[12]

Working method

Once he progressed beyond tempos that could easily fit within a small con-vergence period, such as 3:4:5, Nancarrow needed a working method that would free him from placing barlines to connect voices every few beats. His solution was to make *templates*, long strips of poster paper on which a tempo is marked off. Over the years, Nancarrow has collected templates for dozens of tempo relation-ships the way just-intonationist composer Lou Harrison has collected them for indicating the string lengths of tunings on a monochord. Clearly harking back to Cowell's theories, Nancarrow identifies each template by a pitch name relating it to a basic "C" tempo; the templates he used for Study No. 42, for example, are marked in the score B♭ E D C G B♭ D to indicate tempos corresponding to ratios of 7:10:9:8:12:14:18.

Nancarrow says he always knows from the beginning what tempo relationships a piece will require. In his words,

> When I got into these complex multitempo things, I'd take a blank roll, and knowing before I'd even do it how long the piece would be, and what the proportions would be, draw out those proportions on the whole roll, with the smallest value I thought I'd be needing in the piece. Then I'd take the width of the score paper, from here to here, and draw it off on the roll that size, and take

blank score paper and put all of these things on the blank paper. And then write the piece. Up to then there was no piece, just a tempo relationship.[13]

After he uses the templates to mark off tempos on manuscript paper, he sketches out the piece. From this sketch he draws a more detailed punching score, with beat numbers, dynamic markings, and every indicator he needs to punch the roll. This punching score is often a more accurate guide to what actually happens in the piece than the final score. From the punching score he transposes the notes to a piano roll, first marking off the tempos across the top edge of the roll, with the beats numbered to facilitate keeping the voices of the canon straight. (The cover of Vol. 5 of the Collected Studies in *Soundings* shows his template markings for Study No. 36.) Nancarrow works at a long table, with take-up reels at each end for the piano roll, and a wheeled chair that lets him easily move back and forth across the roll.

The punching machine has a guideline about an inch away from where the hole is actually punched; one problem with getting information from the piano roll (as I had to do with Study No. 47 because Nancarrow had lost the score) is that that gap must be continually accounted for. Once the roll is aligned, Nancarrow pulls the handle and squeezes a trigger to do the actual punching. (James Tenney notes that the handle is quite resistant, and that Nancarrow's left bicep – the handle is on the left – is much more developed than his right.) Formerly, the machine punched only one hole at a time. This made it time-consuming to punch long sustained notes, since each one required a series of holes; the piano mechanism will read a note as continuous if the holes are close enough together. Nancarrow had an attachment made, however, to punch four holes at a time, greatly speeding up the process.

The process is still heavily time-consuming, however, requiring several months to punch one of the more complex studies. Consequently, Nancarrow rarely sketches on the piano rolls, and he envies the ease with which computer composers can make alterations:

> It's too much work. One of the things that appeal to me about these synthesizers is that, if you don't like something in a particular register, or if you want to put something in octaves, whatever, you just change it immediately. You don't have to punch anything. As a matter of fact, in Study No. 21, you remember where the notes get slower and slower? I didn't realize how much the slow voice would be drowned out, and I kept adding octaves to it afterward. Finally, by the end, I think I had all the octaves and you still couldn't quite hear it. For little things like that a synthesizer would be very useful.

He also has little interest in playing with the visual aspect of a roll:

> A long time ago, someone who had seen these patterns said, "Why don't you make an abstract design, don't think of music, just a design?" I did it, I tried to keep from thinking of music, tried to avoid thinking of any specific scale or whatever, just an abstract design. I put it on and it sounded terrible, so I dropped that idea. The others sometimes come out interesting visually, but it's pure coincidence.[14]

Once when I was staring at the formidable quantity of apparatus needed to realize the Studies, and thinking of the years of diligent, even relentless labor that went into them, I remarked to Nancarrow, "It makes me feel lazy by comparison." He replied, "Well, this is lazy work – it's a desk job."

Nevertheless, although Nancarrow rarely sketches on a roll, in 1993 his assistant Carlos Sandoval found sixty-eight discarded piano rolls in his studio, representing abandoned and unfinished works. These rediscovered rolls contain a wealth of information that could lead to more detailed reconstruction of Nancarrow's working methods. For example, one of the rolls, a fairly well worked out three-section piece, had an ostinato from Study No. 2 running through one section, and the opening theme from the String Quartet No. 3 in another, two works separated by at least thirty-five years. Another roll featured the jazz duet that runs through Study No. 41, accompanied by triads and ostinatos more typical of Nancarrow's earliest studies. These incongruities suggest that Nancarrow, when strapped for an idea, rummages through earlier, abandoned works and salvages entire themes and even sections from which to build new structures. (This is what he did with the quintet he wrote for the Parnassus ensemble in 1993.) Like snapshots, the rolls capture private, playful moments: one of them has only the word "Hello" punched diagonally across it, apparently so Nancarrow could hear what the word's shape sounded like translated to sound.

Many of the rediscovered rolls use only a dozen or so pitches, vibrating in static rhythmic patterns; it seems certain that these rolls were intended not for player piano, but for the mechanized percussion orchestra Nancarrow had built and abandoned. Sandoval found the percussion instruments and their mechanisms as well, in rather deteriorated condition. It is questionable whether those percussion works could ever be reconstructed beyond the mere rhythmic scheme.

Notation

After the roll is punched, the only remaining step – and an unnecessary one, from the composer's standpoint – is to copy a final score. With the possible exception of a few electronic composers (who, prior to 1977, were forced to make scores of their created-on-tape works in order to get them copyrighted in the United States), no other composer save Nancarrow has ever had the monumental task of drawing every note in his scores in exact rhythmic proportion to all the others. From 1960 to 1965 he quit composing and labored at scoring the first thirty studies, realizing that the musical world was unlikely to take him seriously unless he put his work in a form that lent itself to analysis. The pinpoint accuracy of those scores, in terms not only of pitch but of placing notes precisely within a fluid temporal continuum, is an achievement no other composer has ever had to duplicate. (Though surprisingly few, there are mistakes in the scores, and some of the more important ones have been pointed out in the analyses, usually in footnotes. It is an indicator of Nancarrow's musical discipline that most errors are immediately obvious as such.)

Nancarrow's proportional notation sets up formidable obstacles for analysis, and they might as well be dealt with at once, rather than scattered through the following analyses. The lack of bar lines and specified relative note durations in about a third of the studies – Nos. 8, 20, 21, 22, 27, 28, 29, 41, 42, 45, 46, 48, 49, 50, and parts of 23 and 35 – gives the impression of a free, rhapsodic rhythmic inspiration. In reality, however, Nancarrow's rhythmic thinking is more often than not systematic, at least to the point of involving a contrast between underlying tempos. Most of the spatially notated scores could be renotated more precisely, though, admittedly, it would be a tremendous amount of trouble in some cases and would not make the music look more like it sounds; the convenience would be only for the theorist. Studies Nos. 8, 20, 35, 41, 42, 48, 49, and 50 have underlying beats, sometimes notated in the punching score but not in the final score, which would make renotation possible. In reproducing examples from these, I have frequently rewritten them in conventional note values, not because I consider Nancarrow's notation inadequate, but so that the reader can see at a glance the exact rhythm he intended. Only the acceleration studies and those with irrational rhythms firmly resist conventional notation.

In the spatially notated studies as they are, how does one find those systems, calculate those tempos? By measuring every last note with a ruler. How does one interpret a series of note durations expressed in millimeters as 14, 13, 9, 9, 10, 5, 16, 5, 13, 14? What the author has done, when it seemed justified by context, is assume that Nancarrow's use of the template fell short of perfect accuracy (in the final score, not necessarily on the piano roll), and that the 13s, 14s, and 16s were intended to represent notes of equal duration, as were the 9 and 10. (Introduce some 11s and 12s into the pattern, of course, and that assumption falls apart.) Even if Nancarrow *did* notate relative durations with microscopic accuracy, two notes within the same melodic line, differing in duration by a factor of thirteen to fourteen, could not be distinguished by ear except under extraordinary and specific conditions. In such a case the analyst has every reason to assume that a line of intermixed thirteen-, fourteen-, and fifteen-millimeter notes will be heard as articulating a steady beat, certainly well within the normal deviations of instrumental practice. The reader should be cautioned, though, that the integrity of the analyses of spatially notated studies is subject to my careful use of my little plastic metric ruler, and that each renotation into more specific note values has been drawn with a sigh of hope that the note lengths on the printed page accurately convey what the composer had in mind. In some cases it has been possible to confirm findings with the punching score.

For whatever reason, Nancarrow's scores since 1978 have been less carefully drawn than the earlier ones. Nancarrow graciously gave me the manuscript punching score for Study No. 48a, and my experience with it dramatized how dependent future Nancarrow scholarship will be on examination of the original manuscripts. Working at first with the final score, I made several misassumptions about the piece's rhythmic nature, and I doubt whether I would have ever correctly determined, say, the opening change from a 21-tempo to a 20-tempo without seeing the relationship of the notes to Nancarrow's marked subdivisions. A page from Nancarrow's punching score to Study No. 48, with attendant explanation, is found in Example 8.51 (on page 230). Beethoven's sketches are intriguing for finding out how a piece developed, but Nancarrow's sketches are often essential just for finding out what he actually intended.

Helpfulness of drafts prior to the final score varies widely. Many of the early studies, for example, reveal no significant differences between the punching score and printed score. In the late studies, however, Nancarrow often includes far more specific rhythmic indications in the punching score, conveying to the final one only proportional rhythmic spacing, and that not always entirely accurate. Imposing on Nancarrow's hospitality as much as I dared, I examined the punching scores to Nos. 23, 25, 41, 42, 45, 46, and others. Brief examination of the punching scores of Nos. 23 and 25 was of no help; they only duplicated the final scores, and earlier sketches will have to be examined for a fuller account. On the other hand, the punching scores to the studies following No. 40 were extremely revealing. Without these my information would have been far less specific, and many of the studies, from No. 20 on, will never be analyzed fully except by someone who has access to facsimiles of the punching scores.

Mind and heart in Nancarrow's music

Perhaps seventy percent of the appeal of Nancarrow's music, the reason it finds admirers among nonmusicians as well as composers, is its pure visceral energy, its combination of speed, melodic variety, timbral force, and clashes of tempo. Most of this book – Chapters 3 through 10 – will be devoted to the other thirty percent of his appeal: the compositional devices, the technical innovations, the formal insights, the ideas ready to flow into the future history of composing. Ad hoc systems appear often and are occasionally transferred from one piece to another, but Nancarrow, contemptuous of twelve-tone and similar methods, is not systematic in the sense that Schoenberg, Boulez, Stockhausen, and Babbitt are. As seemed appropriate for the first comprehensive study of a composer whose methods have been little understood, I have approached each study as a separate work with its own rules, and have tried to group the studies in such a way that restatement of the few transferable principles is minimized.

Given this book's concentration on ideas, technical devices, and structural achievements, it may be well to repeat what James Tenney has written about the other side of Nancarrow's work: "there is enough lyrical freedom, rhapsodic invention, and sheer fantasy to warm the heart of the most outrageously romantic 'intuitionist.'"[15] In following chapters this conviction will be assumed without frequent emphasis. My interest is in how Nancarrow composes, and in the vistas he has added to the geography of musical form and contrapuntal technique. I have come to believe that once Nancarrow's achievements become widely understood, he could eventually have an influence equal to that of Schoenberg, Cage, Stockhausen, or La Monte Young on how twenty-first century music is written. I also feel, however, that a compositional device lacks even anecdotal interest unless it is brought into being at the service of sincere expression.

The most affecting passages in the late Beethoven sonatas are the points at which compositional logic and emotional flow coincide, where a fugal theme suddenly appears in a natural but unexpected context, or where a long-prepared cadence quietly sheds its disguise and reveals itself as the recapitulated main theme. A successful short story is one in which the plot twists make the happiness and disappointments of the characters seem warranted and infectious. Likewise, a convergence point in a late Nancarrow canon is a riveting event, not because the numerical proportions used to achieve it were elegant, but because one hears the motives restlessly echo each other, grow shorter and shorter, pile up more quickly, draw into a sonic implosion, then release, relax, spread out, and die away into a rolling, interminable ritardando. Not only do you respond viscerally to the physical intensity of the sound – Nancarrow's pianos exude a remarkable energy, but anyone with an electric guitar can duplicate that level of enjoyment – you *hear* the process in its inexorable motion, you can tell with increasing specificity *when* it is going to happen, and you hear *why* it happens. Nancarrow is responsible for some of the most inwardly motivated climaxes in twentieth-century music.

The number proportions, tempo ratios, and compositional devices that fill the following pages may look forbidding, perhaps impressive, possibly irrelevant to ultimate questions of musical worth; but every one of them has as its purpose the efficient communication of an image. If Nancarrow's reputation depended on the complexity of his musical structures, he would have a line to wait behind, for many recent composers have spun circles around him in the convoluted analysis department. The measure of his achievement is that music so complicated in description sounds so vivid and direct. The music invites participation by the brain because it first made such intuitive sense to the ear.

2

A biographical sketch

Conlon Nancarrow believes that the appreciation of art neither necessitates nor justifies peering into the private life of the artist. Like Samuel Beckett, he is reticent with biographical information; his frequent comment to interviewers is, "it isn't important." When at ease, however, he relishes telling a story. The following sketch is culled from published and not-yet-published interviews (cited in the notes when the information is available from only one source), along with a number of stories related by Nancarrow personally. Respecting Nancarrow's convictions, I have largely restricted myself to what he freely offered, briefly interviewing a few close relatives and friends primarily for confirmation of details.

Samuel Conlon Nancarrow was born on the Arkansas side of Texarkana on 27 October 1912. John Cage had been born fifty-two days earlier in Los Angeles, Elliott Carter four years earlier in New York City: by the end of the century the three would have become the most influential American composers of their generation. Nancarrow's importance would manifest itself later than that of the other two, both of whom would figure in his career.

Nancarrow's father, Samuel Charles Nancarrow, came from New York state, and worked in Philadelphia for Standard Oil.[1] When Standard transferred him to Arkansas to manage a barrel factory, he relocated to Texarkana. The composer's mother, Myra née Brady, was an Arkansas native. To avoid confusion between the Samuels, the first-born child was called Conlon – a last name from his mother's side of the family – from an early age. A younger brother, Charles, was born three years after Conlon. As one of the community's leading businessmen, the elder Nancarrow entered politics to protect the town's business interests, and served as mayor of Texarkana, Arkansas, from 1925 to 1930, resigning from his third two-year term for health reasons.

The Nancarrows lived in the same home throughout Conlon's youth, on the southeast corner of 20th and Beech Streets, a few blocks east of State Line Avenue. The oak trees that abundantly shade the length of the brick-paved street were planted, according to Charles Nancarrow, by his and the composer's father: oak was barrel-stave material.[2] The house burned down in 1988, and the site is now a vacant lot. Charles occupied the house until it burned, and owned the land until his death in 1993. A few blocks away, in a little park at 9th and County

Streets, grows a magnolia tree with a small monument stating that it was planted on 21 February 1932, by the May Dale Garden Club "in memory of Samuel Charles Nancarrow,"[3] who died in 1931. The neighborhood, full of beautiful old homes with luxurious verandas, is being rezoned as a historical district in connection with Scott Joplin's supposed birthplace several blocks south. Texarkana, Arkansas, has produced its share of groundbreaking composers.

Musical influences were not absent from the Nancarrow home. The house held a player piano (whose significance for Conlon would not emerge for many years), stocked with rolls of Chopin and light classical fare by composers such as Edward MacDowell. Nancarrow claims his family was uniformly tone deaf, although his father enjoyed singing "corny John McCormack songs" such as "Mother Machree."[4] Charles adds, though, that the parents made sure the boys were exposed to Brahms and Beethoven. At the age of six, Conlon studied piano with some "horrible old spinster,"[5] who, in the hallowed tradition of such teachers, destroyed any enthusiasm he might have had. To escape her, he switched to trumpet, studied that instrument with a "nice old drunk," and began playing in the town band.[6] Charles, whose musicality was expressed on the clarinet, remembers that his brother was a fantastic trumpet player with superb lip technique.

Conlon's defiant individualism emerged early. At ten or eleven, he discovered the *Little Blue Books*, a series of mail-order instructional pamphlets published by Haldeman Julius, an old Wobbly. Costing five cents each, these were written on every subject (many by Julius himself) including such taboos as anarchy and sex. Conlon studied them avidly and stashed them away so as not to alarm his parents. Years later, when Nancarrow was grown and his mother found them in the attic, she supposedly said, "Now I understand what happened to him."[7] Nancarrow has mentioned the *Little Blue Books* in several interviews, and a librarian at the University of Arkansas, reading one, once wrote to him, "If you'd like to continue your education, we have a complete set of the *Little Blue Books*."[8]

Conlon's lack of interest in formal education was a continuing problem. When one of his friends was packed away to Western Military Academy in Alton, Illinois, Nancarrow's father decided it might encourage discipline to send Conlon along as well. The plan backfired, for here he "got the music bug," as Charles puts it. Conlon attended the National Music Camp at Interlochen, Michigan, the following summer.[9] He discovered jazz, with Louis Armstrong, Bessie Smith, and Earl Hines becoming his favorite performers. He began composing, he remembers, around age fifteen, and became determined to go into music. His father, however, had no patience for such an effeminate, penurious pursuit and wanted him to study engineering. With outward obedience, Conlon went to Vanderbilt at fifteen to do so. Charles later attended Vanderbilt as well, and remembered getting strange reactions from teachers who asked if he was Conlon's brother. The reactions were explained to Charles by an upperclassman. Among the stories: Conlon once walked into an 8.00 am English class, taught by the distinguished Eddie Mims, at 8.05. Professor Mims stiffly informed Conlon that *no* one entered his class late. Conlon quietly said "Sorry," took his books, and walked out again.[10] Conlon seems to have made attendance a low priority, and the Vanderbilt experience ended after a semester.

These and the following years paint a picture of an impulsive young man, not fond of authority. Nancarrow went to Cincinnati College-Conservatory, studied there for a semester (he now insists, though other accounts differ),[11] and played in the school orchestra and in jazz groups at German beer halls. Here he heard *Le sacre* around 1930, and found the score's rhythmic complexity "a revelation." He also became impressed about this time by the music of Béla Bartók.[12] In Cincinnati, Nancarrow met his first wife, Helen Rigby, a singer and contrabass player. When they married in 1932, Helen was sixteen, still a senior in high school. Her parents tried to persuade them to annul the marriage, but they refused, and for a summer Nancarrow lived in his in-laws' home.[13] The marriage was apparently less than blissful, but Helen accompanied him to Boston where he moved to study composition.

In 1934–35, Nancarrow studied privately in Boston, with Roger Sessions, Walter Piston, and Nicolas Slonimsky. (Composer Alan Hovhaness was a nearby neighbor.)[14] At Malkin Conservatory, Nancarrow's path briefly crossed that of Arnold Schoenberg. The Austrian master had come to America soon after the German government announced that it would remove Jews from academic positions, and, after a year in Boston's wintry climate, would move to Los Angeles and UCLA for health reasons. Nancarrow, no fan of twelve-tone music (though he later used a twelve-tone row in Study No. 25), says only, "I don't remember meeting him. I should have, I knew he was there."[15] Twelve-tone music, Nancarrow comments, "is a dead duck . . . It's a dead end, there's nowhere to go."[16] Further, he has said,

> Of all the 12-tone composers, Webern's one of the few I rather like. Schoenberg bores me to death, doesn't reach me at all. The early music is the German romanticism I don't like, and even the later things are, for me, just an extension of chromaticism.[17]

Nancarrow did, however, study conducting at Malkin with Arthur Fiedler.[18]

One of Nancarrow's favorite stories is of his lessons with Sessions; Conlon would take in his original compositions, Sessions would glance at them briefly, then say, "I think it's fine; now where's your counterpoint exercise?" Because of the brevity and comparative irrelevance of his studies, Nancarrow calls himself basically an "autodidact," but when pressed he admits that Sessions's singlemindedness was a formative influence on his attitude toward counterpoint and voice-leading. As he would later say,

> I wouldn't call Sessions a good composition teacher; I'd call him a good technician. I think a good teacher should have the personality to bring out something in someone. And people who don't have it shouldn't do it. I'm sure I'd be a terrible teacher if I tried it, which I haven't. Because I just don't have the personality for it . . . He was a real rigid personality.[19]

It was just contrapuntal technique, you could apply it to any form. It was just voice leading. That's what I really learned. I still have really no harmonic sense, of harmony as harmony. I never studied it. I've always been interested in voice leading. For me that's the important thing in any piece I make. The sounds that are vertically sounding are *something*, you have to think of that, but I never think of it as harmony . . . And of course, Sessions' studies were very strict, classical Fuxian counterpoint. This fine point of where you make a decision between, say, a bad combination of sounds, bad in the classical sense, or can you sacrifice that to have the voice leading good? And, maybe I got it there, the voice leading was always the important thing. With things that go together, I never got to the point of what Cage says: someone asked him about putting notes together according to the *I Ching*, "What do you do if you put them together and it sounds terrible?" He said, "You get used to it." [laughs] That's very Cagean.[20]

Slonimsky, conductor, musicologist, and future editor of *Baker's Biographical Dictionary of Musicians*, was a more encouraging influence, and later proudly claimed to have "discovered" Nancarrow. It was also in Boston that Nancarrow first heard Indian music at the Ude Shankar Ballet, and he later became an avid collector of Indian music recordings.

In Boston Nancarrow joined the Communist Party. Though never one of its leaders, he arranged a musical program for a Lenin memorial meeting in Boston's Symphony Hall that was sophisticated enough to attract "non-political critics." One of the pieces Nancarrow programmed was his teacher Walter Piston's Sonata for Oboe and Piano, in which Piston himself performed. Harvard, where Piston was teaching, frowned on such extracurricular political activities and warned Piston that he would be fired if he ever did such a thing again. Piston apparently took the warning to heart. Nancarrow has said, "I don't particularly like his music. But I still admire him for playing on that concert."[21]

In Boston Nancarrow began working for the Works Projects Administration, which employed so many composers through the Depression. He worked first as a conductor and "found that I don't have the personality to be a conductor"; if he was as retiring and non-dictatorial then as he is now, the realization cannot have taken long. He switched to writing incidental music for theater, but the first piece he wrote for one play was rejected, so he kept resubmitting it for others – "ten times," he exaggerates. He does not know what happened to the piece, and he remembers it as nothing consequential, "just sounds." The trumpet had been given up long ago, but in 1936 Nancarrow received an opportunity to work his way to Europe by playing in a jazz group for a dance tour, so he brushed his technique back into shape. The trip allowed him a two-month stay in London, Paris (he apparently spent much of his time at the Sorbonne),[22] and Germany.[23] (Later, when he went to fight in the Spanish Civil War, Nancarrow left the trumpet with a friend who moved without forwarding address, ending the trumpet career for good.) By the time of this trip, Conlon and Helen were already separated.[24]

An interesting picture of the young Nancarrow emerges from a friend's recollection from this period. Adeline Lubell was the younger sister of one of

Nancarrow's friends, who asked Nancarrow to teach her piano despite his protests that he could not play the instrument. The going rate at the time was $1.00 per lesson, but she paid Nancarrow $1.50. In 1983 (now married and with the last name of Naiman) she wrote to him, saying she had found a record of his player piano music, and congratulating him on getting around his inability to play the instrument himself. She also said how important it had been to her that, unlike her previous teachers who had emphasized scales and a limited repertoire, he let her imagination "range far and wide." She also recalled how devastated she was when he went off to war and she had to seek out yet another stultifying Boston teacher.[25]

In 1937 Nancarrow returned to Europe under less benign auspices, as a member of the Abraham Lincoln Brigade, who fought with Republican Loyalists in Spain against Franco's fascist government. Nancarrow was a foot soldier; for two years, as he puts it, he fired a rifle and was fired upon, slept in trenches, marched half-asleep when needed, wore the same drenched clothes for days, suffered from hepatitis, fought off lice, and "never saw anything except mud and fields." Recruitment for the International Brigade was organized by the Communist Party, but Nancarrow's reasons for enlisting were more honorable than his government would later admit:

> I was an idealist in those days, and I thought that if Hitler was defeated there, it might avoid the next war, which was obviously coming. Hitler was spreading out, and taking this and that. I thought that might stop him. Of course, it didn't stop him, because the democracies prevented it, with their nonintervention. Well, Hitler intervened, so did Mussolini.[26]

Like so many farsighted comrades, Nancarrow saw the fight as a chance to help the Soviets stop the Germans, a view the U.S. would be forced to share in World War II. At one point he was announced in the newspaper as having been killed, though he only had a shrapnel wound in the neck.[27] Helen, never apprised as to his whereabouts, divorced Conlon by proclamation in 1940, thinking he was still in Spain. She married a cellist named Zimbler, played contrabass in the Houston Symphony and later the Tulsa Symphony, and eventually returned to Cincinnati.[28]

In the meantime, Nancarrow's musical career inched ahead without his knowledge. In 1938, Slonimsky chose Nancarrow's Toccata, Prelude, and Blues to publish in Henry Cowell's New Music Edition. (Cowell, at the time, was incarcerated at San Quentin prison on a "morals" charge; he was eventually released and pardoned.) Aaron Copland wrote a flattering review of the pieces in a subsequent issue, commenting on their "remarkable surety," and their "invention and imagination," and hoping for the composer's safe return from fighting Fascism.[29]

His battalion defeated by Franco in 1939, Nancarrow made a hair's-breadth escape from Fascist-dominated Spain, crammed with his fellow Lincoln Brigade members in the hold of a freighter leaving Valencia in the midst of Italian submarines.[30] He returned to Texarkana to visit his family (his mother was appalled at his undernourished physical condition), spoke by invitation about his Spanish experience to the local Lions Club, and was perplexed to realize that the community considered him a hero as the result of some mistaken belief that he had been battling Catholicism. Nancarrow soon moved to New York, where within a year he made some of the most important musical contacts of his life: among others, composers Elliott Carter, Aaron Copland, and Wallingford Riegger, and Minna Lederman, visionary editor of *Modern Music* magazine.

For *Modern Music* Nancarrow wrote four radio music columns under the title "Over the Air," his only published writings (a fifth article was written soon after in Mexico).[31] Like Cage's articles of the same period, Nancarrow's castigated the superficiality of the new American music that played to nationalist chauvinism by injecting jazz clichés among their "Lisztian dithyrambs," and correctly predicted that American experimentalism would not benefit from the Americana craze. He also showed a shrewd grasp of how commercial interests dilute the significance of the music they sponsor:

> For jazz, radio accepts the "plush" theory followed by certain movie producers (in whose films the poor but honest stenographer comes home from a hard day's work to her modest, eight-room penthouse). Everything must have pomp and splendour, big orchestras, luxuriance, cascades of sound. Jazz of the collective improvisation type is best exhibited by groups of five or six musicians. But apparently soap can't be sold with such a small orchestra – the public might think the soap manufacturer couldn't afford a larger orchestra; and if he didn't have much capital, how could the soap be good?[32]

Nancarrow's habitual laconicism came through in his writing as it does in his speech, making a critical career unlikely. Lederman later recalled her experiences trying to edit Nancarrow's work: "No plea from me could make him add a paragraph, a sentence, even a few words. He said what he had to say and that was it."[33]

Riegger (1885–1961; one of the composers called "the American Five," along with Ives, Ruggles, Becker, and Cowell) got in touch with Nancarrow and tried to lure the disillusioned veteran back into the Communist Party. (Nancarrow describes himself as a Democratic Socialist to this day, but political events of the thirties instilled in him a permanent disgust for Soviet-style Communism.) Soon Nancarrow learned that some of his Lincoln Brigade friends were being hassled by the U.S. Government for their membership in the Communist Party. After they had been denied passports, Nancarrow applied for one just to see what would happen; he, too, was denied. He quickly determined not to live under a government that looked on him with suspicion. Mexico and Canada were the only countries he could enter without a passport, and, having little curiosity about Canada, he moved in 1940 to Mexico City, where he has lived ever since. Had he remained, he might well have been subjected to the persecution visited upon so many artists during the McCarthy Era (including composers such as Copland, Riegger, Siegmeister, and Diamond).

In Mexico City Nancarrow taught a little English, did some translating, lived frugally, and supported himself with help from family at home. He recounts his early living arrangements with considerable amusement. His first apartment overlooked the Zocalo, Mexico City's central square, and cost 120 pesos a month. It faced the cathedral from the top floor of an office building that was deserted at night except for Nancarrow. The apartment needed painting, and when the building manager asked what color Nancarrow would like, he replied (he thinks) "green." It was so painted. Days later, someone with a title such as Minister of Historical Buildings came and told Nancarrow he would have to repaint the apartment red, and when Nancarrow went outside to look at his window from the street, he saw that every window on the square was red except his green one.

Nancarrow rented his second apartment for 75 pesos a month from someone he suspected was not playing with a full deck. When the person in question appeared in Nancarrow's bedroom one night wearing only shirt, hat, and shoes, and demanding to know where his wife was (she was in her bedroom shouting "don't listen to him, he's crazy"), Nancarrow packed up and left before his landlord's eccentricity took a more sinister turn. His next apartment was the maid's quarters at the house of some married friends. Nancarrow's stay here was more tranquil, though he later learned that the couple's jealous husband had accused his wife of having an affair with Nancarrow – who was, as photos from the time show, devilishly handsome.

Nancarrow's first performance experiences, which took place during these years, were disastrous. In 1940 he wrote a Septet for a concert by the League of Composers in New York. Only two rehearsals were arranged, only four players showed up for each, and only one of these was the same for both rehearsals. Predictably, the performance was a disaster. For decades Nancarrow insisted he had destroyed the score, but in 1993 his assistant Carlos Sandoval discovered it in his studio. Once in Mexico City, attempts to make inroads into the Mexican music community met with infrequent success. Nancarrow was befriended by Spanish composer Rodolfo Halffter (1900–87), who had fled to Mexico City in 1939 after the Loyalist defeat, and who later became Mexico's first twelve-tone composer. In 1942 Halffter asked Nancarrow to write a piece for the Monday Evening Concerts he organized in Mexico City: the result was the Trio for clarinet, bassoon, and piano. Rehearsals went badly; the clarinetist refused to play a piece that would, he said, make the audience think he was playing "wrong notes," and ultimately the work was not played.[34]

Luckily Nancarrow had already been struck by a better idea, one that liberated him from dependence on other musicians to an extent many composers would envy. In New York he had obtained Henry Cowell's ground-breaking theoretical treatise *New Musical Resources*, and he devoured it in 1939 and 1940. Among Cowell's innovations was a wide-ranging theory of divisive rhythm, dividing a large rhythmic unit (or measure) into various numbers of equal parts at once, creating an effect of different tempos moving at the same time. Significantly, Cowell hinted (in words quoted in chapter 1) that such rhythms could only be achieved, at that time, by the use of a player piano. Thanks to his father's care for the family's musical interests, Nancarrow was no stranger to the instrument, and he began considering the possibilities. As Nancarrow says today,

> [Cowell's] book *New Musical Resources* is probably the most influence of anything I've ever read in music. In fact, I just reread it again. I hadn't read it in many years, I thought maybe now I wouldn't think so, but I still think it's a very good book. And there are still a lot of ideas in there that haven't been carried out. There are two or three places where he mentions that something would be interesting, but it could only be done on a player piano. And he never did it! That's the thing that surprises me.[35]

In 1940 there was no extra money to put towards elaborate musical technology. But Nancarrow's father had left a trust fund to support his family through the Depression. For fifteen years it was reserved for Conlon's mother, but in 1947 the sons became eligible for their share directly,[36] and Conlon began receiving enough money to live on. Given his frugal lifestyle, the money continued to provide considerable support into the sixties, largely freeing him to compose with only a minimum of nonmusical work. (Nancarrow's present wife Yoko says that he always insisted he would never use his music to make a living, an attitude reminiscent of Charles Ives.) Nancarrow used some of the money to keep up with current musical developments: in later years he would subscribe to *Perspectives of New Music*, *Musical Quarterly*, and *Source*. And in 1947 he used the money to return to New York City to search for a player piano and punching machine.

Staying with friends, Nancarrow spent two to three months in New York. This important episode deserves telling in his own words:

> The main thing I went to New York for was to look into the whole thing of player pianos. I knew nothing about player pianos, or how they were produced, or the rolls, nothing. And so I was going to find out. I went to the QRS, the player piano roll company, which was in the Bronx then. Now it's in Buffalo. At that time it was still a fairly big business for popular music. I met this guy, J. Lawrence Cook, who worked there. They had these big machines that mass-produced player piano rolls, punching a hundred at a time. But he had – it had nothing to do with the factory – a little punching machine for things he wanted to do that couldn't be done on the big machines. Nothing as complicated as I've been doing. At that time I didn't know it was a commercial thing, that I could have bought one. They still exist, you find them in antique stores with player pianos. They're very primitive, but more flexible than the big machines. But since I didn't know that these things could be bought, I asked him – he was a very nice guy – if he'd mind if I got that copied by someone. He said, "Of course not." Maybe he didn't even know that I could have found one if I looked around.
>
> I didn't know who to get to copy it, but I was walking through the Village, and there was a shop there, run by a weird guy who repaired old instruments, lutes, and all kinds of Baroque and Renaissance instruments. I started talking to him, and I happened to mention that I was looking for someone who could copy a roll punching machine. He didn't know anything about it, but by coincidence he had a friend who had a machine shop, who was an absolutely accurate metal

worker. And I got him to go up to the Bronx with me and look at this machine and take all the measurements. And he made that. It took quite awhile, about a month. When I got to Mexico and started using it, right away I saw all kinds of limitations and things that had to be changed. Also luckily, I found this fantastic mechanic in Mexico who rebuilt that machine. The one you see there, that's a big, solid thing. The original was just a little, basic thing. He fixed it up to where I could do all kinds of things. That machine is still holding up beautifully. I've had to change the punches several times, because they wear out.[37]

As agreed beforehand, Nancarrow paid the New York machinist $300 for his work, though the man said, "I told you $300, but if I had to do it again I'd charge you I don't know what!"[38] Years later Nancarrow sent the machinist another $500.

During this same visit to New York, Nancarrow met Henry Cowell, who had unwittingly had such a major effect on his career.

Minna Lederman arranged for me to go meet him, because she knew I admired his ideas. It was after the jail thing, and I sat with him a few hours one afternoon, talking. I had never met him before, so I don't know how he was originally. But the impression I got was that he was a terrified person, with a feeling that "they're going to get him." He may have had that all his life, but I don't think so; I think it had to do with that [jail] experience. And of course, after that, politically, he kept his mouth completely shut. He had been radical politically, too, before. It's quite a sad case.[39]

Nancarrow also happened (possibly at Lederman's insistence) to attend the première of John Cage's *Sonatas and Interludes* for prepared piano (screws, erasers, and other objects attached to the piano strings to make the sound more percussive). The idea obviously intrigued Nancarrow, for years later he used such preparations in his Study No. 30. A more fruitful result of the trip was Nancarrow's meeting his second wife Annette Margolis, an artist and assistant to Diego Rivera. After Annette and Nancarrow married they lived in her Mexico City apartment, but in the meantime, on property she owned from a previous marriage, they built a house and the studio in which all of Nancarrow's player piano music has been written, punched, played, and recorded. Nancarrow's marriage to Annette lasted about five years; when they divorced, they divided the land, and he got the part with the small house and studio. Later, in the seventies, after marrying his third wife, Yoko, Nancarrow would build a new larger house on the other side of the studio.

It is difficult to describe to those who have not been there (and apparently impossible to convince Nancarrow) how like a shrine that studio feels to those who love the music produced there. The room is approximately the size and shape of a three-car garage with a high ceiling. Circling the room are wooden bookcases, containing Nancarrow's extensive library of music books and journals. (His tens of thousands of books on math, psychology, cooking, literature, history, and every aspect of science occupy a separate, crowded library.) On one side of the room stand the two player pianos, their sounding boards facing the room's unoccupied center. (A third player piano, converted into a conventional piano for the use of Nancarrow's son, sits in the living room.) Behind them are shelves holding about seventy piano rolls, including all the Player Piano Studies with their separate movements, as well as a few piano–roll transcriptions of works not intended for player piano that Nancarrow wanted to hear, such as the First String Quartet and *Tango?*.

On the other side of the studio is a long, rectangular table with a cranked roller at each end; here Nancarrow lays out the blank rolls for marking off rhythmic divisions. Until the early 1990s, an artist's clutter lay around the comfortable old easy chair in front of the table: recordings, copies of scores, books about mechanical instruments, unanswered correspondence, sketches, charts, all in a delicate, untouchable disarray that suggested that their owner could quickly locate any item therein. Today the studio is kept scrupulously neat so that the dust will not exacerbate Nancarrow's emphysema. Next to the table is a custom–made cabinet with tiny shelves, full of long strips of paper, each marked off in a different ratio to a common spatial tempo; these are the templates Nancarrow has collected over the years to mark off tempos on his piano rolls. The actual punching is done on a machine in a hallway outside the studio, a machine familiar from many Nancarrow photographs. The space seems full of the vibrations of intense creative activity, accommodated to the very shape of Nancarrow's body over forty years' daily occupancy. The Nancarrows have often dreamed of moving away from Mexico City for health reasons (the area's combination of pollution and altitude would exacerbate even the most benign ailment), but as Nancarrow says,

> if I'm going to continue doing my music for player pianos, I wouldn't dream of trying to move that studio anywhere. I'd spend the rest of my life trying to get one set up like it is here. I put all those things up just the way I wanted to use them. To start all that up again, no. That's out.[40]

Sometime in the fifties Nancarrow bought a second player piano in Mexico with the idea of writing for two pianos, though it was not until the late seventies that the plan would bear fruit. In the late forties, he also experimented for a time with a percussion orchestra mechanically run by a roll, but his mechanical ability was insufficient to get the project off the ground. (Long-persisting rumors that he had written works for mechanical percussion turned out to be true when, among the sixty-eight piano rolls discovered by Sandoval, several, because of their total lack of pitch interest, could only have been written for the percussion machine.) At one point Nancarrow acquired a tape recorder and made a piece of *musique concrète* – electronic tape music using natural sounds – using drum beats painstakingly spliced together in conflicting rhythms; but, as Boulez and Messiaen had done, he became dissatisfied with the result and abandoned both the piece (though the tape still exists) and the medium.

Nancarrow's isolation during the fifties and sixties was as extreme as that of any composer since Ives, but it was not total. He became a close friend of the mural painter Juan O'Gorman, associated with Diego Rivera and David Alfaro Siqueiros; in the fifties, O'Gorman made the beautiful stone mosaic that adorns the front of Nancarrow's small, older house, and in the early seventies he designed the newer house on the other side of the studio as a wedding present. At a dinner party Nancarrow met Ernest Hemingway and was disappointed: "he didn't say two words all evening." Nancarrow also knew the painter Frida Kahlo (Rivera's third wife), and narrowly missed an introduction to Marilyn Monroe when she visited Mexico.

Among musical friends, Nancarrow remained in touch with Elliott Carter, who, in 1951, sent the Rhythm Study No. 1 to *New Music*, which published it. Carter also wrote an article for the June 1955 issue of *The Score*, entitled "The Rhythmic Basis of American Music." In it he acknowledged Nancarrow's innovations in polyrhythms, with an example from the Rhythm Study No. 1 and a brief outline of the rhythmic dissonances involved.[41] Also in 1951 pianist James Sykes gave the world première of Nancarrow's Sonatina in Washington, D.C., its only performance until the 1980s.[42] In the late 1950s John Edmunds of the Americana section of the New York Public Library's Music Division requested tapes from Nancarrow and brought them to the attention of John Cage. Cage, predictably fascinated, gave them to the dancer Merce Cunningham, who choreographed Nos. 1, 2, 4, 5, 6, and 7 in 1960 and took them on a world tour of the Cunningham Dance Company in 1964.[43] In 1962, Nancarrow's old friend Halffter persuaded him to bring his player pianos to Bellas Artes for a concert. It was Nancarrow's only public live concert of his player piano music until 1989, by which time it had become possible to play his rolls live on other MIDI-operated pianos; he found it absurd to play his Studies for an audience of friends who had already heard them in his studio, and he did not move his pianos again until 1990.

At some point during these years, two of the most original minds in the history of music had a brief, disappointing encounter. Harry Partch, composer, inventor of fantastic musical instruments, and visionary tuning theoretician, visited Mexico City and sought out Nancarrow; Nancarrow had ordered one of Partch's self-produced records, and figures Partch was curious enough about who in Mexico would buy his music that he looked up the mailing address. They had drinks, Nancarrow gave Partch a tour of his studio, full of player pianos and drums, and Nancarrow wondered why Partch left without asking to hear a note of his music. (Partch later claimed that Nancarrow had refused to play him anything. As Peter Garland relates, the two had humorously divergent memories of the visit, and Partch remembered Nancarrow talking about his fantasy of going to Paris, spending the remainder of his inheritance in French restaurants, and then committing suicide. Nancarrow claims Partch's story was completely fabricated.[44])

The years 1961–65 brought "sort of a depression." Nancarrow quit composing and put his energies into studying Chinese and preparing readable scores of the pieces he had written. One can see, in the latter activity and in the Halffter concert at Bellas Artes, a desire to bring thirteen years worth of intensively-composed music out of a vacuum and into the public ear. The first commercial recording of Nancarrow's Studies (Nos. 2, 7, 8, 10, 12, 15, 19, 21, 23, 24, 25, and 33) was issued by Columbia in 1969, as a result of interest stirred by the Cunningham tour. (With the company's usual, irritating underestimation of its most historic releases, Columbia deleted this disc in 1973; Nancarrow had never been pleased with its curiously muffled sound quality.) Also in 1969, Nancarrow met composer and radio producer Charles Amirkhanian. Amirkhanian heard some of Nancarrow's studies at a Merce Cunningham dance concert and became fascinated. When he mentioned the music to San Francisco poet George Oppen, an old friend of Nancarrow's, Oppen gave him Nancarrow's phone number. Amirkhanian and his then new bride Carol Law planned a Mexico City honeymoon, and drove down in June of 1969 to meet Nancarrow, at the time an almost total recluse. Amirkhanian, who has since been active in the promotion and recording of Nancarrow's music, says that Nancarrow knew every restaurant in Mexico City that did not play Muzak, and would patronize no others.

Around 1970, after Nancarrow had been single for about seventeen years, he met Yoko Seguira, an anthropologist from Japan, at a mutual friend's going-away party, and let her know through a friend that he would like her to call him. She did, and happily recounts how Nancarrow would show up on their first dates in fancy silk suits. They were soon married and had a son, David Makoto (whom they call Mako), in August of 1971. Yoko suffered complications during the delivery, and afterward was paralyzed on one side for several months. Having become a father at fifty-eight, Nancarrow was suddenly faced with major child-rearing duties (a maid helped out) until Yoko's recovery. Nancarrow's inheritance had nearly run out, and the family lived primarily on Yoko's teaching salary until, in 1982, Nancarrow received the MacArthur Foundation's prestigious "genius" award of $300,000, paid over a five-year period.

Peter Garland, composer and publisher of the important American music journal *Soundings*, began corresponding with Nancarrow in 1972, and two years later drove to Mexico City to meet him. The meeting led to Garland's including the score to Study No. 25 in *Soundings* in 1975. In 1976 New World Records released a recording of avant-garde piano music containing Studies Nos. 1, 27, and 36; the recordings were made by Roger Reynolds with a small, hand-held tape recorder, and Nancarrow is contemptuous of their quality. The following year, though, marked a dramatic turning point in Nancarrow's public fortunes. That year Garland published, as part of *Soundings*, *Conlon Nancarrow: Selected Studies for Player Piano*, with scores of Studies Nos. 8, 19, 23, 27, 31, 35, 36, and 40, along with appreciative articles by Gordon Mumma, Charles Amirkhanian, John Cage, Roger Reynolds, and James Tenney. In the same year, Studies 3, 20, and 41 were recorded by (the now-defunct) 1750 Arch Records, and Nancarrow received his first commission, from the European Broadcasting Union, for a work that would become Study No. 48. By 1984, 1750 Arch would release four records, including the remainder of the studies through No. 41.

In 1981 Eva Soltes, a dancer and performing arts producer who had earlier visited Nancarrow when she was concert director for 1750 Arch, returned to Mexico City and single-handedly tangled with the American Consulate's mammoth immigration bureaucracy to get Nancarrow a five-year visa. This allowed him to visit San Francisco in June 1981, where selected recordings of the studies were played at his first, emotional return to the U.S. since 1947. Soltes became his manager, and arranged and accompanied him on every trip outside Mexico for the next five years. In 1982 Nancarrow was composer-in-residence at the Cabrillo Festival in Aptos, California, where his early instrumental works from the thirties and forties received their world premières: Dennis Russell Davies conducted the Piece for Small Orchestra No. 1, the Kronos Quartet played the String Quartet No. 1, and violinist Romauld Tecco played the Toccata. October and November brought a tour of Graz (the ISCM festival, honoring Nancarrow's seventieth birthday), Innsbruck, Cologne and Paris's IRCAM. At each stopping point Soltes presented her slide/recording show on Nancarrow, and at Innsbruck, Graz, and Cologne, the composer's family was accompanied by Hungarian composer György Ligeti, who had become one of Nancarrow's most enthusiastic fans.

In January of 1984 the player piano studies were featured at the Kennedy Center's Terrace Concerts, and a week later the Los Angeles New Music Group presented the Prelude and Blues, the Sonatina, the Sarabande, tapes of Studies Nos. 25 and 45 (a Betty Freeman commission that also included No. 46 and 47), and Dorrance Stalvey's instrumental arrangements, not terribly successful by Nancarrow's account, of Studies Nos. 14, 26, and 32. Nancarrow also appeared on this tour at San Francisco's Exploratorium, the San Francisco Art Institute, and Betty Freeman's composer series, where he was introduced by his old friend and teacher Nicolas Slonimsky.

June of 1985 brought Nancarrow to the Almeida festival in London where, featured along with Lou Harrison and Virgil Thomson, he spoke publicly about his own music for the first time in his life. This trip was followed by a five-month stay in Berkeley, part of which he spent teaching a small course on his music at Mills College. He also left briefly to attend performances of his music at New Music America in Los Angeles and at the Center for Contemporary Arts in Santa Fe, a performance arranged by Peter Garland. During this time Soltes took Nancarrow to a lawyer to see about the possibility of bringing him back to live in the United States permanently. As Nancarrow tells it,

> Anyone who ever joined the Communist Party is doomed for life as far as America is concerned. By the time I came back from Spain, I was pretty disillusioned about the whole party. Not that I changed my ideas, I still had the same ideas, but the Party didn't have the same ideas, Stalin and all the rest of them. A few years ago, Yoko and I wanted to get out of Mexico on account of my health, and so when we were in California we started investigating what we'd need to do to move legally. The legal thing is, anyone who wants to get residence there [in the U.S.], not citizenship but just residence, has to prove, if they've ever

belonged to the Communist Party, that the five years previous to that time they've been doing active propaganda *against* that ideology. Well, forget about it. I wouldn't even dream of that. Not that I believe in the ideology, but I'm not going to start doing propaganda against it. It's unbelievable, their whole attitude.[45]

The lawyer also advised that Nancarrow would have to sign a statement swearing that he had been "young and foolish" in embracing Communism and renouncing American citizenship. Naturally, Nancarrow, whose political convictions remain firm, declined.

In April of 1986, Joel Sachs's and Cheryl Seltzer's Continuum ensemble played Nancarrow's non-mechanical music at Lincoln Center, including the Piece for Small Orchestra No. 2. The following month he was featured at the Pacific Ring Festival at the University of California at San Diego, where he spoke with Roger Reynolds, Gordon Mumma, pianist Margaret Leng Tan, critic Alan Rich, and computer artist Harold Cohen on a panel entitled "Art and Technology: Is Mastery Still Possible?" The Nancarrows traveled to Amsterdam for performances of his music at the 1987 Holland Festival – Cage and Carter were the other honorees – and on the trip back made a return visit to the Almeida Festival. In 1988 Nancarrow was a guest at the San Francisco convention of AMICA, a player piano society, and in October he was honored at a Mechanical Music Festival in Cologne.[46] The year 1988 also brought major commissions and a return to writing for live performers. The first commission was from England's extraordinary Arditti Quartet, for whom Nancarrow wrote his String Quartet No. 3. The equally impressive pianist Ursula Oppens asked Nancarrow to write a piano piece for a $15,000 commission from Composers' Forum in New York, subsequently entitled *Two Canons for Ursula*, and premièred in New York in 1989.

During this period, the player pianos were silent, fallen into a state of disrepair from which Nancarrow did not expect them to be revived. However, in summer of 1989 Nancarrow's German fan Jurgen Hocker, a chemist and president of the German Mechanical Instrument Association, sent his mechanic protégé Jurg Borchardt to restore the pianos to their original condition at no cost to Nancarrow. One of the year's most significant events was a visit by Trimpin, a brilliant German musician/engineer who has invented machines for playing many musical instruments via computer. For the sake of preserving Nancarrow's piano rolls, Trimpin invented a machine to transcribe them into MIDI-compatible computer information. He copied all of Nancarrow's piano rolls, most of which had existed as unique copies, into computer files, greatly reducing the music's vulnerability to physical disaster, and opening up the possibility of computerized performance elsewhere.

That August Nancarrow participated (along with John Cage, Annea Lockwood, Morton Subotnick, Laurie Spiegel, Anthony Davis, and other composers) in the second annual Composer-to-Composer symposium in Telluride, Colorado. In November 1989 he returned to New York as a guest of the New Music America festival, which featured a performance of Studies Nos. 36 and 48 on grand pianos played via Trimpin's MIDI-computer mechanisms, his first "live" performance of any of the Studies since the one at Bellas Artes. In 1990 New England Conservatory presented Nancarrow with an honorary doctorate. And in October of that year, the University of Mexico City presented a two-day celebration of Nancarrow's music, organized by his composer friend Julio Estrada, Nancarrow's first major honor in Mexico. For the first time in twenty-eight years, he consented to have one of his player pianos moved so that fans could come and hear the piano rolls "live."

Nancarrow's health remained remarkably good until early 1990, despite emphysema and some minor operations (his cholesterol level, for example, is an amazingly low 160). He has continued to maintain the secluded life that gives him such enviable control over his time and privacy. His most frequent complaint is about his poor memory, attributed half-facetiously to Alzheimer's disease (with no correlative evidence). He and Yoko spend weekends at their charming country home near Cuernavaca; in 1990 they sold one weekend home because of its high maintenance and remodeling costs, and subsequently bought another. In January 1990, however, Nancarrow caught pneumonia (brought on by the emphysema) and, falling into a temporary coma, suffered the effects of a small stroke, for which he spent several days in intensive care. For a while his hearing was diminished. His recovery, however, has been remarkable; though his long-term memory is still slightly impaired, he has composed five new works since the stroke. His work has been greatly facilitated in the nineties by the help of an assistant: the composer Carlos Sandoval has organized Nancarrow's studio, recopied scores, and punched the most recent piano rolls.

At 81 Nancarrow is at the height of his fame, celebrated across Europe and increasingly in the United States. His influence on the continuing development of music grows each year, as composers and scholars across the globe become aware of the extent of his phenomenal achievement. The renegade trumpet player from Texarkana who disappeared into Mexico as a political exile is now an inspiring symbol for revolutionary musicians everywhere.

3

Foreshadowings: the early works

Sarabande and Scherzo, Prelude, Blues, Toccata for violin and piano, Septet, Sonatina, Three Two-Part Studies for piano, Trio No. 1, Piece No. 1 for Small Orchestra, String Quartet No. 1

Between 1948 and 1983 Nancarrow composed only for player piano. His dozen-odd works for live instrumentalists, then, fall into two periods: those written before his trip to New York to buy the player piano, and those written in the 1980s and 90s as his growing fame brought commissions from performers. The player piano studies form the core of Nancarrow's output, the reason for current interest in his work, and the primary subject of this book. The non-mechanical works will be considered primarily only to the extent that they shed light on the player piano studies. What discussion of these works will show, however, is that by the time Nancarrow bought a player piano his conceptions of canon, iso-rhythm, ostinato, articulation, phrasing, acceleration, register, motive, pitch row, and polytempo were already formed. The player piano was not just a toy that inspired new ideas: it was needed to satisfy an aesthetic already in place.

Ten works survive from Nancarrow's pre-player piano period. In roughly chronological order, they are:

> Sarabande and Scherzo for oboe, bassoon, and piano (1930)
> Blues for piano (1935)
> Prelude for piano (1935)
> Toccata for violin and piano (1935)
> Septet (1940)
> Sonatina for piano (1941)
> Three Two-Part Studies for piano (early 1940s)
> Trio No. 1 for clarinet, bassoon, and piano (1942)
> Piece No. 1 for Small Orchestra (1943) (also in an extended version for larger orchestra)
> String Quartet (1945)

In addition, some theater music written for a WPA project in the mid-thirties has not survived, and Nancarrow has rejected a tape piece made up of drum sounds which, however, still exists. There is also an unfinished String Quartet No. 2, dating from the late forties; in case he ever got around to completing this early work, Nancarrow numbered his subsequent quartet No. 3.

Sarabande and Scherzo for Oboe, Bassoon, and Piano

Nancarrow has called the Sarabande and Scherzo a "simple-minded piece" and a "childhood effort." Nevertheless, there are some striking qualities here for a work by an eighteen-year-old, and with hindsight one can discern glimpses of his mature concerns. Most notable is the work's preoccupation with canon and fugue: the Sarabande begins with a canon at the fourth between oboe and bassoon, and ends with one at the major sixth. The Scherzo opens with an exchange of melodies between oboe and bassoon, leading to a four-part fugue begun in the piano. The Scherzo's trio is likewise a fugue on a slow, chromatic theme echoed by its inversion, though exact imitation is quickly dropped. Another hallmark of the later Nancarrow is the simple, architectural sense of structure. The Sarabande, for example, can be divided into A (woodwind canon), B (piano counterpoint), and C (A and B simultaneously). One thinks, of course, of the much later Studies Nos. 41 and 48, in each of which the third section consists of the first two played simultaneously; the coincidence is undoubtedly subconscious, but revealing.

Counterpoint in the Sarabande is smooth if unpianistic, and the intervallic style anticipates later works of Bartók and Messiaen. Other factors seem typical of "ultramodern" pieces written in the thirties by such Americans as Henry Cowell, Wallingford Riegger, and John Becker. These include the square rhythms, the sudden and rather arbitrary tonal cadence that closes the Sarabande, and the use of Baroque forms (helpful for grounding the new, atonal style in a simple, non-modulating structure). Less conservative at eighteen than he thinks he was, Nancarrow had already aligned himself with the more advanced composers of the preceding generation. What is missing, of course, is rhythmic experimentation; only the Scherzo's rare septuplet runs provide any unusual rhythmic division, and despite his triple meter Nancarrow abstains from even a hemiola.

Blues, Prelude

The Blues for piano, Toccata for violin and piano, and Prelude for piano were Nancarrow's first published works, the ones that Nicolas Slonimsky issued in *New Music* in 1938 while Nancarrow was fighting in Spain. Nancarrow has called the Prelude and Blues "nothing pieces."[1] They are imaginative, but choppy: they jump from idea to idea with sketchy continuity. The Blues shows some facility with jazz harmony, but the clusters seem thrown in for novelty, and the static, repetitive melody is a type handled better by Aaron Copland. It is easy to see why Copland gave the Prelude and Blues a flattering review; they are in the style of his early jazz works, and not well-written enough to pose competition.

The interest here lies in the few hints of Nancarrow's later ideas that can be found amid the tidbits of 1930s classical stride piano evocation. Playing them, one notices that they use nearly the entire range of the piano, proving that Nancarrow's all-over approach to register was not a result of working with piano rolls, but something that was present from the beginning. The Blues, naturally, uses the dotted (trochaic) rhythm endemic to Nancarrow's jazz style, and the D#–E–G motive at m. 40 is one that will figure prominently in Study No. 3 and elsewhere. The crashing climax strikingly anticipates Study No. 3d, written some thirteen years later. The wandering bass will take on a smoother form in the mature works, and some of the progressions lend credence to Nancarrow's assertion that he has no feel for harmony.

More significantly, the Prelude uses both canon and ostinato. It begins with a three-part canon on a rhythmically square, atonal but not dissonant subject; strict imitation is abandoned by m. 7. At m. 26 a syncopated ostinato begins, which continues through four repetitions. At the final climax the theme laid over the ostinato is brought back in counterpoint with the canon subject (the idea of combining materials first heard separately will become a Nancarrow reflex). At m. 42 the canon subject appears in the bass, augmented and inverted. Nancarrow is fond of these Bachian transformations in his early works, but the mature music will abandon them. In fact the most obvious features of these pieces – the strident pounding on a repeated chord, the jazz melody in parallel semitones, the 4/4 squareness of even the syncopations – never reappear in the player piano music.

Toccata

The Toccata for violin and piano, published along with the Prelude and Blues, is a more conventional and more successful work, primarily because of its unrelenting rhythmic energy. Though the piece requires extreme virtuosity, it is flawed as a violin showpiece by the fact that, after a twenty-six-measure exposition (out of 124 measures total), the soloist fades out for a monochrome, forty-five-measure piano exercise, mostly consisting of scales and parallel seventh chords on the white keys. As we have already come to expect, the piece opens with a canon, the violin following the piano at a three-measure interval. The canon is in B♭ major against an incessant, repeated high E on the piano, and the sharp dissonances that result, perhaps shocking to 1935 ears, tie the piece securely to the iconoclastic aesthetic of the ultramodernists.

Again one listens for the later Nancarrow almost in vain, but one rhythmic tic looks prophetic. Starting at m. 18 the piano has a series of bass chords which outline, in sixteenth note multiples, the rhythmic series 10, 9, 8, 7, 6, 5, 4, 3, 2, 1. Closing the exposition here, that subtractive acceleration will become not only a standard cadential device in the Player Piano Studies, but a premise of Nancarrow's rhythmic thinking. At m. 34 we get an expanding series – 3, 4, 5, 6, 7, 8, 9, underlaid by off-throwing quintuplets in the left hand – and in the last

Example 3.1   Septet, second movement, bassoon theme

few measures another such series: 2, 3, 4, 5, 5, 6, 7, 8, 7, 6, 5, 4, 3, 2. At m. 72 we find an ostinato of five eighth notes beating against the 2/4 meter. The transfer of the beginning of the piano solo to the violin at m. 72, and the switching of violin and piano roles in the canon's recapitulation, are clever in a conventionally musical way that the later Nancarrow rarely indulges.[2]

Nancarrow came to consider the piano part impossible to play at the tempo he wanted, so in the eighties, spurred by requests for live music, he punched a roll of the piano part. The Toccata has since been performed by taped player piano and live violinist.

Septet

Understandably, no music appears from 1937 to 1940, the period in which Nancarrow was fighting in Spain and traveling. The next offering, the Septet of 1940, was the only work Nancarrow completed between fighting in Spain and moving to Mexico. This was the work that Nancarrow claimed he had torn up after its disastrous New York performance, but which Sandoval discovered in 1993. Sandoval reconstructed a bridge section that appeared to be incomplete, and the work received its second performance 11 May 1994 in New York by the Parnassus Ensemble.

The Septet is scored for clarinet, alto saxophone, bassoon, piano, violin, viola, and double bass. Of the three movements, the second is the meatiest, flanked by a less developed introduction and conclusion. The introductory movement, Allegro molto, is based obsessively on a motive of a major second and minor third (A–B–D), and on a clash between a rhythm of dotted eighth notes and one of a quarter note followed by an eighth note, all across a 2/4 meter. The pitch motive generates melodies, but is more often merely repeated in climbing sequences. Several interruptions in the piano reassert the basic rhythmic clash in its most basic terms.

The Allegro moves without pause into a Moderato blues. The opening theme in the bassoon (Example 3.1) returns in the saxophone, violin, and bassoon again (this last time switching to clarinet and viola), in that order. Nancarrow instructs that the trochaic dotted note pattern is to be somewhere between a 3:1 and a 2:1 (triplet) ratio. The theme is accompanied by stride piano patterns that switch off between the piano and pizzicato strings, and later by a walking bass, while the texture crescendos simply via the addition of contrapuntal lines. No particular

Example 3.2   Septet, opening of third movement, piano part

rhythmic complexity runs through the movement, but two moments show a desire to experiment with cross-rhythms: one at mm. 63–67, where a transposing ostinato switches back and forth between the clarinet and violin on every seventh sixteenth note, and at mm. 79–80, where the momentum is suddenly interrupted by triplets. These latter are accented every other note in the strings, every fifth note in the piano.

The final movement is notable for a nervous rhythm in the piano, syncopated at the thirty-second-note level (Example 3.2). This is accompanied by a blues melody in the clarinet reminiscent of the second movement theme, along with its inversion in the saxophone; and a phase-shifting pattern in the pizzicato strings marked by a dotted quarter note in the bass against a pattern of five eighth notes in the violin and viola (the five divided two plus three). The piano remains the center of attention, leading into a brief but crashing cadenza and ending by itself on a note of tonal ambiguity. Overall, the Septet seems overly laconic and underdeveloped, and is primarily interesting for Nancarrow's attempt to write a conventional jazz movement in the middle.

Sonatina

The Sonatina of 1941, Nancarrow's first piece written in Mexico, shows a tremendous advance in ability to conceptualize a work. Gone for good are the rhythmic squareness, the jumping from idea to idea, the clunky parallelisms of the early pieces. Instead, the Sonatina exhibits stunning rhythmic variety and contrapuntal sophistication. In fact all five instrumental works from the early Mexican period are remarkably smooth, well-written examples of the dissonant, ultramodern American style. What they lack is distinctive personality, which suddenly springs into blossom in the first player piano studies. Still, in the Sonatina we are no longer dealing with juvenilia, but with one of the best American piano works of the 1940s.

In the first ten measures alone we find seven five-beat phrases, no two articulated in quite the same way, interrupted by one six-beat phrase. Canon is present, but so well integrated that it does not announce itself. In movement I, mm. 37–43 contain a striking canon of leaping sevenths, the intervals growing progressively smaller until they reach a repeated unison. We also have hints at isorhythm (the same rhythm repeated with different pitches – see chapter 5 for fuller explanation). At mm. 32–36, a dotted quarter pulse in the right hand plays against a 3+2 pattern in the left, for an overall five against three. Likewise, at mm. 61–78 in the first movement, a series of ascending triads keeps up a repeated 2+3 rhythm, while the right hand moves from dotted quarters to quarters to eighths and back: 3+2+1+2+3. Already Nancarrow is interested in juxtaposing different types of rhythmic process, specifically isorhythm against acceleration and ritard.

The second movement blues begins with a five-against-two rhythm, the two articulated by crashing chords. That is only an introduction; the theme in 6/8 follows, marked by the most luscious jazz chords of Nancarrow's output. The second half of the theme inverts the first half, underlaid with some open-spaced triads of a type that will become common in the studies. A *ff* interlude returns to the five-against-two, using some Ivesian fist clusters no doubt suggested by Cowell's book. The remainder of the movement is crafted with exquisite care. Nancarrow wrings unexpected harmonies from the theme by placing the third phrase's accompaniment now under the first phrase. In the last phrase, he superimposes the theme over its inversion, fusing Bartókian and jazz methods as he will again to great effect in the Study No. 1.

The third movement starts out with a perpetual motion canon reminiscent of Roy Harris, and it is worth noting that Nancarrow spaces the entrances asymmetrically: the second voice enters after two measures, the third after five. One can see the beginnings of Nancarrow's rhythmic thinking in mm. 13–27: the rhythmic pattern (3 3 4 – 3 3 2 4 – 3 3 2 – 3 3 4) suggests isorhythm and walks a line between rhythmic motive and isorhythm as certain of the studies, notably Nos. 4 and 35, will do later (see Example 3.3). (This rhythm and its variants run through the movement: note the accents in mm. 63–73.) The theme's primary motive, C–A–G, and its retrograde saturate the movement to the point that one begins to hear canon everywhere.

The contrapuntal difficulties of especially the final movement render the piece nearly impossible to play at the desired tempo, and Nancarrow has generally been unhappy with attempts to play it as written. Piano roll is now the Sonatina's usual method of performance. However, Nancarrow has been quite pleased with performances of the four-hand (one piano) version made by pianist Yvar Mikhashoff.

Three Two-Part Studies for Piano

The Three Two-Part Studies for Piano were discovered in Nancarrow's studio in 1990 by Jurgen Hocker. Though they are not dated, their style – abstract, contrapuntal, with melodies based on perfect fourths and constantly changing meters – is close to that of the Sonatina and the Trio for clarinet, bassoon, and piano. Formally, the piece could have been an early study for the Sonatina,

Example 3.3   Sonatina, third movement, mm. 13–17

Example 3.4   Three Two-Part Studies, No. 1, mm. 34–39

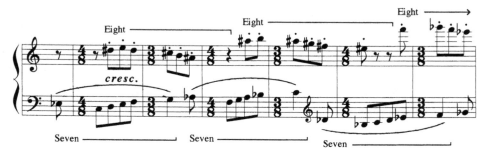

though its rhythmic concerns and melodic intervals are closer to those of the Trio. Based on such internal evidence, I date these Studies around 1941, probably no earlier than 1940 nor later than 1943. All three movements use a consistent, two-voice texture in a rather anonymous idiom that could be characterized as Hindemithian neo-Baroque.

The first Study is interesting for its prophetic use of isorhythm. It opens using virtual 17/8 meter, divided 6+4+3+4. This metric pattern is given nine times in succession at the beginning and eight times at the end, with fragments and variations in between. The contrapuntal lines do not actually repeat themselves rhythmically, but at any given time one of them usually articulates the shift between dotted-quarter- and quarter-note beats implied by the meter changes. As accompaniment and melody switch back and forth between the two lines, the accompaniment flirts with an implied steady beat, usually a dotted quarter against the changing meter. One of the piece's Baroquisms is its dependence on sequence for development, and the middle section of this movement uses sequence to set two phrases phasing against each other in a pattern of seven against eight (Example 3.4). At the end, Nancarrow reduces the melody to a sequence of pure fourths and fifths, setting a 17/8 isorhythm in the right hand against a 3/8 pattern in the left. Here he is measuring the effect of a steady pulse against an irregular isorhythm, an effect which he will explore more powerfully in the Player Piano Studies Nos. 7, 45, 46, and 47.

The second Study sets one of Nancarrow's languid, chromatic blues melodies in 6/8 meter against an accompaniment that implies 2/4, the eighth note being the same in both meters. The six-measure theme is stated twice at the beginning and three times (in different octaves) at the end, with a varied melody in the middle which uses the same rhythm. Separating these sections are two passages which, as in movement I, set two phrases out of phase: here, 3+3+2+2 in the right hand, 1+1+1+1+2 in the left, for an overall ten against six. The first of these episodes reverses Nancarrow's usual melodic formula, descending via a major scale, and ascending via the minor version. The encircling scale patterns distinctly recall the opening of the Sonatina.

The final Study is a canon at the perfect fourth, its Baroque underpinnings skewed *à la* Stravinsky. The 2/4 meter is occasionally crossed by groupings of either three eighth notes or three sixteenth notes. Sevenths and ninths are common melodic intervals, and also serve as the most common harmonic intervals between voices on strong beats. At m. 40 (the only measure of 3/8), the canon switches as though at a convergence point; at first the right hand had been a quarter note ahead, now it is a quarter note behind. It is amazing how well this simple device foreshadows, within a perfectly conventional genre, the structure of the later tempo canons.

Trio for clarinet, bassoon, and piano

The Trio was written for Halffter's Monday Evening concerts, though it was cancelled because of a recalcitrant clarinetist (see p. 42 above). For years the piece was considered a one-movement work, and performed as such by the Continuum ensemble. In the fall of 1990, however, two additional movements were found among Nancarrow's manuscripts.

In the first movement, canon has become a fetish. After an eleven-beat motive is stated in the clarinet and bassoon, it is immediately restated in imitation, and almost every time the music pauses or changes texture, a canon is the next step. Some of these are mere points of imitation, but at m. 81 the three instruments join in a four-part canon with two of the lines inverted. Mm. 161–80 feature Nancarrow's only use of a traditional (2:1) augmentation canon. It is an inversion canon as well: as six lines dwindle down to two, a nine-note chromatic figure is stated seven times in original form, six times in inversion, twice augmented, and three times in augmented inversion. Following this tour de force the piece can only close with a five-part stretto on the opening theme.

The movement's real interest is rhythmic, and the piano functions largely as percussion. In the first eight measures, it plays a chord on every fifth eighth note against the 4/8 and 3/8 meter. Next it articulates dotted quarters against the 4/8 of the woodwind canons and adds a 3+4+2 repeating rhythm in the left hand. In mm. 50–73 piano and winds exchange roles: the piano's canon plays against Webernesque motives, an implied 5/8 meter in the bassoon working against 5/8 + 7/8 in the clarinet. The three-part canon in mm. 110–25 is accompanied by a 5+5+3 octave pattern in the piano left hand. Measures 142–58 pit three meters together, a 2/4 canon in the winds over an involved 3/8 against 5/8 in the piano.

Example 3.5   Trio No. 1, structure of second movement

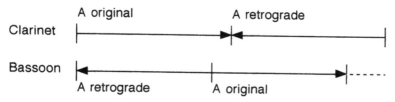

Example 3.6   Trio No. 1, third movement themes

The second movement, which omits piano, is a contrapuntal showpiece: an oddly off-balance self-retrograding crab canon. That is, the first half is a canon in which the clarinet's is the bassoon's line backwards, and the second half of the movement is the first half in reverse. In the first eleven (of twenty-two) measures, the bassoon part plays a backwards version of the clarinet line an octave and a fifth lower. At m. 11 both instruments reverse, each playing its own part backwards. However, a note is added at the end of the clarinet line, so that the bassoon reverses itself a half-measure earlier than the clarinet, and the contrapuntal lines match up differently in the second half than they did in the first. Various figures facilitate the crab canon's audibility: an octave-leaping sixteenth note figure and a long arpeggio of thirds occur once in each instrument in each half. At the end two non-canonic notes are added in the bassoon to allow the two instruments to end together. The structure could be diagrammed as in Example 3.5. The longest rests (dotted quarter) occur in the middle of each half of the movement, where the crab canons cross at the center; this is where Nancarrow has to juggle the phrases that retrograde in close succession, which must work out feasibly in both cases though the center points are different. This trick, leaving rests so the lines do not get in each other's way, is the same type of contrapuntal thinking that Nancarrow will develop more fully in the tempo canons for player piano.

The finale, Molto Allegro, returns to the spirit and technique of the opening Presto: woodwind melodies hurried along by sixteenth note motives, dissonant punctuating piano chords often outlining a quintuple meter cross-rhythm, and occasional canonic passages. The form is roughly a rondo based on three themes: ABCABBCACBA. The themes, given in Example 3.6, begin at mm. 1, 10, and 23, respectively. Note that theme B is derived from the sixteenth note flourish of theme A.

Here canon is neither as obsessive nor as virtuosic as in the first movement, but themes A and B are both "canonized" in their middle statements, while theme C becomes fragmented. The clarinet and bassoon canon on theme A lies in mm. 37–46; then at mm. 47–57, the three instruments play a four-part canon on theme B with entrances at every dotted quarter, despite the 2/4 meter, so that the theme is accented differently in each voice. At the third statement of theme A it becomes a canon in the piano alone, at mm. 100–06. Double canon makes brief appearances at mm. 20 and 66, and a calm final canon on theme B appears at mm. 134–46, just before the percussive ending. It is worth comparing this latter widely-spaced canon in dotted quarter notes with the second movement of the String Quartet No. 3, written some forty years later.

Future melodic tics are more evident here than in the earlier movements. Initial interest is provided by a recurring minor-third motive in the piano – Db C Bb Db – which returns in the bassoon on the final page. Nancarrow's ascending-major/descending minor scale habit is common, growing from the pervasive turn motive Ab G A. For one moment, at mm. 60–66, the clarinet's opening tune is reinterpreted over major/minor blues chords in a brief reference to the style of the *Blues* for piano, or the Sonatina's second movement. Isorhythm, too, appears for brief passages, especially in nonthematic episodes. In mm. 27–36 the top melody of the piano's right hand plays durations of five eighth notes against the 6/8 of the flute and the 3/4 of the piano left hand; at the same time, the bassoon articulates a 3+2 pattern that recurs later in the movement. Cluster chords beat a 2+2+2+3 motive at mm. 113–20, and quartal chords punctuate the final passage with 2+2+3+3.

The third movement takes a few rhythmic risks with its switches between eighth and dotted eighth beats; still, the music never departs from its underlying sixteenth note subdivision, and the anonymous clarinetist who balked at playing the première deserves eternal disrepute. The Trio is a well-crafted bit of 1940s Americana, in which the "Nancarrow moments" stand out like encrusted gems.

Piece No. 1 for Small Orchestra

The Piece No. 1 for Small Orchestra was written in 1943 in Mexico City, presumably with no potential performance in mind; its first performance was at the 1982 Cabrillo festival under the baton of Dennis Russell Davies. The piece appears on some works lists as Suite for Orchestra. It is scored for an orchestra slightly larger than the eighteenth-century model: one each of oboe, clarinet, bassoon, trumpet, and trombone, two horns, strings with contrabass doubling cellos, and piano rather than timpani. The four movements are played without pause, and Nancarrow probably considered the word Suite because they are neither closely related nor completely self-contained.

Example 3.7   Piece No.1, opening of second movement

I Andante

The introductory first movement exemplifies Nancarrow's slow blues style, which had previously characterized his Sonatina and his Prelude and Blues for piano, and would recur in his String Quartet No. 1 and Studies for Player Piano nos. 3 and 10. This introductory, intuitively composed blues begins with a circling bassoon solo (like *Le sacre du printemps*), followed by prominent solos for each woodwind and accompanied by bittersweet jazz chords in the piano. Rhythmic invention is limited to alternating between triplets and a 3+3+2 divided duplet, and there is a moment of canonic imitation at m. 11.

II Moderato

Quiet yet restless, this moderato (in the form ABCAB) is the meatiest movement, for it plays with Nancarrow's favorite device: the effect of different tempos going on at once. The bass line sets up a three against four rhythm vis à vis the piano and higher strings, while the violin, imitated canonically by the trumpet at the distance of a dotted quarter, weaves lithe phrases of five sixteenth notes in length (articulated 2+1+2), for an overall tempo continuum of 3:4:5, or 3/16, 4/16, and 5/16 going on at the same time (Example 3.7). Perhaps picking up its 5/16 meter from that motive, the B section extends the 3:4:5 pattern with an oboe solo marking every third eighth note, a clarinet every fourth, and pizzicato strings every fifth in a 2+3 accompaniment. (The second B section reduces this to solo clarinet and piano.) Metronomic sixteenth notes in the piano add clarity to the briefly climaxing C section, against which the strings pluck a pattern of seven sixteenth notes, the bassoon accenting every third. As in all of Nancarrow's multi-tempo music, the result of these different beats all proceeding at once is a delightfully free counterpoint of individually simple levels, like a game of three-dimensional chess.

III Allegro

Here Nancarrow's canonic tendencies run wild. The piano ticks along with its blues dissonances in clocklike 2/4, while a four-measure theme appears canonically no less than fourteen times in thirty-nine measures. Characteristic of Nancarrow's search for rhythmic variety, entrances of the theme appear at intervals of 6, 8, 4, 6½, 3½, 10½, 2, 5, 1½, 3½, 1, 7, and ¼ quarter notes, and at nine different pitch levels. The last two entrances, only a sixteenth note apart in rhythmic position, are a tritone apart in pitch. The melody is blues-flavored, and recognizable by the trill on its first note, but the piano's perpetual motion is quasi-Balinese, more like something Lou Harrison might have written about that time. Fragments of the theme echo from instrument to instrument to increase the sense of canonic saturation, and the cellos finally give way to the kind of wandering bass line found in so many of the player piano studies.

IV Molto Allegro

This American-sounding finale begins dramatically with a minor-third motive pitting dotted eighths against eighth notes, and that contrast becomes the central idea. But the most prophetic moment occurs immediately afterward. The upper strings alternate between F and E in an isorhythm of 2+3+4+3. Against that, the cellos pluck the motive D♭–C–B♭ over and over in a ritard/accelerando sequence: 3 4 5 6 7 8 7 6 5 4 3 2 3 4 5 6 5 4. This is only the accompaniment, and the bassoon and oboe play a canon above it. But how many player piano studies will later pit an isorhythm against an accelerando, how many will use expanding and contracting number sequences, how many echo an insistent minor third? The fascinating thing about these early pieces is that Nancarrow's habitual responses are all in place, and the early and late studies in particular seem to echo these works more than the more experimental, more differentiated middle studies.

What seems equally significant is Nancarrow's conception of duration, of the fact that the number series is expressed in staccato notes separated by varying numbers of rests. To count durations in Nancarrow's music, one must often take into account not the actual note duration, but the distance between successive attacks in a contrapuntal line. The Orchestra Piece No. 1 proves that this aspect of his rhythmic conception did not stem from the fact that staccato notes, requiring only one hole on the piano roll, were easier to punch, but was with him from the beginning.

The rest of the movement, with its rushing scales and continual accenting of every third sixteenth or eighth note in 2/4, contains little that one could not find in many American works of its period. Nancarrow comes close to establishing another isorhythm in the piano (3 3 3 2 3 6) and in the scale passages he sets up sequences of five sixteenth notes. For all the American energy and jazz intervals,

Example 3.8   Violin melody from Piece for Large Orchestra

the repeated figures devolve into a Stravinskian stasis before an incomplete climax and a disintegrative surprise ending. There is a lot of charming writing here, especially in the gentle Moderato, though the piece does not yet provide much of the feel of Nancarrow's later musical personality. In a test situation, the composer would be difficult to identify – Colin McPhee, Lou Harrison, and Roy Harris might come to mind. What is fascinating, though, is that, despite the charming but impersonal Americanism, all the ideas of Nancarrow's mature works are already present: multiple tempos, canons, repeated rhythmic motives, acceleration and ritard, pitch cells of a second joined to a third, juxtaposition of contrasting rhythmic layers. Nancarrow's personality has not yet gelled, but his preoccupations are found on almost every page.

Nancarrow later used the Piece No. 1 as the basis of a work for larger orchestra; the manuscript is in his studio, though apparently nothing has ever been done with it. (Could this be the orchestral piece he remembers sending to Chavez (see note 34 in chapter 2)? Intriguingly, the score contains what appear to be conductor's markings.) For the large orchestra version, he added a new opening movement of 169 measures, with a four-part canon in the woodwinds. The canon is stated in triplet eighth notes in 2/4 meter with a new voice entering every fourth note, or 2/3 of a measure, so that each voice accentuates the theme differently. In addition, an accompanying 8:9 rhythm is achieved by articulating triplet quarter notes in the brass and every third eighth note in the strings. Later a fiery melody in the violins switches between measures of 2/4 and 3/8 in a volatile manner rare in Nancarrow's other music (Example 3.8). The movement continues with an inversion canon in the woodwinds.

The remaining movements of the Piece for Large Orchestra (to give it a name) correspond to those of the Piece No. 1 for Small Orchestra. A written out jazz cadenza for the piano was added to the blues movement, and new material was added to the final movement's ending. This work, which contains some of Nancarrow's most experimental writing for live performers, awaits future musicological work and performance.

String Quartet No. 1

His last work for conventional instruments before the 1980s, Nancarrow's First String Quartet is easily the most significant and revealing of his pre-player piano

Example 3.9   String Quartet No. 1, opening

Example 3.10   String Quartet No. 1, first movement, theme 2

works. The first movement begins with a Bartókian three-part texture that is canonic by pitch but not by rhythm. (Nancarrow will return to this technique in Study No. 4.) The opening motive, D–E–F♯–G–F♮, hints at the ascending major, descending minor scale prominent throughout the studies (Example 3.9). Though freely handled as regards rhythm, this pitch line will be referred to as Theme 1. Theme 2, which immediately follows, is based on the motive A–B–D (Example 3.10). Canonic episodes begin at m. 33. The movement's strict pitch and rhythm canons occur as follows:

mm.	instruments	distance between entrances	note
21–30	Vc, Vn II, Vn I	3 ♪	
34–41	Vn II, Va	6 ♪	with non-canonic pizzicato bass
43–80	Vn I, Vn II, Va, Vc	8 (12) $♪^3$	
81–110	Vn I, Vn II, Va, Vc	8 ♪	
111–17	Va, Vc	9 ♪	with Theme 2 in Vn II
171–81	Vn I, Vn II, Va	3 ♪	with open fifth drone in Vc
183–89	Vn I, Vn II, Va, Vc	1 ♪	based on Theme 1

Of the movement's 190 measures, canons occupy 121. Most of the remainder, mm. 11–21 and 111–138, elaborates and fragments Theme 2. The climax, in mm. 150–61, deploys repeated notes in a type of isorhythmic sequence common in the early studies: 3 2 3 4 5 4 3 2 3 4 5 4 3.

The second movement, Andante Moderato, is entirely canonic save for a few accompanying pizzicato notes in the cello. (A few notes are displaced by octave here and there for the sake of linear clarity.) The melody is long and through-composed, and canonic entrances arrive at intervals of seven slow measures, so there is little sense of canonic imitation. This is a typical Nancarrow early blues, similar to the slow movement of the Sonatina and Study No. 3d in its rambling melody of shifting subdivisions.

The fiery, American-sounding finale is a microcosm of Nancarrow's compositional concerns and includes a few devices that he has never used since. The rhythmic, wide-ranging theme is typical of American finales of the 1930s and 40s, as is the return near the end to themes from the first movement; see the 1931 Piano Sonata of Roy Harris for a close parallel. Of this movement's 345 measures, 153 involve canon:

mm.	instruments	no. of measures between entries	note
28–40	Vn I, Vc	3	inversion canon
38–46	Vn I, Vn II, Va, Vc		double inversion canon
54–66	Vn I, Vn II, Va, Vc 1		double inversion canon
73–77	Vn II, Va, Vc		brief tempo canon 6:8:9
109–22	Vn I, Vn II, Va	3	isorhythm in cello
131–36	Vn I, Va	2	
142–47	Vn I, Va	2	inversion of preceding canon
173–81	Vn I, Vn II	1	based on Theme 1
182–95	Vn I, Vn II, Va, Vc 1		based on first movement's Theme 2
203–17	Vn I, Vn II, Va, Vc	½ / ⅖	double canon; canon between violins ends at m. 210
237–48	Vn I, Vn II, Va, Vc	2	
260–68	Vn I, Vn II, Va, Vc	2 ♩s	based on Theme 1
269–79	Vn I, Vn II, Va, Vc	1 ♩	based on first movement's Theme 2
326–42	Vn I, Vn II, Va, Vc	3 ♩s	eight-voice canon

The use of double canon (four contrapuntal lines, two separate subjects, each treated canonically) is new, and in the Player Piano Studies Nancarrow has returned to it only in section 4 of Study No. 25 and the rhythm-approximation canons of Study No. 33. Inversion canon, too, is unknown elsewhere in his output. And the eight-part canon for four instruments, even though Nancarrow now calls it "primitive," deserves quotation (Example 3.11).

Aside from this maelstrom of canonic activity, there are plenty of other prescient Nancarrow touches: ostinato, isorhythm, multi-tempos. At mm. 104–22, he introduces a four-note isorhythm, in quarter notes, of 2+2+2+3 (the 2+2+3 rhythm from which this derives first appears in the viola in the opening measures). Across this he overlays a six-note pitch row (or *color*, see chapter 5 for fuller explanation) of A–G♯–F♯–E–D–C♯ (Example 3.12). At mm. 28–324 an ostinato nine half notes long appears in the cello, descending D–C♯–D–C– B♭–A♭–G–F–E. (This recurring descent and that of the isorhythm mentioned above remind the listener of similar ostinatos in the last movements of Charles Ives's Second String Quartet and Fourth Symphony, works Nancarrow could not have heard or seen at this date.)

Example 3.11   String Quartet No. 1, eight-part canon, third movement, theme 2

Example 3.12   String Quartet No. 1, third movement, isorhythm in cello part

Multi-tempos recur throughout the movement, greatly contributing to performance difficulty. In mm. 28–40, violin I and cello play a dotted-half beat (a staccato note every three quarter notes) while violin II and viola play in triplet half notes: a 9:4 ratio. Mm. 72–85 are a polytempo tour de force: violin I marks every fifth quarter note, violin II plays triplet whole notes, the viola plays every third quarter note, and the cello every half note, for a tempo resultant of 15:8:9:6. For a few measures, three of the instruments are playing rising scales, creating a momentary impression of tempo canon. The double canon at m. 202 pits the pairs against each other at a 5:4 ratio, and a 2:5 ratio is common in succeeding passages. In the unison passage in mm. 256–58, Nancarrow takes the daring move (returned to in the Orchestra Piece No. 2 and Study No. 50) of articulating every third note within a quintuplet rhythm.

The climactic passage preceding the final canon again gives each player his own beat: triplet half notes in violin I, quintuplet half notes in violin II, quarter notes with every third accented in the viola, and half notes in the cello. Violin I then changes to triplet quarters, and violin II to dotted halves within quintuplets. In the process, the overall tempo resultant changes as follows, with the simpler, reciprocal duration ratios also given:

tempo		duration
20:36:45:30	or	18:10:8:12
10:24:45:30	or	36:15:8:12
10:36:45:30	or	36:10:8:12

The contrapuntal ambitions here are as tremendous for their time as Ives's were in the finale of his 1896 First Quartet, in which each instrument plays a different theme, two of them in 3/4 meter, the other two in 4/4.

Having proven something to himself with that mammoth contrapuntal achievement, Nancarrow could next abandon the "American" style for a more personal idiom. But in the String Quartet No. 1 every feature of that idiom is already germinally in place – melodies built around minor thirds and the A B D motive, blues, polytempo, canon, isorhythm, ostinato, pitch row, arithmetical acceleration and ritard – except for the wild textural devices inherent to his new love, the player piano.

4

Blues years: the ostinato studies

Studies Nos. 1, 2a, 2b, 3, 5, 9

Introduction to the Studies for Player Piano

The numbering of the Studies for Player Piano needs clarification. The official numbering extends through No. 50, but there are not exactly fifty studies to correspond to those numbers. Studies Nos. 38 and 39 do not exist as such; they became Nos. 43 and 48 respectively because Nancarrow used them to fulfill a commission after having published No. 41, and wanted them to appear later in the series than that number. He also discarded Study No. 30, which was written for prepared player piano,[1] because the preparations – washers, bolts, and strips of felt and rubber placed between the piano strings to dampen them – would not stay in place on the vertical strings of an upright player piano. The piano roll and punching score still exist, however, so I include the work in the analyses below. In addition, Nancarrow has expressed dissatisfaction with Study No. 13, and does not release its score, though he continues to allow it to be recorded. On the other hand, he has revived an early study that he now calls No. 2b. The most recent study received the number 3750 as a kind of joke (though I call it No. 51), another player-piano piece is titled *For Yoko*, and the new study for Trimpin's automatic prepared player piano is called *Contraption No. 1*. So the actual number of studies so far could range from forty-eight to fifty-two depending on whether you count scores, titles, recordings, or numberings. Personally, I count fifty-two: I consider 2b separate from 2a, and include Nos. 13 and 30, *For Yoko*, and *Contraption No. 1*.

With his usual disdain for biographical references, Nancarrow refuses to date his Player Piano Studies, but a few published statements provide a rough framework for general dating. Charles Hamm states that the first thirty were written in the years 1948 to 1960,[2] and Nancarrow himself has said that "about thirty or a few more" were written by 1960. Roger Reynolds, however, states that No. 30 was written in the mid-sixties.[3] Nancarrow notes that Study No. 3, the *Boogie-woogie Suite*, was written first. Study No. 1 followed soon after. Nancarrow modestly claims that in the first fifteen or twenty studies he was "just feeling my way,"[4] although the first twelve raise an astounding wealth of new ideas, and the following seven initiated his exploration of canonic technique.

In the liner notes for the Columbia record, released in 1969, composer Gordon Mumma states that the first thirty-seven studies were finished except for Nos. 34, 35, and 36; and in the 1977 Amirkhanian interview, Nancarrow notes that Nos. 40 and 41 were finished, but not Nos. 38 and 39 (later renumbered 43 and 48). Nancarrow has mentioned that he solves the problem of getting stuck on a piece by working on several pieces at once, and these overlaps confirm that working method. The following table arranges the Studies according to the nearest chronology I can currently provide.

Studies	completed	begun
3	1948	
1	by 1951	
2, 4–30	1948–1960	
31, 32, 33, 37	1965–1969	
34, 35, 36		1965–1969
34, 35, 36, 40, 41	1969–1977	
43, 48		1969–1977
42–50	1977–1988	
51, *For Yoko, Contraption No. 1*	1992–1993	

There is no wholly satisfactory order in which to discuss the Studies for Player Piano. The present book will divide them into chapters based on the primary compositional technique of each study. This has the advantage not only of making technical description more efficient but of keeping most of the studies in roughly chronological order. The disadvantage is that, since many of the studies use more than one structuring technique, the groupings are slightly arbitrary. For example, Study No. 27, an acceleration canon, could have been included among the canons, but I include it in the acceleration chapter for little better reason than that there are fewer acceleration studies than canonic ones. My grouping is pragmatic and, I hope, helpful, but not intended as a hard-and-fast classification.

Written when Nancarrow was in his mid-thirties, the first studies for player piano project a confidence and originality that few American composers achieve by that age. It is true that, even in his recent works, Nancarrow has rarely repeated himself, and hardly a piece fails to include some effect or form that has never been heard before. Still, in terms of new concepts, Nancarrow's early period was his most fertile, for the first twelve studies contain more original ideas, more unheard-of experiments, than any similar group in his output.

When Nancarrow began experimenting with polytempo, he turned first to a simple device that would show it to striking effect: ostinato, a phrase persistently repeated without variation. It was a natural choice, for ostinato was much in the air in modernist music of the 1920s and 30s. Common in European music of the seventeenth century, ostinato lapsed into disuse in Europe throughout the eighteenth and nineteenth centuries, an era in which music was characterised by forms too dramatically developmental for such a repetitious device. After the collapse of Romantic tonality, ostinato was revived into common practice by Stravinsky, Hindemith, and Bartók, who saw in it a means of setting off strange new harmonies in a clear context, as well as making oddly accented rhythms clear through repetition. Deeply impressed by *Le sacre du printemps*, Nancarrow naturally gravitated to ostinato as a potent rhythmic tool.

Nor was *Le sacre* the only source of the ostinato's influence. Stravinsky and Bartók, and Nancarrow as well, all drew on what were considered lowbrow genres, jazz and various folk musics. Stravinsky was fascinated by ragtime, and he and Bartók both found repetitive melody in the Slavic ethnic musics that presented an alternative to the Germanic tradition. Through the thirties Nancarrow had made a living playing jazz trumpet, and jazz, like Baroque music, relied heavily on the ostinato bass as a foundation. Nancarrow's use of ostinato must be credited to both sources, Stravinsky/Bartók and jazz. The I–IV–V ostinatos of Study No. 3 are clearly blues-derived, while the repeating motives of Study No. 5 are more easily traced to *Le sacre*. Because the ostinato, by definition, repeated itself without changing pitch level, it freed Nancarrow from many traditional harmonic, melodic, and formal concerns while he went about forging a radically new rhythmic language.

Study No. 1

Originally, Nancarrow labeled all the studies (on the piano rolls) "Rhythm Studies" up through No. 35. He then decided to drop the word "rhythm" as being redundant, but the first had already been published as Rhythm Study No. 1 (for player-piano) in Henry Cowell's *New Music* in 1952.

This by-no-means-timid piece is more abstract than most of the dozen pieces that followed. Within a framework of two tempos with a ratio of 4:7, Nancarrow builds an arch-like, generally palindromic structure involving no fewer than twelve durations – not selected along a stepwise scale within a 2:1 ratio as in later studies (such as Nos. 28 and 37), but along a quasi-logarithmic scale from 2 to 35. Four of these durations are related to a 4/4 meter of $\downarrow$ = 120, the other eight to a 7/8 bar of identical length, where $\downarrow$ = 210. Unlike his practice in most of the later studies, Nancarrow works primarily with duration, not tempo: that is, not by carving out diverse divisions of a longer period (though he does this too in the overall four-against-seven measure), but through additive rhythm, as in Stravinsky's music, building up a variety of pulses by grouping thirty-second notes into periodicities of 2, 3, 4, and 5. Thus the durations employ a simpler-looking number scheme than the resulting tempo ratios:

Notated duration:	relative duration:		tempo:
♪	♪ = 210	2	420
♪.	♪ = 210	3	280
♪	♪ = 210	4	210
♪♪	♪ = 210	5	168
♩	♪ = 210	8	105
♩.	♪ = 210	12	70
♩	♩ = 120	14	60
♩	♪ = 210	16	52.5
♩♪	♪ = 210	20	42
♩.	♩ = 120	21	40
o	♩ = 120	28	30
o♩	♩ = 120	35	24

If one counts subdivisions related by powers of 2 (i.e., sixteenths, eighths, and quarters) as being "octaves" of the same tempo, there are actually only six different tempos represented (expressed here in smallest whole-number terms): 24, 30, 40, 42, 70, and 105. This is the one study for which it is easier to talk in terms of duration-ratios than tempo-ratios.

Example 4.1 shows the palindromic nature of the structure. In that respect, the piece is imitative of the arch forms of such Bartók movements as the Adagio of the Fifth String Quartet, a Nancarrow favorite. The foundation of the study is a polyrhythmic ostinato of quintal chords (Db–Ab–Eb, moving endlessly I–IV–V) and major triads, heard always in the rhythmic ratio 4:7, but moving along a scale of tempos, accelerating in a 5:4:3:2 progression. That is, the quintal chords occur every 5 beats at first, then every 4 (starting at m. 8, 0:13), every 3 (m. 13, 0:19), and so on. (Throughout these analyses, timings will refer to the second-counter position of each noted event or passage on the Wergo compact disc recordings.) Meanwhile, the triads in the 7 tempo move through a similar process, keeping the ratio constant. Overlaid across the ongoing four-against-seven, these abrupt 5–4–3 speed-ups have a physically jarring gear-shifting effect. The parallel triads, first circling E–C–E–G and then marching up and down the scale from C to G, give the piece its evocative, curiously naive polytonal flavor, especially when a new layer of triads enters at m. 45 (1:05) on a pattern of A–B–C–Bb. The piece is a blend of naivete and sophistication.

Study No. 1 is one of Nancarrow's most imaginative pitch structures, and shows in that respect the influence of not only Bartók but twelve-tone thinking, though it remains intuitive and even tonal. Every note of the melodic material is drawn from a thirty-note row (Example 4.2), divided into segments of nine, eight, seven, and six notes, and first heard in its entirety at mm. 29–32 (measure numbers refer to the constant 4/4 measures of the 120 tempo, so marked in the score). In the first twenty-eight measures, Nancarrow extends these segments first by inverting them, then by intercutting the original form with the inversion in different registers (Example 4.3). He takes full advantage of the invertibility of major triads

Example 4.1   Study No. 1 structure

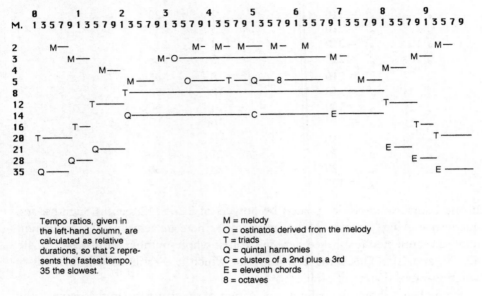

Tempo ratios, given in
the left-hand column, are
calculated as relative
durations, so that 2 represents the fastest tempo,
35 the slowest.

M = melody
O = ostinatos derived from the melody
T = triads
Q = quintal harmonies
C = clusters of a 2nd plus a 3rd
E = eleventh chords
8 = octaves

Example 4.2   Study No. 1, 30-note pitch row

Example 4.3   Study No. 1, intercutting rows, mm. 11–13

into minor ones to create a bittersweet blues feeling throughout. The row finally
appears in its entirety, after which nine- and fourteen-note segments of it turn into
ostinatos. Longer, derived segments (including inversions) flit by in quick sixteenth
notes, finally plunging down the keyboard with a repeating seven-note figure.

Throughout his career, Nancarrow has interpreted the midpoint of an arch
form as an entry into Looking-Glass Land, where everything turns backwards.

Study No. 1 hits bottom registrally at m. 50 (1:15), and from m. 51 everything runs in reverse. From here on, only the retrograde of the row is heard; root-position major triads are up-ended into second-inversion minor triads; bass quintal chords become treble eleventh harmonies; rhythms previously heard in the treble are consigned to the bass and vice versa. The inversion/intercutting process of the opening melodies now repeats itself backwards, highs transposed into lows. As the opening slowly accelerated, the music now grinds to a disgruntled, polytonal halt.

The piece sustains its fastest overall speed for the middle $\frac{3}{5}$ of the form. At the point where the progression reverses itself the melody ingeniously mirrors the chords by decelerating in the same 2:3:4:5 progression, from sixteenth notes to dotted sixteenths to eighths to a five-thirtyseconds-note.[5] The tempo ratios that result from these layers of activity follow a haphazardly complex progression: 2:20:35, 3:16:28, 4:12:21, 5:8:14. These are derived, however, from a continuous potential resultant of 2:3:5:8:14, made up of sixteenths, dotted sixteenths, and five-thirtyseconds notes (a dotted sixteenth tied to a sixteenth) articulated in melodies and chords over the 4:7 ostinatos.

The complexity of these ratio groups already presages those of Studies Nos. 25, 35, and 37, and the process wherein treble lines move to bass, fast becomes slow, and vice versa, hints at a conceptual ancestor for Study No. 21, Canon X. Already in his first essay, Nancarrow has achieved a tremendous level of rhythmic complexity (enough to make a big impression on Elliott Carter), yet the piece is engaging, and not at all difficult to follow.

Study No. 2a

Two ostinatos lay the groundwork for this blues number; in this voyage through uncharted waters, Nancarrow kept his premises simpler than in Study No. 1. The underlying rhythm here is three against five. Surviving scores show, however, that Nancarrow experimented with other tempo ratios: alternate versions (both scores and piano rolls) exist in which the ostinatos articulate beats in the proportions 4:5, 4:7, 5:7, and 5:9.

One ostinato runs through the note sequence F–G–B♭–D, three at a time in a steady rhythm of three eighth notes followed by an eighth rest; within twelve notes, the rhythm repeats four times and the pitches three, after which the process repeats. (This isorhythm-within-an-ostinato anticipates the studies discussed in chapter 5.) The other ostinato is a march-like alternation of A♭ and D♭, played three beats against five of the first ostinato. Every sixteen bars the two ostinatos fall back in sync in terms of both pitch and rhythm, so at sixteen-measure intervals Nancarrow transposes the whole according to a normal blues modulation scheme: I IV I V I.

The first sixteen-measure period passes without melody; we listen only to the ostinatos. Those ostinatos – F–G–B♭–D and A♭–D♭ – look bitonal, but together they form a blues scale, with a flattened seventh and major/minor third ambiguity.

Example 4.4   Study No. 2a, theme

Example 4.5   Study No. 2a, divisions of the dotted rhythm

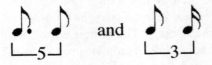

Example 4.6   Study No. 2a, key and tempo structure

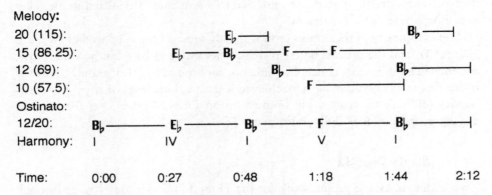

When the melody enters at the second period (0:27), it starts out entirely in that six-note scale. The melody enters at an in-between tempo, creating a 3:4 ratio with the faster and 5:4 with the slower; the overall resultant here is 12:15:20. (This triple ratio becomes the canonic basis of Studies 17 and 19.)

The melody (Example 4.4) is stated nine times at four tempos – 57½, 69, 86¼ and 115 – whose simplest ratios are 10:12:15:20. It also occurs at three transposition levels: I, IV, and V in the key of B♭. In the third and fourth 16-measure periods, the melody is heard bitonally, in tonic and dominant at once. Further nuances are added by different divisions of the tune's dotted rhythm (Example 4.5), though at these tempos the ear barely registers such subtleties. Example 4.6 shows the melody's distribution according to key and tempo layer among the five sixteen-measure periods. An odd feature of the form (though typical for Nancarrow) is that the melody gravitates towards slower tempos in the middle, so that the points of greatest speed are at the beginning of period three and at the end, while the passages of greatest contrapuntal complexity, where the melody is heard in three versions at once, lie around period four. Perhaps Nancarrow gravitated toward slower tempos to compensate for greater complexity, to keep the ear from being overwhelmed.

Study No. 2b

Punched sometime around 1950 and ignored until decades later, Study No. 2b has no real connection with No. 2a. It was originally an arrangement and expansion of the last movement of the not-yet-performed Piece for Small Orchestra No. 1, whose climactic finale Nancarrow must have been desperate to hear. After neglecting this little one-minute piece for decades, Nancarrow picked it up again for inclusion on the Wergo recordings, and assigned it an arbitrary number to fit it into the sequence at an appropriate chronological point. No score exists for the study, and analysis depends for now on what connections one can draw to the orchestral score by ear.

Study No. 2b omits the orchestral movement's fragmented-motive intro-duction and picks up at the *a tempo* at m. 11. As discussed in chapter 3, there are two ostinatos going here at once: pitches F and E alternating in a 2+3+4+3 isorhythm, and a repeating D♭–C–B♭ motive in a ritard/accelerando sequence 3 4 5 6 7 8 7 6 5 4 3 2 3 4 5 6 5 4, expressed in eighth notes in a 2/4 meter. Above this is a canon on the Nancarrovian motive shown in Example 4.7. Before this theme the study adds four ostinato measures not found in the orchestral score, as an introduction. Also not found in the original score are the half-step dissonances (at 0:24) added to the top note of the orchestral piano's 3+3+3+2 cross-rhythms for a bluesier feeling.

The study stays close to the score through m. 46, where it takes a different path. A two-part canon follows on a new but related blues theme (0:39); a bass in dotted eighths forms a syncopated counterpoint to eighth note melodies above (0:50); a blues-chromatic triad progression (similar to a passage in the score's piano part, 1:00–1:07) brings the music to a temporary halt. Rather than slow down and die away before a sudden *ff* finish as in the orchestral version, Nancarrow improves on the form by restating earlier material, first the major second/minor third motive by itself, then the wind melodies and jazzy piano licks.

Nancarrow likes to play this study far faster than any orchestra ever could have, and the overall impression is that of two or three jazz pianists jamming at maximum speed in exhilarating chaos. As the earliest-composed (in part) of the studies (though evidently not the earliest punched) this tiny scherzo may be a mere footnote, but its savage, orchestrally thick texture must have provided inspiration for later experiments.

Study No. 3 ("Boogie-Woogie Suite")

Fewer than a fourth of Nancarrow's sixty-odd works, and only seven of the Studies, contain more than one movement. His conception of multi-movement form allows for contrast of tempo and dynamics between movements, but he creates unity among movements, not by the usual means of melodic or harmonic material, but by means of similarity of structure: form becomes, not a way to vary thematic material, but a theme to be developed itself. Nancarrow has stated that

Example 4.7   Study No. 2b, canonic motive

this so-called *Boogie-woogie Suite*, Study No. 3, was the first study to be completed, and that it was written, not as a multi-movement work, but as five small pieces so much alike in spirit that he later decided to group them together.

This is one of Nancarrow's most popular essays. Movements a, b, and e are more like variations on an ostinato structure than like parts of a suite; all three are built on twelve-measure ostinatos which outline the harmonies I, IV, and V in blues fashion. All movements except the first use the device of combining in counterpoint two melodies previously stated separately (a principle which, in Studies Nos. 41 and 48, Nancarrow will later apply to entire movements). Similarly, the first movement builds its climax through the accumulation of previously heard figures.

Movement 3a comprises twenty-two repetitions, or cycles, of a 4/4, twelve-measure ostinato (plus one introductory measure). The eight-note ostinato figure – C–C–D♯–E–G–D♯–E–D – contains the major/minor triad (C–D♯–E–G) from which most of the study's harmony is drawn, and it is transposed to IV and V according to a standard boogie-woogie pattern: C C C C F F C C G G C C. Of the twenty-two cycles, nos. 2 through 15 constitute a loose set of variations on no. 1's parallel-phrased theme. Cycle 16 (2:16) is a turning point: it strips the texture down to two elements, the ostinato and dissonant chords repeating an irregular isorhythm. From here on, the remaining cycles are united by a linear process in which one new element is added every twelve measures. Nancarrow uses a small, elegantly simple repertoire of variation techniques, but they change with whirlwind speed. The cycles can be boiled down as follows:

1   (0:00) main theme
2   (0:09) theme varied by being filled in with sixteenth notes
3   (0:18) theme in alternating eighths and sixteenths with grace notes
4   (0:27) major/minor chord every seven sixteenth notes; a new, self-inverting theme, of which the third phrase is turned into a brief canon
5   (0:36) a chord every 4+3 sixteenths (reversing to 3+4 at end); the theme reduced to two chords
6   (0:45) an upper melody in 3+2+2 sixteenths rhythm; the theme in 4/4 isorhythm
7   (0:55) a chord every five sixteenths; the theme in a two-measure isorhythm
8   (1:04) an upper melody in 3+2 sixteenths; the theme in 15/16, 6+6+3 isorhythm
9   (1:13) an upper melody in 2+3+4+5+6+7+6+5+4+3 isorhythm; the theme alternating quarters and eighths with grace notes

10 (1:22) chords *and* melody in 4+5+2 isorhythm, making up 11/16 meter

11 (1:31) an upper melody in 5+2+4+5+2+4 (=22) sixteenths isorhythm; the theme as a six-beat isorhythm, inverting itself in alternate phrases

12 (1:40) an upper staccato note every three sixteenths; beat/beat isorhythm theme taken from No. 6

13 (1:49) theme in an expansion/contraction isorhythm, 2+3+4+5+6+7+ 6+5+4+3 . . .

14 (1:58) chords in 13+7+14+5 (=39) sixteenths isorhythm; a motive of repeated eighth notes

15 (2:07) the 13+7+14+5 chords continue; the melody takes up a four-note motive, two half-steps and a minor third, in irregular rhythm

From this point on, the theme disappears, and each element added continues through to the end:

16 (2:16) dissonant blues chords in 13+10+6 (=29) isorhythm (no theme)

17 (2:25) a treble, canonic ostinato in dotted eighths

18 (2:35) chords in 13+3+11+7+5 (=39) sixteenths isorhythm

19 (2:44) the canonic ostinato now in five-sixteenth notes

20 (2:53) chords in 19+10+11+7 (=47) isorhythm

21 (3:02) bass chords in 14+9 (=23) isorhythm

22 (3:11) five-octave chords of F♯s and C♯s in 15+9+12+7 (=43) 16ths isorhythm

The final texture, the suite's most complex moment, is a numerological extravaganza. An eighth note pulse is pitted against dotted eighths and five-sixteenth notes for a constant 2:3:5, over which patterns of 23, 29, 39, 43, and 47 sixteenth notes are superimposed. Study No. 5 will expand this additive texture of prime-numbered ostinatos in a stricter, more abstract manner.

The slower second movement, No. 3b, runs through ten cycles of its twelve-measure ostinato, now in the key of F. Here is the earliest instance in Nancarrow's output of a rhythmic tendency that reappears throughout his early works: the division of a beat into a trochaic rhythm divided, not 3+1 or 2+1, but 3+2, 5+3, or (later, in Study No. 10) 8+5. These numbers, one will notice, occur in the Fibonacci series, the arithmetical chain in which each number is the sum of the previous two: 1, 1, 2, 3, 5, 8, 13, 21, 34, and so on. Each pair of numbers approximates the Golden Ratio (.618:1), a proportion found in nature and considered aesthetically pleasing since ancient times (also widely applied to rhythms by Bartók, though it is unlikely Nancarrow would have known that at the time). More to the point of Nancarrow's early concerns, however, is that this uneven division captures the swing with which blues pianists habitually play melodies notated as either steady eighth notes or dotted eighths plus sixteenths. The difference is subtle, but it puts an intuitive spin on the rhythm which keeps this mechanical instrument from sounding mechanical.

Rhythmic issues here and in movement 3d are simpler than in the faster movements. In No. 3b, one cross-rhythm dominates, that of twelve sixteenths versus the thirty sixteenths of the 4/2 meter, or three against eight. Much of the movement is a straightforward transcription of blues idioms, but there are a few noteworthy points:

Cycle 1   (0:00) a theme generated by an E–F–A♭ motive (the primary motive of 3a as well) begins by drawing five-beat phrases against the 4/2 meter

      2   (0:31) the theme reappears beneath a new melody in quarter notes which toys with triplet (dotted half and dotted quarter) groupings; this begins the movement's characteristic tension between quarter notes and 5+3 sixteenth-note patterns

      3   (1:00) a two-octave space is opened within Cycle 1's dyadic melody to make room for an eighth note countermelody

      4   (1:30) a 12/16 measure is superimposed over the ostinato's 4/2, unsettling the ear by crossing the half-note beat with a dotted-half beat; the theme is traditionally varied, translated into 6/8, with a countermelody in grace-noted dotted eighth notes

      6   (2:28) a treble melody in quarter notes is pitted against one in 3+2+3 sixteenth note values, somewhat as in Cycle 2

      7   (2:56) 6/8 is again superimposed over the 4/2 meter, as the melody continues, doubled four octaves higher

      8   (3:25) staccato triads articulate a dotted-quarter beat, marking four-against-three against the ostinato's beat

      9   (3:52) a new, quick melody plays with an arithmetical ritard, climbing to a note and hitting it in durations of 3, 4, 5, 6, 7, 8, and 9 sixteenth notes; the second half begins a stretto mini-canon

     10   (4:24) the melody and countermelody of Cycle 2 return, slowed down and rhythmically transformed from 5+3 to 3+2

The middle movement, 3c, leaves ostinato behind and plunges into isorhythm, applying a repeating rhythmic pattern to changing pitches. (The reader is referred to chapter 5 for fuller discussion of this device.) Two main melodies and a countermelody recur, all in 6/8 meter and based on a motive of a whole step and a minor third (G–A–C instead of the G♯–A–C of 3a and 3b). They are accompanied by four isorhythms, one merely a variation of one of the others, up to a level of four distinct lines at once. The first isorhythm is given in Example 4.8, a recurring six-note descent phased against a seven-note isorhythm. The remaining isorhythms are derived as follows:

isorhythm 1:	5 4 3 2 3 4 3		= 24 (four measures)
isorhythm 2a:	3 3 4 2 2 2 5	3 3 5 2 2 2 4	= 42 (seven measures)
isorhythm 2b:	3 3 4 4 7	3 3 5 4 6	= 42 (seven measures)
isorhythm 3:	9 5 7 8 7 5 7		= 48 (eight measures)

The texture and elements involved change in roughly twenty-four-measure periods. Example 4.9 shows the basic structure of this relatively simple movement. This type of form, sectionally marked off by various isorhythms and terraced

Example 4.8   Study No. 3c, isorhythmic bases

Example 4.9   Study No. 3c, key, isorhythmic, and thematic structure

Time:	0:00	0:17	0:35	0:52	1:09	1:26	1:42	2:00	2:17	2:39	3:02
System:	1	4	7	10	13	16	19	22	25	28	31	

Melody A   F ———— B♭ —— C ————   A♭ ————   XXE ═══ XC ————

Ctrmel. A   B♭ —— C═══

Melody B   E♭ —— B♭ —— E♭ —— B♭ —— F═══   G ——

Isorh. 1   ·   ———— · · · · · · · :: · · · · · · · · · · · · · ·
Isorh. 2   a ·   b · · · · · ·
Isorh. 3   ————————

Pitch names indicate key transposition   Isorhythm 1: 5 4 3 2 3 4 3
Dotted line = staccato element   Isorhythm 2a: 3 3 4 2 2 2 5   3 3 5 2 2 2 4
Straight line = legato element   Isorhythm 2b: 3 3 4 4   7   3 3 5 4   6
Double line = the same element played in counterpoint with itself   Isorhythm 3: 9 5 7 8 7 5 7
X = free (unrepeated) material

dynamics, will be developed to a higher degree of complexity in Studies Nos. 7 and 11.

Nancarrow develops most of these ideas further in later studies, but the freely-composed fourth movement casts a final backward glance at the Blues and Sonatina. No strict partitioning runs through this brief, charming blues, but mm. 1–6 and 7–12 respectively contain two related melodies which Nancarrow combines contrapuntally in the final seven measures (the recapitulation starting at 1:47). A small staccato isorhythm articulating durations of 3+3+2+4 (= 12) eighth notes accompanies the first melody in both instances. If the thick, nondirectional jazz harmonies look back to earlier works, the clever use of inversion within a blues scale also reminds one of Study No. 1. At m. 11 (0:41), before melody 2 has ended, it is fused with its reentry a fourth higher, but at m. 13 (0:50) Nancarrow

Example 4.10   Study No. 3e, primary melodic formula

flips the melody's second half for a literal inversion. The movement's other notable features are a cadenza-climax that suddenly bursts into thirty-second notes (1:36, reminiscent of the Septet), and the division of a beat not into equal triplets (despite the 12/8 meter), but into jazzed values of 3+3+2 superimposed over the triplet.

The structure of the deafeningly quick finale is so clear, and so similar to No. 3a, that only main features need be pointed out. The ostinato, another boogie pattern spelling out I–I–IV–I–V–I, again takes twelve measures, and this time goes through twenty-four cycles (each of which lasts only six seconds, or 5.25 seconds on the 1750 Arch recording!). Most of the melodic material is drawn from the eight-note melodic formula in Example 4.10. This formula emerges in cycle 2, is stated in quick eighth notes in cycle 3, and ends a longer melody in cycle 4. The melody of Cycle 4 becomes a kind of cantus firmus: it is repeated in various registers in cycles 5, 6, 7, and 17, provides a repeated motive for 10, gets spelled out in dotted eighths in 13, in dotted quarters in 14, and in five-sixteenth values in 15, makes a seven-sixteenth + three-sixteenth pattern in 18, and ten-sixteenth + five-sixteenth in 21 and 22, and is augmented into half notes and quarters in 19 and 20, and finally into dotted halves and dotted quarters to fade out in 23 and 24. That tune does a lot of work in a short time.

In the final eight cycles the bass ostinato undergoes a clever disintegration process, being sifted through an arithmetical grid until there's nothing left. In cycle 17, Nancarrow omits every ninth note, starting with the first; in cycle 18, he omits the notes omitted in 17, plus every eighth note starting on the fourth. Cycle 19 omits those notes and every seventh note starting with the fourth, cycle 20 every sixth note, cycle 21 every fifth note, and so on, the grid becoming finer and finer as the number of bass notes per cycle decreases: 96, 85, 74, 63, 51, 42, 39, 28, 5.

Other rhythmic hijinks include a 7/4 isorhythm in cycles 6 and 10, a 9/8 isorhythm in cycle 8, and some wild counterpoint in cycle 13 in conflicting sixteenth note groupings of 7:5:3:2. The harmonic basis throughout is the C major/minor tonic, which makes equal aural sense in jazz terms whether the bass is on I, IV, or V, leaving the melodies open to any rhythmic placement. In short, Nancarrow draws much from little material, and indulges more redundancy than will be characteristic of later work. But then, this movement's 2,313 "left-hand" eighth notes zip by in 146 seconds, more than fifteen per second, so that the repeated devices found by the eye are just a flash of lightning to the ear.

Study No. 5

The fifth study is the first in a series of experimental works (No. 21, "Canon X," is the famous example, Nos. 28, 29, and 30 are others) which are conceptually simple and perceptually quite complicated. The entire 157 seconds of No. 5 is a thirteen-layered crescendo of activity, the voices brought in one at a time, five of them containing their own built-in acceleration. The experiment implied here is to set up a rhythmic interplay of durations related by all the prime numbers from 5 to 19, and to bring those in gradually enough that the ear can ease its way into the resultant texture. To further complicate things, and create a resounding crescendo, Nancarrow juxtaposes accelerating impulses over the steadily repeating ones. (The idea of one voice marking a pulse while another accelerates will recur in Studies Nos. 23, 27, 28, and 29.)

Like Study No. 2, No. 5 is grounded on two rhythmic ostinatos, this time played at tempo ratios of 5:7. These first two layers (notated on the eleventh and twelfth staves, since Nancarrow helpfully relegates each layer to a different stave) are tonal phrases in, respectively, B major pentatonic and C major. In later years, Nancarrow might have notated them as in Example 4.11 (though without the repeat signs). Instead, he takes the common multiple and notates them in 35/16 meter, so that a sixteenth note unit, however fast (1,160 a minute), remains a constant denominator throughout the piece. It is interesting to note that the F♯–C tritone implied by the juxtaposition of these lines is a pitch analogue to the tempo, since 5:7 is the simplest frequency ratio which defines a tritone.

The next five layers to appear are the accelerating layers, all of which enter in the first sixteen seconds. These are sporadic, mostly diatonic, sixteenth note arpeggios running symmetrically down and then up, and containing 11, 7, 13, 9, and 15 notes respectively in each layer. Within each layer, appearances of the arpeggio become more frequent by a factor of ten sixteenth notes with each repetition: that is, in the layer that occupies the eighth stave (the first to appear), the rest between successive arpeggios is first 192 sixteenths in duration, then 182, then 172, etc., until at last the arpeggio repeats continuously. Each of the other four arpeggio layers follows a nearly identical pattern.

Of the remaining six layers, four are block chords repeated every 11, 17, 13, and 19 sixteenths respectively. Eleven is represented by a D♭–A♭–E♭ chord, 17 by a B♭ D♭ minor tenth, 13 by a B F♯ twelfth in the bass, 19 by a high E F♯ A chord. Layer no. 3 (i.e., on the third stave) is a high chromatic figure in staccato quarters and eighth notes, repeated every thirty-three eighth notes; because thirty-three is divisible by eleven, this line has a consistent relation to the eleven-sixteenths chord. The final layer is the one that stands out most after the ostinatos and defines the character of the piece: a figure of seven triads in staccato dotted eighth notes, on the pitches F, A♭, and A, recurring every fifty-one sixteenths. Since fifty-one is divisible by seventeen, this figure always begins a dotted eighth after every third B♭ D♭ dyad (the 17 chord).

Example 4.11   Study No. 5, ostinatos

The pitch development of this experiment contains a hidden ingenuity. Among the thirteen repeating figures, every pitch on Nancarrow's piano is used except for the top two, and, with one exception – the B next to middle C, found in both ostinatos – no pitch occurs in more than one layer. Nancarrow must have worked out the ostinatos and repeating triad line, then apportioned among the other figures the pitches that were left. The aim, as so often in Nancarrow, was to keep the figures out of each others' way in a rhythmic situation which was bound to be unpredictable.

Study No. 9

The form of Study No. 9 is whimsical, perhaps less elegant than that of some of its neighbors, but not complicated. Except for a small bridge just before the end, the entire study is drawn from three ostinato patterns, each of which has upper and lower lines that are sometimes disassociated from each other. The first, designated below as A, comprises ten measures of 6/8; B comprises eight measures of 5/8 divided alternately 2+3 and 3+2, though sometimes regularized into steady eighth notes by omitting rests; C comprises seven measures of 4/8. In Example 4.12 the melodies are given in the octave registers of their first appearances, though each is transposed by octave during the course of the piece. The purpose of the study is to experiment with these lines played against each other at eighth note tempo relationships of 3:4:5 (2:3 and 5:8 are also obtained by doubling and halving note values). It is almost as though Nancarrow is imagining three continuously running stereo tape loops that he can bring in one track at a time via mixer, with the additional luxury of being able to change speeds.

Four sections are clearly marked, the last two very brief. The first (0:00–1:42, systems 1–18) begins by stating only the lower lines of each pattern against each other at an *eighth note* tempo relationship of 5:4:3. That ratio isn't heard as such, because the rhythms are not yet running in steady eighth notes; the fact that tempos are sometimes manifested in quarters in C, dotted quarters in A, and both in B makes the relationships sound more complicated than they will turn out to be. What one actually hears in the opening clash of ostinatos A and C is a 9:20

Example 4.12   Study No. 9, ostinato patterns

tempo ratio (a half note at 72 per minute versus a dotted quarter at 160). Little by little, Nancarrow fills in the upper lines until, by the end of the section, each pattern is heard complete in the resultant 5:4:3 ratio. (A few metric irregularities are thrown in to bring about a synchronized ending.)

Section 2 (1:42–3:35, systems 19–41) takes the upper lines of each part and pairs them against each other in ten brief episodes whose combinations and tempo ratios can be summarized as follows:

A and B (regularized into 3/8 meter), 4:3	(1:42)
B and C (C always includes both lines), 3:5	(1:52)
B against itself, 5:3	(2:00)
B against the original 5/8 version of itself, 8:5	(2:08)
A and B (back in 3/8 version), 8:5	(2:15)
B against itself, 5:4	(2:26)
B and C, 2:3	(2:36)
B against itself, 4:3	(2:47)
B against the original 5/8 version of itself, 5:3	(3:01)
B against the 3/8 version of itself, 2:3	(3:14)

Through a metric modulation process wherein the slower of each pair is invariably retained for the next episode, the music becomes slower and slower, as if to make the tempo contrasts more and more audible.

The B pattern ends here with a scale, which is Nancarrow's impetus for a bridge section (3:35–3:49, systems 41–43) also using scales. In a tempo ratio of 3:4:5, each of three lines progresses from a collective augmented triad through an arithmetically decelerating series of four eighth notes (though starting with 6 in the third voice), then 5, 6, 7, 8, etc. Next, after a three-second fermata, comes a climactic three-part coda (3:49–4:20, systems 44–49). First the A pattern (upper line only) is stated in octaves and triads, at transposition levels forming an augmented triad, and at tempo ratios of 5:3:4. B, in its entirety, is then put through the same process (4:01). Finally a quick series of thirds (4:10), derived from the A material, plunges downward at a rhythmic ratio of 3:4:5 to crash on a low octave B.

By now we have traveled a long way from Nancarrow's original blues sources toward a thoroughly abstract modernism. After the ostinato studies, Nancarrow's next move will be to detach rhythm from pitch and generate form not from repeating melodies, but from repeating rhythmic patterns, or isorhythms. Ostinato will wane in importance, but the atmosphere and rhythmic devices of blues will return again and again as a source of inspiration, particularly in Studies Nos. 35, 41, and 45.

5

Isorhythm: the numbers game

Studies Nos. 6, 7, 10, 11, 12, 20

Isorhythm is a term introduced early in the twentieth century for a structural device found in motets and mass movements of the thirteenth through mid-fifteenth centuries. Meaning simply "same rhythm," isorhythm refers to the practice of using the same rhythmic pattern, called in fourteenth-century treatises a *talea* ("cutting"), over and over in one or more parts as the structural base for a motet or mass movement. The repetitive series of pitches in which the *talea* was sometimes manifested was called the *color*. When the *talea* and *color* contain different numbers of notes, a phasing process occurs. For instance, in Example 5.1, the tenor from an anonymous thirteenth-century English motet, *Epiphaniam Domino*, has a *talea* of five notes and a *color* of fourteen, so that after seventy notes – fourteen repetitions of the *talea* and five of the *color* – the melody repeats itself. The two primary aspects of melody – rhythm and pitch – are thus disjoined. This abstraction of rhythm from pitch resurfaced as a burning musical issue six centuries later in the serialism of the 1950s. It was also a direction Nancarrow explored independently, and in a manner closer to medieval usage – even if in the spirit of blues and jazz.

Nancarrow's interest in isorhythm, however, more likely arose via Indian music, recordings of which he collected avidly during the forties and fifties. The rhythmic cycle of an Indian improvisation is called *tala* (a word whose closeness to *talea* invites speculation). A *tala* is made up of several (usually unequal) groupings of a smaller subdivision: *Dhamar tala*, for example, is a fourteen-beat cycle divided 5+2+3+4; *Jhap tala* is a ten-beat cycle divided 2+3+2+3. Analyses of the isorhythmic works will make Nancarrow's affinity for Indian rhythmic thinking obvious, whether he drew on the influence consciously or not.

Except for its reappearance in Studies Nos. 45 through 47, isorhythm represented only a brief phase in Nancarrow's early career, yet he added to its history a half-dozen nuances which had lain latent since the fifteenth century. Another composer could devote an entire career to exploring the possibilities outlined in these few studies. There is a fine line between ostinato and isorhythm, since an

Example 5.1   Isorhythmic tenor, *Epiphaniam domino*, 13th century

ostinato reiterates the same rhythm as well as the same pitch, and the studies discussed here form an admittedly heterogeneous group. What they do have in common is some internal dissociation of rhythm and pitch, a use of *talea* independent of *color*. Study No. 20 in particular, so different from anything else Nancarrow has written, does not fit neatly here: it is actually a rhythmic canon, though not a pitch canon, but in its final section it combines *talea* and *color* in an ingenious way that I have found in no other music. Its importance to the theoretical history of isorhythm deserves special acknowledgment.

Study No. 6

Delightful Study No. 6 makes a straightforward 1:1 canon from a western-flavored tune, laying the whole over an ingenious bass line that sounds like an ostinato but does not act like one. Together, tune and ostinato express a tempo ratio of three against an ever-shifting four and five. The quasi-ostinato is actually a fifteen-pitch row, or *color*, in A major, moving from tonic to dominant. The *talea* is more complex, split with stunning originality between two different tempos and subject to two levels of organization. Though only one line is involved, Nancarrow divides it on two staves, one at four eighth notes per second, the other at five. Every four notes the row switches from one tempo to the other; but since there are fifteen notes (into which four does not divide evenly), the pattern shifts one note each time, and the row's rhythmic layout changes slightly with each repetition. Nancarrow keeps the rhythmic contour of the ostinato approximately the same, given his quirky premise, and between the syncopations and the closeness of the two tempos (never heard simultaneously), the ear cannot quite figure where this ostinato's irregularity comes from. The proportionately notated comparison of different statements of the ostinato in Example 5.2 offers some idea of Nancarrow's ingenuity. None of the other early studies uses this idea of splitting one line among different tempos, but it will arise again decades later as the basis of Studies Nos. 44 through 47.

Example 5.2   Study No. 6, proportional notation of quasi-ostinato

Example 5.3   Study No. 6, theme

Over this ingratiatingly eccentric background, Nancarrow lays a simple "cowboy" tune that sounds more or less in 4/4, though it is notated in 3/4 to show its tempo relation to the ostinato; in Example 5.3 it is renotated as it sounds. Statements of the theme are linked together by scale fragments, first in single notes, then in parallel thirds, then in triads, ascending on the major scale and descending in melodic minor, the contrast lending some Spanish flavor. On its third statement (1:32), the melody is echoed in canon a perfect eleventh below, for once among Nancarrow's canons at the same tempo. The first half of the melody is sufficiently pentatonic that such transposition hardly disturbs the tonality, and where it begins to wander chromatically, the canon ends. For some forty measures afterward the tune is accompanied by its own motives in counterpoint of up to three parts. Then (at 2:35), following the statement of the scale motive in triads, Nancarrow states the theme's first and second halves together simultaneously.

Nancarrow makes a charming six-measure coda from the scale motive, but inverts the pattern, descending first and then ascending (with the bass in contrary motion), with triads alternating between the 4- and 5-tempos of the ostinato. A nice effect is that the switch to the 5 tempo on the final chord, though strictly following the pattern, sounds like a coy ritard.

Study No. 7

Without hazarding numerological claims regarding the number 7, one might note that the Study No. 7 occupies the same position in Nancarrow's output that Beethoven's Opus 7 does in his sonatas: the most ambitious among the early works. Not only is this the longest single movement of the first nineteen studies, and the second longest of the first thirty-four (just under seven minutes, but what an intense seven minutes!), it is also one of Nancarrow's most intricate and brilliantly devised contrapuntal achievements. The fifty-two pages of score contain too many tightly-knit sections to describe in detail here, but some idea must be communicated of the lovely naturalness of the counterpoint, and of the masterful way in which Nancarrow builds and sustains tension.

Despite its complexity, this is one of the easiest studies to grasp in a listening or two. For one thing, two main themes help define the form through their recurrences. The first is a Spanish-flavored theme (Example 5.4), marked by Nancarrow's usual major/minor scale ambiguity, and notated in 3/4 for convenience, though it goes by so fast that no distinct meter suggests itself to the ear. Immediately following the repetition of Theme 1 is a flexibly modulating secondary theme (Example 5.5, 0:19), one which re-outlines the opening steady dotted-quarter beat as a yardstick for measuring the changing rhythmic accompaniment. A third theme of syncopated quarter notes (0:27) grows from Theme 1's tail and follows Theme 2 as a separate entity.

With such catchy tunes as landmarks, Nancarrow builds the remainder of his structure from three isorhythms, with lengths of eighteen, twenty-four, and thirty (length ratio 3:4:5), which I shall designate as follows:

18 isorhythm 5+4+2+3+4
24 isorhythm 5+5+2+4+3+2+3
30 isorhythm 3+2+2+3+2+3+3+2+3+2+2+3

The rapid juxtaposition of such patterns should not allow for easy listening, but in this study Nancarrow is uncharacteristically generous with structural repetition. In addition to statements of both themes at the beginning of the first two sections and the canonic reappearance of the second theme just before the end, the themes are repeated immediately at each statement, as are large portions of intervening material.

The isorhythms repeat for pages at a time – the 24 rhythm often by itself – with an insistence that inures the ear to their oddness. Two of the isorhythms are fitted with tunes whose recurrence, though not as recognizable as those of the main themes, offers the ear a subtle impression of continuity. The 24 isorhythm is stated in three tunes, two of them related, which I designate as D, E, and E'. Theme D (Example 5.6) appears at system 17 (0:47), played against its own inversion to complete the isorhythm. Except for the leaping sixth, the tune seems to stem from the study's opening up-and-down scale motive. Later (1:30, system 32), when the texture suddenly reduces to a melodic statement of the 24 isorhythm, we hear that

Example 5.4   Study No. 7, theme A

Example 5.5   Study No. 7, theme B

Example 5.6   Study No. 7, theme D and its inversion

Example 5.7   Study No. 7, theme D

Example 5.8   Study No. 7, theme E

Example 5.9   Study No. 7, theme F

derived melody again in quicker note values, occupying the isorhythm by itself, complete with its distinctive half-step key shift (Example 5.7). The fast, loud repetition of a tune just heard in slower, fragmented form gives the moment an unconscious rightness which, combined with the increasing familiarity of its odd rhythm, makes for an expertly prepared moment of magic.

Tune E (Example 5.8, 1:37) is more of a *color*; growing from a four-note motive, it usually recurs in counterpoint with D, sometimes stated in the 24 isorhythm, often in straight dotted halves, 5/8 values, or half notes. The *color* I call E' is E reduced to transpositions of a chromatic four-note motive, e.g. B–B♭–C–D♭. Tune F (Example 5.9) is associated with the 30 isorhythm; it occurs at five points along with 9.6 repetitions of the 30 isorhythm, the first time in the soprano at system 79 (3:37, p. 24). The 18 isorhythm is not audibly associated with a tune, but it often spells out triads in the bass as a support for the other lines. Example 5.10 contains a system-by-system rundown of the study's rhythmic and thematic elements.

Aside from the three main themes the pitch materials are simple, almost banal, in a way that helps the ear even further in finding its way through the rhythmic intricacies. The scale which opens the piece – major in ascending form, minor descending – reappears in several guises, starting with an eight-note *color* in thirds accompanying Theme A. When Nancarrow needs more pitches than usual to feed the note-hungry 30 isorhythm, he sometimes alternates different forms of the scale passage (Example 5.11, 2:39).

Harmonic movement is generally of three types. The first is a relative stasis in which Theme A takes place, and in which the various *taleas* cavort more or less within one diatonic scale. Theme B incites the second type of harmonic movement, which, as in the earlier studies, often modulates along stylized blues changes. Theme B itself rides a bass which outlines a diatonic chain of descending thirds, E–C–A–F–D–B–G; the seven keys, each expressed by four notes, fit neatly across four bars of the seven-note 24 isorhythm *talea*. Even more ear-catching is the recurring chain of parallel major triads modulating via a cycle of fifths, A D G C F B E; expressed in a five-note pattern, this takes five bars to fall back into sync with the 24 isorhythm.

The fascinating thing about such inner workings is that they transform the *color/talea* opposition of isorhythm from a hidden medieval structural device into audible boogie-woogie patterns. Harmony and rhythm live separate lives; the obvious repetition fools the ear into perceiving a regularity that is not there, while the friction keeps the mind intrigued. In the line from p. 22 (3:21) given in Example 5.12, the rhythm repeats the augmented 18 isorhythm, 5+4+2+3+4. Pitch, however, follows a three-note harmonic pattern, creating a harmonic rhythm of 11+12+9+13+9 (= 54) that runs across three repetitions of the *talea*. The duration outlined by each harmony fluctuates, but always averages out to 10.8 beats. In a way this is an extension of the syncopated 3+4+5+4 idea used in Study No. 4, the idea of playing just around a background beat; the technique will assume signal importance in the first canons, Studies Nos. 14–19.

Example 5.10   Study No. 7, structural diagram

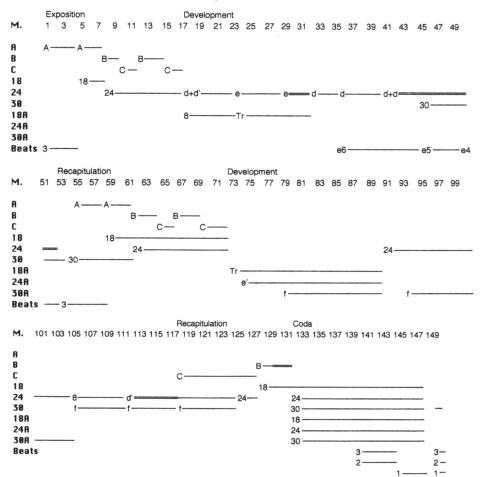

Key: Numbers along the top refer to systems in Nancarrow's score. A, B, and C mark occurrences of the three primary themes. Lowercase letters d, d', e, e', and f refer to subsidiary melodies used with the isorhythms, and variants of those melodies. 18, 24, and 30 indicate the corresponding isorhythm stated in 8th-notes, and 18A, 24A, and 30A the quarter-note augmentations of those isorhythms. A double line shows more than one form of an isorhythm in counterpoint with itself. 8 refers to an isorhythm expressed in pairs of notes an octave apart, and Tr to an isorhythm expressed in arpeggiated triads. The lowest lines, bearing the numbers 1 through 6, indicate steady beats of from one to six 8th-notes, respectively. Words above the system numbers relate the sections of the piece to a modified sonata form. Each of the piece's 149 systems lasts approximately 2.7" on the Wergo recording, 2.38" on the 1750 Arch recording.

Example 5.11   Study No. 7, 30 isorhythm with alternating scale figures

Example 5.12   Study No. 7, isorhythmic bass outlining irregular harmonic rhythm

Example 5.13   Study No. 7, isorhythm with boogie-woogie patterns

Example 5.14   Study No. 7, isorhythm with out-of-phase phrasing

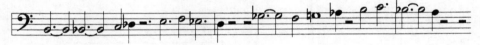

Another wonderful device is the descending triads along the cycle of fifths (kept diatonic, blues-style, by insertion of a tritone). In Example 5.13 (0:26), the 24 isorhythm *talea* uses seven attacks and the harmonic pattern five, so that seven modulations are spread across five measures. The triads, whose banality begs the ear to regularize them, keep changing implied duration – 3+2+3, then 2+4+3, 5+5+2, 2+3+5, 4+3+2, 5+2+4, and 3+5+5. The ear recognizes the discrepancy, but not the system that accounts for it; rather, it sounds like the rhythmic license taken by a jazz player. Nancarrow adds a further wrinkle through an imaginative use of phrasing. Example 5.12 is accompanied by a version of the 24 isorhythm which, although it contains seven notes, is phrased in groups of four (melody E') as in Example 5.14. The constant working of harmony and phrasing against the bar line destroys any sense of isorhythmic repetition, making every measure sound fresh and intuitively out of whack. Nancarrow is repeating the same rhythm over and over, but the rhythm you hear is not the one he is repeating – a remarkable concept, and a remarkable achievement.

On a larger scale, Study No. 7 is emotionally compelling because of the directedness of its overall melodic and harmonic movement, which parallels that of a classical sonata in ways too numerous to ignore. As in so many sonatas,

Theme A is harmonically stable, Theme B begins at once to explore surrounding tonal areas. Furthermore, Theme B clearly derives its opening arpeggios in each phrase from those of Theme A, and its four-note cadencing scale motives from Theme A's second phrase, so that one theme seems to grow from the other as naturally as in a Beethoven sonata. The first athematic section of contrapuntal isorhythms, systems 17 through 52, acts as a development, primarily of the 24 isorhythm: beginning at system 41 (1:54), tune D is even developed as a canon.

Nancarrow's handling of rhythmic progression creates a quickening excitement similar to that of a classical sonata. At system 35 in this development (1:37), the E *color* articulates a dotted half-note beat against the 24 isorhythm. At system 45 (2:04) this is replaced by a beat five eighth notes in length, then at system 49 (2:15) by a half-note beat. This 6–5–4 progression leads directly back to the dotted-quarter beat (3) beginning the recapitulation at system 53 (2:26), and in case there is any doubt that Nancarrow had this consciously in mind, he notates the 3-beat on the same stave as the previous 6, 5, and 4.

The divergences from sonata form, of course, are not to be glossed over (for example, the primary themes are never transposed), but neither are they marked enough to prevent the *feel* of the genre. Even Haydn wrote a symphony (No. 89) in which the functions of development and recapitulation are reversed, which is hardly less strange than what happens here. The recapitulation proper (systems 53–72, slightly longer than the exposition to accommodate added isorhythms) is followed by a second, longer development, which eventually leads back to a smaller recapitulation (systems 121–32) using only Themes B and C – Theme A is memorable enough not to require restatement. This second development (at 3:21, system 72) *sounds* more developmental than the first, reducing as it does to augmented forms of the 18 and 24 isorhythms; like Brahms, Nancarrow often lowers the intensity of his middle sections (cf. Studies Nos. 2, 9, 31) to build toward a more effective final climax. At system 91 (p. 28, 4:07), just where the texture becomes thinnest, he brings truly Beethovenian focus to bear on that four-note motive, propelling it through a gripping series of modulations (Example 5.15).

Nancarrow hardly resorts to the kind of tonic/dominant polarity that lies at the basis of the classical sonata, but there is here a tension between the keys of E (sometimes ambiguously close to A) and C, first of all in the scales which open the work, E major ascending and all-natural descending. Theme A, after the first four phrases, flirts with the C major triad before centering again on E, and Theme B paradoxically establishes the key of E with a chain of triads outlining the C major scale to establish the key of E: E C A F D B G E.

Typically of Nancarrow, the coda (5:49, system 132 to the end) brings back all three isorhythms, plus their augmentations, for a monolithic, climactic block of sound. No themes are heard here, but the harmonies change key following the bass line with kaleidoscopic nonsynchronicity. The first seven and a half systems – 360 eighth notes, the smallest common multiple in which the 18, 24, and 30 isorhythms can come back in sync – are repeated in the next seven and a half with

Example 5.15 Study No. 7, isorhythmic motivic development

minor changes beneath a soprano filigree of steady quarter notes, dotted quarters, and eighths. The coda's own brief coda (at 6:32), which, like that of Study No. 9, uses an arithmetical progression, drives home one of Nancarrow's most convincing cadences, and shows the relationship between the keys of E and C in the process. Having painted himself into a C major triad, he interprets it as a flattened submediant chord, going through a harmonic progression of a step down, a fourth up – C B⁹ E D⁹ G F♯⁹ B A⁹ C B⁹ – over a rhythm of 10, 9, 8, 7, 6, 5, 4, 3, 2, and 12 eighth notes. The final dominant ninth on B provides the impetus for a resounding cadence on E, accomplished via a quick scale passage down the Phrygian scale on E (all naturals) and back up the major scale (four sharps), showing succinctly how the C major/E major duality derives from the major/minor scale which opened the piece.

Generally, Nancarrow is not much of a believer in sonata form. As he told me,

> You know who Marvin Minsky is, don't you? The artificial intelligence expert? He had an interview once, and in the introductory note it said that he's a very good amateur musician, and that he improvises fugues on the organ. Which means he's not exactly illiterate musically. And in the interview he said that sonata form and all the classical forms are based on key relationships. "That doesn't mean much to me," he said. I'm not quoting exactly, but he said, "Brahms starts a piece in F major, and then after awhile he modulates to A–flat, and goes on for awhile. And then he goes back to F," as he put it, "*to relieve my tension* about leaving F. I've long since forgotten about F." I feel the same way. It doesn't mean anything to me at all.[1]

Nevertheless, what makes Study No. 7 unique in Nancarrow's output is the thoroughness with which its ideas are varied and developed. Most of Nancarrow's melodies (including the D and F tunes here) are too long, most of his studies too short, to require much in the way of classical developmental technique. Musical interest in the late Studies lies elsewhere, in the perceptual structures that unfold from the canonic process. The isorhythmic ideas of Study No. 11 are similar to those of No. 7, but the blocks of material in No.11 are huge, and Nancarrow has never gone further in the direction of No. 7. In the larger debate of 20th-century music, his sympathies lie squarely in Stravinsky's non-developmental camp, to which this one essay is a masterful exception.

Study No. 10

With Study No. 7 Nancarrow capped a period of impressive early achievement. In the String Quartet, the Sonatina, and the first seven player piano studies, he had behind him a small but original body of work whose quality any forty-year-old composer could have been proud of. This was a turning point: the next three studies, Nos. 8, 9, and 10, are patent experiments, interesting more for the technical questions they raise than for their solutions. Study No. 8 will eventually lead to the acceleration canons, and the tempo contrasts of No. 9 will be explored in Nos. 14–19 before becoming the basis of his greatest body of work. Study No. 10, though, remains torn between the blues style and the number systems so brilliantly deployed in No. 7. Not until the studies numbering in the twenties will Nancarrow again display the same perfectly confident balance of form and process as in the first seven.

After Study No. 3, No. 10 stays closest to blues piano style, though instead of relying on ostinato it makes tentative moves toward isorhythm. Nancarrow obviously had trouble with the form. When submitting it to *Soundings* for publication, he dropped a four-and-three-quarter-page slow introduction that had been included on the Columbia recording. He was arguably right: the introduction is not well developed melodically. And yet, the original version contained rhythmic correspondences between the introduction and closing which imparted to it an overall ABA shape; deprived of the opening A, the fourteen pages that remain seem lopsided. The numbers do not work out as elegantly as in the Studies Nos. 7 and 11, and everything points to a makeshift form, an uneasy compromise between arithmetical structure and intuitive melody. Still, No. 10 has its blues charms, and its application of isorhythm to chords rather than single notes is original.

The overall structure is most easily observed in the chordal "left hand" accompaniment. Study No. 10 breaks into two sections, one marked by sustained, the other by staccato chords, and the latter falls into three further subsections distinguished by rhythmic pattern. The opening chords express a half-note pattern of:

5 4 3 2 1 2 3 4 5 4 3 2 1 2 3 4 5 4 3 2,

for a total of sixty-two half-note measures. Superimposed on this twenty-note *talea* is a harmonic *color* of four chords: E♭ minor, F⁷, G♭⁹, C¹¹. The resulting series states the chords first in lengths of 5, 4, 3, 2, then again at 1, 2, 3, 4, creating a

Example 5.16   Study No. 10, simultaneous acceleration and deceleration

kind of harmonic balance, since each chord is heard for a total of six measures. That overall pattern then repeats a whole step higher – F minor, G^7, $A\flat^9$, D^{11}.[2] (Both times the last chord becomes a 13th chord the second time for reasons of voice leading.) Lastly, the pattern begins *another* whole tone higher, and proceeds only half-way.

At each chord lasting five measures (0:00, 0:25, and 0:51), a new melody voice enters, until finally three are going at once; this is, arguably, a canon with subjects in identical tempos, though the entrances are too distant for much canonic effect. The melody is a rhapsodic blue-note figuration with little relation to the notated beat, beginning with a diminishing thirty-second-note sequence, 8 7 6 5 4 3. As each new harmonic sequence begins a whole step higher, the next melodic voice enters canonically, also a whole step higher, while the previous melody takes on a subsidiary role. The voices complete this section by superimposing the augmenting and diminishing forms of the thirty-second-note sequence at once (Example 5.16, 1:01). As later studies will show, Nancarrow loves the effect of an acceleration and a ritard occurring simultaneously.

The study's second section (at 1:05) governs a fourteen-chord *color* via a systematically changing rhythmic pattern. Expressed in sixteenth note durations, these chords articulate the following syncopated rhythmic structure:

pattern starts at

(8 8 8 5 8 8 8 11) × 3	(1:05)
(8 8 5 8 8 11) × 3	(1:31)
(8 5 8 11) × 3	(1:50)
(5 5 5 3 5 5 5 8) × 3	(2:02)
(5 5 3 5 5 8) × 3	(2:17)
(5 3 5 8) × 3	(2:29)

Then, in thirty-second notes:

(13 31) × 7	(2:37)

Except for the last, these patterns are little more than syncopations, a shifting of the accent to the middle of the measure following Nancarrow's standard 5+3 division of the half note. The now-abandoned introduction foreshadowed these patterns but, because of the tempo and the rhythmic amorphousness of the melodies, the effect did not quite communicate to the ear. Nancarrow will enjoy greater success with such syncopations in Study No. 11.

In the first part of this second section (1:05), the fourteen-chord sequence modulates upward a minor third with each repetition. In the second part (2:02), Nancarrow introduces a tritone intervallic change so that it modulates *downward* by minor thirds. Each time, though, he also introduces other irregularities to prevent the sequence from following minor thirds through an entire diminished seventh chord, and to allow for the fact that fourteen does not divide evenly into the number of measures (fifty-four) in each section. The third section, eccentrically dividing an 11/8 measure into 13+31 thirty-second notes, runs once through the fourteen-chord sequence with the final chords modified for a cadence on F. The keys (suggested by a I–IV–V–I progression opening each sequence) proceed according to the following pattern:

1st section	F A♭ B G
2nd section	C A F♯ D
3rd section	G cadencing on F

Two melodic lines grace this second half, based on uneven triplets in imitation of blues: 3+2+3 in thirty-second-note groupings. Every rhythm articulates this irregular "beat" except for a few contrasting repeated-note motives. Nancarrow freely composed the first fifty-four-measure section around his 3+2+3 rhythm, then recomposed it to fit the registers and tonalities of his new, descending harmonic sequence, adding a short coda. The alterations include shifts of register, movement of motives from one voice to the other, and a series of changing transposition levels from the original, determined by the transposition relationships of the fourteen-chord sequence evident in the key scheme above: first a perfect fifth (F to C), then a major third (F to A), minor second (A to A♭), major second (A♭ to F♯), etc. The symmetry of the plan is intriguing – ascending harmonies in one half, descending in the other, the sequence determining the melodies' pitch level – but it leaves the first half of the study out of account, and, atypically for Nancarrow, remains a little too vague to be audibly meaningful.

Study No. 11

Jaunty Study No. 11, related to No. 7 in its isorhythmic technique, sounds simpler than it looks in the score. Its secret is that it is based entirely on an isorhythmic 120-note melody (that is, a melody containing an internal isorhythm). Like so many of Nancarrow's lengthy melodies (for example, those of Nos. 6, 8, 19, and 21), this one starts out in a clear key (C major/minor) and becomes increasingly

Example 5.17 Study No. 11, isorhythmic chord sequence

atonal, though it returns to the tonic at structural points. The 120 notes comprise eight repetitions of a fifteen-note isorhythm, which further divides into three segments of twenty eighth notes each:

5 5 6 4 5 5 3 4 3 5 4 3 3 3 2

Such a division is emphasized in the first line by the return to the tonic chord at the beginning of each phrase. The first forty-five notes, along with the chords that harmonize them (all with parallel fifths in the bass), are given in Example 5.17, lined up to make the isorhythm clear.

That this melody is not entirely through-composed becomes apparent from the melodic correspondences between the first two systems especially: both start with a rising minor-triad motive, both contain the motive C–D–G in the middle, and both end with half-steps. The isorhythm's effect of near-normalcy stems from the emphasis on fives within the twenty-beat cycle, which conditions the ear to take 20/8 as the virtual meter, dividing it into four with a unit of five eighth notes as the beat. Across this meter, the 6+4 grouping sounds like a syncopation, and the 3+4+3 like an uneven triplet. Once again, Nancarrow uses the player piano to produce the impression of a jazz pianist who can reproduce his freedoms with exact precision.

From this oddly-rhythmed chorale Nancarrow fashions rhythmic sequences which act as ostinatos and determine the structure. The isorhythm is sixty eighth notes in length, and the entire study comprises forty sixty-beat periods, enough for five statements of the entire melody. (In the printed score, each period takes four beats less than two systems.) These statements divide the piece into five sections. In the first fifth of the piece (periods 1 through 8; 0:00–0:46), the melody is heard in staccato chords; in periods 9 through 16 (0:46–1:30), it is spelled out by sustained notes. In the next $\frac{2}{5}$ of the piece, periods 17 through 32 (1:30–2:53), the melody as such is absent (except for periods 20–24, where it is partially stated in octaves). Instead its notes, and those of the accompanying harmony, appear in derived rhythmic sequences. The final eight periods, 33 through 40 (2:53–3:41), state the chorale in its original staccato-chord form again, with running eighth note accompaniment.

However, over those forty periods is imposed yet another level of rhythmic organization. At first it seems odd that the introduction of new material often does not coincide with the beginning of a new period, and that patterns derived from the isorhythm sometimes begin $\frac{1}{3}$ or $\frac{2}{3}$ of the way through. As it turns out, a textural change takes place every 160 beats (every five systems), so that while the isorhythm divides the study into forty periods, changes of texture divide it into fifteen. If fifteen sections are stretched across forty periods, three of one will coincide with eight of the other, so that Study No. 11 contains five repetitions of a three-against-eight structural cross-rhythm. The largest common denominator between period and section is the implied 20/8 measure, one-third of the isorhythm. At the other end of the scale, the smallest common multiple of 60 and 160 is 480, so the most significant articulations, those where texture and melody change both at once, occur every 480 beats, one-fifth of the entire piece.

The fifteen texture-defined sections of the piece progress as follows:

Systems 1–5 (0:00–0:16) The first two and two thirds periods of the isorhythm are stated unaccompanied.

Systems 6–10 (0:16–0:31) The isorhythm is played against a bass note marking every fourth eighth note, setting a half-note beat against the basic five-eighth-note beat; each pitch anticipates the bass note of the following chord.

Systems 11–15 (0:31–0:46) The half-note beat is replaced by a blues pattern of 3+3+2.

Systems 16–20 (0:46–1:01) The isorhythmic chord sequence begins sustaining the top note of each chord. A new rhythmic pattern (hereafter designated as Pattern A) enters in arpeggiated triads like those of Study No. 7. This pattern, which runs throughout the middle three fifths of the piece and another section at the end, sometimes in out-of-phase counterpoint with itself, is derived from the isorhythm through unequal divisions, creating syncopations in the third phrase:

```
5     5  6    4     5   5  3  4  3  5    4   3  3   3 2
2 2 1 2 3 3 2 1 2 1 1  2 1 2 2 3 1 2 1 3 3  3 1 2  2 1 2 2  1 3  3
```

Systems 21–25 (1:01–1:15) The top two notes of each chord move into a high register, so that the sustained note representing the melody is now in a middle voice.

Systems 26–30 (1:15–1:30) The sustained melody notes drop to the lowest voice of the chords.

Systems 31–35 (1:30–1:44) The melody drops out. Pattern A restates its original form from system 16 (period 9), now accompanied by Pattern B, also derived from the isorhythm and displaced from A by a sixteenth note:

```
5  5   6   4 5 5   3 4   3   5   5   3 3 3  2
2 3 2 1 2 1 2 3 4  3 2 2 1 3  3  1 2 1 2  1 3 2  3 2  3  1 2 1 2
```

Systems 36–40 (1:44–1:58) The isorhythmic melody reappears in octaves in a middle voice.

Systems 41–45 (1:58–2:12) The isorhythmic melody in octaves moves to a higher voice. Pattern B is replaced by a rhythmic anomaly, a repeating ninety-nine-beat pattern full of eighth note groups that outline minor third motives, sometimes in immediate repetition.

Systems 46–50 (2:12–2:26) Everything drops out except Pattern A, whose gloss on the isorhythmic melody will be described below.

Systems 51–55 (2:26–2:39) A slightly varied form of Pattern A enters playing against itself, 20 beats out of phase and displaced by a sixteenth note.

Systems 56–60 (2:39–2:53) A third voice enters with Pattern A, twenty beats out of phase with both of the others.

Systems 61–65 (2:53–3:07) Recapitulation: the isorhythm returns in its original, staccato chord form, with an accompaniment of steady eighth notes grouped 3+3+2.

Systems 66–70 (3:07–3:21) The accompaniment switches from 3+3+2 to a steady eighth-note pulse in alternating octaves. Pattern A returns.

Systems 71–75 (3:21–3:41) Pattern A enters in a lower voice, over which the other version of A becomes irregular, primarily filling in the rests in the lower version of A. Octaves give way to running scales, leading ultimately to a triumphant cadence on C.

(One can note, in the increasingly shorter timings of these theoretically equal sections, the acceleration that takes place naturally as the roll becomes thicker on the player piano's take-up spool.) Example 5.18 attempts to give, in a glance, a more concise view of the organization.

It contributes to the remarkable perceptual unity of this "blues motet for player piano" that the melodies of the faster rhythmic patterns are derived from the primary melody by a technique analogous to the paraphrase technique applied to the cantus firmus in Renaissance masses. In the excerpt from systems 46 (2:12) through 48 in Example 5.19, the notes marked with crosses are taken from the melody, and the others are mostly pitch repetitions to fill out the greater number of notes needed; the masses of Dufay, Ockeghem, and Josquin are filled with similar examples. Ultimately Study No. 11 creates an impression not of abstract rhythmic structure, but of a melody almost jazzy enough for big band arrangement. Despite the formidable ingeniousness of the piece's rhythmic arsenal, it is one of Nancarrow's catchiest, most hummable works.

Example 5.18   Study No. 11, structural diagram

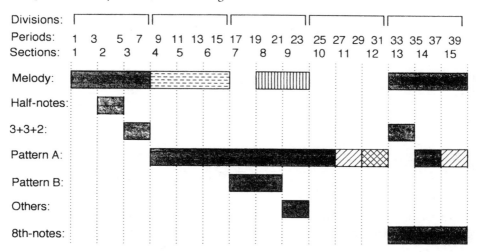

Example 5.19   Study No. 11, paraphrase technique

Study No. 12

Study No. 12 is an aural delight and a structural enigma. It does not use isorhythm in the same sense as the other isorhythmic studies, and it is included here partly because there is nowhere else to put it. Tenney hears flamenco guitars in its superfast, punctuating arpeggios, for which I tend to call it the "Spanish" Study. There is also, however, an almost medieval quality to the work, not only in its

Example 5.20   Study No. 12, opening chords

inexhaustible supply of modal melody, but in the long, irreducible number arrays of its rhythm, deployed in a manner that seems at once capricious and rigid.

The piece is built from four long sequences of block chords, each with its own detailed, nonrepeating rhythm; for purpose of analysis I call these sequences chants 1–4. The chords are in three voices, resulting from three lines all in Phrygian mode. The top voice in each chant is almost always in Phrygian mode on E, the middle voice on A, and the lowest on D; the one exception is the first statement of chant 3 (systems 48–51), where the E and A voices exchange places. A nonrhythmic layout of the chords as in Example 5.20 shows that the counterpoint is melodically, not harmonically, conceived. The melodies of the top voices of all the chants are remarkably similar in contour: each begins by neighboring and circling the tonic, all leap up to the fourth scale degree, and all except that of chant 4 establish the orthodox Phrygian reciting tone on the sixth scale degree before descending to the tonic cadence. Divorced from their rhythm, these lines look inexplicably like Gregorian chant. I searched the entire *Liber Usualis* for possible chant quotations, and when I asked Nancarrow if Study No. 12 reflected any influence of Catholic music he picked up in Spain, he laughed heartily:

> It's funny, my Spanish influence in music was before I went to Spain, not after. I didn't hear any music in Spain. It had nothing to do with it. In fact, [in Arkansas] the Catholics were practically subversive as far as the culture goes. I came from a Protestant family, Congregationalist. I think in the whole town there were two Catholics, and they were considered like Communists or something. I had never even thought of any kind of religion one way or the other.[3]

The first section consists of four repetitions of the top voice of chant 1, an amazing seventy-two-note melody with a complex through-composed rhythm. First expressed in three-note chords and in quarter-note units, the chant begins with a 5+4+3+2+1 duration series; this is the study's main recurring rhythmic motive, later broadened to 13+11+9+7+5. The rhythm exhibits a general, nonlinear acceleration, ending in strings of quarter notes. The second statement of chant 1 (0:36), top voice only, is expressed in dotted eighths, or at three-quarters the

Example 5.21   Study No. 12, section 1 structural diagram

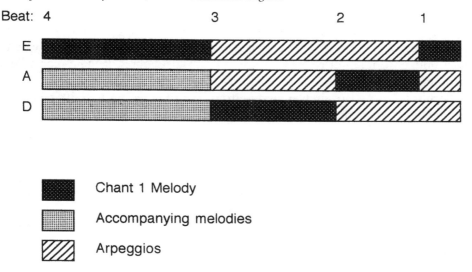

Example 5.22   Study No. 12, Phrygian model for arpeggio lines

tempo of the first; the third statement (1:02) is in eighths, at one-half the original tempo, and the last (1:20) is in sixteenths, at one quarter the tempo. Thus the entire first section illustrates a structural 4 3 2 1 acceleration.

Although the latter three statements of chant 1 are expressed monophonically, they are sporadically accompanied by lines expressed in quick arpeggios of alternating fourths and fifths (i.e., C G C), so that, except for a transition at systems 38–40 and the final section, three voices are always present. First, chant 1 is on D in the bass with arpeggios spelling out Phrygian lines on A and E above; then chant 1 is in the middle on A, with arpeggios on D below and E above; then chant 1 is in the treble on E, with arpeggios on D and A below. The first section (0:33–1:33, systems 1–34) could be reduced to the scheme in Example 5–21.

However, three separate voices are not what the listener hears. The fact that the two arpeggio lines never coincide encourages the ear to hear them as a single element: except in the third subsection, they are neither distant enough in range nor close enough in rhythm to be heard as separate. One has to notate the arpeggio lines separately, as in Example 5.22, to see the Phrygian modal basis on which they were conceived. The arpeggios continue as the section closes with a brief bridge made up of elaborate Phrygian cadential figures, landing repeatedly on E, then cadencing on A in a wild quasi-cadenza of octaves.

Sections 2 and 3 are simpler, and perhaps best summed up in a diagram that outlines the form of the entire study:

Section 1		starting at
Systems: 1–13	chant 1 in chords, quarter-note beat	0:00
14–23	chant 1 with arpeggios, dotted-eighth beat	0:36
23–30	chant 1 with arpeggios, eighth note beat	1:02
30–34	chant 1 with arpeggios, sixteenth note beat	1:20
35–40	bridge: quasi-cadenza in E Phrygian, then A	1:33

Section 2		
41–46	chant 2 in chords	1:51
46–48	second half of Chant 1 in single line, on A, sixteenth note beat	2:06
48–51	first half of Chant 3 in bass chords	2:10
52–54	second half of Chant 3 in treble chords	2:19

Section 3		
55–69	three-part canon on chant 2 on D, A, and E, arpeggios added internally with each line	2:27

Section 4		
69–73	first half of chant 3 on F over chant 4	3:04
73–78	chant 2 on A with altered ending over chant 4	3:15
78–81	second half of chant 3 on C♯ over chant 4	3:29
81–84	chant 1 on F; chant 4 continues with arpeggios	3:37
84–98	bridge/cadenza material; chant 4 continues without arpeggios	3:45

Section 3, a three-part canon based on chant 2, uses an odd rhythmic canon technique that Nancarrow had suggested in Study No. 4 and would later use again in No. 33: notationally, the voices are in the same tempo, but they proceed through their material at different rates because the faster voices have sixteenth notes subtracted from each measure. The result approximates a 10/12/15 canon; set side by side, the duration in sixteenths given to each note of the chant in each voice begins as follows (the lower rhythm duplicates that of the original statement of chant 2's original statement, with minor modifications):

upper:	16	10	7	7	5	1	1	18	8	10	8...
middle:	19	12	8	9	6	2	2	22	9	12	10...
lower:	23	15	9	11	8	3	3	27	10	15	12...

Example 5.23   Study No. 12, triad roots of chant 4

In imitation of the arpeggios of Section 1 Nancarrow adds triadic arpeggios preceding some of the notes.

Section 4, the climactic finale, contains two elements: a single line in octaves, borrowing from the top voices of chants 3, 2, and 1; and chant 4, a sequence of block chords made up not of three notes, but of three major triads. Chant 4 is the only one that modulates from mode to mode, and the line above it modulates with it. Also unlike the others, chant 4 is not through-composed (except for the rhythm), but repeats a twelve-chord sequence seven times (twice only partially) at different pitch levels. Reduced to the roots of each triad, the sequence is as in Example 5.23. Between the third and fourth sequences (systems 81–84) Nancarrow adds triadic arpeggios which zip through all three voices. As in section 1, the chant 1 melody leads to the cadential cadenza figures. These change mode when they change range, maintaining the perfect-fifth relations which have obtained between voices throughout: e.g., the melodies switch between F♯, C♯, and G♯ in systems 87–89, then B♭, F, and C, later C♯, G♯, and D♯, etc. At last the arabesques stabilize around B, move to E, and then A, as the chordal rhythm accelerates 15, 14, 13, 12, 11, down to 1 for a rousing finish. The overall effect is satisfying, and the inexhaustible generation of Phrygian melodies seems a compositional tour de force.

Study No. 20

Study No. 20 has been one of the most popular of the studies, not only for its originality (which is even greater than appears on the surface), but because it shares concerns with much European music of the 1970s, and is thus easier to place in the context of an international avant-garde than anything else Nancarrow has written. Its quasi-statistical deployment of repeated pitches within a limited range is similar in effect to the stochastic textures of Iannis Xenakis's music, and to the effects György Ligeti has achieved since his flirtation with minimalism. In particular, Study No. 20 reminds one vividly of two piano pieces, Xenakis's

Example 5.24   Study No. 20, opening line renotated

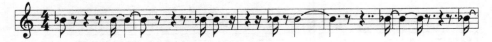

Example 5.25   Study No. 20, transformation of hexachords

Evryali (1973) and Ligeti's *Monument-Selbstporträt-Bewegung* (1976), though it is worth emphasizing that Nancarrow's work antedated those pieces by at least fifteen years. I like to call this the "Cloud" Study, because it captures the textural feeling Ligeti sought in his *Clocks and·Clouds*, and because its gentle patter of random-sounding notes evokes a light rain.

The main difficulty of analyzing Study No. 20 is notational. This is one of the few studies whose notation hides rather than reveals its structure. Careful measurement shows that the length of every note and rest (allowing for some tiny degree of imprecision) is divisible by $\frac{1}{3}$ of a centimeter. Nancarrow's marked tempo equates $1\frac{1}{3}$ centimeters with a beat of 120, which means that he could have notated the study's tempo as $\quarternote = 120$, with the constant $\frac{1}{3}$ cm. subdivision represented by sixteenth notes. This more conventional notation would have made analysis easier, but given the purely quantitative nature of the rhythms, it would also have resulted in needless complexity. The first line, for example, a repeated B♭, would appear as in Example 5.24. The notation Nancarrow chose provides a clearer picture of the piece's intentions and aural effect than any standard notation would have done.

Actually, it is logical that even a spatial piece written by Nancarrow at this point would contain an underlying constant subdivision. Study No. 21 is the first piece in which he rigorously explored the effect of gradual acceleration, and it was the piece that made the limitations of his punching machine too frustrating to ignore. After No. 21, Nancarrow had the machine altered so that, instead of punching holes at points indicated by notches on the mechanism, it would move along a smooth continuum, capable of placing a hole at any point. For No. 21, he went through a tedious process of placing the mechanism one half or one quarter of the way between notches. Since No. 20 uses no acceleration, there would have been no reason to endure such a process. Here, the notches have the effect of creating an underlying subdivision.

Study No. 20's most obvious distinguishing feature is its reduction of pitch to groups of six diatonically adjacent notes, as though Nancarrow wanted to make sure nothing distracted the ear from the time aspect of this "study in durations." There are five sections, the last two overlapping in time. The first introduces only three pitches in its first half – B♭, A, then G – according to a rhythm canon with duration values : 11 16 10 3 23 16 7 13 9 11 7 5 10 14. (All rhythms in this study will be expressed in units of $\frac{1}{3}$ cm. in the score, or $\frac{1}{48}$ of a system, and as measured from note head to note head, not counting rests.[4]) At system 11 (1:00), D, E, and F are brought in: F states the first 1/3 of the B♭ rhythmic series (minus the first note, missing in both score and recording), E in the second 1/3, and D in the final $\frac{1}{3}$. As cadence, Nancarrow adds values at the end to bring all six pitches together in unison as a cluster chord.

Section 2 (systems 15–25, 1:25) transposes that hexachord up a fifth and transforms it, one note at a time, into a lower chromatic hexachord via a consistent canonic process. Two rhythmic series are used, one for the first hexachord and one for the second, both 180 units in duration:

$$8 \ 20 \ 17 \ 10 \ 14 \ 21 \ \ 7 \ 21 \ 15 \ 16 \ 14 \ 17 = 180$$
$$19 \ 15 \ 12 \ 14 \ 19 \ 12 \ 11 \ 16 \ 12 \ 19 \ 13 \ 18 = 180 \text{ (plus a final note)}$$

Distances between entries of each pitch and series diminish by multiples of six as follows:

	42		36		30		24		18	
C		B		A		D		E		F

these distances remaining constant throughout the section. Perceptually, of course, the canon is inaudible as such; what one hears instead is the transfiguration from one hexachord into another shown in Example 5.25.

Section 3 (systems 26–29, 2:26) is little more than a bridge. In the piano's lowest three octaves, each of three voices intones an E♭–F–G♭ pattern, in a duration series identical to the D–E–F layer of section 1.

Section 4 (systems 30–39, 2:47) continues the process of section 2, canonically transforming through a series of five hexachords. A tritone-transposed version of the original section 1 hexachord emerges at the following canonic distances, the pitches entering in the same relative order they occupied in section 2:

	34		29		32		21		30	
B		A♯		G♯		C♯		D♯		E

The sum of those distances puts 146 units between the entrances of each hexachord's first and last pitches, and, since a new hexachord begins every 180 units, each hexachord is barely established (for less than five seconds) before its transformation begins. As it merges into the final section, the canon runs through the series of hexachords shown in Example 5.26. Each 180 units contains twelve notes and, starting with the third hexachord, the canon begins repeating duration patterns that had been used earlier in the work.

The final section (systems 40–60, 3:40) departs from the textural stasis of the rest of the study and, in a piece that has rarely used more than a tenth of pitch space at a time, suddenly bursts across the entire keyboard. At system 39, a low

Example 5.26   Study No. 20, hexachords

Example 5.27   Study No. 20, staggered–octave line renotated

melody starts in the bass, soon echoed an octave above and two octaves above. But not echoed at consistent rhythmic intervals: successive entrances of this new line are canonic as to rhythm, but their pitch remains in unison with the lowest line. At system 48 (4:32), these three voices end and the process spreads into the six voices that heretofore had been reiterating single pitches. Here Nancarrow creates an amazing heterophonic melody in which six voices are playing the same line in different octaves, according to a rhythmic canon which is applied to the pitches differently in each case. Though all lines are running through the same rhythmic sequence, each one is at a different point in that sequence, even though they are all at the same point in the pitch sequence. This is the only use of isorhythm I know of in which the *color* and *talea* are identical in all parts, but *correlated* differently; that is, each line associates any given pitch in the *color* with a different duration in the *talea*. The result, renotated in Example 5.27, is a grand, lumbering line in randomly broken octaves, in which one never knows where the new pitch will be sounded first.

At the same time, Nancarrow reintroduces the original B♭, A, and G in octaves (to better sound through the texture), which serve as fixed points against which the melody can be more clearly perceived. These three pitches are deployed in the same rhythms as in the opening canon, though with the entrances now separated by four systems instead of three. The study ends rather suddenly at the same point in the B♭ line at which section 1 ended, immediately following a unison attack on the three pitches. The final texture sounds almost stochastic, its methods inaccessible to the ear, yet its underlying process is both simple and unprecedented.

108

6

Canon: phase I

Studies Nos. 4, 13, 14, 15, 16, 17, 18, 19, 26, 31, 34, 44, 49, 50

Nancarrow's 1975 statement to Roger Reynolds – "My interest has always been in tempo"[1] – was made in hindsight. Nancarrow's first interest, like that of many American composers active in the 1930s, had been in cross-rhythms, specifically the patterns made by groupings of 3, 4, 5, and so on, against each other in counterpoint. The first dozen studies move away from a conception of rhythm based on diverse groupings of an individual unit to, in Study No. 9, the superimposition of tempos whose common denominator is sufficiently small to be notationally inconvenient and finally forgotten. With the close-knit group of Studies Nos. 14–19, Nancarrow takes the daunting next step that no other composer had dared make, and focuses on tempo in a way that abandons the realm of *Le sacre du printemps* and the other rhythmically experimental works written under its influence.

To make that futuristic step, Nancarrow used an ancient device. "Canon" is Latin for "rule" or "law"; in medieval music, it was the strict rule by which one part of a composition could be transformed to provide the remaining part or parts, usually a transposition or rhythmic modification needed to create a second contrapuntal voice structured to fit consonantly with a first. For purposes of setting one tempo against another, canon appealed to Nancarrow for perceptual reasons. As he put it, "Let's say you have two tempi going at the same time . . . if you have them both at the same . . . *melodic* proportions, it's easier to follow the temporal changes."[2] When Beethoven wanted to make large-scale harmonic movement *thematic* (in the phenomenological sense, as a focus of attention), he restricted variations in melody and harmony, transposing large passages in their entirety (as in the Adagio of the "Hammerklavier" Sonata). Similarly, in order to make *tempo* thematic, Nancarrow minimized differences in other parameters.

Nancarrow was not the first to write tempo canons, though he revived the practice after a hiatus of almost 400 years (unless one counts the augmentation or 2:1 canon, which survived into the eighteenth century). When composers of the

109

Example 6.1 Josquin des Prez, Agnus Dei 2 from *Missa L'homme armé super voces musicales*, published 1502

fifteenth and sixteenth centuries wrote *prolation* or *mensuration* canons, they were limited, Renaissance notation being what it was, to differentiating tempos by having one notated line interpreted according to different prolations (meters). Mensuration canons generally ceased to be tempo canons once the music moved to briefer note values, because those did not change duration under different prolation signs. The Agnus Dei from Josquin des Prez's *Missa L'homme armé*, however, reprinted in Example 6.1 in its original notation followed by its canonic solution in modern notation, is an exception in that the 2:1:3 tempo ratio holds throughout – it is a tempo canon as well as a mensuration canon.[3] In that sense, Nancarrow can be said to be the first explorer of the true tempo canon. More recently, György Ligeti has written tempo canons in his Etudes and Piano Concerto, and younger composers have written tempo canons in response to Nancarrow's influence.[4]

The studies examined in this chapter are not all early ones, but they are the ones that represent Nancarrow's early conception of canon, the ones in which contrast of perceptibly different tempos is the primary focus. In the studies discussed in chapter 8 the canonic discipline remains as stringent as ever, but aurally the works begin to blur into another, unprecedented genre. In the early canons discussed here, the relationship of the opening subject to its tempo-varied reappearances remains the center of perceptual interest. These canons *sound* like canons, though in an utterly innovative way.

Study No. 4

Study No. 4 fits uneasily in this chapter, but there is no other place to put it. It is not a strict canon, for there is no transformational rule by which one part could be derived from another, and only at moments does it approach tempo canon. It is, however, an unusual essay in heterophonic canon, unique in Nancarrow's output in being canonic by pitch only. Starting at system 6, the three voices run through the same pitch sequence, but not in the same rhythm, nor at any consistent temporal distance. The charming effect is like that of three small, timid animals walking parallel paths, each hesitating and charging ahead at its own whim.

The study opens with a twenty-seven-measure introduction containing five ideas, four of which will be further developed in the rest of the piece. Three are based on a descending or (in one case) ascending arithmetic sequence. The first, alluded to in the opening six notes, is a sequence of durations in the descending order of 9, 8, and 7 sixteenth notes. The third and most important is a sequence of 3, then 2, then 1 quarter notes interrupted by sixteenth notes, shown in Example 6.2. The last is the repeated 2+3+4+3 series shown in Example 6.3. The fourth is a blues rhythm of syncopated triplets common in these early studies. And the remaining idea is two rapid strings of sixteenth notes, the second of which contains forty-eight notes that start out encompassing the outer ranges of the piano and converge toward the middle; Nancarrow does not develop it further here, but figures like it appear in the later studies beginning with Study No. 25.

Example 6.2   Study No. 4, primary motive

Example 6.3   Study No. 4, isorhythmic idea

The pitch sequence on which Study No. 4's first and third canons are based is an ingenious fifty-one-note series (hereafter called Row 1) using eleven pitches – A is omitted – that branches out over and over from the same first notes:

B	C	E♭	F	B♭	D♭			
B	C	E♭	F	A♭	B		B♭	
B	C	E♭	F	A♭	B	G♯	E	
B	C	E♭	F	A♭	B♭			
B	C	E♭	G♭	F	A♭	B♭	D♭	
B	C	E♭	F	A♭	B	B		
B	C	E♭	F	D	B♭	G	E♭	G♭

Part of the charm, along with the inter-row redundancy, is that the C–E♭ interval is equally likely to be either a rising third or a falling sixth. I can never play through this row (or indeed, hear the piece) without calling to mind T. S. Eliot's similar word technique in *Ash-Wednesday* (1930):

> Because I do not hope to turn again
> Because I do not hope
> Because I do not hope to turn . . .
>
> Because I do not hope to know again
> The infirm glory of the positive hour
> Because I do not think
> Because I know I shall not know . . .

The effect, in both words and notes, is lovely. How many of Schoenberg's followers have used a tone row so poetically?

Except for the introduction, No. 4 is written throughout in three voices. The first canon (0:33–1:28, systems 6–16) is composed of two parts, the second of which (beginning at system 11, 1:01) is identical to the first except for a voice exchange: the bass line moves to the soprano, the soprano to the tenor, and the tenor to the bass. This canon's rhythms are easily characterized, though not systematic. The soprano begins with groups of two or three sixteenth notes

Example 6.4   Study No. 4, isorhythmic idea

leading to longer, sustained notes. The tenor changes its underlying beat, from dotted eighths to quarters, back to dotted eighths, to five-sixteenth notes. And the bass, after a brief triplet blues rhythm, accelerates from quarters to dotted eighths to eighths, a 4 3 2 progression (Example 6.4). All three voices end with the blues triplets, quarter notes alternating with eighths. Though no voice sustains any one rhythm for long, the general effect is of the same pitches moving along in contrasting durations of either two, three, four, or five sixteenth notes.

The second canon (1:28–1:52, systems 16–21) is more systematically derived from the introduction's interruptive sixteenth note idea. This section runs through one statement of a forty-note melody similar to the fifty-one-note melody of the first and third canons, but with a few elements permutated:

		E♭	F	A♭				
B	F	E♭	C	C	F	B♭	A♭	
B	C	E♭	F	B♭	D♭			
B	C	E♭	F	G♯	B	G♯	E	
B	C	E♭	G♭	F	A♭	F	B♭	D♭
B	C	B♭	A♭⁵	F	A♭			

Henceforth this will be called Row 2. The bass moves in quarter notes interrupted by sixteenths, the tenor in dotted eighths interrupted by sixteenths, and the soprano in eighths interrupted by sixteenths. This canon is nearly strict, but with two rules instead of one: the tempo ratio is 4:3:2 with the exception of sixteenth notes, which remain 1:1. However, Nancarrow varies the durations of the end-notes of the phrases arbitrarily for textural variety.

Canon 3 (1:52–2:41, systems 21–31) returns to Row 1 and parallels the first canon in starting capriciously and moving towards greater order. Their beginnings are similar; all three voices switch between the blues triplets, steady eighth notes, dotted eighths, and (lowest voice only) quarters and five-sixteenth values. At last (systems 25–28) the top voice latches onto a repeating 2+3+4+5+4+3 isorhythm,

113

which it plays against dotted eighths in the bass and eighths in the tenor. At the unison bar line in system 29, all voices switch to Row 2 and run through the sixteenth note interruptive idea in another two-rule canon at a 5:3:2 tempo ratio, the strictest canon yet.

The final section (2:41–3:14, systems 31–37) contains the simplest and most arithmetically consistent statement of the tone-now. All three voices move in unison (two octaves apart) through the second half of Row 2 in an arithmetically expanding series: 1 sixteenth note, then 2, 3, 4, 5, and so on up to 11. Then, reversing the order of voice entrances for the first time, the soprano plays a line (derived from elements of both rows) in the repeating rhythmic sequence 1+2+3+2, the tenor in 2+3+4+3, and the bass in 3+4+5+4. After these finish, fragments of the rows are stated one last time as a coda (2:59), jumping octaves throughout the range and sustaining notes to build a cadential chord, using the interrupted quarter-note pattern found in the introduction.

In Studies Nos. 12 and 33, Nancarrow later found reason to write canons in which perceived divergences of tempo are created by having different rhythmic values in each line. But he has rarely used the technique so delicately and whimsically as here.

The "Seven Canonic Studies"

Now we come to the true canons. Nancarrow originally intended to unite Studies 13 through 19 as a group under the title "Seven Canonic Studies," no doubt partly because of their brevity (all seven combined clock in at under thirteen minutes), but more importantly because of their near-identity of structure. Every rhythm in these studies (with a handful of exceptions that I feel certain are mistakes) is determined by overlays of the additive formula that had figured in Study No. 4: $n-1$, n, $n+1$, n. Specifically, all seven studies result from combinations of four rhythmic patterns:

$$3 + 4 + 5 + 4 \ (= 16)$$
$$4 + 5 + 6 + 5 \ (= 20)$$
$$5 + 6 + 7 + 6 \ (= 24)$$
$$6 + 7 + 8 + 7 \ (= 28)$$

In Study No. 16, Nancarrow makes these patterns explicit through notation and register, placing each in a separate voice; in No. 19, through register alone; in No. 13 through temporary melodic isolation; in No. 18, through hidden patterns that are difficult to unravel. In the other studies he collapses all four into a single resultant. Consequently, all seven use a similar rhythmic "language," though he ensures through small irregularities that no two are identical.[6]

The smallest common multiple of 16, 20, 24, and 28 is 1680; that (plus 1 for the final cadence) is the length in eighth notes of either voice of Study No. 18. Studies Nos. 14, 15, 17, and 19 invariably (except for the addition of a final cadential note) use canonic voices of 336 eighth notes each; 336 is the smallest common multiple of 16, 24, and 28. Study No. 16 has an opening section of 336 eighth notes, then another of 560 – the tempo ratio between the two is 5:3, and 560 = 5/3 × 336. 336 is, then, the number whose multiples (either times 1, 2, 3, or 5) determines the length in eighth notes of Studies nos. 14 through 19. Within each section of each canon, the 3+4+5+4 pattern is repeated twenty-one times (21 × 16 = 336), the 5+6+7+6 pattern fourteen times, and the 6+7+8+7 pattern twelve times. 20 does not divide evenly into 336 (it repeats sixteen times with sixteen beats left over), so the 4+5+6+5 pattern is the one Nancarrow moves around to keep those six canons from all having the same rhythm.

Although such a structure inevitably remains hidden from ear and even from eye, it gave Nancarrow what he needed for his purposes: an easily varied nonmotivic rhythmic language which guaranteed consistent density throughout a composition. Searching without any modern precedent for a clearly audible way to juxtapose simultaneous tempos, he was more interested in hearing the temporal juxtaposition itself than in creating the kind of changing event-structure that would become the focus of the later canons. Since each pattern always contains four attacks within sixteen, twenty, twenty-four or twenty-eight eighth notes, the number of attacks within any given length will average out, approximately, to a constant number. And, since Nancarrow marks coincidences among the patterns with chords whose number of notes indicates the number of the pattern involved (except in No. 17), the system provides textural variety in a way that articulates the larger rhythm. Perhaps more importantly, the system creates the illusion of a unified rhythmic language, one in which motives can still appear, though in synthetic and largely unpredictable ways. Example 6.5 shows how the 16-, 24-, and 28-series combine to create similar rhythmic characters in these canons' every subject (except for Nos. 13 and 18, for reasons to be discussed later).

Below, the "Seven Canonic Studies" will be discussed not in their numbered order, but in order of increasing conceptual (not always perceptual) complexity: 16, 14, 19, 15, 17, 13, 18. One is tempted to speculate that they might have been composed, or at least conceived, in this order; at the very least it seems safe to assume that they were composed quickly one upon the other. The final numbering may indicate an order in which Nancarrow felt the pieces might have coalesced into a dramatically satisfying suite, with the climactically three-voiced Studies Nos. 17 and 19 nearer the end, separated by the most rhythmically sophisticated of the set, No. 18. He may have abandoned such a grouping precisely because of the too-great similarities of the studies concerned, as not providing sufficient contrast for a multi-movement work.

Study No. 16

Actually, Study No. 16 is not a true canon, but one of Nancarrow's isorhythm pieces. As such it properly belongs in the previous chapter, but its rhythmic

Example 6.5   Studies Nos. 14–19, rhythmic coincidences

pattern is so clearly the blueprint for Studies 14–19 that to separate it from them would be to indulge a foolish consistency. Study No. 16 is Nancarrow's first piece since the early Sarabande couched in the form : AB(A+B). This structure will later form the basis of Studies No. 41 and 48, manifested on a more momentous scale.

Every rhythm in Study No. 16 is based on an undulating four-note duration series of either 3+4+5+4, 4+5+6+5, 5+6+7+6, or 6+7+8+7; Nancarrow had earlier used such series in Nos. 4 and 8. He combines cyclic repetitions of these patterns in a four-voice block whose resultant rhythm is ever changing. The overall effect is a halting chorale whose voices rarely move at the same time. As counterpoint, the individual lines do not mean much; they are clearly conceived as a collective, and they cadence repeatedly in A, even though they begin and end on D. The first such block is played at approximately $\downarrow$ = 84. The second (starting at 1:09), $\frac{5}{3}$ as long, is played at 140, or $\frac{5}{3}$ so fast as to be identical in temporal length. Finally (at 2:15), the two blocks are played simultaneously, their individual lines strategically limited in range for minimal overlapping.

Study No. 14 – Canon – 4/5

Apparently the first in a series of canons that now numbers over two dozen, Study No. 14 is structurally direct. The higher of the two voices, transposed two octaves and a perfect fifth above the lower, is played $\frac{5}{4}$ as fast as the lower, therefore lasts $\frac{4}{5}$ as long, and is placed over it symmetrically in the middle. (The isomorphic lines that make up the different layers of a canon will be referred to as "voices" throughout these analyses, even though the reader should keep in mind that they often, as here, contain chords and even contrapuntal lines.) With 337 eighth note beats in each part, the two lines reach the same melodic point in their melodic material at the midpoint of the study, beat 168 (0:40); hereafter in this analysis and others the point at which voices so coincide will be referred to as the convergence point. (Refer to chapter 1 for discussion of tempo canon terminology.) Thirty-three beats of the lower voice are heard before the upper voice enters, and thirty-three are heard after it finishes.

Again, each of the voices of Study No. 14 is a resultant of four rhythmic patterns: 3+4+5+4, 4+5+6+5, 5+6+7+6, and 6+7+8+7. Beats where those patterns coincide are marked by chords whose number of pitches (e.g., four on the first beat – see the opening in Example 6.5) indicate the number of patterns coinciding. However, unlike the situation in Studies Nos. 16, 18, and 19, the pitches are not related to the rhythmic patterns in a systematic manner. Nancarrow apparently set out his rhythm, then composed the melody into it intuitively. The one exception is in the case of the sustained notes, which always exist only between two notes of the same pattern. For example, the sustained G♯ leading to F♯ in the first measure and B leading to D in the third (lower voice) are all from the 3+4+5+4 pattern, even though in the second case notes from other patterns intervene. With two exceptions in the first seven measures, all such sustained notes

Example 6.6   Study No. 14, entrance of second voice

"resolve" by half-step. Sequences of such resolutions create much of this canon's characteristic sound.

Nancarrow's one concession to tonal canonic conventions is the clever pun surrounding the entrance of the second voice. It enters on a B major triad, in the middle of the lower voice's first V^7–I cadence to its home base of E; for a quick moment, the ear hears it as part of the cadence, and not until the upper melody continues C♯–B–G does one realize that this voice is in a new key (Example 6.6, 0:08). Elsewhere, evidence of harmonic control is spotty, though there are few dissonant clashes. In general, the question of consonant vs dissonant counterpoint in these tempo canons is a vexed one, since the differences in tempo tend to preclude any great number of unison simultaneous attacks between voices. Here there are twenty-three simultaneous attacks out of a possible sixty-six coinciding beats in the canon's length; that slim ratio was not sought by Nancarrow, but merely resulted from the rhythmic process. Of those simultaneities between voices, several create major triads, but there is also a G♯–A clash in system 6 and a C–C♯ clash just after the convergence point, indicating that dissonance treatment was not high among Nancarrow's priorities in his early conception of canonic practice. In the later, less conventionally textured canons, such questions are not really solved, but simply fade from relevance.

A word about the notation of these middle studies: the constantly changing meters here have nothing to do with the way in which the rhythm was composed, but are rather an intuitive response to the way the rhythm sounds. In No. 14, Nancarrow has generally arranged the bar lines so that the frequent half-step dyads resolve onto a downbeat, and the longer note groupings end with their last note on a downbeat. Reynolds reports that Nancarrow once renotated No. 14 with straight 5/8 in the higher voice against 4/8 in the lower in order to make the tempo relationship clear.[7] Given the arbitrariness of the accents relative to the rhythmic system, and the fact that Nancarrow does not use the player piano's

Example 6.7   Study No. 19, rhythmic strata separated

Example 6.8   Study No. 19, diagram of cadential harmony (by Philip Carlsen)

volume function to accent downbeats anyway, Reynolds' concern about the "significant quality of metrical interplay"[8] assumes a more intuitive rhythmic ordering than actually took place. The same is true of the notation of Nos. 15, 17, and 18.

Study No. 19 – Canon 12/15/20

Study No. 14 took two voices and placed one symmetrically over the other; No. 19 uses three voices and delays the second and third so that all three end simultaneously, at a convergence point. Although the canonic tempo ratio is 12:15:20, Nancarrow is still working within his 3, 4, and 5 limits. 12:15=4:5, 12:20=3:5, and 15:20=3:4.

Each voice taken by itself is a resultant of the same four rhythmic patterns, this time with the 5+6+7+6 isorhythm begun on the first note, but with the 4+5+6+5 rhythm begun on its first 5. This is the clearest canon in its expression of the rhythmic structure, since the rhythmic strata within each voice are separated by octaves, and each occupies a different register. For example, the notes in the piano's lowest octave spell out a 6+7+8+7 rhythmic pattern, the notes in the next octave up spell out 5+6+7+6, and so on. Nancarrow collapses these rhythms onto two staves; in Example 6.7 they are separated. All four strata express the same melody, or pitch row – C♯–D♯–E–C♯–D♯–F♯–D–C♯–B, and so on – except that, because the lines with quicker values have more notes, certain pitches are omitted from the slower lines to keep all four in sync. The fastest voice expresses the entire row, but the lowest voice omits the E, then the second D♯, then the D, and so on.

Each of the other two voices is a sped-up transposition of this entire resultant, and each enters a perfect eleventh higher than the one before it; Nancarrow abandons that transposition level in each voice's last two pitches for a unison ending. In fact, this is the most traditionally tonal of Nancarrow's tempo canons. Philip Carlsen has shown that the harmonies created by the three voices are primarily triadic, and that there is considerable justification for analyzing the piece in E major, even though it ends with a surprising cadence on F♯. By abstracting pitches from the final two and a half systems, he arrived at the progression of triads and seventh chords in Example 6.8.[9] Such passages are not common in the later canons. Study No. 19's staggered octaves make this the most distinctive sounding of the "Seven Canons," and Nancarrow will reuse those staggered octaves to excellent effect in Study No. 20.

Study No. 15 – Canon 3/4

Study No. 15 is the sole work among Nancarrow's studies whose rhythms are simple enough, and whose sonorities are restricted enough, to be played by a live, single pianist: Yvar Mikhashoff has done so. Again, the rhythmic structure of each of the two lines is a composite rhythm resulting from the same quatrain of rhythmic patterns used in No. 16. Here, though, the separate rhythmic patterns are not kept distinct by range and notation, but are rather collapsed into a single line.

Study No. 15 is the simplest statement of Nancarrow's ad hoc rhythmic system. Here the system determines the number of notes heard at any one time: two notes at once indicate that two of the rhythmic lines coincided at a beat, a three-note chord indicates that three coincided, and the closing four-note chord results from all four lines. There is no internal evidence that Nancarrow allowed the rhythmic lines to influence pitch or register. The melody appears to have been filled in intuitively after the rhythms were calculated. All of the two-note chords are either minor thirds or octaves (with two exceptions, one of them a D and C functioning as the penultimate cadential seventh chord), and all of the three-note chords are major triads. A note adjacent to a triad is usually a half-step from one of its members, and where three or four single notes are contiguous, they usually define a scale segment or turn figure.

This canon adds a new wrinkle not found in Nos. 14 and 19: a tempo switch. There are two voices, one three octaves higher and $\frac{4}{3}$ as fast as the other. Each voice goes through its 336 eighth notes-long material twice, switches to the other tempo, then repeats. This means, since the voice at the 220 tempo finishes sooner (0:23) than the voice at 165 (0:31), that for a period of eighty-four eighth notes ($\frac{1}{4} \times 336$), both voices proceed at the same, slower tempo. (Canonic voices temporarily falling into the same tempo occur again in Studies Nos. 17 and 24.) There are a few spots in which Nancarrow's contrapuntal intentions become clear, mainly places in which triads in one voice are consonant with the note appearing in the other. Each of the tempo switches is marked by a G major sonority, the first (middle of system 11) sounding particularly cadential.

There are also noticeable V–I cadences on G at two arithmetically significant points, the beginning of system 7 (0:13), and the middle of system 19 (0:41). Each of these occurs on a G major triad 192 beats into the fast voice and a D leading to G 144 beats into the slow voice (Example 6.9). $144 \times \frac{4}{3} = 192$. $192 + 144 = 336$. 144 is, then, the solution to the equation $x + \frac{4}{3}x = 336$. Looking at the distribution of beats before, between, and after those points (Example 6.10), the mathematically inclined may see why those are the only points at which the sonorities that came together in the first half of the canon will also fall together in the second half. Nancarrow picked those points, along with the tempo switches and the final beat, for the canon's only V–I cadences. Although he does not remember making any such calculation, it could not have happened by accident.

Study No. 17 – Canon 12/15/20

Study No. 17 is to No. 15 as 19 is to 14: same idea, one more voice added. In addition, Study No. 17 is the only one in the set to use three separate canonic subjects. Each is a 336-beat resultant of the same four isorhythms, with the 20-line (the only number not divisible into 336) shifted to keep the voices from being rhythmically identical. The rhythmic distribution is as follows:

Upper voice:	$3 + 4 + 5 + 4 = 16$
	$(1 + 6 + 5 +)\ 4 + 5 + 6 + 5 = 20$
	$5 + 6 + 7 + 6 = 24$
	$6 + 7 + 8 + 7 = 28$
Middle voice:	$3 + 4 + 5 + 4 = 16$
	$(5 + 6 + 5 +)\ 4 + 5 + 6 + 5 = 20$
	$5 + 6 + 7 + 6 = 24$
	$6 + 7 + 8 + 7 = 28$
Lower voice:	$3 + 4 + 5 + 4 = 16$
	$(3 + 5 +)\ 4 + 5 + 6 + 5 = 20$
	$5 + 6 + 7 + 6 = 24$
	$6 + 7 + 8 + 7 = 28$

Example 6.9   Study No. 15, points of symmetry

Meter signatures have been omitted.

Example 6.10   Study No. 15, articulation of structural points

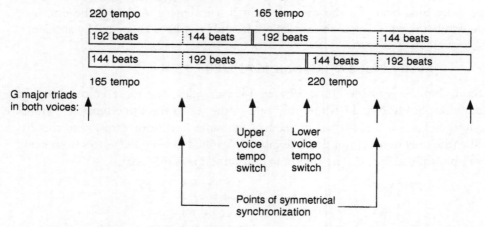

Labeling the canonic subjects A, B, and C, the distribution of subjects, voices, tempos, and entry points is as follows:

top voice	A at 172.5	B at 138	C at 230
middle voice	B at 138	C at 230	A at 172.5
bottom voice	C at 230	A at 172.5	B at 138

Because the subjects are the same length in eighth notes but at different speeds, the changes from one subject to another are staggered and hidden within the contrapuntal texture. There are moments when two voices proceed at the same tempo, but none in which all three voices are in the same tempo. Except for No. 26, the 1:1 canon, this is Nancarrow's only tempo canon in which each canonic subject appears throughout in only one tempo.

Because of the contrapuntal density of three different voices destined to combine as invertible counterpoint in ways not foreseeable without a computer, Nancarrow keeps his tonal materials simple. With occasional exceptions, he marks the beats on which more than one note of his rhythmic system coincide with dyads, but he uses only octaves, and never more than two notes at once per voice. The melodies themselves are among his most diatonic; almost every sharpened or flattened note in the piece is either a leading tone (preceded or followed by a half-step) or the sharpened third of a triad "functioning" as a secondary dominant. Adjacencies of the pitches D, E, and F alone account for over a fifth of the piece. Even so, the plurality of subjects makes this one of Nancarrow's most difficult canons to perceive formally.

Study No. 13

As stated in chapter 4, Nancarrow's attitude toward Study No. 13 is ambiguous. He apparently never made a final copy of the score, and no punching score or sketch has been found in his studio. He has, however, allowed the piece to be recorded along with the other studies. Specifically, he considers it an "outline of tempo possibilities," intelligible only as an introduction to the "Seven Canonic Studies," and since he no longer considers them a group, No. 13 has lost its purpose. Still, aside from the work's unlucky number (and Nancarrow despises superstition in any form), it is difficult to see why he has half-disowned it, for it is structurally as interesting as some of the other pieces in the set.

Because of the absence of a score or even sketches, the following analysis is slightly conjectural, based on an analysis of the piano roll. The study contains twelve different contrapuntal lines, divisible into three groups of four. Within each group of four, the first voice articulates a rhythm of 5+6+7+6, the second a rhythm of 3+4+5+4, the third a rhythm of 4+5+6+5, and the fourth (which enters much later) a rhythm of 6+7+8+7. The opening, with the entrance of the first three voices, could be notated (in neutral 4/4 meter) as in Example 6.11. The second set of four voices enters a perfect twelfth higher and $\frac{4}{3}$ as fast; the third set of voices enters yet another minor seventh higher than the second set and $\frac{5}{3}$ as fast as the first set. Though the use of isorhythm is not as elaborate here as in Studies Nos. 7 or 11, No. 13 is the first study (along with No. 16) to combine isorhythm with simultaneous contrasting tempos. In terms of pitch, however, Study No. 13 (also like No. 16) is not a strict canon, for the voices leave off canonic imitation after several measures, whereafter the harmony proceeds mostly in octaves, thirds, and triads.

With respect to tempo, then, this is the most complex of the "Seven Canonic Studies," for after it combines those isorhythms into a resultant, it plays that

Example 6.11 Study No. 13, opening (conjectural notation)

Example 6.12 Study No. 13, structural diagram

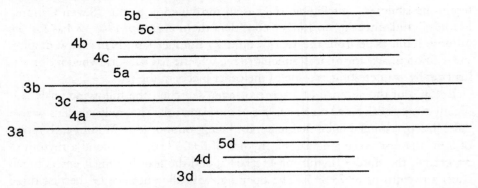

resultant against itself at tempo ratios of 3:4:5. The faster sets of voices are placed fairly symmetrically above the slower, providing a simple arch form, almost a rhythmic palindrome. Calling the lines of the 3-tempo 3a, 3b, 3c, 3d, and so on, the structure of the study could be diagramed as in Example 6.12. The piece is not so perceptually clear, however, for the ranges of the different lines overlap considerably, making it impossible to distinguish which note falls in which line by ear or sometimes even analytically. Because of its slowly shifting tonality and octave-leaping texture, Study No. 13 is similar in sound and technique to Studies No. 16 and 19, making Nancarrow's subsequent abandonment of the work even more puzzling.

124

Study No. 18 – Canon 3/4

Study No. 18 is the most rhythmically intricate of the early canons, not only using isorhythms, but expressing them in varying units of three, four, and five eighth notes (as does No. 13 in a less clear way). Consequently, the rhythm is a resultant of not the usual four, but six isorhythms:

$$(4+5+6+5) \times 3 = 60 \text{ repeated } 28 \text{ times}$$
$$(3+4+5+4) \times 5 = 80 \text{ repeated } 21 \text{ times}$$
$$(6+7+8+7) \times 3 = 84 \text{ repeated } 20 \text{ times}$$
$$(5+6+7+6) \times 4 = 96 \text{ repeated } 17.5 \text{ times}$$
$$(6+7+8+7) \times 4 = 112 \text{ repeated } 15 \text{ times}$$
$$(5+6+7+6) \times 5 = 120 \text{ repeated } 14 \text{ times}$$

Because of such complexity, this is Nancarrow's only canon in which the canonic parts are of dissimilar texture; that is, the lower voice consists of a melody with a harmonic accompaniment of up to six parts, while the upper voice, an octave higher, uses only the melody. Were the harmony echoed in the upper voice as well, the texture would become impossibly thick, obscuring the canonic relationship.

The rhythmic structure that is characteristic of these studies is more clearly articulated in the lower voice accompaniment of No.18 than it is anywhere else except for Study No. 19. Each of the above isorhythms is articulated in a certain register and along a certain scale, with accidentals added for variety and harmonic consistency with the other voices. For example, the low notes which punctuate the piece spell out the $(6+7+8+7) \times 4$ pattern, or $24+28+32+28$, appearing at eighth notes numbered 0, 24, 52, 84, 112, 136, 164, 196, 224, and so on. The highest voice below the melody runs down the minor scale and up the major in typical Nancarrow fashion according to the pattern $(6+7+8+7) \times 3$, or $18+21+24+21$, appearing at eighth notes 0, 18, 39, 63, 84, and so on. A schematic diagram for all six voices would look as in Example 6.13, which shows the six isorhythms that make up the texture on the six lower staves and the melody drawn from the resulting addition of patterns on the top line.

Thanks to the arithmetical properties of this system, No. 18 possesses the most elegant rhythmic language among the "Seven Canonic Studies." The rhythms of Nos. 14, 15, and 17 group themselves into unpredictable, indiscriminate phrases, but by multiplying the units in which the isorhythms are expressed, Nancarrow created a system that, by limiting arithmetical possibilities, would grant his rhythmic language *motivic* as well as consistent density. One peculiarity of the system (though it is difficult to see how Nancarrow could have anticipated this) is that there are never attacks on more than two adjacent eighth note beats, so that the two–note grouping becomes a motive of the work. Other influences are more subtle, such as the duration groupings of twelve eighth notes into which so many adjacent measures fall.

Significantly, since the voices of this canon have a tempo relationship of 3:4, the $(6+7+8+7) \times 4$ isorhythm in the upper voice is fated to coincide at every note

Example 6.13   Study No. 18, derivation of contrapuntal rhythm

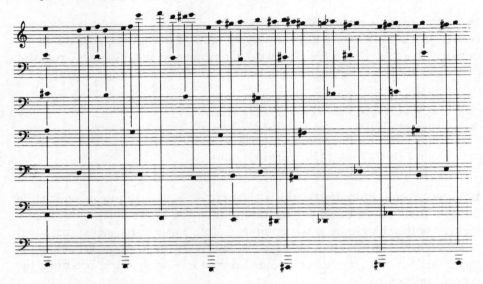

Example 6.14   Study No. 18, simultaneities

Example 6.15   Study No. 26, structural diagram

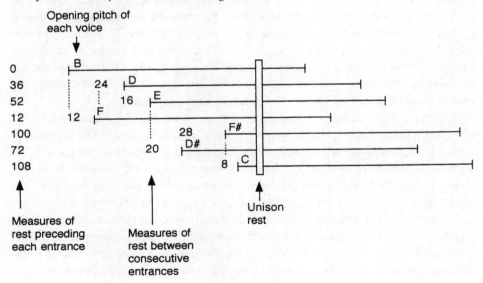

with the lower voice's (6+7+8+7) × 3 isorhythm, since a half-note in one passes at the same speed as a dotted quarter in the other. Thus for the first time Nancarrow has programmed a minimum level of coincidence into the structure of the canon, a subtle idea which will not bear its fruit until the late canons starting with No. 32. This, if anywhere, is a place where we might look for Nancarrow to exert systematic harmonic control between voices, since one sixth of the simultaneities are given *a priori*. But if we isolate the upper notes that spell out these two series, as in Example 6.14, we find that while the resulting simultaneities are more often consonant than not, their haphazard variety suggests that linear, not harmonic, thinking was the determining factor behind this melody.

Ultimately, the canonic melody itself is the unstructured element of this Study. With its Spanish-sounding Neapolitan F ever leading to E, it is reminiscent of the melody of Study No. 12. Typically for Nancarrow, it clings to the E as a sort of reciting tone, but wanders ever further afield harmonically before finally cadencing a fourth above on A.

Study No. 26 – Canon 1/1

Following the "Seven Canonic Studies," Nancarrow moved to isorhythmic canon in Study No. 20 (discussed on pp. 106–8) and acceleration canon in Studies Nos. 21 and 22 (which will be discussed in chapter 7). Study No. 24 marked the beginning of the new conception of canon discussed in chapter 8, but as this chapter's remaining examples show, he never abandoned the simpler type of tempo canon he began with.

Study No. 26 is an anomaly of Nancarrow's output, in which context its deadpan simplicity seems almost humorous. This is a seven-voice canon, notated completely in whole notes, all voices related at a tempo ratio of 1:1. Nancarrow wrote the piece, he says, as

> Not exactly a joke, but a relief from complicated tempos. Like, "This is just the basic thing where everything starts." At one point I was thinking of discarding it, but Cage was here, I played it for him, and he said, "Oh, what wonderful harmonies." I thought, well, if he thinks that, maybe I'd better leave it. In fact, I hadn't even thought of it as harmonies.[10]

Cage apparently appreciated the harmonies for their quasi-random unpredictability. The 122-note canonic subject is a chant-like melody centering around E in the first voice, with a strong Phrygian feel provided by F and a surprising final cadence of Bb–Eb. The subject occupies the entire chromatic space of an octave, and is doubled in octaves in each part. Over a fourth of its intervals are half-steps, though the minor sixth skip from B to G (in the opening voice) appears four times as such, several other times filled in with other notes.

As diagramed in Example 6.15, the seven voices enter at respective rhythmic distances of twelve, twenty-four, sixteen, twenty, twenty-eight, and eight measures (four times three, six, four, five, seven, and two) and at transposition levels involving a chromatic scale from B up to F♯ with C♯ omitted. It may be worth noting that entrances of the first, third, fifth, and seventh voices are separated by thirty-six measures each.

Rests divide the 151 measures of each voice into twenty-seven phrases of various lengths ranging from three measures (two notes and a rest) to twelve (eleven notes and a rest). At one point in the study, m. 121 (2:20), rests coincide dramatically in all seven voices. To ensure this, Nancarrow had to calculate seven rests within the canonic line, separated by the same numbers (in reverse order) which separate the entrances of each voice:

measure no. of rest	13		21		49		69		85		109		121
distance in measures		8		28		20		16		24		12	

These are the only rests whose positions are necessitated by the canonic structure, and the twenty-seven others are scattered in such a way as to promote variety of texture. The silent measure 121 forms a kind of negative climax, occurring in the middle of the twenty-one-measure passage which contains the only ten measures in the piece articulated by notes in all seven voices (thus the notation; actually, as a result of coincident pitches among voices there are only eight such measures). This passage, mm. 115–135, includes the midpoint of the piece's 259 measures, and the fact that the dramatic hiatus occurs just before that midpoint throws the piece's weight squarely in the middle.

Obviously, this is the one canon in which Nancarrow could have most easily controlled the resulting harmonies, though the evidence leaves unclear how much he was concerned to exert that control. The transposition levels of the first three voices make up a diminished triad (B F D), and the same is true for the last three; these are the sets of voices left most exposed at the beginning and end of the piece. Since the voices enter in multiples of four measures, Nancarrow could conceivably have taken every fourth beat from some scale that would have given him some intervallic consistency among three-note chords. Separate the melody into four strata – every fourth beat in one, each beat after the fourth in another, etc. – and you will find passages that suggest a whole-tone scale. Since triads govern the transpositional relationship of voice trios 1–3 and 5–7, this may account for the fact that major and minor triads and whole-tone chords appear more often than could be accounted for by chance. However, the results of such analysis are so inconsistent that one hesitates even to suggest that Nancarrow was thinking along these lines.

An atypical touch for Nancarrow is that the lowest three voices are more spread out in range than the upper ones, which, when all voices are present, weights the sonority toward the top of the piano (see Example 6.16). Since the lower voices enter last, however, the sonority gradually descends from top to bottom over the course of the piece. The fact that the second and fourth voices to enter are only a half-step apart causes them to cross frequently and often land on the same pitch. Clearly polyphonic distinctness was not Nancarrow's aim here, and the voices

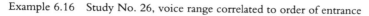

Example 6.16   Study No. 26, voice range correlated to order of entrance

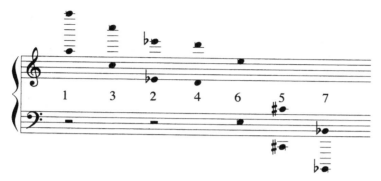

merge into a monolithic set of block chords. In denying his usual rhythmic inter-est, Nancarrow has not compensated very much in the areas of pitch or texture. The main purpose of Study No. 26 may be to provide the attention some welcome relief when listening to a large group of the studies.

Study No. 31 – Canon 21/24/25

Possibly the first study Nancarrow wrote following his five-year hiatus, Study No. 31 is a relatively uncomplicated canon, as though he were trying to get the old compositional pitching arm back in shape. The piece is simply structured, briefer than any study since No. 19, and more similar to the group of canons from No. 14 through No. 19 than to either the intervening studies or the monumental works that would follow.

The piece divides into three sections, the outer ones in nervously syncopated eighth notes, the middle one in calmer quarter notes. Taking the structure of only the opening voice, one finds a forty-seven-measure theme in the treble register, consisting of only the seven pitches within a diminished fifth; eight measures of rest; a seventy-three-measure theme in the bass, using the same motive as the first but extending its range to a major ninth; another eight measures of rest; and finally a thirty-two-measure theme in octave-displaced octaves. Except for some steady eighth notes in the final drive to the cadence, this last theme is derived from the first, using the same rhythm and articulating its tonics (E as opposed to G in the first section) at the same points, as the comparison in Example 6.17 will attest.

The second and third voices enter a perfect fifth and major ninth higher, respectively, in a tempo ratio of 21:24:25. In the second and third sections, those pitch intervals are increased by an octave. In the first two sections the ranges of the themes are small enough that the voices never overlap; in the third, because of the octave displacements, adjacent voices overlap by two octaves. The slowest voice begins first and the fastest last, so that throughout the canon they become closer and closer to synchronization, but this is Nancarrow's only canon in which the convergence point lies outside the canon's temporal frame. Had the canon

Example 6.17   Study No. 31, comparison of first and third canons

extended for another thirty-six eighth notes in each voice, the voices would have converged. By the second eight-measure rest, they are close enough together in time that the rests overlap, causing a brief caesura between the second and third canons.

Study No. 34 – Canon $\dfrac{9}{4/5/6}$ | $\dfrac{10}{4/5/6}$ | $\dfrac{11}{4/5/6}$

Study No. 34 has one of the most complex and even confusing systems of tempo relationship of any of the canons. In effect, it is an acceleration canon, but unlike the canons examined in chapter 7, the acceleration is by steps rather than gradual; in addition, the acceleration is not unidirectional, but rather weaves up and down toward its goal before plummeting into a final ritard. Nancarrow achieved an effect of accelerative contrasts with a theme that, in each instance, retains a steady beat. The three voices manifest a tempo relationship of 9:10:11, and within that pattern of *simultaneous* tempos, each voice runs through a system of *successive* tempos. The tempo succession of each voice is shown in Example 6.18.

The three voices do not manifest these tempos at the same time, since the 9-voice enters first and the 11-voice last, and there is no convergence point until the last note. The letters refer to the form created by the melodies, one of which, A (Example 6.19), recurs at alternate sections for most of the work. The 4:5:6 ratio of the title refers only to the tempos of the first six A melody statements, which run, in the lower voice:

72	90	108	144	180	216
4 :	5 :	6 :	8 :	10 :	12

the second three tempos doubling the first three. One can see, however, that the 9:10:11 tempo ratio is not sustained throughout the piece, but primarily only in the sections marked A. For the most part, the tempos move along a scale whose ratios work out as:

10 12 15 16 18 20 24 30 32 36.

Example 6.18   Study No. 34, tempo scheme

Section:	A	B	A	C	A	D	A	E	A	F
11-voice:	88	106²/₃	110	(110)	132	(132)	176	146²/₃	220	176
10-voice:	80	96	100	117¹/₃	120	(120)	160	146²/₃	200	160
9-voice:	72	96	90	106²/₃	108	120	144	133¹/₃	180	144

	A	G				A————————————			
	264	234²/₃	176	146²/₃	132	117¹/₃	110	88	73¹/₃
	240	213¹/₃	200	133¹/₃	120	106²/₃	100	80	66²/₃
	216	192	180	120	108	96	90	72	60

Example 6.19   Study No. 34, theme A

Example 6.20   Study No. 34, tempos converted to pitch ratios

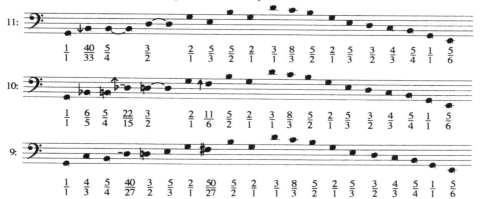

Pitches are notated according to the exact just intonation notation developed by Ben Johnston. Sharps raise a frequency by 25/24, flats lower by 24/25. An upward arrow raises a frequency by 33/32, a downward arrow lowers it by 32/33. A minus sign lowers by 80/81. Major triads FAC, CEG, and GBD are assumed to be tuned to perfect 4:5:6 pitch ratios.

However, in the B, C, D, and E melodies (none of which is repeated), each voice takes its own idiosyncratic course. Converting tempo ratios to pitch ratios, one could say that the three voices follow the slightly heterophonic lines shown in Example 6.20 (arbitrarily using G as representing the initial tempo in each voice).

The highest tempos in each voice are not reached until the final seven (of forty-five) systems (3:49), after which the 9:10:11 canon remains strict through, for all perceptual purposes, a gradual fast ritard (if that is not an oxymoron) in which the tempo changes come every two measures on the average. Note that where the voices differ, the faster voices have the proportionately slower tempos. Perhaps Nancarrow worked out a consistent tempo scheme, then decided that he did not like the way the A melodies fell together, so moved things around.[11]

The seven statements of the A melody are fairly evenly spaced; in the lower voice they occur about every forty-five seconds.[12] This means, since the tempos increase and the A melody is played more quickly each time for the first eighty-five percent of the piece, that the melodies and rests that separate sections must increase in length. The three lines overlap pretty continuously: after all have entered, the longest passage in which fewer than all three are heard at once is only six seconds. At systems 39–40 (3:49), the voices are finally close enough for a real stretto, entering in quick succession after a rest. However, the theme occurs so often that we have already heard it in close proximity with itself: the second A passage in the lower voice occurs just before the top voice enters (0:53), where these two voices state it at a nearly-identical ratio of 88:90. The final A statement comes in the middle of the final ritard, and it sounds exhausted by its dizzying tempo climb. This is one of Nancarrow's coyest endings, and it is the only one in which the voices end simultaneously on a ritard. Last-minute acceleration is his usual gesture, and here he subverts his own cliché.

The changing transpositional relationship of the voices is interesting: in the lowest voice the A melody is stated successively on six chromatically contiguous pitch levels – E, Eb, Gb, G, F, and Ab – and in the middle and upper voices a major third and perfect fifth higher respectively, forming structural major triads. The melodies are so overlapped and so little tonal, however, that the structure has no appreciable aural effect, and transposition of the non-A material is irregular. At system 41, where the voices switch from single notes to octaves, the interval distance changes to two octaves between adjacent pairs and remains so to the end. As in Study No. 31, a light, airy feeling is created by keeping the voices separated by at least a perfect twelfth.

With its ratios within ratios, this is one of Nancarrow's most experimental studies, and it is his last canon in which no strong connection is made between form and content. In Studies Nos. 24 and (if it *is* an earlier work) 32, he had already found a path from structure to ear, and in the canons from No. 33 to No. 48 he will tread that path with increasing confidence. When he returns to the idea of tempo changes within tempo contrasts in Nos. 41 and 48, it will be on a very different basis. In the meantime, Study No. 34 has a striking tune, and we hear that tune 21 times. With its quirky rhythms and widely spaced voices, it makes a delightful companion piece to Study No. 31. Encouraged by the Arditti Quartet's brilliant performance of difficult tempo relationships in his String Quartet No. 3, Nancarrow has made a string trio arrangement of Study No. 34 (at the time of this writing, not yet performed).

Study No. 44 – Aleatory Canon (Round)

Although Studies Nos. 44, 49, and 50 were written later than all or most of the canons examined in chapter 8, they constitute a return to Nancarrow's earlier conception of canon, for their concern is not texture or collective effect, but contrapuntal clarity and tempo contrast. Numbers tell part of the story, for Studies Nos. 49 and 50 return to small-number tempo ratios of 4:5:6 and 5:7 respectively, and such low rungs on the tempo overtone scale are not conducive to subtle inter-voice effects: the voices move away from each other too quickly. And in Study No. 44, where the tempo is left to chance, such effects could not be predicted.

Only forty-four measures long as if in reference to its number, Study No. 44, like No. 26, is an almost humorous anomaly among Nancarrow's canons: one in which the two lines can be played against each other in any tempo relationship, starting at any point. The impetus of the piece was to apply a Cagean solution to the problem of synchronizing two pianos, a Gordian knot Nancarrow had never been able to untie to his requisite perfection. In addition in No. 44 each part can also be looped as often as desired to bring about different echoings within each performance and to bring the two parts to fairly equal length; for this reason Nancarrow qualifies the title, calling the study technically a *round*, not a canon. As in Study No. 17, where the resulting canonic simultaneities are unforeseeably complex for different reasons, the tonal materials remain extremely simple: the lower part uses only six pitches in A major (with a D♯ thrown in at the end), the higher part similarly in E.

For the bass line, Nancarrow revives a technique he had used in No. 6, distributing a simple pitch row among different tempos – two in No. 6, here three, at a ratio of 3:4:5. The pitch line is no ostinato (as in No. 6), but rather a systematic permutation of (in the lower voice) the pitches E, F♯, A, and B, each repeated immediately an octave higher (the system is broken in the final five notes to create a cadence on B):

```
E F♯ A B      F♯ E A B
E F♯ B A      F♯ E B A
E A B F♯      F♯ A E B
E A F♯ B      etc.
E B A F♯
E B F♯ A
```

With each pitch immediately echoed an octave higher, the irregular rhythm suggests a boogie-woogie left hand played by someone with a nervous disorder. Though the pitch sequence is systematic, the rhythmic layout appears freely inventive, distributing usually three or four notes in each measure, with no simultaneous attacks. (That is, no pattern could be found using computer-assisted analysis.[13] See the discussion of No. 45b on page 258 for a diagram of a similarly written accompaniment.)

Over this halting bass Nancarrow lays an innocent melody in 14/16 meter, using a pentatonic scale plus a leading tone, and based largely on the interval of the

Example 6.21   Study No. 44, melody

Example 6.22   Study No. 49a, three versions of primary motive

Example 6.23   Study No. 49a, major-triad motive

third. Of the melody's twenty-three phrases and events, two simply move back and forth between triads on E and A (B and E in the upper part); four are isolated major triads; three others are small sixteenth note runs. Aside from the latter two types of event, every phrase in the melody is drawn from a blues pattern of 3+2+3+3+2+3 sixteenth notes followed by either a staccato or a sustained note or chord, as in Example 6.21. Instead of the 7:5:4:3 tempo ratio suggested by the meters, the melody's dotted eighth notes create (on a micro level) an even more complex 14:15:12:9.

Although Nancarrow leaves the tempos and spacing of the canon free, he not surprisingly has his own preference: one part, he thinks, should last approximately a minute (i.e., ♪ = 308 in the top, 14/16 line), the other a little more or less, and each should loop about ten times to allow sufficient variety in the relationship between the two lines.

Study No. 49 – Three Canons, 4/5/6

The triple-canon Study No. 49 bears the enigmatic subtitle "excerpts from the forthcoming Concerto for Pianola and Orchestra." The pianola is a nonelectric mechanism, operated by foot pump, which plays a conventional keyboard with mechanical fingers. Dynamics and tempo are operated during performance by a live performer, which means that the pianola can be played as part of an ensemble. Rex Lawson, an English pianola virtuoso, interested Nancarrow in the instrument, and Nancarrow responded by writing the three canons of Study No. 49 with the idea that they would form central movements of a pianola concerto. He originally had some ideas for the remaining, accompanied movements, but at this writing he does not seem to have worked them out at any length. As it stands, Study No. 49 is quite self-contained, a simple middle movement flanked by more complex outer movements parallel in structure, all using the same tempo ratios.

Nancarrow's late return to simple tempo ratios in this study seems to have encouraged a more visceral, less precompositionally determined approach than he had used since the early 1950s. Except in No. 49c, no collective effects are attempted, and there are no complicated number schemes to work out. The outer canons end at their convergence points, the middle canon has its convergence point in the middle. Movement A is a straightforward subject of approximately 790 beats,[14] echoed above at intervals of, respectively, two octaves and a fourth and three octaves and a fifth. The notation is proportional, but that there is an implied beat seems evident from the fact that the between-notehead durations in the lowest voice are all divisible by a common unit. The background material consists primarily of a minor-third motive with grace note, never stated twice in quite the same way (more conventionally renotated in Example 6.22). This motive is also thematic in movements 49b and 49c, forming a link between the three canons. For once Nancarrow unifies his movements motivically *as well as* by structural device.

The foreground motives, which stand out from the overall staccato, single-note texture and echo between the voices, are primarily of two types: at first, fast arpeggios and scales, then a motive of four major triads given in Example 6.23. In general, the arpeggios appear in the first half of the piece and the quadruple-triad motives characterize the latter half. Nancarrow times the events to unify the three voices perceptually. For example, the second arpeggio is timed in the first voice to cover the second voice's entrance, and the first arpeggio in the second voice similarly covers the entrance of the third voice. Toward the end, the quadruple-triad motives are spaced so that they echo from lowest voice to highest with little overlap. Each voice ends with a progressively growing series of glissandos, starting with four notes and adding by twos for a final glissando of twenty-two notes. Example 6.24 gives a rough idea of the distribution of elements.

The "slow movement" 49b is equally straightforward. One of the simplest and most lucid movements Nancarrow has ever written, it has a warm feel that stems

Example 6.24   Study No. 49a, structural diagram

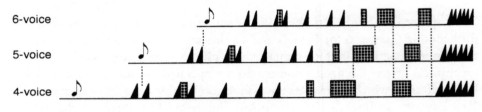

🎵 = first appearance of grace-note motive

◢ = long arpeggios and scales

▦ = quadruple triad motive

from the fact that it generally eschews staccato: its melodic notes are sustained even when not legato. However, there is a major discrepancy between the score and recording, and Nancarrow appears to have revised the piece's second half considerably. The version on the Wergo recording returns to the opening melody following the convergence point, which does not happen in the score I have for the work. Perhaps Nancarrow felt the piece was not sufficiently unified in its original form. The voices imitate, lowest to highest, at intervals of a perfect twelfth, and there are seven sections, grouped around a central, simultaneously struck triad.

1   (0:00) A melody in mostly sustained notes, wandering (in the lowest voice) from the key of C to G to A to E to B (23.1% of each voice). (The second voice enters at 0:17, the third at 0:28.)

2   (0:38 in the lowest voice) Staccato notes using, as motives, octaves, chromatic scale segments, and a rhythm of four eighth notes followed by an eighth rest (10% of each voice).

3   (0:55 in the lowest voice) The return of 49a's grace-note/falling minor third motive, stated on three pitch levels in each voice, with staccato notes in mid-section (10.8%).

4   (1:13 in the lowest voice) A scalar wave, alternately falling and rising, of alternating octaves, accelerating in five stages from a quarter note in the 5 tempo to $\frac{13}{5}$ of that tempo, ending on a major triad at the central convergence point (1:23) (7.8%).

5   (1:26) A brief, falling-triad melody using two of the grace-note/falling minor-third motives, then quoting from the beginning of the movement (quotation absent in the score) (18.7%).

6   (1:39 in the highest voice, which is now ahead) A series of up-and-down wandering scales (in the score, a series of slow repeated notes falling in thirds) (16.2%).

7   (2:02 in the highest voice) Return of the grace-note/falling minor-third motive, with a few more scales before the final motive (13.3%).

Example 6.25   Study No. 49b, structural diagram

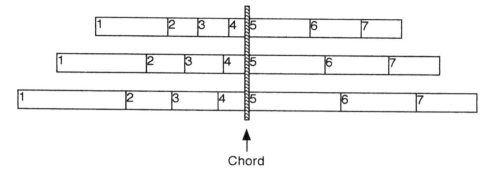

Example 6.26   Principle of repetition within each voice for collective effects

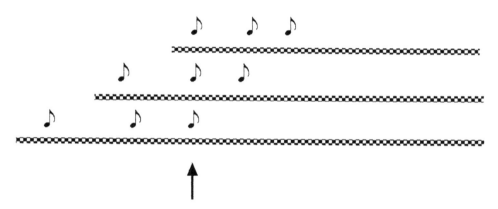

Except for the final lonely statement in the slowest voice, no voice leaves a section until the others have reached it. The proportions of the sections look something like Example 6.25. Nancarrow is more interested here in the textures created by all three voices using the same material than by playing off a texture in one voice against different ones in another – a return to his early canonic style.

Movement 49c, however, is more complex, and might be better discussed among the "sound-mass" canons of chapter 8, its simple tempo ratios notwithstanding. Nancarrow's strategy here is a kind of free counterpoint punctuated by points at which the voices combine for a unified effect; aside from those points, motives bounce around with little regard for order. The operative principle of this contrapuntal vein is that, for all three voices to combine in a unison effect *not* involving a convergence point, the relevant material must occur within each voice as many times as there are voices. For example, if effect A is to occur in all three voices simultaneously, it must occur three times in each voice, as in Example 6.26. This is the same principle used to place the dramatic rest in Study No. 26. Elsewhere, it does not appear in the canons in this chapter, but it becomes a common organizing principle in the late canons.

Example 6.27a   Study No. 49c, three glissando patterns

Example 6.27b   Study No. 49c, staccato triad figure

Example 6.27c   Study No. 49c, chromatic eighth–note strings

Example 6.28   Study No. 49c, structural diagram

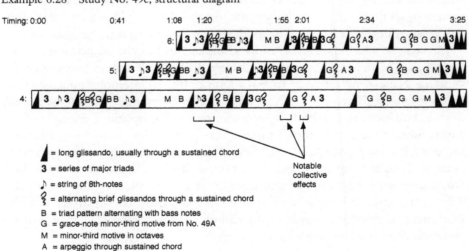

The movement is composed of formulas, repeated at any pitch transposition. The most individual material occurs at the very beginning, where, in the solo exposition of the 4-voice, it is most exposed. From then on, the materials become a little generic, and as the upper voices become more active, rests in the lower voice become longer and more common. The major formulas are as follows:

1   Chromatic glissandos through a sustained chord (fourteen occurrences in each voice). Except for the first, they follow one of the three patterns in Example 6.27a (in varying transpositions: the chord in brackets is sustained from the pitches of the glissando).

2   Staccato triads. At the very beginning, these form a rhythmic motive. Afterward, however, they are stated either in staccato quarter notes, alternating with eighth notes in a 2+3 rhythm (Example 6.27b) or shaped as the grace-note minor-third motive of No. 49a.

3   Strings of eighth notes filling out an octave or ninth chromatically (Example 6.27c).

4   A minor-third run (D C♯ B) in octaves, with a 2+2+1+2+3+4 rhythm also alluded to in the triads.

In addition, there is a dramatic quintuple arpeggio (/\/\/) in each voice, a double arpeggio (/\) just before the end, and a final series of chromatic glisses (/\/\\/).

The way in which these formulas are laid out to form the movement's structure is intuitively clear, if not reducible to a formula. The first half of the movement is largely determined by a climactic quasi-unison among the three voices in systems 17 and 18 (1:15 to 1:21 on the Wergo recording). Here, all three voices coincide in the following sequence:

1   a string of eighth notes, twenty-four in the 6 voice, twenty in the 5 voice, and sixteen in the 4 voice (so that given the tempo contrasts the strings have the same duration in each voice);

2   a series of major triads, sixteen in the 6 voice, fifteen in the 5 voice, and twelve in the 4 voice;

3   a rising, forty-two-note chromatic glissando.

In order for this eighth note/triad/glissando sequence to appear in all three voices at a non-convergence point, it has to occur three times in each voice. That is, the sequence's first occurrence in the 4 voice coincides with its second occurrence in the 5 voice and its third occurrence in the 6 voice. The creation of that effect, then, determines about half of the material in the first sixty percent of the piece (twenty-seven of forty-four systems). Example 6.28 gives a rough idea of the placement of ideas throughout the movement.

A few other pre-planned effects account for much of the movement's remaining structure. At systems 25 and 26 (1:55), a three-octave glissando in the 4-voice is followed by one in the 5-voice, then in the 6-voice. Next, at system 27 (2:01, immediately following the final eighth note/triad/glissando sequence in the 6-voice), the jagged alternating-glissando figure echoes from the 4-voice to the 5-voice to the 6-voice, an effect which again determines the placement of three such figures in each voice. Then, as the echo distance approaches zero, figures begin echoing from voice to voice without structural recurrence. At system 34 (2:34), the grace-note figure starts bouncing throughout the texture. At system 41 (3:04), the minor-third motive does the same. At system 42, the triads pound out a repeated D major, and, finally, a series of up-and-down glissandos (each the equivalent of three quarter notes long and six quarter-notes for the last) brings the movement to its closing convergence point.

The gestures of Study No. 49c are so varied that one never hears much sense of tempo contrast. The stringent technique of tempo canon provided a discipline to compose against, but the movement's vivid textures could have been achieved without it. Unlike most of the canons, this is not an experiment reaching for unknown effects but, appropriate for a concerto, a flashy showpiece showing what the player piano (or pianola) can achieve.

Study No. 50 – Canon $\frac{5:7}{3}$

Study No. 50 started out, not as a player piano work, but as the canonic second movement of the Piece for Small Orchestra No. 2. Perhaps realizing the immense difficulty of getting an ensemble to play tempo ratios of 3:5:7 accurately (a feat for which he has talked about developing a computerized video-conductor), Nancarrow made a piano roll of the piece and now considers it a separate study, claiming to prefer it, in fact, to the original. The player piano score is atypically inaccurate for Nancarrow, and the further one gets from the final note, the less exact the vertical alignment of notes is. Specifics of the piece are more easily obtained from the orchestral score, which (unlike the piano score) contains bar lines. For that reason, measure numbers will be used in addition to system numbers in the following analysis.

Except for a few internal canons such as those of Studies Nos. 25, 35, and 45c, this is the only canonic study which contains a noncanonic voice. The two upper voices make a (not perfectly strict) 5:7 canon. The lower voice, however, in the 3 tempo, is freely written, though its rhythms and motives follow those of the other voices closely. Conceptually, the canon proceeds according to simple rules, though the working out of those rules looks complicated in the score. The rhythmic idea is a brilliantly simple result of superimposing two rhythmic schemes – additive and divisive rhythm. In the first place, a constant measure is assumed, at a tempo of 90 per minute, divisible into 5, 6, or 7 parts. (The 3 in the designation $\frac{5:7}{3}$ is a little misleading; the 6/8 measure in the 3-tempo is often divided into three quarter notes, but frequently into two dotted quarters or six eighth notes as well.) Thus there are three possible tempos for the smallest subdivisions: 450 (90×5), 540 (90×6), and 630 (90×7).

Within the individual melodies, the subdivisions are grouped according to durations of one, two, three, four, and six subdivisions, plus eight subdivisions in the 6 voice, along with irregular, much longer durations which need not concern us yet. For example, a melody can march along articulating every fourth eighth note of either the 5, 6, or 7 tempo. There are, therefore, sixteen basic durations or tempos, each eighth note grouping creating a different tempo in a different voice.

	Divisions:		
	5 voice	6 voice	7 voice
Groupings			
8 × ♪		67.5	
6 × ♪	75	90	105
4 × ♪	112.5	135	157.5
3 × ♪	150	180	210
2 × ♪	225	270	315
1 × ♪	450	540	630

Assume for a moment an arithmetic array – 1, 2, 3, 4, 6 – in which, for any member designated by x, the following member is designated by (x+1). (The problem is so stated because the array skips the five eighth note grouping, and we need 6 adjacent to 4.) The two canonic voices, those at the 5 and 7 tempos, use phrases consisting of three elements:

1 staccato notes articulating beats of x subdivisions,
2 staccato major triads at beats of (x+1) subdivisions, and
3 a final minor third (falling or rising), usually stated in octaves, whose first octave has duration x+1, and whose second an indeterminate longer duration.

Echoes of this last element, as shown in Example 6.29, form the study's characteristic sound.

The numbers are simpler than their algebraic expression sounds. For example, when the 5 voice enters (0:44, system 11 in the player piano score, m. 65 in the orchestral score), x = 4. The staccato notes articulate every fourth eighth note, the triads every sixth eighth note, and the first sustained octave is six eighth notes long (Example 6.30a). At the end of system 23 (m. 145, 1:37), x drops to 3. The staccato notes articulate every *third* eighth note, the triads every *fourth* eighth note, and the first sustained octave is *four* eighth notes long (Example 6.30b). And so on. At system 34 (m. 214, 2:21), x becomes 2. The staccato notes articulate every second eighth note, the triads every third eighth note, and the first sustained octave is three eighth notes long. Finally, at system 43 (m. 274, 2:59), x becomes 1, the staccato notes become triads arpeggiated in eighth notes, *some* of the triadic chords appear on every second note, and the first sustained octave is two eighth notes long. In fact, Nancarrow is more interested in the rhythmic vitality of each line than in his system, and the individual phrases contain exceptions to these rules, mostly in the manner of hemiolas (triads alternating between two and three groupings, for example).

At two points in each voice (3:36 and 3:50 in the 5-voice), Nancarrow combines the sustained minor-third motive and triad idea (Example 6.31). The

Example 6.29   Study No. 50, primary motives

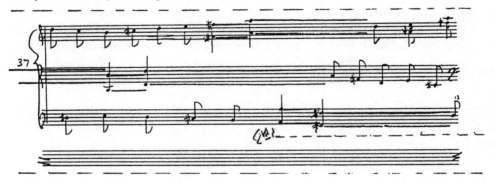

Example 6.30a   Study No. 50, durations when X=4

Example 6.30b   Study No. 50, durations when X=3

two appearances of this line, one ascending and one descending, are timed so that the first in the 7 voice coincides contrapuntally with the second in the 5 voice (3:50). Otherwise, for whatever reason, the upper voices are not *exactly* canonic, as becomes clear only in the orchestral score. The differences lie in the length of the second note of each sustained minor third motive, which is varied between the two voices by as much as five eighth notes.

The lower, noncanonic voice follows a different set of rules. In the first sixty-five measures (ten systems), its rhythmic groupings are irregular. Then, when the 5 voice enters, the lower voice falls into consistent patterns. From systems 10 to 20 (0:44–1:24, mm. 61–129) it articulates a beat of eight eighths (a measure and a

Example 6.31   Study No. 50, combined minor third and triad idea

third), with the first note of each sustained minor third six eighths (one measure) long. At system 21 (m. 130) it drops the minor-third motive (except for two isolated recurrences) and assumes an accompanying role, stated pizzicato through-out, in the contrabasses. From systems 21 to 34 (1:25–2:21, mm. 130–213) it emphasizes a beat of six eighth notes (one measure), with frequent syncopations, i.e., 4+8 instead of 6+6. From systems 34 to 37 (2:21–2:34, mm. 214–236) it emphasizes a 4 eighth note beat, then moves from a 3-beat to a 2-beat until system 45 (3:05, m. 283). Finally, a free interplay of 2- and 1-beats is maintained for the remainder of the piece.

Example 6.32 gives a proportionate overview of the progression of basic pulses of the three voices. As can be seen, the voices are timed to move to faster units almost in unison, thus limiting the number of tempo relationships used from the vast number possible within the tempo system. The result is a series of tempo contrasts as follows—

	21	28	(28)	42	(42)	84	(84)
15	20	30	(30)	60	(60)	(60)	(60)
9	12	18	24	36	72	(72)	36

– reducible, moment by moment, to the following lowest values:

	21	14	(14)	7	(7)	7	(7)
5	20	15	(15)	10	(10)	5	(5)
3	12	9	12	6	12	6	3.

As the overall tempo accelerates by steps, the staggered movement from 6- to 4- to 3- to 2- to 1-eighth note groupings brings a stepped simplification in the tempo relationships, and only at the end, where the music is fastest, does the piece reach its basic 7:5:3. (This same type of tempo clarification occurred during the first section of Study No. 9.) To the ear, this series of steps translates as a succession of bursts of energy, all three voices picking up speed at *not quite* the same moment, as though independently motivated by some outside force – an exhilarating effect.

143

Example 6.32   Study No. 50, structural diagram

Numbers indicate number of subdivisions in basic pulse throughout a
passage

▨ = sustained-triad motive

Example 6.33   Study No. 50, staggered 5-against-3

The bare numbers, however, obscure Nancarrow's ingenuity. The 5:3 ratio
heard when the 5 voice enters is not merely five notes heard against three within a
repeating period, but a five shifted so that *it never coincides* with the three
(Example 6.33). A practiced ear can pick out a three-against-five rhythm from its
periodic unison attack, but this skewed placement sounds irrational : in fact, unlike
Nancarrow's irrational tempo ratios, it *guarantees* that the two lines will never
coincide. Added to that are the triads and sustained notes, which, being always
one unit longer than the staccato notes, further complicate the tempo contrast
with a hemiola-like effect.

Aside from its simplicity, Study No. 50 also resembles the canons from
Nos. 14–19 in its tonality, which is more statistical than functional. The only real
motive is the sustained minor third which echoes among all three parts; otherwise,
the melodic material is drawn from generic scale segments and triads. Of the
sustained minor-third motives, seventy percent consist of the four minor thirds
(B–D, E–G, F♯–A, A–C) within the G major scale. That number increases to
seventy-four percent if only the canonic voices are considered, and the next most
common third is D–F, still within a flattened-seventh G scale. Sixty-two percent
of the triads are on G, A, C, or D, and distantly related chords such as C♯, D♯, and
G♯ occur only as leading tones within a scale segment. Within a passage, the "key"
can rarely be pinned down as C, G, or F, but the diatonic content ever gravitates
toward that trio in the circle of fifths, distant notes appearing only coloristically.

The layout of the orchestral version (see the discussion of Piece for Small
Orchestra No. 2 on pp. 276–8 for scoring) is designed not to keep contrapuntal
lines separate, but to separate the motives in each line from each other. After the

introduction of the 6 voice (stated by oboe, then bassoon), the staccato notes move into the strings (first pizzicato, then arco), the triads are taken by the piano (played by two performers to handle the 5:7 contrast), and the sustained minor-third motives echo among the woodwinds and French horn.[15]

Nancarrow has not returned to strict canon (through an entire piece) since Study No. 50. His most compelling secrets of canonic structure, however, will appear in chapter 8.

7

Stretching time: the acceleration studies

Studies Nos. 8, 21, 22, 23, 27, 28, 29, 30

None of Nancarrow's achievements is more original, more uniquely his own, than the sense of curved time he has created by means of long, slow, smooth acceleration and ritardando. He clearly likes the illusionary effects acceleration can offer: particularly the contrast of an acceleration in one voice against a deceleration or steady tempo in another. The exquisitely gradual convergence of two tempos, or the paradox of a faster beat becoming the slower without changing, are auditory delights which, so far, only Nancarrow's music has provided in purest, most perceptible form. Gradual tempo change has always been imprecise in Western practice, and music has never before even had a notation in which it could be handled as a subtle element. Although there are precedents for ostinato, isorhythm, and even tempo canon, there is no history of acceleration prior to Nancarrow to delve into for precedents. The literature is his invention.

The two types of acceleration/deceleration Nancarrow uses, arithmetical and geometric, produce different effects, require different notations, and should be carefully distinguished. In arithmetical acceleration, he simply subtracts from (or adds to, in the case of deceleration) each succeeding note the same duration unit, arriving at a rhythm such as that in Example 7.1. This rhythm appears as early as 1935 in the Toccata for violin and piano, as late as 1993 in *For Yoko*, and at many, many points in between.

The other type, geometric acceleration, involves decreasing each successive duration by the same proportion, and is virtually impossible to notate conventionally. Nancarrow sometimes indicates it with percentage signs: an 8% acceleration, for example, is one in which each duration is eight percent shorter than the one preceding it, or each duration is multiplied by .9259 ... (1/1.08) to obtain the next. Since multiplication by small percentages will not automatically yield a chain of integers, this rhythm can only be notated proportionally. Geometric acceleration occurs in most of the studies in this chapter – Nos. 21, 22, 23, 27, 29 – and in part of No. 25. Its use eventually demanded that Nancarrow have his punching machine rebuilt so that it could punch a hole at any point along a smooth continuum.

Example 7.1   Additive acceleration

How different are these two types of acceleration? Is it necessary to go to the trouble of the proportional notation? Say we want to accelerate over a phrase of ten notes to a tempo six times as fast as our starting point. Arithmetical and geometric methods will give us the following comparative values for duration, tempo, and note-to-note proportional tempo increase (selecting 120 as our arbitrary endpoint):

arithmetical:			geometric:		
duration	tempo	percent increase	duration	tempo	% increase
12	20		12	20	
11	21.82 . .	9.1	10.032 . . .	23.92 . . .	19.62
10	24	10	8.386 . . .	28.62 . . .	19.62
9	26.67 . .	11.1	7.01 . . .	34.24 . . .	19.62
8	30	12.5	5.86 . . .	40.95 . . .	19.62
7	34.29 . .	14.3	4.899 . . .	48.99 . . .	19.62
6	40	16.7	4.095 . . .	58.6 . . .	19.62
5	48	20	3.424 . . .	70.1 . . .	19.62
4	60	25	2.862 . . .	83.86 . . .	19.62
3	80	33.3	2.392 . . .	100.32 . . .	19.62
2	120	50	2	120	19.62

The arithmetical acceleration, obviously, is achieved by subtracting one invariable unit from each note to obtain the duration of the next. The geometric acceleration requires more sophisticated mathematics. Since there are to be eleven notes altogether, ten decreases in duration must be spread evenly among them. And since the final note is to be six times as fast as the first, the rate of increase per note is the tenth root of six, which is 1.1962312. . . . That means each note is approximately 1.1962 times as fast, or 119.62% as fast, as the one before it, and the rate of acceleration (119.62% minus 100%) is 19.62%. Thus, the first note is 119.62% as long as the second note, the second note 119.62% as long as the third, and so on. This is a generalizable formula. If n is the number of notes in the total string (including first and last), and x is the proportionate speed between the first and last notes, then the acceleration rate is the $(n - 1)$th root of x, minus 100%.

The differences are striking. Articulated in sound, the arithmetical acceleration, starting off with a nine rather than a nineteen percent change, sounds slow to take off; in the first few notes one might not be sure an acceleration is beginning, then at the end it becomes a quick blur. Nancarrow often likes this effect: Studies Nos. 3 and 10 use it for an ingratiating, jazzy rubato. The arithmetical acceleration in Study No. 42 begins 134, 133, 132, 131, and so on; the first few minutes of the piece are static, and one could be halfway through the work before realizing an acceleration is taking place. In longer streams of notes, however, arithmetical acceleration quickly becomes unwieldy. Study No. 23 contains an accelerando over 303 notes; to structure it arithmetically, the first note would have to last 303 times as long as the last note. The acceleration would not be audible for some time, since a duration series like 303, 302, 301, 300 would be perceived as a steady beat.

Arithmetical and geometric duration variations are not perceptually equivalent. The rhythms 8+8+7+7+7 and 3+3+2+2+2 might be equivalent in an arithmetical acceleration sense, but they are unlikely to be perceived as similar in most musical contexts. However, the rhythms 3+3+2+2+2 and 6+6+4+4+4 are easy to hear as functionally identical, as "octaves" of the same rhythmic motive. There is a percentage limit past which most of us hear durations as identical (as much as sixteen percent, according to some studies), and, Study No. 42 aside, Nancarrow rarely goes past 12:11 in arithmetical accelerando (though in Study No. 8 he goes to 24:23). Arithmetical acceleration was fine for the small-scale effects of the short-phrased blues pieces, but when he wanted a long, smooth, structural accelerando that could be heard as such, he was forced to come up with a notation and methodology for geometric acceleration.

Study No. 8

Nancarrow's first acceleration experiment, Study No. 8, makes do with arithmetical acceleration, but uses it ingeniously. It is the first spatially notated study, though when it was punched, Nancarrow's machine still had the notches that made punching in between them inconvenient. Because of that physical limitation, the piece is still tied to a small, invariant background durational unit. Based on careful measurement with many averages taken to account for slight inaccuracies, I have found that the durations in this study all seem to be divisible by a unit of approximately 1.7166 millimeters in the published score. My hypothesis in the following is that 1.7166mm of duration in the score (which is reduced from Nancarrow's original manuscript) is analogous to one notch, or some invariant number of notches, on Nancarrow's punching machine, and that the rhythms in this study are easily analyzable when divided by that unit.

Three isorhythmic series are used, each deployed in a manner of alternating accelerandos and ritards. There are two general patterns: either to start with the longest duration, accelerate to the briefest, then decelerate back, or to accelerate and decelerate in a zig-zag pattern – for example, 1 2 3 4 3 2 3 4 5 4 3 4 5 6 . . . – and then reverse the process. Series 1, found in all three sections of the piece, is a row of nineteen durations, accelerating (or, in retrograde, decelerating) arithmetically from notated lengths of forty-one or forty-two millimeters down to ten or ten and a half. Between these extremes, the durations are marked off virtually equally, each duration about 1.7mm shorter on the page than the one before it. Since 41/1.7166 is about twenty-four and 10.25/1.7166 is about six my guess is that Nancarrow marked off the longest duration as twenty-four notches on his

Example 7.2   Study No. 8, conjectural notation of opening line

punching machine, the next as twenty-three notches, the next twenty-two, and so on down to eight, seven, and finally six. Whether this exactly recreates what happened or not, it is clear that the accelerando is arithmetical, not geometric, and that the same unit is subtracted from each duration to get the next. Series 1, then, can be designated as 24, 23, 22, 21 . . . 9, 8, 7, 6, 7, 8, 9, 10 . . . 20, 21, 22, 23.

At the beginning, duration series 1 is made a basis for triple rhythm. Staccato notes mark off the duration series, each preceded by a legato note about one-third of the duration of the previous note. According to Carlsen, to whom I am indebted for several points here, Nancarrow originally notated this line in 3/4 meter with tempo changes and acceleration markings.[1] Given my hypothesis about the arithmetical duration series, however, one could conceivably recast the line in the cumbersome notation of Example 7.2.

Section 1 (0:00–1:10, systems 1–18) contains three gestures. The first begins quasi-canonically, as one of Nancarrow's rare 1:1 canons (Studies Nos. 6 and 26 are other examples); that is, the acceleration rate is the same in the second voice as in the first, because the same isorhythm and durations are used. The second voice enters when the first reaches its shortest duration (0:12), and the third enters when the second reaches its shortest duration (0:24). The third voice, though canonic by pitch, begins with the *quickest* durations and decelerates, unlike the other voices, which began slow and sped up. The upper two voices then keep up a reciprocal relationship in which one switches to acceleration every time the other switches to a ritard. The lower voice is at its slowest point when the third enters, and remains slower on the average. At the third voice's entrance, the second (for no clear contrapuntal reason) ceases its canonic imitation.

The second and third gestures (systems 11–18, beginning at 0:40 and 0:55 respectively) are both 1:1 canons at the octave, one the exact inversion of the other, on the symmetrical duration series (as measured between staccato notes, with the tempos arranged downward from fastest to slowest) given in Example 7.3. The melody is based on part of the opening voice from the beginning of section 1.

Example 7.3   Study No. 8, section 1 duration series

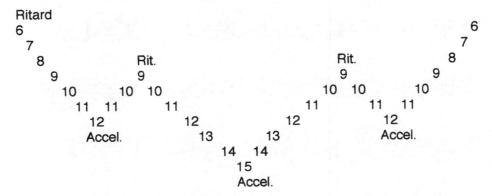

Section 2 (1:10–3:05, systems 19–50) switches at first to entirely staccato notes. The three staccato voices use duration series 1, this time with no internal subdivisions. In each voice, the durations diminish from twenty-four to ten and increase back through four cycles. In an anticipation of Studies Nos. 20, 27, and 37, Nancarrow here sets extreme limits to his pitch range. The first thirty-six notes in each voice use only F, G, and A♭, the next thirty-six only A♭, B♭, and C♭, the next thirty-six B, C♯, and D, and the next 36 D, E, and F, rising a minor third with each cycle.

The sustained treble and bass melodies laid over this staccato background use an eight-duration series which I will call series 2. In millimeters, the durations of series 2 run approximately as follows:

  55 43 33 24 17 12 8.5 7.

Dividing by the 1.7166mm unit, this series follows roughly the proportions:

  32 25 19 14 10 7 5 4.

These values are easily derived by addition of ever greater units:[2]

$$4 + 1 = 5$$
$$5 + 2 = 7$$
$$7 + 3 = 10$$
$$10 + 4 = 14$$
$$14 + 5 = 19$$
$$19 + 6 = 25$$
$$25 + 7 = 32$$

Given Nancarrow's numerous additive-acceleration strategies, this looks like a scheme he could have come up with. However, whether these are the durations he had in mind or not, the series is clearly an attempt to come closer to a geometric, rather than an arithmetical, accelerando: note by note, the acceleration rates run approximately

  28% 32% 36% 40% 43% 40% 25%.

Example 7.4   Study No. 8, system 31, melodies with durations

Example 7.5   Study No. 8, second duration series

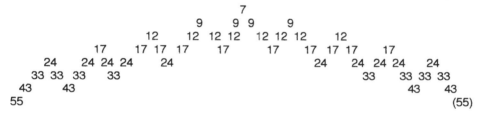

Part of the interest of this section is the superimposed contrast between the two types of accelerando, arithmetical and quasi-geometric.

At system 31 (1:55), Nancarrow superimposes two sustained melodies over the staccato background. First the ascending major/descending minor motive is stated in the treble, accelerating and then decelerating according to duration series 2, then the inversion of this gesture occurs in the bass. Next come the melodies of Example 7.4 (which marks their approximate durations in millimeters). Between them, the two voices spell out the accelerating/decelerating form of series 2 given in Example 7.5. Nancarrow divides the melody between treble and bass via an interesting process: all the accelerating passages are given to the treble line, the ritard passages to the bass, making a pattern first of four treble notes plus three bass notes, then three treble plus four bass notes. Besides the major/minor figure, this melody is based on a motive of F♯–B–D–C♯. The final third of section 2 (starting at 2:43) is a canon between the treble and bass voices, each line stating individually the form of duration series 2 that, in the preceding passage, both had stated together in alternation. Once again, the bass voice enters with its longest duration at the treble voice's shortest duration, and the melody spins off of the minor triad motive, E A C B.

Section 3 (3:05–4:21, systems 51–73) is based on a self-retrograding acceleration/ritard rhythm similar in shape to those of sections 1 and 2. Divided once again by 1.7166mm, the durations fall into a regular twenty-six-note pattern given in Example 7.6.[3] First the bass states this rhythm in a "stride piano" melody in which every other note (with one recurring exception) is an octave above its predecessor. The articulation further complicates this pattern by sustaining every third note, the

Example 7.6   Study No.8, section 3 duration series

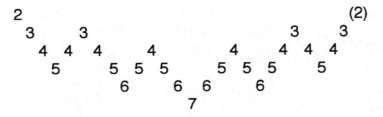

Example 7.7   Study No. 8, harmonies

Example 7.8   Study No. 21, 54-note row

others being staccato. Over this, Nancarrow brings back the study's opening line in treble octaves, and in the same rhythmic values as its first appearance. When this line ends, a "tenor" voice is introduced in the new rhythmic row, a melody in which alternate intervals are rising perfect fifths. Over these the melody of section 2 returns, beginning E–A–C–B–A, in another zig-zag pattern based on duration series 2: 55 43 33 24 17 12 17 24 33 24 17 12 9 7 9 12 17 24 33 24 17 12 17 24 33 43 (55).

At last a third, treble voice enters (3:58) with the new isorhythm, alternate intervals rising minor thirds. Three voices are now stating the same rhythm, but in a staggered manner: the tenor's shortest note coincides with the bass's longest. The melody in each voice repeats after seventy-eight notes, and the voices are clearly written to harmonize together in root-position triads and seventh chords (see Example 7.7). Over this frenetically repeating chorale Nancarrow superimposes one final accelerando in octaves, representing (in 1.7166mm units) an arithmetical sequence: 26, 25, 24, 23, and so on down to 3, 2, 1.

In certain spots, notably the beginning, Nancarrow's experimentation with simultaneous accelerando and ritard pays off with rich aural delights. At other places, such as most of section 2, the voices simply blur together. But though the aims of Study No. 8 will not be realized with full success until later, its originality in handling new problems is amazing. It anticipates the major acceleration study, No. 27, in both its simultaneous use of ritard against accelerando and its limitation of a canon to a range of only three pitches after earlier canons of much larger pitch range.

Study No. 21 – Canon X

Study No. 21, subtitled "Canon X," is one of the conceptually simplest in the collection, and one of the most perceptually fascinating. Reducing the central idea of No. 8 with minimalist fervor, Nancarrow begins the lower voice at a tempo of approximately 3.4 notes per second and speeds it up with excruciating gradualness (an acceleration rate of about .117 percent) to 110 notes per second; the higher voice does the opposite, beginning at 36 notes per second and slowing down (at *circa* .179 percent) to 2.3 per second. At first the treble is eleven times faster than the bass, by the end it is forty-eight times as slow. The subtitle refers to the crossing the two voices make when their tempos momentarily coincide (at system 32 out of 89), though there is no canonic effect at this center, since the hitherto slow lower voice has not gone through nearly as much of its material as the fast higher voice, and the two are not at the same point in their cycles. A quick convergence point passes unnoticed after the treble's first eight notes, and another at the first treble note of system 61, where the pitch canon starts over in each voice.

The melody is little more than a prop for the illustration of the tempo effect, and uses a fifty-four-note row, given in Example 7.8. The row begins in fairly clear F minor, but soon begins a false modulation towards B♭ before abandoning any sense of tonality. Nancarrow repeats this row fifty-four times in each voice, dropping one more initial note with each repetition: that is, the second statement omits the first note and contains fifty-three notes in all, the third omits the first two notes, the fourth the first three notes, etc., until the number of notes ends up three, two and one. This strategy anticipates the linear additive and subtractive processes of minimalist music of the sixties: Frederick Rzewski's *Attica* and *Coming Together*, and Philip Glass's *Music in Fifths* are the closest analogies.

At system 61 the process runs out of notes; the treble, now slower, voice runs through the fifty-four notes one last time (with two pitch alterations for a final V–I cadence),[4] and the now much faster bass repeats the entire subtractive process. So, because of the much greater tempo difference at the end when compared with the beginning, the canon is not exact in terms of number of notes; the bass contains 2,971 notes to the treble's 1,540. When Nancarrow first played back the roll, he could no longer hear the slower treble voice near the end, so he added more and more octaves to keep it audible.

Clearly, a melody so complex and run through such strict arithmetical procedures is little more than a prop for the illustration of the tempo effect, which is sufficiently fascinating to listen to for its own sake. Given the strictness of the system, there is no way (outside of a specially-designed computer program) Nancarrow could have predicted simultaneities between the two voices, and the transposition levels of the row seem chosen to create variety within each line, not to influence any way the two lines might combine. Given the structure Nancarrow aims to create here, pitch becomes secondary.

Study No. 22 – Canon 1% / 1½% / 2¼%

Study No. 22 is the first of two canons (No. 27 is the other) Nancarrow describes not by tempo ratios, but by percentages. In the first section, the lowest voice accelerates at a rate of one percent, which means that each note is 101 percent faster, or 99.0099 percent as long, as the one of the same notated value before it. The highest voice, which enters second (at 0:17), accelerates at a rate of 1½ percent, and the final middle voice (which enters at 0:33) at 2¼ percent. The lowest voice begins at a tempo of approximately 45 (75mm per note) and, over the course of ninety-six smoothly accelerating beats, reaches a tempo of about 115.8 (29mm per note). The highest voice increases from a virtually identical tempo[5] at a rate of 1½ percent to 185.1 (18mm), and the middle voice increases at a rate of 2¼ percent, to about 372.6 (9mm).

1.5%	tempo:	45×1.015^{95} [4.114] = 185.1
	duration:	75mm $\times$ .9852^{95} [.243] = 18.23mm
2.25%	tempo:	45×1.0225^{95} [8.2797] = 372.6
	duration:	75mm $\times$ .978^{95} [.1208] = 9.06mm
1%	tempo:	45×1.01^{95} [2.57354] = 115.8
	duration:	75mm $\times$ .99^{95} [.3849] = 28.87mm

I whipped up these calculations in ten minutes with a $12 hand-held calculator, but how Nancarrow accomplished that and more difficult feats with available 1950s technology is a mystery; he does not remember.

The structure of Study No. 22 is easily described. First of all, it is a palindrome; from system 39 (2:01, bottom of p. 11) the first half is repeated backwards, the accelerandos having become ritards. It is the only actual palindrome in Nancarrow's output, though arch forms and other palindromic ideas are frequent. In the middle section, however, contrast between staccato and sustained notes does slight injury to the integrity of the palindrome, for attack-point retrogrades differ from note-duration retrogrades; here, motives containing both sustained and staccato notes do not preserve their phrasing when reversed (as shown in Example 7.9). Too, the last chord of the first section is staccato in the first half, sustained in the second. Like Studies Nos. 24, 33, and 37, No. 22 is not really a single canon,

Example 7.9 Study No. 22, retrograde motivic transformation

becomes

but a series of canons, since intervals of transposition and delay do not remain constant. In the outer sections, the interval of transposition between lowest and middle, and between middle and highest, voices is two octaves and a minor third; in the middle section it is two octaves and a major third.

The piece is divided into almost perfect thirds in an ABA form, one A being the other backwards, and the B being palindromic in itself. The first A section (first twenty-six and two-thirds systems) is a straightforward canon using a sustained melody which occupies, in all, two octaves and a minor third, the same as the interval of imitation. Thus the ranges of each pair of contiguous voices interlock by only one note, dividing almost the piano's entire range into equal thirds. In a non-linear rhythmic tour de force that must have cost Nancarrow considerable calculation, the three voices converge on the final note.

The middle section (1:26–2:35) consists of six melodic fragments in each voice, generally decreasing in length from thirty-five beats to thirty-two to eleven, five, ten, eight, scattered with no temporal canonic consistency, but in such a way as to contrast rates of acceleration in different voices. Acceleration rates between the lowest and middle voices are switched here, so that the lowest speeds up at two and a quarter percent, the middle at one percent. The lowest voice picks up its tempo from the end of the first section, as if smoothly continuing its acceleration, but the others restart at slower tempos than they had already been heard in. Now at two and a quarter percent, the lowest voice accelerates from 120 to about 1120, the highest, at one and a half from 179.2 to 840, and the middle from 210 to 560, each acceleration remaining conceptually continuous through the long rests: that is, after each pause each voice continues at the new speed it would have reached had it been continuous. Once segments get down to five or eight notes, it is no longer possible to hear acceleration rates as slow as one percent, and the middle pages are more a contrast of tempos than of accelerations.

The first (and last) twelve pitches in each voice fill out a complete chromatic set, but the piece is not twelve-tone. As so often in Nancarrow the pitch element seems through-composed, with some reliance on certain motives. A rising fourth followed by a scale segment is common, and in the middle section chains of perfect and augmented fourths are frequent. Diatonic and chromatic scales are often interrupted by notes in a different register, then continued, and this intermittent linearity renders the rhythmic counterpoint easy to follow without becoming stale or predictable. Despite accumulated speeds of over eighteen notes per second, the midpoint of the palindrome (2:01) is unmistakably heard as such, largely because of the directionality of the ascending gestures, next heard in echoing descent and the gradual ritard of the second half makes a patent mirror of the first's accelerando. This little piece belongs more on the experimental than the inspired side of Nancarrow's creative ledger, but the points it was meant to make are clearly audible.

Study No. 23

Study No. 23 is one to give music analysts headaches, but it helps secure Nancarrow's position as one of the great innovators of the 1950s, at least for those whose conception of that period assumes a European model. For Study No. 23 is a pioneering work – Nos. 28 and 29 are others – in the dependent association of frequency with duration, an idea that was very much "in the air" between 1949 and 1960. Messiaen had experimented with giving each pitch its own duration in his *Modes de valeurs et d'intensités*, and he, Stockhausen, and Boulez pursued the implications of the idea throughout the decade. Independently, Milton Babbitt had arrived at similar methods in his *Three Compositions for Piano* (1947) and *Composition for Four Instruments* (1948). Although Nancarrow could not have known about what was going on in Paris, Darmstadt, and New York at the time, he had read Cowell's *New Musical Resources*, which anticipated these issues. In Study No. 23, however, Nancarrow took an approach different from Cowell's, and closer to the European experiments.

In this unusual study, not only is there no canonic imitation between the two voices, as Carlsen notes,[6] but they seem totally unrelated in character, one being derived from motivic development, the other through abstract rhythmic formulas. The different types of contrast between the motivic (usually metered) voice and the formulaic (unmetered) one define four main sections, the fourth of which is an altered mirror of the first.

In Section 1 (0:00–0:25, systems 1–7), the unmetered voice plays seventy-one staccato notes, covering a chromatically contiguous range without repetition (the piano's entire range except for the top octave) in a general rise and a continuous accelerando from a tempo of 44.4 to approximately 1650, an acceleration rate of *around* 5.3 percent (though acceleration rates are impossible to calculate exactly when dependent on measurements made by hand). The metered voice contains

Example 7.10   Study No. 23, primary motive

dyads and single notes: most of the motives consist of an interval of a second or seventh followed by an adjacent note on either side. Different forms of the motive in Example 7.10 act as momentary cadences, and a relief from the predominantly staccato texture.

In sections 2 (0:25–2:54, systems 8–51) and 3 (2:54–4:18, systems 52–78), Nancarrow draws a correspondence in the unmetered voice between pitch and duration (or rather, implied duration, since the notes are staccato). From B_0 to A_6, each of the seventy-one pitches is associated with a duration slightly shorter than the one a half-step below it. Carlsen found the ratio to be such that each pitch was about twice as short as the one a major ninth below,[7] and that calculation seems correct; in other words, there is a 5.076 percent acceleration rate (1.0576 is approximately the fourteenth root of 2, and there are fourteen half steps in a major ninth), with each note moving up the chromatic scale. For example, B_0 is marked by a duration of about 60mm, $C\sharp_2$ by 30mm, $D\sharp_3$ by 15mm. In an exact pitch/ratio correspondence, each pitch would have been twice as short as the one an *octave* below, but Nancarrow skews the durations a little in favor of the lower notes. The result is a texture in which, as in Messiaen's *Modes de valeurs*, the low notes last many times longer than the high notes.

Starting at system 8 (0:25), the unmetered voice articulates these durations in five-note groups. Within each group, all the notes take the duration associated with the first note, so that each five-note group briefly establishes a steady tempo. Each initial pitch is also associated with an invariant pitch figure; for example, every time the G below middle C occurs, it is followed by E♭–B–F–E. The metered voice, meanwhile, continues in the manner of section 1. Section 2 is divided into subsections by changes that occur simultaneously in both metered and unmetered voices. They can be characterized as follows:

system 19 (1:05)	metered voice	Tempo jumps upward to 141, dyads are replaced by three-note chords (mostly seventh chords with a missing fifth). After system 23, two-note motives decrease in favor of strings of more than three melodic notes.

	unmetered voice	four-note groups replace five-note groups. The melodic figures associated with each pitch remain the same, but the last note is dropped.
system 29 (1:40)	metered voice	The tempo increases to 149. Three-note chords are replaced by four-note chords (either seventh chords or ninth chords missing a fifth). Starting at system 32, the single notes are mostly replaced by minor third dyads. Melodic motives of more than four notes become more prevalent.
	unmetered voice	three-note groups replace four-note groups; another final note is dropped from each figure.
system 40 (2:18)	metered voice:	The tempo increases to 156. The texture drops back to dyads and two-note motives, as in section 1. Intervals are mostly seconds and sevenths again.
	unmetered voice	two-note groups replace three-note groups.
system 46 (2:37)	metered voice	Tempo jumps to 162. Minor third dyads reappear. All else remains the same.

These changes are summarized in Example 7.11.

In the metered voice Nancarrow's tempo shifts are arrived at arithmetically rather than geometrically: the succession 132, 141, 149, 156, and 162 is derived by adding, respectively, nine, eight, seven, and six. This means that the percentage of tempo change *decreases* – 6.8%, 5.7%, 4.7%, 3.8% – and the tempo changes are not clearly audible. If one ignores the shift from 156 to 162, the tempo changes divide section 2 into four subsections of almost identical length. Occasional localized patterns occur in the metered voice. For instance, a six-note motive at system 25 recurs at system 27; at system 29 another six-note motive is given sequential treatment; a passage from systems 47–48 is transposed at system 49. Such intuitive developmental procedures create a sense of melodic unity.

Section 3 (2:54–4:18, systems 52–78) opens with a first, dramatic five-note chord sustained for eight seconds. This section has no metered voice; the contrast here is between a steady accelerando and a stream of seemingly arbitrary durations. Staccato notes spell out a 303-note accelerando in the piano's top octave (a register avoided in earlier sections) at *about* 1.12 percent, from a tempo of 56.5 to about 1650. The lower voice, still using the lower seventy-one pitches, continues the unmetered voice's progression; it drops to single notes, now sustained, each lasting the duration associated with it, for a seemingly random texture dominated by low notes.[8] This "random" voice, however, does move toward higher pitches (and thus quicker durations) at systems 77–79 for a brief climax leading to the concluding section.

In section 4 (4:14–4:41, systems 79–86) the unmetered voice repeats its seventy-one-note run from section 1 in exact retrograde, descending and decelerating, with an added cadential note at the end. The metered voice moves quickly back from four-note to three-note chords to dyads, borrowing some section 1 material along the way.

Example 7.11   Study No. 23, structural chart

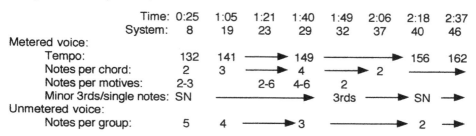

Example 7.12   Study No. 27, sectional characteristics

Section:	Systems:	Clock line:	Canonic voices:
1	1-44	single notes	sustained notes
2	45-58	octaves	trills
3	58-69	single notes	staccato notes
4	69-83	major thirds	sustained quadruple octaves
5	84-92	major triads	triads with trills
6	92-97	variable 4-note chords	triads, octaves with trills
7	97-99	single notes	sustained chromatic lines
8	99-104	quintuple octaves	trills

It is difficult to make aural sense of some of this. The textures of Study No. 23 are delightful and not duplicated elsewhere, but in few of Nancarrow's works is there so great a gap between process and audition. The main thing one hears is the perceptual shift when a moving tempo passes a stationary one. In section 1, the metered voice seems very fast compared to the staccato bass, but as the latter speeds up the metered motives sound slower and slower by comparison; in section 4, the reverse happens. In between, we hear a steady tempo contrasted with randomly varied patches of slow or fast beats, then a slow, steady accelerando against random durations. The effect is a worthwhile illusion, a lively sonic analogue to the optical tricks involving seemingly convergent parallel lines. The correlation of pitch and duration, though, complicates matters: since the fastest notes in section 2 are so high in pitch, they sound disconnected from the unmetered voice, and fly by as little flurries unrelated to the overall rhythmic structure. Study No. 23 attacks two fascinating rhythmic methodologies at once, and they conflict in interesting, maddening ways.

Study No. 27 – Canon 5%/6%/8%/11%

Despite its thrilling timbral effects, Study No. 27 is a fairly mechanical exploration of varying combinations of simultaneous acceleration and ritard. I like to call it the "Ontological Clock" Study, in reference to an offhand remark Nancarrow made to Roger Reynolds that the nonaccelerating eighth-note line that runs the length of the piece represented "the ticking of the ontological clock."[9] What I will call the "clock line" – an intermittent staccato pulse on the pitches D#, E, F, and G♭ above middle C, sometimes doubled at the octave, major third, and so on – provides a perceptual yardstick against which all the accelerating and decelerating voices are heard. Nancarrow's remark implies that, in the midst of the illusions of bending and stretching time, the clock line gives our ears a bit of unambiguous reality to hold on to.

The clock line is the piece's horizontal axis of symmetry; everything that happens above it in the treble is eventually reflected (though not by inversion) in the bass, and vice versa. Its textural changes also divide the piece into eight sections, characterized in Example 7.12. Altogether there are eleven canons in the series, four of them in section 1. Each canon contains four voices (though in the first, one pair does not overlap with the other pair), accelerating and decelerating at rates of five, six, eight, eleven percent respectively.

Section 1, by far the longest, is divided into four canons. The first canon (0:00–1:19, systems 1–20) contrasts two melodies beneath the clock line, one accelerating and then decelerating at six percent, the other doing so at eleven percent. These are followed by melodies above the clock line using eight percent and five percent acceleration and deceleration. The melodies employ a sixty-four-note row, complicated by rests and subdivisions of the prevailing beat. Of this study's ten pitch rows, none appear to be significantly related. This first row, though, is the only one to use virtual eighth- and quarter-note rhythms (though the canon in section 5 does include rests). Perhaps Nancarrow felt that, since this is the only part of the piece in which only two voices are heard together, the rhythms should be more interesting than the steady pulses of the succeeding canons.

The second canon (1:19–1:40, systems 21–26) uses only ritards, of five percent and six percent in the bass melodies, eight percent and eleven percent in the treble, timed to converge at their endpoint at system 26. The canon's twenty-three-note row uses only four chromatically adjacent pitches and no rhythmic irregularities. The third canon (1:40–2:14, systems 26–35), with its twenty-three-note row within the space of a major sixth, has the bass lines accelerate and ritard at six percent and eleven percent respectively, while the treble lines ritard first and then accelerate at eight percent and five percent. The fourth canon (2:14–2:46, systems 36–44) has each voice accelerate and then ritard, bringing in the voices from lowest to top, eleven percent to five percent. Its eighty-eight notes per voice are made up entirely of transpositions of a five-note chromatic motive, A–B–A–B♭–A. Using A for accelerate, R for ritard, and a central line for the clock line, the form of section 1 could be encapsulated as in Example 7.13a. The section provides plenty of chances to hear simultaneous acceleration and deceleration.

Example 7.13b charts, in a roughly proportional manner, the basic tempo scheme of the remaining sections. In Section 2, the E and D# of the clock voice are doubled an octave below, the F and G♭ an octave above. This is a canon in half-step trills, the trills following a fifty-seven-note row within a major ninth. The

Example 7.13a   Study No. 27, structural diagrams

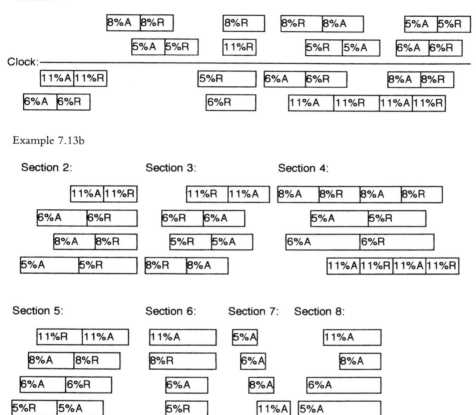

Durations not strictly proportional

tempo pattern follows that of section 1's fourth canon. Section 3 reverses the pattern, following ritard with acceleration. Here each voice, now all in staccato notes, descends into the bass in a ritard, then begins again at the top of the piano and accelerates downward and upward. (The final thirteen notes in each voice invert the first thirteen.) In section 4 each canonic voice in the bass is doubled four octaves above in the treble, on both sides of the clock line, giving this passage in the score the appearance of an eight-voice canon.[10] This canon has the unusual feature that, while the 5% and 6% voices each accelerate and ritard once, the 8% and 11% voices go through their acceleration and ritard twice.

In section 5 it becomes difficult to distinguish the canonic lines from the clock line, since both are playing triads (though the canonic lines sometimes include trills on the triads' middle notes). Section 6 provides the four voices overlapping

Example 7.14   Study No. 27, transposition levels of canonic voices

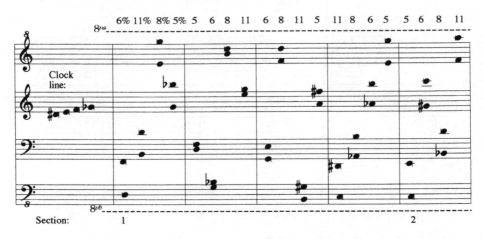

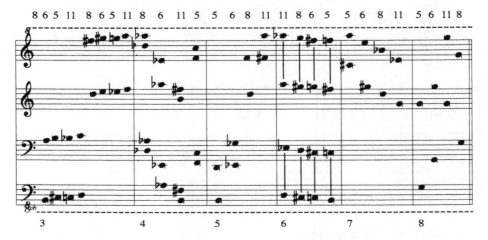

symmetrically. Each canonic voice includes bass octaves and treble triads alternating pianistically at the extremes of the piano, giving the effect of an eight-part
double canon. Brief section 7 merely states four chromatic glissandos accelerating
at five, six, eight and eleven percent the clock voice marking time, so that we
have one last chance to hear the contrasts clearly before the explosive finale.

Like section 2, final section 8 is a canon in trills, this time major seconds. The
clock voice itself is a kind of slow major-second trill: it has abandoned its usual
pitches to alternate irregularly between E♭ and F. The canonic voices skip widely,
using only pitches from the C major scale for their lower notes. The intervals of
transposition are all octaves, so that all voices can cadence on a climactic G; even
the clock voice jumps up to A♭ at the end leading downward to G, as though its
D♯–F♯ ascent had been aiming at that pitch all along.

Example 7.14 provides the transposition levels for each canon, the range of each voice, and the order of entrance. Treatment of range varies greatly among the eleven canons: in sections 1, 2, 4, and 5 the voices stay scrupulously out of each other's way, but in 3 and 6 they are separated only by half-steps. These fluctuating registers provide as accurate a picture of the piece's overall sonic shape as anything could.

The finale brings up an interesting point about the theory of acceleration canons. In a "normal" tempo canon, if two voices have a 4:5 tempo relationship, one of them will be $\frac{5}{4}$ as long as the other. Acceleration canons, however, involve no necessary proportion between the length and acceleration rate. The total duration of a given line is a function of not only the acceleration rate, but of the length of its longest (or shortest) note. In Study No. 22 Nancarrow began each voice with (virtually) identical durations, and timed the voices to end at the first convergence point; thus, each voice had to begin at a precisely determined point. Here he takes advantage of the greater structural freedom the acceleration canon allows, and can begin each voice wherever he chooses.

For example, in the final canon, the 11% voice begins *earlier* than the 8% voice, yet they conclude together. In order for this to happen (since the 11% voice accelerates at a faster rate), the 11% voice's initial durations have to be considerably longer than those of the 8% voice. In section 1's second canon, Nancarrow arranged for all the voices to attack their last note together and to cut off together; given a specific final note-length, the proportions of each line were determined, as in Study No. 22, and the 11% voice *had* to begin later than the others, the 5% voice first. In the first half of section 3, on the other hand, the 5% and the 11% lines are nearly identical in length; to achieve this, Nancarrow had to begin the 11% ritard with much shorter durations. Consequently, the usage of convergence points and significant canonic points is entirely different than in the tempo canons. The canons of sections 3 and 7, for example, contain no convergence points. Section 4 has a few between certain pairs of voices, but they are scattered haphazardly, and no more than two voices ever coincide; the same goes for section 6. Except at the ends of three canons – canon 2 of section 1, section 2, and section 8 – convergence point is not an important issue in this study. Indeed, acceleration canon is less conducive to making it one.

In creating this wealth of variations on the idea of a curved rhythmic space, Nancarrow allowed us to hear something that many musicians have doubtless wondered about, but which had never before been possible. However, acceleration canon does not have the kind of clean structural implications Nancarrow found in the straight tempo canon, the built-in correspondences between form, echo distance, and phrase length. This may be why, after Study No. 27, Nancarrow abandoned the acceleration canon (except for the quick, virtuoso finale of the Third String Quartet). Perceptually fascinating, it did not lead to the kind of compositional richness he found elsewhere.

Study No. 28

Study No. 28 is a structuralist experiment, as relentlessly mechanical as Studies Nos. 5 and 21. However, unlike the situation in the acceleration canons, the acceleration here does not take place gradually, but in discrete steps. Two major scales run up and down the keyboard throughout the entire piece, in the same keys and both shifting up a half-step each time they reach top or bottom. One (notated on the next to lowest stave) remains at a constant tempo throughout, of about 360. The other scale (notated on the lowest stave) begins more slowly, at about 252; each time it returns to the bottom of its range it shifts tempo up a notch in a pattern that relates to the constant-speed voice in the same ratios in which a justly-tuned chromatic scale relates to the tonic. If we take the "tonic tempo" as being C = 1/1 (♩ = 360), we find the acceleration voice moves stepwise along the following "scale".

252	7/10	F♯	480	4/3	F
270	3/4	G	504	7/5	F♯
288	4/5	A♭	540	3/2	G
300	5/6	A	576	8/5	A♭
315	7/8	B♭	600	5/3	A
337.5	15/16	B	630	7/4	B♭
384	16/15	C♯	675	15/8	B
405	9/8	D	765	17/8	C♯
432	6/5	E♭	810	9/4	D
450	5/4	E	864	12/5	E♭

Note that the acceleration increments are fairly uniform except for the skips from 337.5 to 384 and 675 to 765, which are about twice as large as average; this is because the moving voice skips over C (360 and 720), which would bring it into tempo unison with the "drone" voice.

Through these scales Nancarrow threads a layer of repeated notes in small, nonsynchronous chromatic clusters. Eight pitches, each frozen in register, form the centers of these clusters, and each dots out its repetitions at a different tempo – the lower the pitch, the slower the tempo, as shown in Example 7.15. Around each of these pitches, two half-step neighbors pulsate irregularly, the upper one articulating a tempo approximately $\frac{17}{16}$ the speed of the main note, the lower one $\frac{15}{16}$ that speed. Thus these are tempo clusters as well as pitch clusters, because a 15:16:17 ratio defines two half-steps. The piece moves among these eight pitches in an irregular fashion; each returns either 6, 7, or 8 times in a pattern that seems to have no permutational regularity.

The third and final layer is a line in sextuple (sometimes septuple) octaves that accelerates at a rate of about five percent from an initial tempo of 7.45 (duration = eight seconds) to a final tempo of about 1106. At first this line merely reiterates the tonic of each major scale during which it occurs; but as the line begins to repeat faster than the scales modulate (there are ninety-nine notes in the octave-line and

Example 7.15   Study No. 28, tempo/pitch correspondence

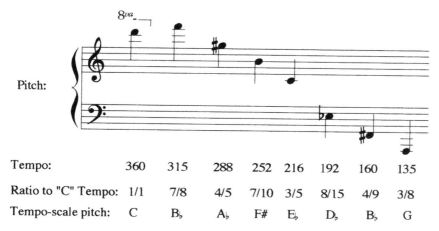

Tempo:	360	315	288	252	216	192	160	135
Ratio to "C" Tempo:	1/1	7/8	4/5	7/10	3/5	8/15	4/9	3/8
Tempo-scale pitch:	C	B♭	A♭	F#	E♭	D♭	B♭	G

only about forty-one modulations), other notes start being added in between, first the fifth of the scale, then the fifth and fourth, then fifth, fourth, and second, finally adding the third. At first, because of the long durations, this line is the least present element, but towards the end, its tendency to double in speed every thirteen or fourteen notes makes for a rip-roaring finish.

Nancarrow has repeatedly mentioned that Study No. 28 and its successor are not among his favorites, possibly because they use such simple materials to explore strict conceptual ideas. However, the perceptual processes they are designed to explore are fascinating, and they are especially thrilling to listen to if you know what is going on. Even if its scales give Study No. 28 a "practice room" sound, its successive tempo contrasts provide a wonderful study in ratios in a particularly clear context.

Study No. 29

Characterized by repeated notes that sound like a jumble of Morse code transmissions, Study No. 29 is an elaborate companion piece to No. 28, manifesting the same type of structural relations in a more complex manner. This is an ABABABABABABAB form, A and B each undergoing its own acceleration process, which the other interrupts.

Though the texture is multilayered and the numbers require considerable analysis, the sections can be concretely characterized. The A sections contain three elements. The first is a line of sustained octaves which accelerates, in the course of the seven A sections, from a tempo of 14 to about 1392, at an average rate of about 5.7 percent. After each B section interruption, the acceleration picks up where it left off. The second element is a layer of repeated notes pulsing at different tempos, almost all above F_3: at first only two at a time, increasing to three in A2, and four in A4. The tempo of each pulse is related to pitch through a scheme whereby tempo ratios are roughly proportional to pitch ratios. That is, since the interval of G to F represents a 9:8 pitch ratio, the tempos of repeating Gs and Fs exhibit the same ratio, 270 to 240, and so on for the rest of the scale:[11]

pitch	mm	tempo
C♯	11.9	384
C	12.5	367.7
B	13.6	337.2
A♯	14.3?	320
A	15.3	300.5
G♯	16.1	285.6
G	17.0	270
F♯	18.2	252.3
F	19.1	240
E	20.4	224.4
D♯	21.1	217.4
D	22.7	202.1

In the A sections, only a few pitches are used as repeating notes in more than one passage, and a few of the notes, especially in a high register, repeat at double tempo. A section by A section, the repeated notes and octaves (only the upper note of the latter is given) run as in Example 7.16.

The third element is an isorhythmic bass, outlining triads in a seven–note pattern that repeats every eleven eighth notes (Example 7.17). The roots of these triads travel in the ascending major/descending minor pattern favored by Nancarrow, and the tempo remains constant throughout all A sections, at about $\quad = 360$. Thus the three elements represent three different tempo patterns: acceleration in the sustained mid-register octave line, layering at different speeds in the mostly higher repeated notes, and unchanging isorhythmic repetition in the bass.

The B sections reverse some of these relationships: here it is the bass that accelerates, the soprano lines that remain largely constant. There are four layers of activity. The bass line, mostly (with three exceptions on the final page) occupying the piano's lowest octave, uses the same seven–note isorhythm as the A sections but with acceleration, beginning at a tempo of about 85 and accelerating to about 1,392. Like the A sections, the B sections contain a layer of repeated notes, but only one at a time and always in a low register, from F♯$_2$ to D$_3$. Only nine pitches are found, pulsing at tempos *not* corresponding to those of the A-section repeated notes, but approximately (or possibly) related by a not-too-complex system of ratios.

pitch	F♯	G	G♯	A	B♭	B	C	C♯	D
tempo	157	204	242	288	339	432	508	628	720
ratio	13	17	20	24	28	36	42	52	60

The highest layer consists of three upper voices of single notes, parallel third dyads, and triads. Each note, dyad, or triad repeats three times within the repeating seven–note isorhythm (given in Example 7.18) at tempos corresponding to the five fastest tempos of the repeated notes (possibly reducible to 14, 18, 21, 26, and 30).

Example 7.16 Study No. 29, repeated notes and octaves in A sections

For the first four B sections, only one strand of this highest layer is heard at a time. At B5, triads begin to overlap with dyads, then single notes with triads, and in B6 and B7 all three layers are heard together, single notes on top, triads in mid-register, and dyads in between. By now the single notes have fallen permanently into the 720 tempo, the dyads into the 628 tempo, and the triads into the 508 tempo; Nancarrow's manuscript shows that, when C, C♯, and D repeat in the bass, they coincide with, respectively, the triads, dyads, and single notes.[12]

The remaining layer of the B sections consists of two lines in bass clef which mostly wander up and down the up-major/down-minor pattern in quarters,

Example 7.17   Study No. 29, isorhythmic bass

(Stems not present in Nancarrow's notation)

Repeating isorhythm

Example 7.18   Study No. 29, isorhythm in dyads

Example 7.19   Study No. 29, structural chart

	A1	B1	A2	B2	A3	B3	A4	B4	A5	B5	A6	B6	A7	B7
Time+:	0:00	0:29	0:37	1:00	1:10	1:21	1:38	1:52	2:15	2:23	2:47	2:55	3:19	3:24
Starting octave tempo*:	13		18		27		36		60		99		205<c.1392	
Repeated notes:	2		2-3		3		3-4		4		4		4	
Dynamics:	mp		mp		mf		f		f		ff		ff	
Seconds+:	29		23		11		14		8		8		5	
Seconds+:		8		10		17		23		24		24		32
Dynamics:		ff		ff		ff		ff		ff		ff		ff
Upper layers:		1		1		1		1		2		3		3
Starting bass tempo*:		85		91		97		107		134		184		249 <c.1392

*According to the score
+According to the Wergo recording

eighth notes, and dotted quarters, sometimes using the seven–note, eleven–beat isorhythm, but with many gaps. These lines change tempo frequently and simultaneously, and the lower line is always *about* $\frac{9}{10}$ or $\frac{8}{9}$ as fast as the higher; if the ratio remains constant, the score is not precisely enough drawn to be more exact. Like the A sections, the B sections contrast acceleration with unchanging tempo and changing steady tempo, but each rhythm type has moved to a different register.

Between these two texture complexes Nancarrow builds his form. Contrasts are at first dynamic: the A sections begin *mp* and crescendo by stages, while the B sections are *ff* throughout. The A sections decrease in length, starting at twenty-three seconds for A1 and decreasing to only four (although A4 is longer than A3), and the B sections mirror that decrease by lengthening from six to twenty-five seconds. Example 7.19 shows the pattern of interruptions, and the intermittent crescendo that takes place on alternating levels. Aural distinction between the A and B sections fades as the dynamics reach a uniform *ff* but the contrast between the repeated notes (the Morse Code effect) of A with the moving, triply-articulated triads and thirds of B remains audible.

Study No. 30

Study No. 30 was the piece Nancarrow wrote for player piano in response to John Cage's *Sonatas and Interludes*, and the study he later abandoned. He once bought a player grand piano to try to make the piece feasible, but its mechanism was unreliable, and kept breaking down. As he told me,

> I had so much problem with the mechanism, I decided it just wasn't worth it. I wasn't dissatisfied [with No. 30], but it was pure rhythm, there wasn't anything melodic. I still have the roll, but the roll has no indication of what the preparations were. I don't think I'd remember.[13]

Sandoval has discovered a list of preparations in Nancarrow's studio, though it does not quite jibe with the pitches in the piece. And, while Nancarrow has never copied out the score to No. 30, I found a rough punching score and copious sketches for it in his studio, evidence of considerable thought, calculation, and work. (An old reel-to-reel tape of the piece also apparently exists.) More research will be needed to reconstruct the piece in performance, but there is easily enough information to provide some analysis, and the work is interesting enough conceptually to be worth reviving with today's technology.

Combining canon with isorhythm in an overall accelerative pattern, the work forms part of a natural group with Nos. 28 and 29, and is quite similar to the latter in its intercutting of textural blocks. To begin with, Nancarrow set up five textural resultants, each using a different pitch set, a different register of the piano, and among them, thirteen different tempos altogether. Each line repeats in an endless loop of sixty beats. The textural blocks are differentiated as follows:

1 The lowest block involves a rhythmic canon at a 3:5 ratio between two staccato voices, accompanied by two thick, alternating chords.

2 The second block contains three voices, each a simple alternation between two pitches, outlining a rhythmic canon at an apparent tempo ratio of 4:5:7.

3 The third block contains two voices with five pitches each, in a canon at a 5:7 ratio. This is not a canon in the conventional sense of one voice being a transposition of the other; rather, given their two different interval sets, the two voices follow the same contour, each pitch in one voice invariably mapped to a companion pitch in the other.

4 The fourth block is not a canon, but involves two voices, one containing two pitches and the other three, articulating between them a tempo ratio of 9:10.

5 The highest block, also noncanonic, contains three voices, each consisting of three chromatically contiguous pitches, outlining tempo ratios of 24:25:30.

Example 7.20   Study No. 30, pitches of each textural block

The pitches and ratios of the five textural blocks are given in Example 7.20.

As in No. 29, Nancarrow's technique in Study No. 30 is simply to cut back and forth between these blocks without overlapping, as though they were so many strips of fabric to be sewn together. A segment of texture 1 is followed by a segment of texture 4, then segments of 2, 3, and 5. Then, when texture 4 returns, it picks up at the same point in its repeating cycle at which it had stopped the first time around. Similarly for the segment of texture 3 that follows, and so on. The piece contains about 103 segments, which generally become shorter toward the end with an accelerating note of sectional contrasts. (In Nancarrow's sketches, a final chaotic page juxtaposing all five textures simultaneously was crossed out, and this is absent from the piano roll.)

The work's most interesting technical device is the transference of a melody's rhythm and contour from one level of organization to another. Nancarrow composed a five-note melody sixty beats long, and applied its contour and rhythm not only to the canonic voices of textures 1 and 3 (and possibly 5), but also, in a fusion of macro- and microstructures, to the large-scale movement among textural blocks. Example 7.21 compares the 5:7 canon of block 3 with the lower canonic voice of texture 1, and also with the movement and relative durations of the textural segments. The pitch movement within each five-pitch melody parallels the structural movement among the five textural blocks, and the rhythm of the melodies is grandly augmented to become the rhythm of the intercutting. Toward the end of the study the segments become shorter and shorter, to the point that near the end a block may contain only two or three notes, and the ability to distinguish different blocks breaks down.

Once acquainted with this structure, the list of preparations Sandoval found (along with the preparations themselves) does not make much sense. First of all, the list, given in Example 7.22, shows only thirty prepared pitches, while the study uses forty-eight. Secondly, there is no indication of how such items as a metal washer are to be placed in the piano strings. Thirdly, the list reveals great

Example 7.21 Study No. 30, comparison of contours and rhythms on macro– and micro–levels

Block 3:

Block 1:

Movement among textural segments (numbers indicate approximate duration of segment):

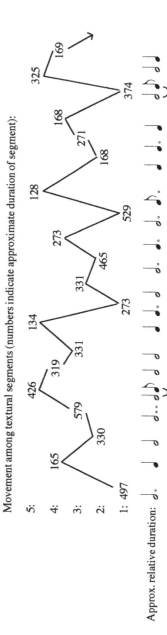

Approx. relative duration:

Example 7.22 Study No. 30, Nancarrow's list of preparations

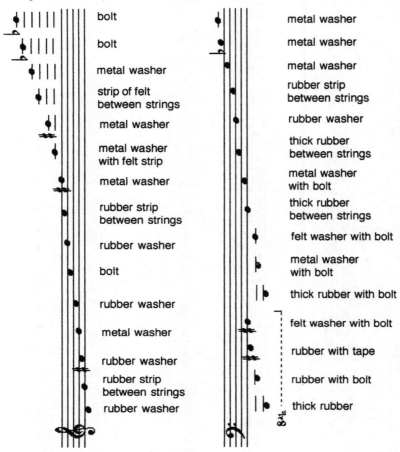

variety in the preparations from note to note along the range, which does not seem to match the work's construction in blocks of sound. The conclusion seems inevitable that what Sandoval found was perhaps an early form of the preparations, not the one Nancarrow finally used.

Nancarrow's entire output is infused with the idea of acceleration and deceleration, but his actual use of smooth, geometric, *literal* acceleration only lasted for only a handful of studies; perhaps he became exhausted by the calculations involved. In this last group of acceleration studies, Nos. 28–30, acceleration becomes generalized from a contrapuntal device to the level of overall form. Having contrasted changing tempos with constant tempos in Study 28, Nancarrow obviously wanted, in the next two studies, to retry the experiment in a nonlinear way, in a context where form and memory could play a part. When he returns to acceleration in Studies Nos. 42 and 48, it will no longer be to experiment so literally, but to provide a structural basis for other processes in a grandly climax-oriented formal conception.

8

Beyond counterpoint: the sound-mass canons

Studies Nos. 24, 32, 33, 36, 37, 40, 41, 43, 48

> If the tortoise has the start of Achilles, Achilles can never catch up with the tortoise; for, while Achilles traverses the distance from his starting point to the starting point of the tortoise, the tortoise advances a certain distance, and while Achilles traverses this distance, the tortoise makes a further advance, and so on ad infinitum. Consequently, Achilles may run ad infinitum without overtaking the tortoise.
>
> Zeno

The ancient paradox above comes close to expressing the essence of the tempo canon discipline. For whenever the faster, later voice of a tempo canon arrives at a certain event, the slower, earlier voice has already passed it and moved on to something else. And yet, with each such movement that something else becomes less and less far away. Finally, in the tempo canon as in real life – Zeno's impeccable logic notwithstanding – the voices *do* converge, and in that moment surrounding the convergence point an infinity must be squeezed into an instant, even as it explodes into yet a new field of continually expanding distances. Listen to the ending of Conlon Nancarrow's Studies Nos. 40 or 48, or the middle of Nos. 36 or 41: like Diogenes, he takes the simple, earthshaking step that refutes Zeno in a triumph of unstoppable, irretrievable motion.

It is in the exploitation of the convergence point that Nancarrow reached his greatest compositional achievements. Convergence points – the points at which faster voices "catch up" with slower voices and corresponding notes coincide – are of little importance in the canons of chapter 6. At most (as in Studies Nos. 15, 17, 18, 19, 34, 49a, and 50), the final CP offers a punchy ending as voices collide. In the canons of this chapter, however, the placement of CPs determines details throughout a canon: phase length, type of gesture, distance between gestures, texture, dynamics, density, synchronicity, audibility.

Typically, in the late canons, the following motion occurs: immediately following any convergence point, a quick echoing of brief figures creates excitement signalling the entrance to a new section of the piece. Usually voices lose their distinguishability in a bristling texture, then slowly separate. Short figures are

Example 8.1 Study No. 24, top system of page 13

gradually displaced by longer and longer motives which sound calmer (by virtue of their temporal stability) but also more complex, even developmental. As a new convergence point is approached, the echo-tempo picks up again, and figures splinter into ever briefer motives, creating a deliciously gradual feeling of cumulative climax. In the canons that end with convergence points (Studies Nos. 24, 32, 33, 37, 40, 48), that feeling of climax is pushed up to the last note. In the canons that do not end at convergence points (Nos. 36, 41, 43), the climax comes in the middle of a large arch form, and the end dies away in a textural decrescendo. And in the canons that contain more than one convergence point (Nos. 24, 37, 43), the process occurs over and over, with meanings as different as those of the several cadences of a Beethoven sonata.

The basic, underlying principle is that Nancarrow often links motives from two voices without overlapping them. Thus a motive or figure will occur first in the fastest voice, then, just as it enters in the next-fastest voice, the first voice will move to a contrasting figure. Passages in which all voices are playing the same figure are used for special, usually climactic, effects. The interesting thing about tempo canon, though, is that the temporal distance between occurrences of any given figure in different voices changes continually. This means that the length of a figure, if its end in one voice is to dovetail with its beginning in another, varies with its distance from the nearest convergence point. In Example 8.1 from p. 13 of Study No. 24, the convergence point is at the beginning of the system. The first glissando is heard as a blur among the three voices. By the three-note trill figure in the fourth measure of each line, the voices are far enough apart in time for the figure to overlap by only one note. The six-note trill figure in the seventh measure is twice as far away, it is twice as long, and it overlaps by two notes. Two pages later (Example 8.6 below) the echo distance is fifteen beats, and the phrase length is fifteen beats. And so on.

Though not always as literal as in Study No. 24, this process is pervasive; Nancarrow tends to use his longest phrases, his longest passages of unvaried texture, *furthest* from the convergence point, and his briefest, quickest gestures *close* to convergence points. What this means is that canonic structure has a determining effect on canonic materials: what kind of figure Nancarrow uses at a given point *depends on where it occurs in the canon.* Process and materials interrelate: figures within a structure are derived from it, and their relation to it is audible. Here Nancarrow achieved the minimalists' dream of *audible process*, without any sacrifice of pitch or rhythmic complexity. (Nancarrow is contemptuous of the minimalists' rhythmic simplemindedness, and does not realize how interestingly his music relates to theirs.) And the proportionality between phrase length and distance from a convergence point means ultimately that the logic of tempo canon results in geometric acceleration on a formal level: as a CP approaches, section lengths become geometrically shorter. An examination of Study No. 40 will demonstrate this point with particular clarity.

This is the central difference between what I am calling the early and the late canons. The early canons distributed their materials evenly, with little regard for placement, and sometimes arbitrarily: given minor harmonic changes, the melody of Study No. 15 could just as easily have served for a 4:5 or a 3:5 as for a 3:4 canon. As in any fugue, the entrance of the opening figure in each voice is a primary event, but echo distances, particularly under odd pitch transpositions, can be difficult to hear. Convergence points can even pass by unnoticed. The late canons, on the other hand, *sound* less like canons: instead of hearing a melody recur in fugal entrances, one tends to hear mass effects and major structural points. Individual voices disintegrate at these moments to participate in collective masses of sound – for which reason I like to call these canons the "sound-mass" canons. Their interpermeation of form and motive makes them a high point in the ancient art of counterpoint. Every study discussed in this chapter is arguably a masterpiece: these are, along with perhaps four or five others, Nancarrow's greatest works. Adequate analysis of any two of them could fill an entire book. There is space here for barely an outline of each study.

A final note: The pseudo-issue of whether one can "actually hear" simultaneous tempo ratios of 19 to 20, 24 to 25, 60 to 61, arises again and again in connection with Nancarrow's late work. In the early canons, he had restricted himself to ratios involving 3, 4, and 5 because he wanted to hear them. When, in Study No. 24, he ventured as far as 14:15:16, it was precisely because his focus had changed. The canons in chapter 6 are the ones in which keeping the voices distinct was a concern of paramount importance. In the sound-mass canons, the very point was that no one could *possibly* hear a discrete difference; here Nancarrow is not illustrating tempo differences, he is using subtleties of tempo to create forms and textures that had never been heard before, and which could have been created no other way. Webern has often received credit for the creation of *diagonal texture,* texture in which harmony and counterpoint merge and cease to oppose each other as horizontal and vertical. Nancarrow not only recreated diagonal texture in a new and vivid way which owed Webern nothing, he created a *continuum* through which the horizontal could flow through the diagonal to become vertical, then flow back again. In the final few notes of Study No. 32, or the opening notes of No. 37, one hears the horizontal melt into the vertical (or vice versa), with the diagonal as a poignantly ephemeral intermediary stage. To fret about tempo perception during such an illusion is to miss the ocean through wondering which wave is which.

Study No. 24 – Canon 14/15/16

The 14/15/16 canon is the first of Nancarrow's truly sophisticated canons, the first to use canonic technique not primarily to differentiate tempos, but to create textures and collective effects. As such, it is closer in sound and technique to Studies Nos. 32, 36, 37, 40, and 43 than to its immediate neighbors, and seems to occupy a later place in Nancarrow's output than its number would indicate. If No. 24 indeed preceded Nos. 25, 26, 27, and 31 (as Nancarrow says it did), then it is a remarkable anticipation of the direction his future development would follow.

The most striking aural feature of this study is the feathery arpeggio effect created by the closeness of the tempos and the fact that the transposition intervals between the three voices usually spell out either major or minor triads. The first thing one hears is a series of widely-spaced, arpeggiated major triads, eight of which go by before the voices are too far apart to hear the triads as such. Because of the frequency of convergence points (thirteen in the entire study), this effect is repeated many times, infusing the whole with the sweet consonance of arpeggiated triads despite considerable dissonance.

Like Studies Nos. 27, 33, and 37, No. 24 is a series of canons with diverse structures and intervals of transposition rather than a single canon. The distinct sections alternate *pianissimo* pointillistic canons in relatively long note values with *fortissimo* canons filled with trills, octave tremolos, and repeated notes. I count twelve sections, even though two of them (8 and 9) are no more than brief interludes; and while my criterion is a simultaneous change in both dynamics and interval of transposition, the lengthy tenth section is unusual for twice changing transposition interval mid-canon. The pattern of transposition intervals is itself revealing.

section	1	2	3	4	5	6	7	8	9	10			11	12
slow,	A		E		E		G#		D				A	
pp	F#		B		B		E#		A				E	
canon	D		G		G#		C#		F				C#	
fast,		F#		C		F#		B		D	B	Ab		Ab
ff		D		C		F#		F#		B	B	Eb		Ab
canons		B		C		F#		C#		G	B	B		Ab

These notes are not in close position, of course, but always separated by at least two octaves. As the chart shows, the slow canons (slower in that they use half

Example 8.2   Study No. 24, structural diagram

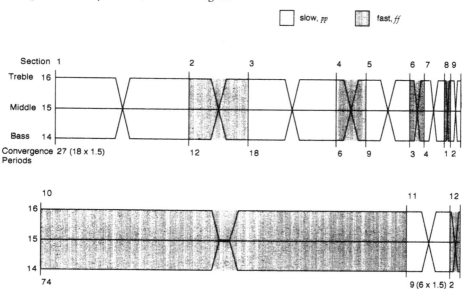

notes and quarters rather than eighths and sixteenths) are all set in triadic trans-positions, four of them major. The triadic effect is too subtle to be perceived in the fast canons, which in four cases are transposed at the double octave, the better to perceive echoes between quickly moving lines. The tenth section seems almost like a structural attempt to integrate major and minor in one canon by "modulating" from one to the other.

The tempo-structure device in this study, which will recur in Study No. 43, is equally subtle and elegant. The basic tempos of the piece are 224, 240, and 256 (14:15:16) for the dotted quarter, except in sections 1 and 11, which are exactly two thirds as fast: 149⅓, 160, and 170⅔. Tempo changes occur not at conver-gence points (except at the beginning of sections 9 and 12), but halfway between them, so that each voice enters each new section in the same tempo in which it ended the previous one, then switches. Thus starting at canon 2, the top voice first lags behind the others, then switches to the faster tempo, catches up, synchronizes, gets ahead, switches to the slower tempo, synchronizes, lags behind, etc., in a continual give-and-take between the upper and lower voices. (The middle voice maintains the same tempo almost throughout.) Example 8.2 gives some idea of the tempo crossovers, as well as the alternations of loud and soft and the durational proportions of the twelve sections.

This is one of the few canons (along with Nos. 15, 17, and 37) that both begin and end at convergence points, and the way Nancarrow plays with those points is intriguing. The canons of sections 2, 3, 4, 9, 10, and 12 begin not *on* the conver-gence point, but in an arpeggiated motion slightly afterward, and canon 7 begins one measure *before* its convergence point, creating a slightly off-center interplay between canonic form and tempo structure. The convergence period I use for this analysis equals fifteen eighth notes in the middle voice, alternately fourteen or sixteen eighth notes in the upper or lower voices. That period is the largest common denominator of the lengths of the canons, which, counted in multiples of fifteen eighth notes, fall into the following proportions:

27:12:18:6:9:3:4:1:2:74:9:2

Since sections 1 and 11 progress at tempos only two thirds as fast as the rest of the study, they actually contain eighteen and six periods respectively, but I have multiplied by 1.5 to show the actual temporal relations to the other sections. If we separate the proportions of the slow, soft canons and fast, loud canons –

pp	27	18	9	4	2			9
ff		12	6	3	1	74		2

we find two parallel accelerandos, a 27–18–9–4–2 decrease in the lengths of the soft canons, and a 12–6–3–1 decrease in the lengths of the loud ones, followed by the mammoth (by comparison – it is over 100 seconds) tenth canon, which occupies over forty-four percent of the length of the entire piece.

It is amazing how well Nancarrow unifies the soft canons as one group, and the loud canons as another, almost without any common motives or structural devices, via the sheerly physical means of texture and contour. In a way, the more linear, partly isorhythmic soft canons relate more to his early canonic practice, the loud canons with their frenetic trills and tremolos to his later work, giving the study a transitional feel. Even so, the soft canons display a new mastery of counterpoint, an ear-gratifying audibility of structure that none of his earlier works possess.

The very first notes (Example 8.3) provide the only real motive in the piece. That "tune" returns in the last third of the first canon (end of the second system, p. 3) and forms a basis for more focused development in canon 11, which, in terms of both motive and tempo, forms the "recapitulation." The lilting triple rhythms make canonic echoes easy to recognize, and Nancarrow occasionally thins out the texture to allow a motive to play itself out in slower voices.

To discuss the odd-numbered, *pp* canons first: The delicate third canon (1:03–1:31) is notated in 9/8, but structured mainly in two- and three-note phrases articulating durations of eleven eighth notes, offset by an occasional group of twelve. The middle third takes up a charming little repeated-note motive (1:12), easily picked out from the counterpoint by the ear, expressing eleven as either 4+2+5, 4+3+4, or 5+2+4 (Example 8.4). Twentieth-century music has produced few moments of such exquisite poetry, even though played by a mechanical parlor instrument. The final third falls into an eighth-note isorhythm of 4+4+4+6. Similarly, the scalar, dotted-quarter melodies of canon 5 (1:39–1:52) are accented with three-note chords in a 3+2+2 pattern. Canon 7 (1:56–2:03) is in quarter notes, accented by two-note chords into patterns of two, three, four,

Example 8.3   Study No. 24, opening melody

Example 8.4   Study No. 24, eleven-beat motive

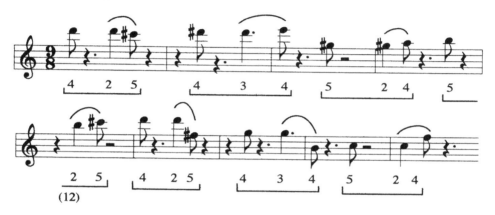

and five. Canon 9 (2:04–2:07) is a 2.5-second, two-chord-plus-one-note interlude, and canon 11 (4:03–4:16), as already mentioned, is a shortened return to canon 1.

The fast, *ff* canons use, not melodic lines, but the kind of frenzied, virtuosic figures that make Nancarrow's later work so exciting: staccato repeated notes, trills, and octave tremolos (not, as yet, many glissandos to speak of). Canon 2 (0:43–1:03) ties together the 160/240 tempo contrast of the first two canons by using both eighths and dotted eighths, in a catchy, partly motivic melody that sets the ascending/descending pattern for these sections (Example 8.5). The trills and tremolos occur in canons 4 (1:31–1:39), 6 (1:52–1:56), and 8 (2:03–2:04), deployed in triads and cadential figures; if the materials seem generic when examined closely, the resultant textures are distinctive, and unprecedented.

Canon 10 (2:07–4:03) is worth examining in considerable detail, because it exemplifies in relative miniature many of the principles that will govern Nancarrow's late, larger canons. We have already seen an example from this canon of phrase length varying with lengthening echo distance: in Example 8.1 (from p. 13 of the study), the trill figure first has a length of three sixteenth notes at an echo distance of two, then a length of six sixteenths at an echo distance of four. Even the quasi-isorhythms are expanded, from 3-based meters like 9, 6, and 12 sixteenth notes to near-multiples of 7: 20, 7 and 15. By the top of page 15 (2:28, period 88), the echo distance has increased to sixteen eighth notes, and Nancarrow is working with phrases of fifteen eighth notes (Example 8.6). At the top of page 17, the echo distance has increased to thirty eighth notes, and the phrase occupies thirty-one.

Example 8.5   Study No. 24, melody of canon 2

Example 8.6   Study No. 24, top system of page 15

Example 8.7   Study No. 24, canon 10, passage with all voices in same tempo

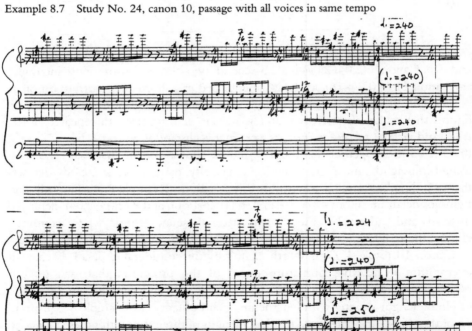

Example 8.8   Study No. 24, variation technique

Example 8.9   Study No. 24, top system of page 22

This canon, constituting the climax and bulk of the study, is also the place for Nancarrow to integrate the soft and loud canons, and he does so on p. 14 (2:18), reducing the dynamics to *p* and breaking down his figures into widely-spaced single notes and chords, imitating the greater sparseness of canons 3, 5 and 7. Immediately following, the repeated staccato eighth notes of canon 3 re-enter for the first time (see Example 8.4).

Here (at 3:03) occurs a phenomenon found nowhere else in Nancarrow's music. Instead of tempos switching between the upper and lower voices at the midpoint, as happens in every other section, all three voices break into the same tempo – ♩. = 240 – for eight measures (two periods), and then switch to the opposite tempos.[1] Even more striking, the voices are in rhythmic unison for those two periods, which means that each voice has to repeat that rhythm three times: i.e., in order for there to be a rhythmic unison when the echo distance is not zero, the first voice must be playing the rhythm for its third time, the second voice for its second time, and the third voice for its first time. Melodically, this passage (see Example 8.7) does nothing more than rotate an eight-pitch row – F♯–G–G♯–B–A–F–E–C♯ – which Nancarrow throws out of phase with the figures that occur between each repetition (otherwise the lines would be in pitch unison as well). This use of an isorhythm and a pitch row combined differently in each of several voices was an ingenious trick Nancarrow had developed in the final section of Study No. 20. Afterward, he points up both the palindromic feel of this canon and the relation between the repeated notes and the trills by bringing back earlier material in variation (Example 8.8). By page 22 (3:44), the echo distance has once again decreased to twenty-two sixteenth notes, and so have the phrase lengths (this is one of the points at which the interval of transposition changes), as evident in Example 8.9. At the bottom of this page, Nancarrow finally begins allowing his phrases to overlap for one last textural explosion before the *subito **pp*** recapitulation. Canon 12 (4:16) is simply a thundering cadence in repeated eighth notes landing on D, the key in which canon 1 appeared to open.

It is instructive to keep in mind that these twelve sections, exposed here at some little length, zip by, with all their contrasts, palindromes, tempo changes, variation devices, isorhythmic patterns, climaxes, twists, turns, and vicissitudes, in a matter of exactly 263 seconds (on the 1750 Arch recording, only 237). The briefest part, what I have called canon 8, lasts less than two seconds. One feels after study of the score that one has emerged from a symphonic work of at least Bartókian dimensions, but these thousands of bewilderingly organized notes actually take up the same timespan as the average Schubert lied: a sobering thought for the analyst, a challenge for the listener.

Study No. 32 – Canon 5/6/7/8

Study No. 32, the canon 5/6/7/8, represents a second step away from Nancarrow's early canonic practice. Study No. 24 created mass effects from indistinguishable voices, but each voice in itself remained linear, separated from its companions by register. In No. 32, pointing ahead to Studies Nos. 41 and 48, Nancarrow begins to destroy the integrity of the individual line, to break each voice up into different registers so that it becomes, perceptually, a plurality of voices. Although no voice ever uses more than one pitch at a time (no triads or octaves here), the opening ten measures establish three registers within the first voice alone, with such clear pitch linkage between noncontiguous phrases that the ear has no reason to hear them as belonging to a single voice (see Example 8.10). As a result, when the other three voices enter (each a perfect fifth higher than the last), the net effect is not one of four voices at different tempos, but of *three* voices in separate registers, not canonically related. For the first time (and not the last), Nancarrow has used a strict canonic technique to subvert canonic perception.

As difficult as the details of this study are to pin down, the structure is extremely clear. Each canonic voice is divided into three sections whose functions are determined by a desire for contrapuntal transparency. In expository section 1 (164 beats long, out of a total of 431; systems 1–14 and 0:00–1:01 in the lowest voice), three registers are distinguished: a high melodic line, made up of both staccato and sustained notes, whose tessitura descends to leave room for the next voice; an intermittent line of sustained notes in the bottom half of the bass clef; and a staccato line of deep bass notes. Section 2 (77 beats, systems 14–20 and 1:01–1:30 in the lowest voice) is a meandering, mostly descending contour of sustained notes in a low register. Section 3 (190 beats, systems 21–36 in the lowest voice, starting

Example 8.10   Study No. 32, opening melody

Example 8.11   Study No. 32, registers of the lowest voice in the three sections

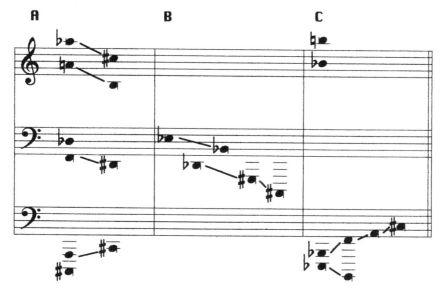

at 1:30) uses both sustained and staccato notes in two registers, initially separated by a chasm of three octaves. Although Nancarrow does not separate the registers by any strict method (the way serialists at the same period were demarcating "bandwidths"), the general register movement, given for the lowest voice, is as given in Example 8.11.

In section 1, where the voices are furthest apart, motives echo in the upper registers from one voice to another at slightly different speeds; it is easy to hear the repetition of motives, but any feeling of canon is destroyed by the fragmentation of the individual lines. Three motives predominate: a rising minor third (heard fifteen times in each voice overall), sometimes interlocked in pairs (A–C, B–D); a rising and descending minor third filled in by step; and a descending major triad. (The linked minor thirds over a bass line create a strong affinity with Studies Nos. 44 and 50.) Clarity is paramount: the first voice has a long rest at the entrance of the third voice, and descends into section two as the fourth voice enters. Section 2 is the "get out of the way" section, the passage in which each voice retires into a background role of sustained bass notes. Section 3 brings back both the motives and the registral separation of section 1, but with a new purpose. Now, approaching the convergence point, the voices are closer together, and echoes become more and more audible. Phrase lengths are increasingly tailored to dovetail a motive from one voice into another. In the final moments of this 161-second piece, as single notes plink upward in the perfect fifths of the transposition levels, the canonic process dawns on the observant listener just in time for the final chord.

No collective effects result here from the closeness of temporal echo, as happened in No. 24. Even the convergence point is marked (as later in No. 37) not by a final attack, but by the unison release of a chord that has almost died away. But like No. 24, No. 32 draws its proportions from the canonic ratios. As the study's structure diagram in Example 8.12 shows, section 1 is never heard in all four voices at once, which would lead to too great melodic complexity. Section 2 is never heard in more than two voices, and never heard alone, for its accompanimental line has little melodic interest in itself. In section 3, however, the sparseness of the melodic motives and decreasing echo distance provide enough clarity for all four voices to coexist.

In order to keep these contrapuntal lines from getting in each other's way, certain proportions must fall into place. Section 1 must occupy exactly the first $\frac{3}{8}$ of the piece, because the fourth voice, being $\frac{5}{8}$ as fast as the first, enters $\frac{3}{8}$ of the way through. Likewise, Sections 2+3 in the fastest voice equals 3 alone in the second (i.e., there is a 5:7 ratio between 2 and (2+3), since the second and fourth voices have a 5:7 tempo ratio). The point is not that Nancarrow worked out these proportions in advance (he may have proceeded more intuitively), but that the canonic structure ultimately determined the sectional proportions of each voice. This is why, despite its spare, one-pitch lines and absence of timbral effects, Study No. 32 falls squarely within the later sound-mass phase of Nancarrow's canonic thinking.

Study No. 33 – Canon $\sqrt{2}/2$

Austere, episodic, and angular, Study No. 33 is one of Nancarrow's strangest and most striking works, and the first canon (within his output and ever) to make use of irrational tempo relationships. If ratios offer a conceptual analogy to pitch intervals, then irrational ratios are analogous to sheer dissonance, irreducible disharmony. The square root of 2 (1.4142136 . . .) is the interval of the equal-tempered tritone, and Nancarrow had already used one of its common approximations, 5:7, in earlier works, notably Study No. 5.

The allure of irrational ratios is more conceptual than audible: theoretically, they ensure that, given steady beats in the voices so related, no attack in one voice will *ever* coincide exactly with *any* attack in the other except at convergence points. In practice, however, just as irrational pitch intervals are "rounded off" by

Example 8.12   Study No. 32, structural determination of section lengths

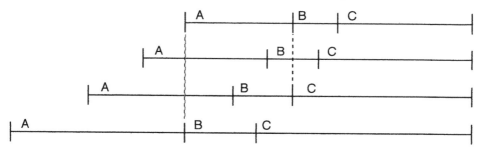

the ear, irrationally-timed attacks eventually come too close together for the ear to distinguish. The square root of two is approximated within 99.97% by the ratio 41:29, and, at tempos (as here) of $\quarternote = 280$ and $\quarternote = 140 \times \sqrt{2}$ (197.9899), after forty-one quarter notes in one voice and twenty-nine in the other the succeeding attacks will differ by less than 1/384th of a second – virtual synchronicity. Still, in the outer sections of this first irrational canon, Nancarrow works with slow, blocklike chords which give the ear as faithful an experience of tempo irrationality as technology can provide.

Like Studies Nos. 22, 24, and 27 before it, No. 33 is not a unitary canon, but a series of distinct canons. The first canon (0:00–0:55, systems 1–13) begins at a convergence point, switches tempos in the middle, and ends when it reaches an (unarticulated) convergence point. This is a canon of regularly paced (save for an occasional rest or subdivision), sustained block chords, mostly made up from widely spaced, five-note diatonic or whole-note scale segments, in irregular alternation with staccato quintuple octaves. The tempos switch after twenty-seven whole-note beats in one voice and nineteen in the other – 27:19 being another approximation of $\sqrt{2}$ – yet already the first chords of system 5 (after seventeen measures in the faster voice and twelve in the slower: 17:12 = 1.416667) sound, to my ears, simultaneous. The striking feature, though, is that there are virtually no identical durations between one attack and the next. Nancarrow overlaps the voices considerably in register (the transposition level is a perfect twelfth, but many of the chords occupy over four octaves), so that one hears, not two easily distinguished voices, but a cumulative, irrational, nonrepeating rhythm unlike anything heard before or since.

Canon 2 (0:55–1:36, systems 14–24) doubles each tempo to half-note values, each voice outlining a lower melody punctuated by high major/major seventh chords, like a couple of bizarrely unpracticed oompah bands. The convergence point here occurs at system 19 (1:15) somewhere in mid-measure, and so is not articulated as such; the point is marked, however, by being the only place at which as many as four seventh chords appear consecutively in either voice, a device which helps the pre-warned recognize the convergence.

Structurally, Canon 3 (1:36–2:41, systems 24–42) reiterates canon 1 by beginning and ending at convergence points with a tempo switch in the middle. This

Example 8.13   Study No. 33, canon approximation

canon's most distinguishing feature is its repeating major thirds which, since the voices are a perfect fifth apart, combine into seventh chords, whose now-broken sonority forms a link with canon 2. Further acceleration is created by moving into staccato quarter notes and eighth notes, and in the second half (starting at 2:11) the canon adds notes in a bass register in an accelerating eighth-note pattern: nineteen eighth notes between attacks, then eighteen, seventeen, sixteen, etc. The accelerating bass lines in all voices make a smooth transition into the lightning-quick bass melody of canon 4, and this device is typical of the procedure of Study No. 33: episode follows episode, but within each texture some element is developed which flows into the next texture and provides continuity.

The final canon (2:41–6:13, systems 42–104) is a monster, comprising eleven or twelve distinguishable sections, occupying about sixty percent of the piece, and proceeding backward nonlinearly through the materials of the earlier canons to make a rough arch form. The rampaging bass melody leans heavily on a sixteenth note leaping to a syncopated repeated note below, a motive developed further in the rest of the canon. This line culminates in a convergence point (3:05) negatively accentuated by a rest – we are not ready for a climax yet – and then a bridge based on the chromatic scale which, articulating a steady quarter-note beat, offers a quick clear glimpse of the $\sqrt{2}$ tempo contrast. Next re-enter elements from three earlier sections: the seventh chords with bass line of canon 2 (3:10), the jumping major thirds of canon 3 (3:16), and the motive leaping downward to syncopated repeated notes heard at this canon's inception.

At this point Nancarrow uses a truly odd technique found nowhere else in his music. At system 56 (3:27) the top voice begins to duplicate within itself *both* voices of canon 2; but instead of using two different tempos, the lower part maintains its relation to the upper part in a notation rounded off to the nearest sixteenth note (see Example 8.13). This means that, when the second voice reaches this material at system 58, the original canon 2 is being played against itself, and the lower part of the upper voice is essentially the same tempo as the higher part of the lower voice, give or take the rounded off sixteenth note:

lower part of upper voice ($\downarrow$ = 280)								
note values	11/16	11/16	23/16	5/16	13/16	5/16	11/16	17/16
durations in seconds	.589	.589	1.232	.268	.696	.268	.589	.911

upper part of lower
voice ($\downarrow$ = 197.9899)

note values		2/4	2/4	4/4	1/4	2/4	1/4	2/4	3/4
durations in seconds		.606	.606	1.212	.303	.606	.303	.606	.909

Four tempos, rather than two, are now implied, but two of them are virtually identical, and the others are related by a 2:1 ratio:

Upper voice	280		
	197.9899 approximated	$\sqrt{2}$	$\dfrac{2}{\sqrt{2}}$
Lower voice	197.9899		
	140 approximated	$\sqrt{2}$	$\dfrac{\sqrt{2}}{1}$

Since to divide by the square root of two twice is the same as to divide by two, the slowest tempo is virtually half the fastest.

The rounding off to sixteenth-note values makes the process approximate, and there are no aural clues given to make the equivalences audible. In the three systems in which the sections overlap in both voices, only two consecutive quarter-note beats are articulated clearly enough so that a forewarned ear *might*, with close attention, hear the effect. But the temptation to multiply structurally the square root of two by itself must have been irresistible, and the section sits smiling in this thorny context like an arcane mathematical joke. What one *can* hear clearly is that the third canon has returned twice briefly in the middle of the fourth, once at its original tempo, then at a slower tempo, so the joke has its formal, unifying and varying purpose, even if the punch-line is hidden.

The remainder of this canon, until the final section, runs through octaves, seventh chords, octaves, single notes, and octaves in rhythms continually thrown off beat by mixing eighths and quarters, sixteenths and eighths, to articulate groups of three, five, seven, nine, and eleven sixteenth or eighth notes. In few Nancarrow studies does the ear become so thoroughly lost as here: in the whirlwind speed of the syncopated sixteenth notes, the striated, unintegrated textures of single notes versus seventh chords, the relation and continuity of the two voices becomes a blur. Yet, as the chaos deepens gradually, it returns to some strange kind of coherence in a series of barely distinguishable stages fascinating to hear. After one final seventh chord arpeggio flourish at system 85 (5:05), the move to slower rhythms begins. The staccato octave line in systems 86 through 93 (in the upper voice) uses only durations of three, five, seven, and ten sixteenth notes, ultimately falling into an expanding quasi-isorhythmic pattern (the pitches do not repeat), shown in Example 8.14. The use of 5, 7, and 10 lends continuity, for 7/5 and 10/7 are approximations of $\sqrt{2}$; the five and seven sixteenth-note values of the slower voice create effectively the same tempo as the seven and ten values of the faster voice, which continues after the former has already passed into the sostenuto final section — another esoteric joke on the tempo-tritone approximation.

At last the five-note block chords re-enter (at 5:39), now stated in dotted halves rather than whole notes, and so one and a third times as fast as the opening

Example 8.14   Study No. 33, 3–5–7 rhythms in canon 4

3	3	5		3	5		5		3	5		5		5		3
5	5	7		5	7		7		5	7		7		7		5
7	7	10		7	10		10		7	10		10		10		7
10																

section. The movement grinds to a halt via an arithmetic ritard, adding one more eighth note's duration to each chord: 6, 7, 8, 9, 10, 11, 12, 13, 14, 14 (*sic*), 16, 30. The final violent flourish is preceded by one last little appearance of the alternating major thirds a fifth apart (6:09), a pre-cadential gesture that calls to my mind the flute/piccolo gesture in the penultimate measures of *Le sacre*. Aside from that one unconscious reference, though, Study No. 33 is a remarkably self-contained work. Primal and primitive as to sonority, mathematically subtle, devoid of reference to jazz, melody, or any known style, the piece lives by its own law, like an isolated musical offering from another planet.

Study No. 36 – Canon 17/18/19/20

If Study No. 24 explored the numbers 14, 15, and 16, Study No. 36 continues the climb up the next four rungs of the overtone ladder. By any reckoning, this is one of Nancarrow's most beautifully structured and transparent works. The four voices are placed *almost* symmetrically: out of 842 half-note beats in each voice, 426 elapse before the convergence point, leaving a denouement of 416. At first the study is easily perceivable as a canon; closer to the synchronization point the voices merge (with exquisite gradualness) into one of Nancarrow's most electrifying textural effects. Half the fun of the second half consists in what Nancarrow does to prevent the ear from falling back into recognition of the canon, to prolong the textural effects as long as possible. Symmetry is the subject of this study: how to create it, how to avoid predictability by subverting it.

The study contains fifty convergence periods, i.e., fifty groups of seventeen half notes in the lowest voice, or fifty groups of twenty half notes in the highest. (For score-marking purposes, the first full convergence period begins halfway through the lowest voice's first measure.) The voices enter at pitch transpositions of, respectively, a major tenth, minor tenth, and major tenth between successive statements: a widely-spaced (and symmetrical) major/major seventh chord. Because of the close temporal spacing, that sonority assumes a greater significance than it could in the canons based on 3:4:5 ratios. Surely Study No. 36 owes some of its transparency, its lightness of texture, to its harmonic basis in the triad, manifested within each individual voice as well as in their cumulative relationship.

Example 8.15   Study No. 36, opening melody

Echoing the transposition levels in a horizontal manner, the opening theme outlines a major/major seventh chord in all accented notes except the first, and is otherwise easily recognizable for its quasi-grace notes, repeated staccatos, and major/minor feel (Example 8.15). The small chromatic runs characteristic of this study are a jazz reference from a style of jazz playing that Nancarrow would have known intimately in the thirties. The resemblance to the pianism of someone like Art Tatum is unmistakable.[2]

This theme is the same length as the opening echo distance, so that it echoes immediately from voice to voice. Throughout the piece, it appears four times in each voice, twice before the convergence point, twice afterward. The second occurrence (1:01 in the lowest voice) comes exactly halfway between the opening and the convergence point, and is twice as fast, expressed in half notes rather than whole notes. Because this is the midpoint, the echo distance is now half what it was at the beginning; and since the theme is twice as fast, this recapitulation preserves the same temporal relationship between voices as at the beginning. In other words, the entire opening section is repeated twice as fast, and a tritone higher. However, after the first twenty-six measures the restated theme departs from its original form. Balancing the themes in the first half, the theme returns in the second at half-note values at m. 618 (2:59, an octave higher than the original statement), then at full values at m. 649 (3:08, a minor sixth higher). The first comes about seventy-two percent of the way through the second half, the last at about eighty-one percent of the way. These occurrences are symmetrical by order, but not in terms of distance from the CP, for reasons that will be discussed below.

Most of Study No. 36 consists of textures built from the theme's simple elements: single staccato or sustained notes, often approached via thirty-second notes expressing either a chromatic scale segment or arpeggio of thirds. This background material is expressed in progressively shorter durations: from double and even quadruple whole notes at the beginning, to a half-note beat at m. 44, to a quarter note at m. 137, to an eighth note at m. 298. Departures from this texture constitute the study's major events. First are the upward-arpeggiated, sustained, root-position, four-note major triads that echo from voice to voice starting at m. 56 (0:31) and again at m. 162 (1:15). In the latter instance, the chord-phrases are sustained just longer than the echo distance so that their occurrences in successive voices overlap. After the CP they return at m. 371 (2:08), but now they are second-position major triads, arpeggiated downward. Having passed through the CP, we are in a looking-glass world, and everything which went up now comes down. This happened in Study No. 1 merely because we had reached the midpoint; here, the transformative moment is a climactic CP of bizarre timbral effects.

The other flashy pre-CP effect is a rising, sixty-seven-note, chromatic glissando involving all four voices (1:37). In order to achieve this effect, Nancarrow has to place smaller glissandos at four points in each voice so that the fourth glissando in the lowest voice can immediately precede the third in the tenor voice, the second in the alto, and the first in the top voice – a formal idea he had first worked with in the tenth canon of Study No. 24. Had he wanted the glisses to coincide, he would have placed them at measures marking a 17:18:19:20 ratio before the CP (for example, eighty, seventy-six, seventy-two and sixty-eight measures before). To make the four-voice glissando continuous between voices, however, he has to place the glissando in the lowest voice a measure *earlier* than that in the tenor voice, which must in turn be a measure earlier than the one in the alto, and so on. So, Nancarrow calculates: delay the second glissando in the lowest voice by one measure, the third by two, the fourth by three, thus, eighty, seventy-seven, seventy-four, and seventy-one measures before the CP. Multiply these distances by $\frac{17}{18}$, $\frac{17}{19}$, and $\frac{17}{20}$ to place each glissando in its corresponding lowest-voice measure, and you come up with the figures (rounded to the nearest 0.1) and the aural shape represented in Example 8.16. Had this mega-glissando occurred closer to the CP, the earlier glisses in the lower three voices would have overlapped it, obscuring its sweep. Had the mega-glissando come earlier, farther from the CP, there would have been gaps between it and the glissandos preceding and following. Nancarrow probably calculated by eye rather than by algebra; but this is the one point in the study at which the effect he wanted is arithmetically convenient, and the placement of all sixteen glissandos (four per voice) is determined by the canon's 17:18:19:20 tempo structure. Form and content have merged.

The upward mega-glissando is balanced in the second half of the study by a downward glissando the same distance after the CP as the upward one was before it: i.e., four convergence periods. In fact, mm. 388–399 are a strict pitch inversion of mm. 240–251, with minor rhythmic alterations.

The convergence point (1:54), dividing point of the piece's symmetry, is one of the most arresting moments in Nancarrow's music. It is approached, starting at m. 300 (1:50), via a series of shorter glissandos and arpeggios, smaller images of the mega-glissando; but now that the echo distance has shrunk to a measure or less, each glissando is immediately echoed in the next voice, and continuity no longer depends on repetition within each voice. In the measure before the CP, all four voices sweep through glissandos to a high register. The climax, starting at the CP, consists of brief thirty-second-note glissandos in all four voices, two per measure, all ending on the same pitch. The first contains eight notes, then there are two seven-note glissandos, three of six notes, four of five notes, five of four notes, six of three notes, seven of two notes, and eight of one note, before a final crashing arpeggio of alternating major and minor thirds – again, timed to sound continuous from voice to voice. The effect of all four voices running through short glissandos in a high register and in different tempos is stunning: even Nancarrow was astonished.

Example 8.16   Study No. 36, diagram of mega-glissando

Distances (in lowest-voice half-notes) of each glissando from the CP:

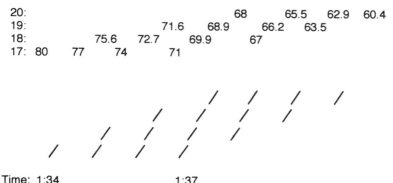

20:						68	65.5	62.9	60.4
19:				71.6	68.9	66.2	63.5	
18:		75.6	72.7	69.9	67	
17:	80	77	74	71	

Time: 1:34   1:37

> Long ago, every so often, I'd get a new surprise – the effect of some combination when it was played on the player piano. For a long time I hadn't had any, but with that particular point in No. 36 . . . I got a shock. Really, I didn't expect it. It's in the score, exactly what I got there, but . . . I liked the result, but it wasn't what I was expecting.[3]

Given a symmetrical denouement after such a dramatic climax, the second half of the piece could quickly fade in interest, but Nancarrow's keen sense of form prevents disappointment. For the next six and a half convergence periods, until m. 454 in the highest voice, Study No. 36 retraces its steps fairly literally. Exceptions are the replacement of little thirty-second-note runs (mm. 285–97) with lines of eighth notes and sixteenth notes; thirty-second notes would have had little effect so soon after such a knock-out climax. At m. 454 (2:25), though, Nancarrow expands the arpeggiated-sustained chords (formerly triads in the first half) to dominant thirteenth sonorities. That is only a hint of what is to come.

At measure 479 in the uppermost voice (2:30), the fun begins. The soprano voice rips upward through a three-octave glissando, sustaining every seventh note for a chord of stacked perfect fifths. This chord sustains for four half-note beats before another three-octave, sixty-fourth-note glissando rips downward, sustaining an irregular six-note chord. When the alto voice follows with the same figure, the soprano punctuates with various staccato chords at the beginning, middle, and end of the glissandos. The alto then provides that service for the tenor, and the tenor for the bass.

The upward-glissando/sustain/downward-glissando pattern occurs four more times in each voice: 187, 198, 209, and 220 half notes after the convergence point. Divide those four numbers by eleven, and you get: seventeen, eighteen, nineteen, and twenty. The fourth pattern in the soprano coincides with the third in the alto, the second in the tenor, and the first in the bass. The placement of the midpoints of these figures, stated in distances of lowest-voice half notes from the CP, is as follows (add 320 to find the measure numbers):

159	168.3	177.7	187			
	167.3	177.2	187	196.8		
		176.6	187	197.4	207.8	
			187	198	209	220

In addition, the amount of time between the glissandos in each pair decreases. The duration in thirty-second-notes of each upward glissando, sustain, and downward glissando is as follows:

		up	sustain	down
half-notes from CP	187	8	52	10
	198	10	36	10
	209	12	16	10
	220	7	0	10

This ensures that each set of glissandos fits inside its predecessor's echo, so that the pile-up at p. 38 (m. 540 in the highest voice, 507 in the lowest) presents two continuous glissandos through all four voices, adjacent both temporally and as to pitch. The overall scheme is diagrammed in Example 8.17. This series of glissandos produces a wavelike effect dominating the music for four convergence periods, from mm. 486 to 540 in the lower voice.

The recapitulation of the opening theme, in half-note values, comes at m. 618 (2:59), but the glissandos have pushed this restatement so far from the CP that only forty half notes elapse before the final, whole-note statement arrives at m. 649 (3:08). In fact, the bass voice is still playing its half-note version when the soprano and alto have already moved on to the whole-note version, making a momentary canon within a canon. In the final statement, each voice plays the first thirteen bars of the theme, then adds a few long notes before dropping out on a final diatonic glissando. Greatly simplified, the overall event-shape of the study could be summarized as in Example 8.18.

Around the central convergence point, the themes and glissandos build a symmetry, skewed by the addition of another up/down glissando, itself symmetrical, which pushes the reappearances of the theme closer to the end of the piece than the first appearances were to the beginning. Within this off-symmetry, events spaced in each voice at multiples of seventeen, eighteen, nineteen, and twenty refer to the convergence point, like windows in an ancient temple placed to point to the solstice and equinoctial positions of the sun. In no other Nancarrow work are the convergence periods so frequently marked by events; out of fifty, about twenty are marked by a glissando through all voices, large staccato chords in more than one voice (periods 35 and 36), or thirty-second notes leading to the down-beat in several voices at once (as in Example 8.19, the opening of periods 24 [1:45] and 28 [2:03], equidistant from the CP). No other study so elegantly demonstrates the arithmetical properties inherent to tempo canon. And yet, precisely because of its structural articulation, Study No. 36 is no sterile exercise, but one of Nancarrow's easiest works to keep one's place in by ear.

Example 8.17   Study No. 36, diagram of interlocking glissandos

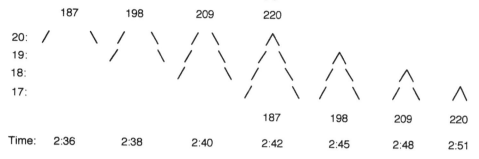

Example 8.18   Study No. 36, structural diagram

T = main theme in whole-note values
t = main theme in half-note values
3 = arpeggiated triads
╱ = glissando through all four voices
c = complex sustained chords
⋀ = upward and downward glissandos
* = convergence point, rapid glissando effects

Study No. 37 – Canon 150 / 160⁵/₇ / 168¾ / 180 / 187½ / 200 / 210 / 225 / 240 / 250 / 262½ / 281¼

Those who value most of all in Nancarrow the elegance of his structures and the audibility of his tempo processes will find Study No. 37 one of the most brilliantly lucid musical works of the twentieth century. Despite the number of voices (three times that of any of the other canons) and sections, this is really one of Nancarrow's simpler canons. Only a little material is needed, sometimes as few as two to five pitches per section, since everything is repeated through twelve voices. But the tempo structure is so intricate that Nancarrow needed only apply a few bold strokes of counterpoint to create transparent, ear-arresting textures of a type never before heard. In addition, Study No. 37 is the longest uninterrupted movement in Nancarrow's output. At 10:27, it exceeds any of his other single piano rolls by over three minutes.

Though the array of twelve tempo numbers looks forbidding, its premise is simple. The tempos express the same proportions as the twelve contiguous pitches of the justly-tuned chromatic scale, as given by Cowell in *New Musical Resources*.

Example 8.19   Study No. 36, articulated convergence periods

(To this day the walls of Nancarrow's studio are lined with charts developed from those in Cowell's book.) Taking the slowest tempo, 150, as C, the tempos correspond to ratios and pitches as follows:

281¼	15:8	B
262½	7:4	B♭
250	5:3	A
240	8:5	A♭
225	3:2	G
210	7:5	F♯
200	4:3	F
187½	5:4	E
180	6:5	E♭
168¾	9:8	D
160⅝	15:14	C♯
150	1:1	C

The give-away of Cowell's influence is the one unorthodox ratio, 15:14 instead of 16:15 or 17:16 for C♯; I have never seen anyone except Cowell use this ratio for a normal half-step. Out of the dozens of tempo contrasts available from super-impositions of these twelve, Nancarrow limits his choices by proceeding in each canon through the twelve-tempo "scale" by either half-steps or minor thirds.

Example 8.20   Study No. 37, tempo structure

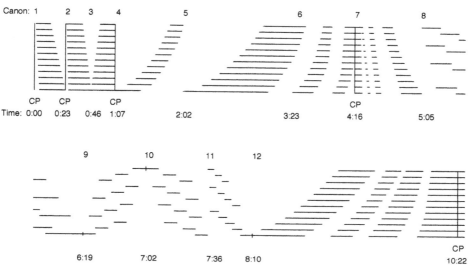

Like Study No. 24, No. 37 is a series of twelve canons. The proportions of these canons are as follows:

canon	percent	canon	percent
1	3.5	7	7.7
2	3.3	8	12.1
3	2.9	9	7.4
4	7.7	10	5.8
5	13.5	11	6.0
6	7.9	12	23.9

The percentages add up to over 100 percent, for canons 5 and 6 – uniquely in Nancarrow's output – overlap by two pages. Example 8.20 shows the overall tempo structure, though a larger scale might be necessary to give a clear idea of the tempo progression of canons 8–11. The diagram, with its curves of silence sculpted from layers of ongoing tempo, bears a striking similarity to Stockhausen's tempo diagram of a section from *Gruppen* in his famous 1957 article ". . . how time passes . . ."[4] In Stockhausen's case, however, the diagram is primarily a theoretical tool for understanding how the music was conceptualized; in Nancarrow's, keeping in mind that the speed increases toward the top of the page, the diagram can be a vivid analogue to what one actually hears.

Convergence points are brilliantly de-emphasized in this study, for this is the work in which Nancarrow learned how to create beautiful effects with convergence points by *omitting* them. CPs occur at pp. 1 (0:00), 4 (0:23), 11 (1:07), 40 (4:16), and 107 (10:27), and every one is marked with either a rest or (in the last case) a continuation of sustained notes. (Admittedly, at p. 40 the rest is only a sixty-fourth note long: this is the one audible CP.)

Example 8.21   Study No. 37, relationship of tempo to transposition level

What the diagram does not reflect, as the score does, is the variations in the coupling of tempo with register. One of the subtlest aspects of the study is the way in which Nancarrow plays with the relations between high and low, fast and slow. In canon 1 the fastest tempo is associated with the highest notes, the slowest tempo with the lowest; canon 2 reverses these relationships. Through canon 4 the tempo becomes faster as the pitch descends, canon 5 accelerates as it ascends. Canons 9 and 11 create the striking effect, less clearly achieved in Study No. 23, of a vivid tempo-to-register proportion: although the music jumps around the keyboard, the lower a passage is, the slower it is. Example 8.21 shows the order of tempo entrances and transposition levels in each voice.

The opening of canon 1 (0:00–0:23, pp. 1–4) is arresting in its simplicity. Each voice of this canon contains only five notes, two breves followed by three whole notes. In a stroke of inspiration, Nancarrow places the convergence point at the beginning on a rest: the first notes heard occur a measure *after* the CP, just as they have begun to spread out temporally. The interval of transposition is a perfect fifth: each voice begins a fifth below the preceding one. As a result of these two conditions, the first gesture is a rippling, downward series of eleven perfect fifths. The rhythm does not quite outline a smooth curve, because the successive tempos do not all have the same proportion. There are four possible "half-steps" in Nancarrow's justly-tuned chromatic scale – 15:14, 16:15, 21:20, and 25:24 – and those ratios account for the slight durational discrepancies between one note and the next. It is an amazing perceptual transformation: the interval variations inherent to just intonation have been graphically translated for the ear in the form of rhythmic quantities.

The second downward ripple is twice as slow as the first, since it is twice as far from the convergence point. The third enters before the second is finished, and by the fifth the lines are so intertwined that contour becomes obscured. The way in which clear processes are piled up until they are obscured, then become clear again as the texture thins, is one of this study's most fascinating properties.

Transposition levels change from canon to canon, but the use of all perfect fifths in this first canon sets up two tendencies for the remainder of the Study. First, the intervals from one voice to the next tend to be equal. In canons 2 and 3 the voices are separated by perfect fourths, in canon 4 by major seconds, in canons 6 and 9 by three sets of minor tenths a perfect fourth apart, in canon 7 by minor thirds. Secondly, the transposition levels include all twelve pitches, except for canons 4 (major second transposition level), 7 (minor third transposition level), and 12 (where the opening notes, as in No. 36, spell out a major/major seventh chord).

The next two canons are as simple as the first, and merely expand its principle. Canon 2 (0:23–0:46, pp. 5–8) is a quasi-inversion of canon 1, with staccato rather than sustained notes. The notes ripple upward instead of downward because the fastest tempo is at bottom rather than top, and the intervals are fourths rather than fifths. The canonic line at first rises chromatically, and each voice remains within a major third.

Canon 3 (0:46–1:07, pp. 8–11) is the retrograde of the process used in canon 1 expressed in major triads. The convergence point – again unheard because it falls on a rest – is at the end rather than beginning. The triads start out in the bass, and the upward ripples become faster and more audible as such as the CP is approached. Thus in the first three canons we have a pattern of original–inversion–retrograde expressed in sustained notes–staccato notes–triads.

Each voice in canon 4 (1:07–2:02, pp. 11–19) is given only two pitches, a half-step apart, and each voice enters a whole-step lower than its predecessor, filling out a chromatic space by minute increments. This is the first of seven canons in which no convergence point is involved, and the spacing is free. Canons 4, 5, and 6 all involve a gradual decrease in the duration between the entrance of one voice and that of the next: this pattern keeps the texture thin at the beginning and places the thickest part near the end of each canon. In canon 4 Nancarrow at first spaces the entrances according to beats of the 150 voice, but when the 150 voice drops out he switches to beats from faster tempos. Expressed in 150-tempo beats, the spacing between voice entrances is:

voice no.	1	2	3	4	5	6	7	8	9	10	11	12
150-beats	10	9	9	7	6	5	4	$3^{33}/_{56}$	$2^{23}/_{56}$	$2^4/_7$	$3^1/_{21}$	

The temporally curved spacing begins with an arithmetical decrease, then broadens at the end; had Nancarrow continued to subtract a beat from each interval, the final two voices would have been only $^1/_5$ of a second apart. (There is no indication why the third and fourth voices are nine beats apart instead of eight as the pattern would imply.)

In canon 5 (2:02–3:32, pp. 19–33) the pitch range is barely expanded, to three chromatically contiguous pitches instead of two, and the voices are widely separated at irregular, mostly whole-tone intervals. Temporally, they are spaced according to a simpler, more linear, if still inconsistent, pattern:

voice no.	1	2	3	4	5	6	7	8	9	10	11	12
150-beats	12	11	10	9	8½	7½	7	6	5½	5	4½	

Canon 6 (3:23–4:16, pp. 32–40) suddenly bursts out of the extreme pitch limitations that each voice has endured thus far. (Note the nine-second overlap with canon 5.) The canonic line consists of eighteen 4/16 measures of a chromatic sixteenth-note line, twenty-two measures of rest, a few more measures of chromatic sixteenths, some thirty-second-note arpeggios, a few more chromatic notes, and a final arpeggio and chromatic scale in thirty-second notes. Again the voices are spaced according to a decreasing duration pattern:

voice no.	1	2	3	4	5	6	7	8	9	10	11	12
150-beats	7¼	$6^3/_{10}$	$5^7/_{10}$	4¾	4½	3½	3	2½	2	1½	1	

The voices are timed such that five of them end with their thirty-second-note rip within a beat of the opening convergence point of canon 7.

This is the most complex canon of the piece, and, for the first time in Nancarrow's output, convergence points occur between some pairs of voices *independently* of other pairs. For example, the 262½ and 281¼ voices converge on a rest at p. 38, the 225 and 281¼ voices at the last measure of p. 39, and the 250 and 262½ voices just before their 17/16 measures on p. 40. Needless to say, these CPs are not an audible feature of the work, merely a theoretical point of interest.

Canon 7 (4:16–5:05, pp. 40–48) is a sort of mid-piece climax, beginning as it does with a convergence point marked by flurries of sixty-fourth notes, reminiscent of Study No. 36. (Actually, the CP itself is on a sixty-fourth-note rest.) First, six *ff* groups containing one, two, three, four, five, and six sixty-fourth notes echo from top to bottom. As they end in the 150-voice, a group of twelve thirty-second notes enters in the 281⅓ voice and flashes through the registers. This is followed, *pianissimo*, by flurries of twelve sixteenth notes each containing an entire cycle of fourths, a beautiful, feathery effect. The remainder of the canonic line is made up of chromatic cells grouped in rhythmic motives mostly nine sixteenth notes long. The line's second half, after a brief rest, climbs through three octaves.

Canon 8 (5:05–6:19, pp. 48–61): Here for the first time successive tempo contrasts begin to move, no longer by "half-steps" through the tempo scale, but by "minor thirds." There are five possible minor third ratios in Nancarrow's tempo scale: 6:5, 7:6, 25:21, 32:27, and 75:64. The ratios that result, therefore, are quite complex. On pp. 52–53, for instance, we hear four voices create a tempo resultant of 27:32:36:42. On pp. 55–57, the resultant can be reduced no further than 450:525:588:700. The canonic line here develops a simple motive from canons 4 and 5 – A–A–G♯–A – by inverting it and punctuating it with major triads. A descending chromatic scale in the middle gives the ear an extra element to listen for. As in canon 6, independent convergence points occur between pairs of voices: between the 168¼ and 262⅓ voices at p. 53, and the 160⁵⁄₇ and 250 voices at p. 56.

It should be clear in Example 8.20 that canon 9 (6:19–7:02, pp. 61–69) reproduces the tempo progression of canon 8 in retrograde, and canon 10 reproduces it in the original, the three canons forming a doubly-nested tempo palindrome. (Actually, the voices are spaced so that what should be the fifth voice enters just before the fourth, rendering the pattern slightly asymmetrical.) This canon's brief, *ff* line transfers the A–A–G♯–A motive to staccato triads.

Canon 10 (7:02–7:36, pp. 69–75) is the *pp* aftermath of *ff* canon 9, with an even briefer subject. Its 25 *pp* staccato notes decorate major triad arpeggios with adjacent chromatic notes.

Canon 11 (7:36–8:10, pp. 75–81), with the briefest canonic line in the study (only 13 beats), reduces the repeated note/triad idea to its pointillistic essence, a sustained triad with two staccato taps. The tempo pattern descends through the tempo scale via major triads rather than minor thirds, while, interestingly enough, the transposition levels *double the intervals of the tempo progression.* Typically holding back in preparation for the climax, all voices stay in the middle of the keyboard.

The finale, canon 12 (8:10–10:27, pp. 82–107), which occupies almost a fourth of the piece, begins with what looks like a twelve-tone fugue in sustained half notes; in fact, in the first twelve-note phrase in the lowest voice, F is repeated once, C is omitted. The half notes last for thirty-one measures, followed by fourteen measures of rest. Next, like the tolling of a bell, come seven repetitions of one pitch, and, since the transposition levels follow three statements of the same major/major seventh chord, that repeated note is always either D, A, F♯, or C♯. Then come twelve more measures of rest, eleven measures of half notes based on the canon's opening motive, and eleven more measures of rest; these rests travel through the tempo structure diagram like diagonal columns of silence, lightening the texture and giving the canon breathing room. Next, as if quoting canon 3, twelve staccato triads appear at half-note intervals, their roots all within a major third in each voice. The canonic line ends with three resounding, *ff* notes – B♭, G♭, A♭, C in the lowest voice. The notes are carefully chosen, for the major/major sevenths on B♭ and G♭ have two notes in common, and so do those on A♭ and C. The result, shown in Example 8.22, is a complexly colored flattened-dominant-

Example 8.22   Study No. 37, final transposition levels

to-tonic feeling, as out of the welter of transpositions the final seventh chord, CGEB, finally emerges in all twelve voices.

Trimpin, who has translated Nancarrow's complete piano rolls into computer MIDI information, can print out the notes of each study on a time/pitch axis. Example 8.23 contains his graphic analysis of canons 7 and 8 from Study No. 37. Note the descending flurries at the beginning of canon 7, and the twelve diagonal smudges – descending chromatic scales – of canon 8. The images suggest natural ice formations, or birds floating in parallel flight: the music looks as beautiful as it sounds. Study No. 37 is one of Nancarrow's most popular works, and its popularity is at least partly due to the fact that Nancarrow's tempo-scale, such a daring conceptual move, is completely convincing to the ear.

Study No. 40 – Canon e/π

Having tested the waters of irrationality in Study No. 33, Nancarrow plunged in Study No. 40 into the first-ever musical use of transcendental numbers, numbers not derivable as roots of algebraic equations. (I like to call this the "Transcendental Canon," for both its numerical properties and its iridescent sound effects.) The tempo ratio between the two voices of No. 40 is that between e (the base of natural logarithms) and π (the ratio of the diameter of a circle to its circumference). In decimal terms, that ratio is 2.7182818279 . . . : 3.1415926536 . . ., and e/π = .86525597925. . . . Were one to reduce that forbidding fraction to an integer ratio, the e:π ratio is well approximated by 13:15 (.86666 . . .), though, more accurately, it lies between 45:52 and 77:89, closer to the latter. The nearest superparticular ratio is 6:7 (.85714 . . .). At the tempo of Study No. 40 the duration difference between thirteen eighth notes at the slower tempo and fifteen at the faster tempo is less than 1/500th of a second. That makes 13:15, as they say, close enough for jazz.

The two-movement form is also unique. This is surely the only piece of music in existence whose second movement is its first movement squared. In the score, Nancarrow indicates that the piece is to be played first on one piano with a duration of 4:00, then, as second movement, on two pianos at once, one with a duration of 4:20, the other entering after 5⅓ systems of the first with a duration of 4:00. (He punched the two identical rolls at once.) In principle, this would

Example 8.23   Study No. 37, Trimpin's MIDI diagram of canons 7 and 8

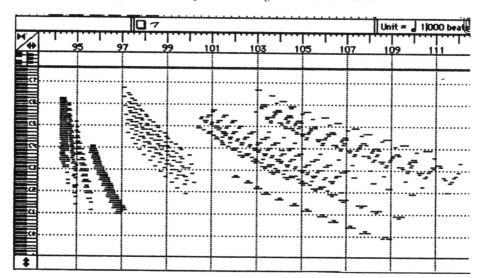

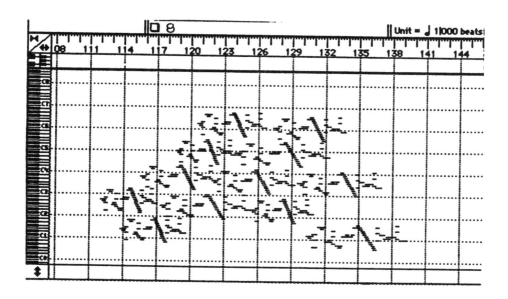

Example 8.24a Study No. 40, motive 2

Example 8.24b Study No. 40, motive 3

Example 8.24c Study No. 40, motive 4

superimpose a 12:13 ratio over the e:π, since 4:00/4:20 = 12/13. Were a 12:13 ratio exactly what Nancarrow wanted, however, he should have notated the faster roll's entrance after 6½ systems rather than 5½. And neither recording follows either the instructions or the notated score perfectly:

	Faster roll duration	Slower roll duration	Proportion
Score instructions:	4:00	4:20	1:1.08333 . . .
Score notation:	79.5 systems	85 systems	1:1.06918 . . .
1750 Arch recording:	3:58	4:26	1:1.11765 . . .
Wergo recording:	4:25	4:40	1:1.0566 . . .

The 1750 Arch recording was made on two pianos. The Wergo recording, made when one piano was in need of repair, uses only one piano, and the two parts were overlaid in the studio; the recording engineer Robert Shumaker could have given Nancarrow any proportion he desired. But any ostensive ratio between the tempos of Nancarrow's two pianos is rendered suspect anyway by the physical fact that, as the paper on the receiving roll increases in thickness, the tempo increases slightly. All of this is to say that the tempo ratio between parts in No. 40b is not something about which we can be theoretically meticulous. It is a real-world problem, not a paper problem.

The canon's transposition level, a major tenth, marks it as the beginning of a group of late, two-voice canons based on that interval: Studies Nos. 40, 41, 43, and 48 (actually, No. 43 uses a major third). Having written groups of canons based on transposition levels of perfect fourths and fifths (Nos. 31, 32, 33, 37) and levels that spelled out major and minor triads and seventh chords (Nos. 24, 34, 36, 37), Nancarrow settled on the major third and its octave as being the preferred interval for his longest and most complex works. The major third offered three advantages. One, particularly apparent in Nos. 40 and 43, is that his ubiquitous minor-third motives, combined in one voice with their major-third transposition in the other (e.g., C–E♭ with E–G) create a bittersweet and ambiguous major/minor harmony. Another, used with great effectiveness in Nos. 41 and 48, is that a tonal motive echoed a major third above heightens tension, since the echo moves toward the sharp side of the scale more dramatically than virtually any other interval would have. The third advantage is simply that, given Nancarrow's emphasis on the major triad, the major third offers a flexible, medium amount of dissonance, allowing him such controls as being able to cadence quasi-tonally at a convergence point on B♭ in one voice and D in the other. The transposition interval subtly colors a canon, and "major third" is the hue of Nancarrow's late, great canons.

Study No. 40, for the amount of frenetic energy it builds up (the first page is ferociously marked *ff sempre*), is one of Nancarrow's most economical works. Four gestures make up almost the piece's entire vocabulary:

1   Sixty-fourth-note glissandos ending in either a sustained note, a sustained triad, or a staccato note. A few of the glissandos are interrupted by eighth-note rests, the glissando resuming after the rest where it would have been had its descent or ascent been continuous.

2   A motive in staccato repeated octaves (Example 8.24a), usually in groups of two and three separated by a minor third, often using the rhythmic motive 3+3+2, which is accented internally by chromatically moving minor thirds as inner voices (hereafter called the 3+3+2 motive).

3   Sometimes merging with the preceding, a Morse-Code-like motive of repeated staccato eighth notes (Example 8.24b), the first in a group often preceded by two chromatically contiguous sixty-fourth notes (hereafter called the repeated-note motive). In general, the "grace-notes" alternate, approaching from above one time and from below the next.

4   A half-step, sixteenth-note trill figure, often in dyads, often in minor thirds, sometimes using larger intervals, and sometimes in contrary motion (Example 8.24c).

At two points in the work (systems 37–38 and 44–45 for the lower voice) the trills turn into widely spaced tremolos, and for much of the second half the second and third ideas are accompanied by octaves in the bass.

In few of Nancarrow's canons is his contrapuntal strategy so clear, even though the details are difficult to describe systematically. Study No. 40 goes through a three-part process, the three phases distinguished by the changing relationship of the two voices.

1   An introduction in which motives are thrown about in quasi-random fashion, making no distinction between the two voices.

2   A middle section in which prolonged ideas in one voice are simultaneously contrasted with different prolonged ideas in the other.

3   An approach to the convergence point in which the two voices merge indistinguishably on the same motives.

In addition, there are isolated passages during phase 2 in which the two voices merge, anticipating phase 3. In general – this is a tendency that began in Study No. 32 and reaches its climax in the last few canons, including No. 49c – Nancarrow preserves clarity by contrasting high-profile material in one voice with low-profile material in the other. Glissandos, in his music, are always high-profile material (as are arpeggios, though none occur here). The repeated-note motive is low profile, though the 3+3+2 motive is usually high-profile. When one voice goes through a series of glissandos, Nancarrow moves the other into the repeated notes, except for an occasional tour de force such as system 64, just before they merge into the same texture, where the glissandos in the two voices overlap.

Phase 1 consists of the first eighty-five measures (1:35 or twenty-nine systems in the lower voice), which are filled with sporadic appearances of the four motives. Once the second voice enters (0:39, system 12), the lines are interwoven so that no high-profile motive in one interferes with a high-profile motive in the other. The glissandos are highly varied, and follow no specific pattern. Where there are three trill figures in a row, they are spaced in a decelerating pattern, the third further from the second than the second is from the first. Fragments of the repeated-note motive articulate eighth-note durations of four, five, seven, and nine, anticipating its behavior later in the piece.

By system 37 (1:59) phase 2 has begun in both voices, and the Achilles and the tortoise metaphor becomes especially applicable. From this point on Nancarrow's strategy is generally: the moment Achilles (the upper voice) catches up with the tortoise (the lower voice), the tortoise moves to something else. For instance, at system 37, when the upper voice reaches the repeated-note motive that the lower voice has been playing, the lower voice switches to tremolos. The lower voice switches back to repeated-note motives, and in systems 39–43 (2:04–2:18) both voices merge in a texture of staccato bass notes. At system 44 (2:18) both voices switch to tremolos. At system 45 (2:23), the upper voice goes back to the repeated-note motive, the lower switches to glissandos, alternately up and down, leading to triads. When, at system 49 (2:37), the upper voice goes through the second tremolo set and then the glissandos, the lower switches to the repeated-note motive with bass-octave accompaniment. And so on. Finally, at system 68 (3:33), Achilles' gain on the tortoise becomes too close (echo distance = seventy-two eighths in the e tempo), and the two voices hammer away in similar texture for almost the remainder of the piece.

This strategy determines the lengths of sections, which must decrease as the convergence point gets closer. The e-voice's first extended repeated-note section (systems 30–37) lasts 227 beats. When this passage occurs in the faster voice, it is counterpointed by a tremolo and repeated-note passage 195 beats long (227 × .865256 = 196.413). The next few sections run as follows:

time	1:35	1:59	2:18	2:37	2:51
systems	30–37	37–43	44–49	49–54	54–58
℮-voice		repeated notes	tremolos + repeated notes	tremolos, glissandos	repeated notes
Beats (℮ tempo)		227	195	146	148
Beats (π tempo)	227	195	146	148	129
π-voice	repeated notes	tremolos + repeated notes	tremolos, glissandos	repeated notes	3+3+2 motive, repeated notes

The arithmetic does not work out consistently (the 146 should be closer to 168), because at system 49 there are a few beats of overlap between the voices. And at the speed of this music, smudging a few beats hardly matters. Overall, each section is about eighty-six percent as long as its predecessor, for a sectional acceleration of about sixteen percent; *taken to its conclusion, the logic of tempo canon results in geometric acceleration on a formal level.*

The long repeated-note section (systems 30–37 in the lower voice) is followed by tremolos which articulate, with minor departures, a repeated 3+2+2 pattern with tremolos and rests (i.e., three eighth notes of tremolo, two of rest, two of tremolo, three of rest, and so on). Next follows another repeated-note passage, the lower voice playing only C♯ and E, as the upper voice reaches its first long repeated-note passage playing only D♯ and F♯. One contrapuntal purpose of this long, random interplay of four notes within a perfect fourth (which anticipates similar effects in the *Two Canons for Ursula*) will become clear in the second movement, No. 40b. Next, tremolos return in the lower voice (Example 8.25, 2:18–2:23), this time interrupted by triads rather than rests, at the point where the first tremolo passage appears in the upper voice. Uncharacteristically of Nancarrow, each set of tremolos is composed of repeating pitch cells in four voices, with a minor-third motive doubled at the octave in the middle.

upper voice	lower voice (triads not included)
|: C E G D F :|	|: G E :|
|: B♭ G A :|	|: G B♭ A :|
|: B♭ G A :|	|: G B♭ A :|
|: E :|	|: C F C :|

The merging of the two voices anticipates the ultimate merging in the final section, and has a vibrant, sparkling sound similar in excitement to the climax of Study No. 36.

Three subsequent high-profile passages are parallel in their effect: series of glissandos leading to either sustained triads (2:23–2:37 and systems 45–49 in the lower voice), major- and minor-third tremolos (3:09–3:24 and systems 60–65 in the lower voice), or trills (4:11–4:15 and systems 80–81 in the lower voice). In the first of these passages, sixteen-note glissandos alternate in direction, and the durations of the triads follow an *almost* accelerative pattern: 9, 10, 8, 7, 6, 5, 4, 3,

Example 8.25   Study No. 40, tremolos

2, 1, 11, 10, the last two followed by forty- and forty-eight-note glissandos. The second passage, starting with an intermittent E–F trill, contains a series of sixteen- or twenty-four-note glissandos (again alternating up and down) leading to major- or minor-third tremolos in a loosely accelerating series: 27 tremolo notes, then 26, 23, 22, 17, 14, 11, 6, 16, 13, 12, 13, 8, 6. The last such passage occurs during phase 3, overlapping with its own echo, and does not accelerate.

At system 68 (3:33), phase 3 begins. The voices become difficult to distinguish by ear, though there are still points at which they undergo simultaneous changes of register and texture (notably the role-switch at the opening of system 74). At system 68, the top line of the upper voice plays octaves on C and E♭ against D and F in the lower voices, an effect similar to the long, "minimalist" section of four pitches at systems 39–43. Meanwhile, the "left hands" are playing a minor-third motive, B♭–A–G, in the upper voice against G–A–B♭ in the lower. At system 74 (3:52) the lower voice brings back the repeated-note motive in octaves, joined at system 75 by the upper voice. The former fix on F and A♭, the latter on A and C. Overlapping slightly, both voices run through another glissando/trill passage at systems 80–81 (4:11). The succeeding material interrupts trill figures with bass octaves in a shimmering clash akin to that of the earlier simultaneous tremolos. Five-octave glissandos in both voices bring the activity to an extremely brief halt; then triads on the 3+3+2 motive provide a strongly tonal cadence as a final flourish.

So much for No. 40a. What about No. 40b? Was No. 40a originally planned to combine in meaningful counterpoint with itself, or did Nancarrow, having once made it clear what was going on, simply want to double the noise? In fact, the counterpoint that went into making No. 40a combine with itself is as ingenious as that of the original canon. First of all, the introduction to No. 40a is sufficiently sparse (and this will be even more true in Studies Nos. 41 and 48) so that the random gestures of the introduction will little interfere with each other. Since in the first movement no more than one glissando is heard at a time, no more than two will coincide in the overlay, no matter at what system the second layer begins. (On the Wergo recording, the second roll's opening glissando at 0:15 is covered by the first roll's glissando of system 5; it is difficult to hear that another voice has entered.)

The key to the counterpoint in phase 2 is the long repeated-note sections, and the fact that the original canon itself alternates between high-profile and low-profile passages. As the repeated notes of the e-voice made an accompaniment for the glissandos of the π-voice in No. 40a, so the section of repeated notes in both voices, systems 39–43, will retreat to accompany the second piano's final introductory glissandos in No. 40b. Then, conversely, the second piano's repeated-note section forms an accompaniment to the first piano's accelerating glissandos and triads (systems 45–49). This, at least, is what happens on the recording, and it depends on one piano's tempo being about eighty-five to eighty-nine percent that of the other (which is not quite true of either recording). If Nancarrow's specification of 12:13, or 92.3%, were adhered to, the repeated-note sections of the two pianos would overlap by over two systems (to little musical point, since the same four pitches would be resounding in both pianos). Nancarrow, of course, has often overridden his own tempo specifications, and was wise to do so in this case.

The intermittent fits of glissandos in No. 40a (systems 45–49, 51–53, 60–68, 80–81) become nearly continuous with the overlayering of No. 40b. The final pages, in which every note in the slower piano is echoed within seconds in the faster at its own pitch level, blurs into indistinguishability (an effect intensified by contrast if the earlier part of the movement is kept fairly distinct). At this point, "more noise" is exactly what Nancarrow wants. The sound ceases to be canonic or even rhythmic; the hectic mass of vibrations is truly transcendental.

Study No. 41 – Canon $$\dfrac{\dfrac{1}{\sqrt[3]{\pi}} \Big/ \sqrt[3]{13/16}}{\dfrac{1}{\sqrt{\pi}} \Big/ \sqrt{2/3}}$$

Studies Nos. 41 and 48 may be, by most obvious standards, Nancarrow's magna opera. They are his longest works: on recording, 20:14 and 19:47 respectively. The tempo ratios of their canons are his most extreme, extreme as to irrationality in No. 41, and as to closeness of proportion in No. 48. They are among his most elaborate forms, though their basic ideas are not complicated. They differ in mood and contrapuntal strategy, yet there are significant parallels in structure and method – even though the canons converge in the middle of No. 41, at the end of No. 48. They are also among Nancarrow's smoothest, least sectional works, defining between them a new concept of musical continuity.

It is easy to imagine Nancarrow's urge, having embarked on the study of irrational tempo ratios, to work with such familiar irrationals as the square root of 2, e, and π. How he arrived at the convoluted ratios of Study No. 41, however, defies imagination. When I asked him where he found them, he replied,

I've been criticized for that by a mathematician. At that time, I was looking for some irrational relationships. I had this book of engineering, and I looked up some relations that were roughly what I wanted. I didn't want something that was so separated they didn't even relate, or too close that you couldn't hear it. I found that those particular numbers, transferred into simple numbers, gave the proportion more or less that I wanted. Not exact, but near enough. This was before I had written a note. And some mathematician wrote me and said, "This is ridiculous, you could have gotten the same proportion with such-and-such a ratio." Not too simple, but not too complicated. But by then I had already done it, and I said, just leave it. And furthermore, what I had was not exactly the ratio the mathematician gave me.[5]

The two voices of No. 41a proceed at a ratio of $1/\sqrt{\pi}$ to $\sqrt{2/3}$: that is, .5641896 . . . to .8164966. . . . That ratio, .6909883 . . ., is about 9:13, or, even closer, 29:42. The two voices of No. 41b are related by a ratio of $1/\sqrt[3]{\pi}$ to $\sqrt[3]{13/16}$, or .6827841 . . . to .9331278. . . . This ratio, .7317155 . . ., is close to 11:15, even closer to 30:41. For rough calculation, superparticular ratios 4:5 and 3:4 are close.

Like the other canons with central convergence points (Nos. 22, 36, and 43), No. 41a is a loose arch structure. Its primary materials are the rushing streams of grace notes which irregularly fill in chromatic scale segments, and a two-voice layer of blues counterpoint, prominent at the beginning, disappearing for awhile, and returning at the end. In the final score Nancarrow uses no meter or barlines, but the punching score is marked off into regular beats, and the music could conceivably be more conventionally renotated; we eventually need an annotated score which will make analytical aspects of the work clearer. Altogether, there are 3770 beats – 2614 before the convergence point, 1156 afterward – each subdivided into three. The CP appears three-quarters of the way through system 92, in the middle of an indistinguishable mass of notes between 5:41 and 5:50.

The opening theme (0:05, system 2), recurs several times in both developed and original forms. Taking off from variations on a three-note pentatonic motive, it is accompanied by two-note motives in a lower voice. The punching score confirms that, taking a dotted eighth note as the basic triplet beat (10.625 mm. equaling one dotted eighth in the published score), it could be renotated as in Example 8.26. Its opening motive generates much of the movement's jazz-flavored melodic material. At system 11 (0:47) this theme returns minus its first motive, and at system 18 (1:13) it is repeated with the lower voice above the higher one. At systems 25–27 (1:42), just before the second voice enters, the main tune is condensed from thirteen to seven beats, and accompanied by an isorhythm of 3+3+2 eighth notes, a jazz polyrhythm clearly suggestive of trumpet and bass, and worthy of Ornette Coleman (Example 8.27). (I cannot help but think that Nancarrow's valve-fingers twitched as he wrote that.) This cheery passage sets up the entrance of the second voice as a dramatic interruption.

The two voices throughout create a fragile, intermittent texture, and Example 8.27 represents their fullest exposition. Following the entrance of the second voice (1:53, system 27) this jazz texture recurs in the lower voice only in small

Example 8.26   Study No. 41a, primary theme (renotated)

Example 8.27   Study No. 41a, variation of primary theme (renotated)

fragments, and after system 37 (lower voice) it drops out completely until after the convergence point (system 92). When it reappears, first in octaves and later in the original undoubled melodies, the various segments are repeated in reverse order: the second (in octaves) at systems 108–109 (6:33), the main theme bringing the movement to a close at systems 130–131 (7:45). The effect is that of a dream boogie-woogie, constantly in danger of fading away, interrupted by tornados of notes which overtake it and drown it out, then subside to allow it a final, tentative reappearance.

The movement's other primary material, the fast-note runs or "Nancarrow licks," seem infinite in their variation, but they reduce easily. Nancarrow created twenty-three patterns, one of two notes, one of three, four, five, six, and so on up to twenty-four; except for transposition level, all of the movement's eleven-note patterns are the same, all the seventeen-note patterns the same, etc. As evident in Example 8.28, many of them fill out, or nearly fill out, a small chromatic scale

Example 8.28   Study No. 41a, selected grace-note patterns

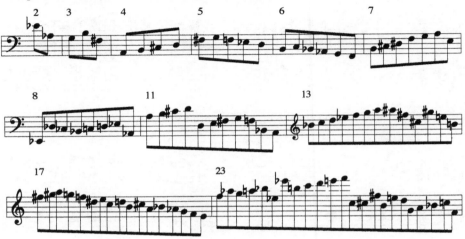

segment, for which purpose they rely heavily on the Nancarrovian major–minor motive C Bb Ab G A B. The 24-figure is a rising chromatic scale, though it sometimes contains more or fewer than twenty-four notes. The entire series of patterns (except for 2 and 3) is found in increasing order, rising from the lowest note on Nancarrow's keyboard (in the lower voice) to the highest (in the higher voice), at systems 93 to 96, the climax and convergence point (5:41–5:50); to the ear, the exact CP is lost in the whirlwind of notes. At large-scale articulation points, where Nancarrow wants more than twenty-four notes, he combines these patterns into longer strings. A breakdown of some of the more prominent strings (in the lower voice) follows:

system	1	21+6+20 (plus a few extra notes)
system	39	20+11+17
system	40	24+13+9+7 (24 lacks three notes)
system	60	9+12+13+16
system	61	22+8
system	129	23+13+15
system	131	20+11+17
system	132	13+9+8+24 (the closing gesture; 13 lacks one note, 24 has a few extra, extending the chromatic scale upward)

Nancarrow will throw his system out the window for a good contour, and several of the strings take liberties in the form of omissions and additions.

In most of the fortissimo figures, Nancarrow sustains the final notes, creating one of this movement's most unusual features: drone notes which sound almost continuously in one voice or the other. Except for systems 16–18, 91–98 (the climax of continuous fast-note runs), scattered moments after the CP, and during the fast-note runs that establish the drones, there is always a single note or octave sustained, with a *ff* attack, in the background. (Actually, some of the notes die

210

Example 8.29   Study No. 41a, counterpoint of drone pitches, systems 1–57

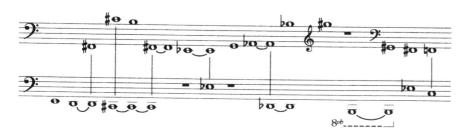

out before their successors arrive.) When sustained tones are present in both voices, the pitches are usually a fourth, a fifth, or perhaps a third apart, creating a subtle background of resonant consonance, the counterpoint of which is laid out in Example 8.29.

The first section (0:00–1:53, systems 1–27, 804 beats), which one could call the exposition, contains only fast-note glissando figures and jazz fragments. Almost all of the glissando figures are stated once each. The two-voice jazz material is *pp*, while most of the fast runs (including all the drone-initiating ones) are *ff*. The next section (at system 28, just after the entrance of the second voice at 1:53) introduces a new idea: irregular *ff* motives in octaves. In the first 48 systems of the lower voice, these are mostly nonrepeating three- to seven-note melodies. At system 46 (3:06), though, the octaves spread alternately into two diverging polyphonic lines in a pattern which is repeated in the lower voice at systems 67 (4:29), 75 (4:57), 102 (6:09), and 105 (6:21). This pattern could be renotated as in Example 8.30. (The fifth "right-hand" octave is sometimes a whole-step lower.) At systems 64, 70, 81, 98, 99, and 121 an isorhythm is derived from this melody's rhythm and octave distribution (with the sixth "left-hand" octave omitted) for use in passages where each "hand" runs repeatedly up a minor third (e.g., G–A–Bb in one "hand," C#–D#–E in the other).

Other, similar octave melodies follow different isorhythms. Bits of two-register octave melody at systems 50 and 54 each engender their own isorhythms to be used later. The latter melody's rhythm is repeated and extended in a one-register melody at system 76. The isorhythm expressed at system 50 (Example 8.31a) is used again at systems 66, 77, and 82 (this last at half tempo) for figures with a

Example 8.30   Study No. 41a, recurring octave melody (renotated)

Example 8.31   Study No. 41a, isorhythms

Example 8.32   Study No. 41a, triad motive

minor-third motive in each "hand." At systems 66 and 82, two statements of the isorhythm are followed by a different one, drawn from the system 54 melody (Example 8.31b). All of these rhythms have in common a sextuple beat interchangeably divided 4+2, 3+3, and 2+4, with notes "tied" to create syncopations. That these patterns exist, invisible in the notation of the final score, demonstrate how often Nancarrow thinks in terms of beats and syncopations even when he does not notate them as such.

The only remaining material is a recurring melodic fragment scattered throughout the movement. Given in Example 8.32, it occurs only once in each voice before the CP, at system 48 (3:15). After the climax it reappears eleven more times in each voice, eight times stated in triads, three as single notes, echoing back and forth and dominating the movement's dénouement. The few remaining triadic melodies (lower voice, systems 51–52, 68, 74, 103, 115) are freely composed, using quarter and half notes with an occasional dotted quarter. The melody at system 74, however, is a major tenth transposition of that at system 68, and this creates an interesting effect, for a major tenth is the study's transposition level. The triads at system 68 are echoed by the higher voice at system 74, coinciding with the new, transposed line. This creates, at system 74 (4:54), a false convergence point – the two voices play the same notes simultaneously at different tempos – a device found nowhere else in Nancarrow's music until the *Two Canons for Ursula*. Afterward, of course, the voices immediately go into different material, and the informed ear barely has time to register the formal pun.

This movement, No. 41a, marks the most significant return to jazz inspiration of Nancarrow's late work prior to Study No. 45 (a "second boogie-woogie suite") – although there were significant jazz touches in Studies Nos. 35 and 36 as well. The mixture of syncopated melody and "Nancarrow licks" at the beginning and end sound strikingly improvisatory, like a pianist tossing off riffs as he works on a theme. The octave melodies, which, when they enter in the lower voice, underlie the jazz theme in the higher, seem conceived as a bass accompaniment. The movement's midsection – systems 78–99 – becomes more obsessive and abstract, like the "outside" stage of a Thelonious Monk solo before the return to the theme. The movement is a deceptively natural fusion of Bartókian arch form, jazz improvisation, and canon.

The second movement, 41b, brilliantly combines acceleration with canon (as will No. 48a). Nancarrow's punching score is marked off into 3468 beats, 2286 before the convergence point, 1182 afterward. The acceleration before the CP and deceleration afterward are articulated by a repeated-note pulse in the bass, reminiscent of Study No. 27's "ontological clock." Much of the movement's excitement and tension derive from the noticeable tempo changes of these underlying beats. The "clock" runs in both voices through the first 1404 beats (to system 54 in the lower voice, 63 in the higher), changing pitch and tempo as follows:

pitch (lower voice)	F♯	B	C	F	E	B	E♭	D	E♭	C	D♭
beats in pulse	10	9	8	7	6	5	4	4	4	3	2
number of notes	10	11	24	20	17	36	38	32	10	54	57
beats in section[6]	100	99	192	140	102	179	152	128	39	161	112

As one can see, the pulse moves through an additive acceleration, though neither the number of pulses nor the length of time on each note follows a consistent pattern. In systems 24–54, the pulse is heard in both voices at once, often at close tempos. The harmonic intervals between pulse pitches, shown in Example 8.33, vary from maximum dissonance to maximum consonance.

The pulse is absent from systems 55–87, but twenty-two beats after the convergence point (4:27, system 88) it reappears in an accelerating pattern. Following the CP, however, it is heard in only one voice at a time: whenever the pulse's echo appears in the slower voice, it drops out in the faster, and when it

Example 8.33   Study No. 41b, counterpoint of pulse pitches

Upper voice:

Lower voice:

Example 8.34   Study No. 41b, pulse progression in second half

Voice:	Pitch:	Pulse-length*:	Number of pulses:	Duration:	
Higher	F	1	8	8	
Lower	C#	1.367	8	10.933	
Higher	B♭	1.333	11	14. 667	
Lower	D	1.822	11	20.044	
Higher	G	2	13	26	
Lower	B	2.733	13	35.533	
Higher	B	3	17	51	
Lower	E♭	4.1	17	69.7	
Higher	E	4.333	9	39 +	
"	F	6	9	54 =	93
Lower	A♭	5.922	9	53.3 +	
"	A	8.2	9	73.8 =	127.1
Higher	A♭	8	4	30 +	
"	E♭	11	13	143 =	173
Lower	C	10.933	4	41 +	
"	G	15.033	13	195.433 =	236.433
Higher	D	16	11	175 +	
"	A♭	19	6	114 +	
"	G	?	1	1=	290
Lower	F#	21.867	11	239.166 +	
"	C	25.967	6	155.8 +	
"	B	?	1	1 =	395.966

*in terms of the higher voice's tempo

runs out in the slower, it comes back in the faster. This back-and-forth discipline imposes a decelerating order on the number of repetitions, and the slowing pulse alternates between the original tempo of the higher voice and its $\frac{41}{30}$-as-slow echo in the lower. Example 8.34 documents this decelerative progression. The durations in the final column, which measure the points at which the pulse switches from one voice to another, increase throughout. The deceleration of the pulse, evident in the furthest right column of numbers, is nearly if not quite linear.

Aside from the pulse, there are six types of gesture in No. 41b:

1   The dramatic, sixty-six-note arpeggio, or "Nancarrow lick," found three times in each voice, twice near the beginning, and once at the end (systems 1, 10, and 130 in the lower voice). Out of the sixty-six, only one pitch (D$\sharp_5$) is repeated, and eight different pitches are sustained from this jagged sweep across the keyboard. At the figure's final appearance in each voice, Nancarrow sustains not a complex chord, but five octaves of a single pitch class – E♭ in the higher voice, B in the lower – to create a semblance of tonic finality.

2   A rhythmic motive of 3+3+2 (sometimes 3+3+2+4) outlined by either staccato chords, sustained chords, staccato triads, or, in one case, single notes (Example 8.35). These are among the rare Nancarrow chords that do not exhibit parallelism. However, two of these passages, one in triads (Example 8.35b), the other in two semi-inversional lines (Example 8.35c), repeat motivically and verbatim at different transpositions.

3   A repeated pitch motive with offbeat neighboring tones either a half-step or a minor third away. This motive can outline either a brief additive accelerando or, more often, a steady pulse of three (eighth-note) beats (Example 8.36a and b). At four points in each voice (systems 30, 35, 109, and 125 in the lower voice), this motive skips through a series of triad arpeggios (Example 8.36c). The final occurrence turns upward rather than down.

4   Glissandos, either chromatic or diatonic, leading to a sustained triad (or occasionally a single note). A brief series of progressively longer glissandos, lacking the final triad or sustained note, occurs once in each voice (lower voice, systems 49–50).

5   Major triad arpeggios, either isolated or leading to an (often complex) chord.

6   The first 58 systems use only these first five motives. At system 59, however, octaves – first double, then triple, then quadruple – inaugurate a new section, and take over the repeated-pitch motive at a speed three times as fast (Example 8.37). In the punching score, the repeated pitch is always notated on the beat, the others on an adjacent ⅓-beat. This figure often moves around to outline diminished seventh chords on its repeated pitch.

The first 600 beats, or 23 systems (0:00–1:18), of No. 41b could be called the exposition, in which the ideas are introduced one by one. Glissandos and arpeggios

Example 8.35a   Study No. 41b, systems 32–34 (renotated)

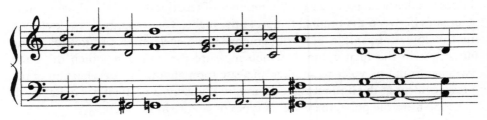

Example 8.35b   Study No. 41b, systems 15, 98, 127 (renotated)

Example 8.35c   Study No. 41b, systems 112, 121 (renotated)

are mostly *ff*, the pulse, chords, and most of the repeated-note motives are *pp*.
At system 24 (1:18) the higher voice enters, and for the next 467 (lower-voice)
beats until system 41, the lower voice strips down to little more than the pulse,
generally staying out of the way of the second voice's exposition. The second
voice's relatively quiescent period lasts until system 53 (2:47), whereafter the two
voices freely trade *ff* glissandos, arpeggios, and chords over the *pp* pulse.

A transition to a new texture takes place from beats 1538 to 1642 (lower
voice: 3:04–3:15, systems 59–63), where the first octaves enter on a decelerating
chromatic scale in the lower voice (just as the upper voice starts its progressively
longer glissandos). From beats 1642 to 2286 (3:15–4:27, systems 63–87), the
music, entirely *ff*, alternates irregularly between quadruple octaves stating the
repeated-note motive and the chords in the 3+3+2 pattern one and a half times
as fast as in the exposition (i.e., 4+4+2⅔ beats rather than 6+6+4). Nancarrow
strives for maximum dissonance in this passage, usually emphasizing in the
lower-voice octaves a pitch a half-step away from the one in the higher voice.
Major-triad arpeggios are freely interspersed among the octaves and chords. A
final glissando at system 87 rips its way up to the convergence point (4:27),
landing on a brief, dramatic pause.

The final third of the movement moves gradually from a whirlwind of
glissandos and arpeggios back to the more discrete motivic materials, replacing the

Example 8.36   Study No. 41b, repeated-pitch motives (renotated)

Example 8.37   Study No. 41b, repeated-pitch octaves (system 76 renotated)

quadruple octaves with double octaves and, gradually, single notes once again. The first six systems contain only arpeggios, scales, and the repeated-note pulse. Nancarrow borrows the drone technique from No. 41a and sustains the lowest note of each arpeggio and glissando until the next occurs, creating two background chromatic bass lines through system 93 (4:44). Beginning at system 92 (4:40) fragments of the repeated-note motive return, in both triple-speed octaves and the original form. Several phrases from the first half are brought back, most of them cited above. And, as mentioned, the pulse resumes at system 88 (4:29) and continues, alternating between voices and decelerating by steps, until the very last note.

As for the simultaneous playing of Nos. 41 a and b to make No. 41c, careful synchronization is difficult when attempted "live." In the score, Nancarrow is not specific about when No. 41b should begin. His diagram suggests that the center of 41b should fall slightly before the center of 41a and seems to imply (given that the convergence points come at proportionately different places in the two movements) that 41b's CP should fall around 41a's system 83. That is about where it occurs on the "live" 1750 Arch recording, in which 41b enters at the beginning of 41a's system 13. On the Wergo recording, 41b begins and ends about 30 seconds later than on 1750 Arch:

	41b enters	41b drops out
1750 Arch recording	system 13	system 120
Wergo recording	system 20	system 131

The Wergo recording achieves the salutary effect that the brief, climactic pauses in both movements – 5:50 in 41a and 4:27 in 41b – coincide perfectly, a dramatic moment that would be nearly impossible to capture outside the recording studio.

However, Nancarrow might respond with his favorite "It doesn't matter much," since varied contrast rather than synchronicity is the general principle of all three movements. The low bass pulse and soft, sustained chords of 41b mix well with the high, pointillistic jazz material of 41a, and the arpeggios of one and "Nancarrow licks" of the other fuse the two for the ear. At the climaxes, No. 41a's minor-third motives in octaves also blend with No. 41b's octave repeated-note motives. The *synchronous* merging of two-piano textures is a subtlety which will occupy Nancarrow more fully in Study No. 48.

Study No. 43 – Canon 24/25

In its elegantly asymmetrical working out of an arch form involving close tempo ratios, Study No. 43 continues the form and method of No. 36. (Remember that it was originally numbered No. 38; the two were chronologically closer than the numbering indicates. Nancarrow seems to have begun No. 43 *before* Nos. 40 and 41, which are considerably more complex.) This 24/25 canon is more nearly palindromic than No. 36; no extravagant post-CP event appears to throw the symmetry off balance. Instead, the textures and motives of the first half of the piece return in almost exact reverse order in the second half, though varied, some of them more elaborately developed, others shortened. If the canons of Nos. 36, 37, 40, and 41 are mountain ranges, No. 43 is a landscape of rolling hills, less dramatic, but brooding nonetheless.

The striking form of No. 43 results from the tempo switch device Nancarrow had discovered in No. 24. The slower, lower 24-tempo voice starts first, as usual, and after the CP (m. 177 out of 483) the 25-voice gets ahead. Then, however, the tempos switch at m. 228, causing a second CP at m. 281, and the lower voice, now in the 25 tempo, ends first. Studies Nos. 43 and 22 are the only ones which neither begin nor end with a convergence point, but which contain more than one internally. Interestingly, Study No. 22 is a fairly strict palindrome, and No. 43 is palindromic in spirit, although there are no actual retrograde passages.

For once, the dénouement following the CPs is longer than the original exposition; the proportions of the piece are shown in Example 8.38. Because of the close tempo relationship between the two voices – 24:25 – the piece spends about a third of its duration with an echo distance of twelve or fewer quick beats. In pitch, as well, the voices are unusually close, transposed by only a major third. At both CPs, where the voices appear to be playing in parallel major thirds,

Example 8.38   Study No. 43, proportions

	Exposition	CP	CP	Denouement
Convergence Periods*:	50	24		68.5
Beats:	1198	588		1643

*given in quarter notes

Nancarrow uses diminished seventh chord arpeggios, their harmonic color "neutralized" by the diminished seventh a major third away in the other voice. No other of Nancarrow's canons keep its voices this close in both pitch and time for so long, and this gives the study its distinctive sound. In addition, the entire study plays with the tension between the major third of the transposition level and the minor third of Nancarrow's favorite motive. Major and minor thirds permeate the piece like the warp and woof of its fabric, the minor third running horizontally through the motives of each voice, the major third running vertically between the voices. And both intervals are prominent in the primary motives of the piece.

The study's palindromic form is charted in Example 8.39, and its primary motives are shown in Example 8.40. The canon begins simply with a theme made from single staccato and sustained notes, covering over three octaves in range (Example 8.40a). The major/minor triad spelled out in mm. 8–9 (A♯ C♯ F♯ A) becomes an important feature of the work. This melody, referred to as Melody A in Example 8.39, leads to what I will call the triad motive (B), which follows a major triad with either one or two adjacent steps, the second making a minor third (Example 8.40b). Descents and ascents through triads (C) provide relief from both the chromaticism and the rhythmic irregularity (Example 8.40c).

At m. 37 (0:41 in the lower voice) an extended period of staccato repeated notes begins, decorated by half-step neighbor-notes and using an additive acceleration motive (D, Example 8.40d). This leads to a recapitulation of the A melody and the triad motive. At m. 94, Nancarrow develops the major/minor motive from A, first descending, then ascending in expanded, twenty-six-note chains (E) which allow us to hear the 24:25 ratio unadorned (Example 8.41). This row appears partly in inversion as early as m. 94 (1:19), and starting at m. 125 (1:47) it becomes the basis of quick, eighth-note arpeggios. Note that the triads it generates ascend via major seconds; this ascent will soon take on new significance. Interspersed among the arpeggios are staccato triads outlining minor thirds (G, Example 8.40e). These lead to subclimactic arpeggios on diatonic thirteenth chords (H).

The build to the first convergence point begins with a section (1:59, mm. 137–149) in which Nancarrow plays with half-step motives (I) reminiscent of tonalized Webern, expanded in Nancarrovian language into major triads and octaves (Example 8.42). At m. 150 (2:11) octaves begin a minor-third motive in eighth-note tremolos (J), anticipating the long section between the CPs. Then, at 158 (2:17), minor-third tremolos (K) begin. The lowest voice rumbles in minor-third alternation, echoed a major third higher to create major/minor triads

Example 8.39   Study No. 43, near–palindromic arch form

Before Convergence Points				After Convergence Points	
Mm.	Beats		Description	Beats	Mm.
1-11	84	A	Melody	117	472-483
12-14	51	B	Triad motive	57	468-471
15-22	54	A	Melody	78	459-467
23-36	118	C	Descent through triads to triad motive	73	450-458
		C'	Ascent through triads to triad motive	178	428-449
37-58	107	D	Repeated notes with half-step neighbors	152	406-427
59-73	70	A	Melody with major/minor motive	98	393-405
74-76	22	B	Triads leading to triad motive	30	391-392
77-93	88		ascent (descent) through fourths, descent through triads (absent), scale	63	380-390
		E	major/minor motive	35	375-379
		B	triad motive	32	371-374
		C	scale, ascent through triads	46	364-370
94-97	28	E	major/minor motive	18	362-363
98-102	40	B	triad motive	33	358-361
	5		rest	7	
103-110	63	E	26-note ascending runs with triad motive	68	350-357
111-120	60	F	staccato 3rd motives leading to octaves	70	345-349
			rest	8	
121-124	20	G	ascending (desc.) 3rd motive in triads	22	342-344
	3		rest	4	
125-126	27	E	ascending (desc.) 8th-note arpeggios, based on 26-note run: 15, 13, 11	31	339-341
	9		rest	7	
127-134	43	G	staccato triads: 3rd + major/minor motives	57	333-338
	6		rest		
135-136	12	H	ascending (desc.) diatonic 13th chord	11	332
	6		rest	15	
137-149	90	I	triads followed by octaves; half-step motive	83	322-331
150-157	39	J	minor 3rd motive in octaves		
		H'	minor triad arpeggio	4	321
158-168	78	K	tremolo minor thirds, rising whole-tone scale	87	307-320
	2		rest	1	
169-175	60	JH	3rd motive in octaves, ascending 8th-note 13th chord at 172 (glissandos)	100	292-306
176	13	H"	ascending (desc.) diminished 7th chord(s)	58	281-291

Convergence points: mm. 177 and 281
Mm. 177-280   588 beats   J 3rd motive in octaves

Items in parentheses indicate alternatives different in second half.

Example 8.40a   Study No. 43, opening theme (original notation)

Example 8.40b   Study No. 43, motive B

Example 8.40c   Study No. 43, motive C

Example 8.40d   Study No. 43, motive D

Example 8.40e   Study No. 43, staccato-triad motive (G)

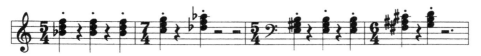

Example 8.41   Study No. 43, 26-note chains

Example 8.42   Study No. 43, half-step motives

Example 8.43   Study No. 43, minor-third tremolos

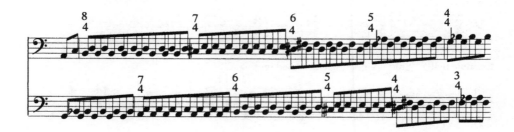

between the two voices. These figures, in additively accelerating durations, ascend by major seconds, just as the triads ascended in the twenty-six-note row of m. 103 (Example 8.43). The ascent climbs through the whole-tone scale, and, since there are no minor thirds in this scale, both whole-tone scales are present in each voice. Actually, this passage is so low on the piano that the major/minor sound is hardly heard as such. Instead, one hears an impressively restless growl of a kind unanticipated even among Nancarrow's timbral effects. Minor thirds return to the octaves (J) at m. 168 (2:26), and a couple of diminished-seventh arpeggios bring us to the first convergence point (2:36).

The 24-convergence-period section between the two convergence points consists entirely of eighth-note tremolos outlining a minor-third motive (J). First the rhythm is sporadic, and both voices are in high register. Starting at m. 199 (2:52), the voices progressively descend into the bass. By m. 224 the rhythm is continuous, and at m. 245 the voices begin leaping in register, the higher voice jumping upward when the lower voice leaps downward and vice versa. Two ascending diminished-seventh arpeggios in eighth notes lead to the first CP; after the second, a myriad descending such arpeggios in sixteenth notes lead away from it, and the piece retraces its steps back to melody A.

The piece's hairpin form can be read down the left side of Example 8.39 for the first fifty convergence periods and back up on the right for the last sixty-nine and a half, with the section between CPs at the bottom as a turning point. It is easy to see that most of the ideas, especially those from the work's first quarter, are developed at greater length in the dénouement than in the exposition. As in Study No. 36 (echoing Study No. 1), the CPs have a looking-glass effect. The triad motives that rose in the first half are answered in the second by their falling counterparts; the triads and staccato notes that fell 5–3–1 now rise 1–3–5; the downward arpeggios now turn upward and vice versa. With its thin, crisp textures and ear-catching melodic turns, this is the simplest of the late canons, a kind of textbook case of a tempo canon with only one structural irregularity. Reduction to such a transparent context, however, only enhances the charm of Nancarrow's melodic idiosyncrasies.

Study No. 48 – Canon 60/61

In Study No. 48 Nancarrow expands the combined use of canon and acceleration which he had experimented with in No. 41b. Shorter than No. 41 by half a minute, Study No. 48 is his third canon to use two pianos, and the second (after No. 41) in which the third movement consists of the first two played simultaneously. In No. 41, however, the second movement was to be spaced symmetrically within the temporal frame of the first; here the movements are timed to end together at their convergence points, making synchronization crucial. Study No. 48 also uses Nancarrow's closest-ever tempo ratio, a ratio so small that the ear cannot distinguish that a gesture's echo in the 61 voice is any faster than its statement in the 60 voice. What one *can* hear is the exquisitely slow change in the echo distance, which decreases from (in the case of No. 48a) a mere eight seconds at the beginning to zero over the course of six and a half minutes.

It is difficult to derive precise data on the rhythm of No. 48 from the final score. However, the punching score (which Nancarrow kindly presented to me) indicates that No. 48a plays off of a background beat that accelerates throughout the movement. The manuscript is marked off into 1500 beats, each containing six subdivisions. At the beginning, a tempo is articulated that corresponds to ten and a half of those subdivisions. After 172 on the 1500 scale, the tempo accelerates to ten subdivisions, then nine and a half at 314, nine at 405, and so on down to one. In other words, the tempo increases (and beat-duration decreases) by ratios of 21, 20, 19, 18, 17 . . . 4, 3, 2. Nancarrow marks in the manuscript (though not in the final score) the points at which one beat changes to another. In most cases, the new beat is not manifested until several beats of rest have passed, but the marking usually coincides with a *ff* figure: often an arpeggio, sometimes an erratic rhythmic motive of a type found only at these junctures. Such points occur as shown in Example 8.44.

As one can see, the length of a section through which a given beat predominates decreases throughout the movement, but in neither a linear nor a systematic fashion. Everything in this movement points to a gradual acceleration, but few aspects of it are systematically ordered. That acceleration is perceptually curved, far more audible toward the end than at the beginning. Logarithmically adjusted to indicate actual perceptual change, the curve could be graphed as in Example 8.45. (The "B-sections" are explained below.) Some seventy percent of the perceived tempo change takes place in the last fifth of the movement. No one is likely to notice the move from the 10½-tempo to the 10-tempo, hidden as it is by extraneous material, as an acceleration. By the end, though, the tempo moves through a 7/6/5/4/3/2 progression within a few seconds, with obvious effect. The decrease in length of sections exaggerates the built-in nonlinear character of the additive accelerando.

This underlying beat-acceleration is manifested in a background texture of voices leaping pointillistically between two widely separated registers, running through the piece like the "ontological clock" of Study No. 27 – only this time the clock's tempo accelerates by steps. Renotated to show the duration values evident in the manuscript, this texture appears at the beginning as shown in Example 8.46. This material, which crescendos by stages from *pp* to *ff* throughout the course of the piece, consists primarily of grace-noted single notes ticking off the beats, often spelling motives on the minor third (evident in the above example), and interlaced with staccato triads. However, eight brief passages (the B sections of Example 8.45) increase the background's activity level. These passages play off the current beat with rhythmic motives derived from the beat-length, such as a 5+2 or 3+2+2 motive in the seven-beat section, or a 2+2+1 motive for the five-beat one. Three such passages are renotated in Example 8.47.

Example 8.44   Study No. 48a, placement of tempo shifts

Beat duration:	Number marked in MS:	Duration of section:	Page beat begins:	Signaled by:	Timing (Wergo):
10.5	4	168	2	*ff* arpeggio	0:00
10	172	143	16	*ff* irregular motive	0:49
9.5	315	90	30	*pp* arpeggio	1:31
9	405	111	35	*ff* arpeggio	1:56
8.5	516	104	45	*ff* irregular motive	2:25
8	620	94	54	*ff* arpeggio	2:53
7.5	714	98	62	*ff* irregular motive	3:17
7	812	85	70	*ff* octaves	3:41
6.5	897	78	78	*ff* arpeggio	4:04
6	975	79	85	*ff* irregular motive	4:23
5.5	1054	72?	91	*ff* arpeggio	4:44
5	1126?*	68?	100	*ff* motive + octaves	5:01
4.5	1194	58	103	*ff* octaves	5:18
4	1252	54	108	*ff* arpeggio	5:32
3.5	1306	46	112	*ff* irregular motive	5:44
3	1352	40	116	*ff* arpeggio	5:55
2.5	1392	32	120	*ff* arpeggio	6:06
2	1424	29	122	*ff* arpeggio	6:15
1.5	1453	23	125	*ff* arpeggio	6:23
1	1476	24	127	*ff* arpeggio	6:28

*Nancarrow neglected to mark the onset of the 5-beat in both of two MS scores. Timings refer to the (usually) *ff* figure that signals the onset of each new beat, not to the first appearance of that beat.

Example 8.45   Study No. 48a, perceived tempo

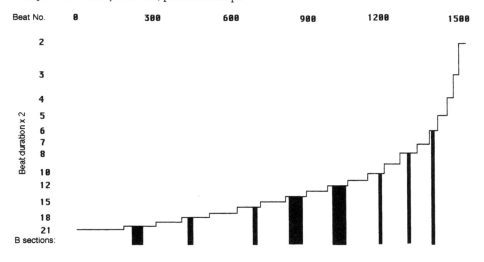

225

Example 8.46   Study No. 48a, opening "clock" material (renotated)

The eight sections, creating a kind of ongoing ABABABA form, are outlined in Example 8.48.

The first B section introduces triads into the texture (which thereafter remain). The second introduces a bass open-position arpeggiated triad motive (Example 8.49) which increases in frequency and becomes important in No. 48b. Note that these more active passages occur only during sections in which the beat-duration is a whole number of subdivisions: i.e., during the 9-beat and 8-beat, but not the 8½-beat or 7½-beat. For whatever reason, Nancarrow will divide 9 into 4+3+2 and 5 into 2+2+1, but he avoids dividing fractional-length beats into fractional subdivisions. By the time the tempo reaches the 2-beat, it is too quick to subdivide, and the distinction between A and B passages disappears.

So much for the background, or low-profile, part of the canon. Since the tempo ratio between the two voices is so close (60:61), and the voices skip through such wide registers, the background textures of the two voices cannot be distinguished by ear alone. The echo of the lower voice's steady beat a few seconds later in the higher voice often sounds like a continuation of the same beat, and the motives are too neutral to catch the ear. So within this, so to speak, "pointillist soup" Nancarrow places the gestures that *can* be heard echoing from one voice to the other: arpeggios, tremolos, stride octave patterns, and rhythmically irregular minor-third motives, most of them distinguished from the surrounding material by being louder or softer.

Most frequent are the arpeggios (or rather, jagged-contour "Nancarrow licks") whose speed is either one note per marked subdivision (six per beat) or occasionally twice that. This means that, at the beginning, the arpeggios are ten and a half times as fast as the steady-beat material, which latter gradually accelerates until it is the same speed the arpeggios have been all along. This is one of the ways in which a disparate variety of motives at the beginning becomes more and more unified as the piece progresses.

Example 8.47 Study No. 48a, openings of selected B sections (renotated)

10-beat (1:05)

7-beat (3:55)

5-beat (5:11)

Example 8.48   Study No. 48a, chart of B sections

Page of score on which section begins:	Lasts from X to X beat*:	Duration in beats*:	Beat-duration used:	Timings (Wergo)+:
p. 19	208 - 259	52	10	1:02 - 1:21
p. 37	423 - 446	24	9	2:01 - 2:12
p. 59	679 - 700	22	8	3:09 - 3:17
p. 70	812 - 883	72	7	3:42 - 4:04
p. 85	990 - 1042	53	6	4:27 - 4:43
p. 100	1164 - 1177	14	5	5:11 - 5:15
p. 109	1271 - 1282	12	4	5:36 - 5:40
p. 116	1355 - 1362	8	3	5:56 - 5:59

*Refers to beats marked up to 1500 in the punching score, not to the variable-length beat.
+Timings indicate the duration through both voices.

Example 8.49   Study No. 48a, triad motive

(9-beat)

Example 8.50   Study No. 48a, arpeggio source figures

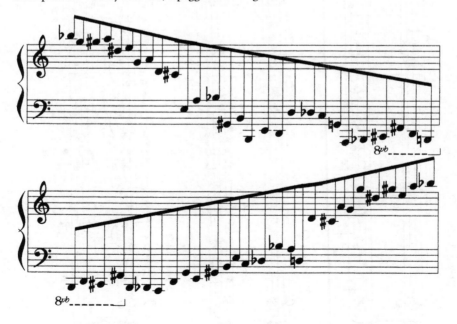

Of the first six "Nancarrow licks," five are freely composed. The exception is that the figure on p. 35 (1:56) is a $\textbf{\textit{ff}}$ repetition of the $\textbf{\textit{pp}}$ arpeggio from p. 28 (1:33). Afterward, Nancarrow becomes more systematic. Of the forty arpeggios in No. 48a, twenty-four are drawn from two figures (Example 8.50) stated at pp. 41 (2:15) and 43 (2:20), both using the same twenty-eight pitches, and the second an *almost*-retrograde of the first. From p. 41 on, all $\textbf{\textit{pp}}$ arpeggio figures are drawn from these figures in alternating pairs: e.g., on pp. 67–68 a thirteen-note fragment from the descending form of the row is quickly followed by a thirteen-note fragment from the ascending form. The two figures of each pair always contain the same number of notes, decreasing by one with each pair. These figures are spaced as follows:

pages	notes	time	pages	notes	time
56–57	14+14	3:04	117	7+7	6:00
67–68	13+13	3:37	121	6+6	6:11
81–82	12+12	4:17	123	5+5	6:19
93	11+11	4:51	125	4+4	6:24
101–02	10+10	5:16	126	3+3	6:27
108	9+9	5:43	127	2+2	6:29
113	8+8	5:49			

Times given are for the points where the second voice's first figure coincides with the first voice's second.

They are always timed in such a way that the second arpeggio of each pair in the lower voice coincides with the first arpeggio in the higher voice. Thus, the distance between the arpeggios of each pair decreases throughout the work, and is always $\frac{1}{61}$ of the distance to the final convergence point. By the last three pairs, that distance is so small that each pair is combined into a single figure. The distance between pairs also decreases in an irregularly accelerating pattern; in terms of the number sequence in the manuscript, those distances run 171⅙, 130, 160, 135, 98⅓, 80⅔, 56, 50, 40, 30, 20, 10, and 8 (measured, in reference to the lower voice, from the midpoints at which the arpeggios coincide). All other arpeggios from p. 41 on are $\textbf{\textit{ff}}$ and are inserted at the points where a new beat-duration begins; they are freely composed, often around triads, except for the figure on p.77, which is a $\textbf{\textit{ff}}$ repeat of the $\textbf{\textit{pp}}$ arpeggio on p. 8.

One pair of the arpeggio fragments can be seen in Example 8.51, which is a facsimile of p. 51 from Nancarrow's punching score. The page offers some insight into Nancarrow's working method. The arpeggios appear in the lower system, beginning at beats 1317 and 1320. The fragment that appears in the lower voice at 1320 coincides with that in the upper voice at 1317. Since the voices converge at beat 1500, these points are 183 (1500 − 1317) and 180 (1500 − 1320) beats before the convergence point. 183/180 = 61/60. Also on this page are found the points (in the upper system) in each voice where the 4-beat changes to the 3½-beat,

Example 8.51   Study No. 48a, page 51 from Nancarrow's manuscript

marked (3½ − 3½); vertical lines beneath the subdivisions mark off the beat durations. The long vertical lines connecting the two voices at 1310 and 1320 in the lower voice show coincident subdivisions, which occur every 60 subdivisions (10 beats) in the lower part, every 61 subdivisions in the higher. Short lines drawn from the noteheads to the subdivision markings keep track of where each note belongs. Other numbers beneath the staff indicate dynamic markings in player-piano language. The marking (6–4–2) indicates which holes to punch for *ff*, (−4−) for *mf*, 0 for *pp*, and (−6−) for *f*. The circle with a plus sign in it (+) is Nancarrow's sign for the endpoint of a note previously sustained. The portion of the piece represented here falls between 5:44 and 5:51 on the Wergo recording.

The coincident timing of arpeggios marks a major contrapuntal difference between Studies Nos. 41 and 48. There is no convergence period in No. 41, since the tempo ratio is irrational; theoretically, no note in one voice will ever coincide with a note in the other except at the CP. Therefore, Nancarrow makes few attempts in No. 41 to create collective, merging effects between the two voices (nor between the superimposed movements of No. 41c), and they rarely hit the same type of gesture at the same time. Study No. 48, however, has a relatively long convergence period of ten beats of the slower voice. Nancarrow uses that convergence period, and, in all three movements, makes the coincident timing of similar gestures an important structural feature. If one were to draw a line between the extremes of chaos and synchronicity in Nancarrow's canonic technique, with Study No. 41 at the chaos end and No. 36 at the other, No. 48 would lie in between.

The loud tremolos that blare forth from the texture, perhaps the most distinctive feature of No. 48a, progress in similarly near-systematic fashion. Over the first seventy pages, six sets of tremolos appear at various points, progressing upward across the keyboard. Each pair is a whole step narrower than its predecessor, from an octave down to a major second (except that what should be a minor sixth is major), and (save for the last) also longer in duration. (See Example 8.52a.) At p. 71, tremolos − now decreased to a half-step and better called trills − ascend as in Example 8.52b. From p. 85 on, the trills/tremolos occur as shown in Example 8.52c, decreasing in duration and accelerating in frequency, the second of each pair in the lower voice coinciding with the first in the higher voice. Transpose the first tremolo of each pair up a major tenth, compare it to the second, and you will see what effects Nancarrow intended for the combination of the two voices: fluttering chromatic clusters in the first three cases, dominant seventh chords in the fourth and fifth.

What remains of this movement's raw materials is the stride-octave lines and special rhythmically irregular motives, most of which are placed, signal-like, at the onsets of new tempos. (These parallel the irregular octave motives of No. 41a but now serve a specific formal purpose.) More than any other elements, these echo audibly from one voice to the other, and thus serve as counters for keeping track of the slowly decreasing echo distance. All of them are fortissimo, and most of them use a prominent B–C♯–D motive (or some transposition thereof), its placement

Example 8.52   Study No. 48a, pattern of trills and tremolos

*all pages, times, and pitches given for lower voice

within the phrase highly varied. Example 8.53 gives eight of these gestures, each renotated to provide an accurate idea of rhythmic placement with reference to Nancarrow's punching score. In the last few pages, at the peak of the overall accelerando, minor-third motives, stride-octave figures, *pp* and *ff* "Nancarrow licks," and trills merge at speeds so fast as to become nearly indistinguishable. They lead to a final major-triad arpeggio on F in the lower voice, A in the higher, which then cadences after an infinitesimal pause on B♭ and D. Thus No. 48a.

Movement No. 48b (notated in the final score as the upper two voices of No. 48c) has no underlying accelerando to parallel that of No. 48a.[7] The tempo ratio is again 60:61, the transposition level a perfect fifth, rather than the major tenth common in the late canons. Lacking the gradual textural crescendo of most of the long canons, the texture of No. 48b remains thin throughout – rarely more than one idea or two notes at a time in either voice – until p. 116 (5:44), where the texture explodes to tremendous density (to match No. 48a when they combine as No. 48c). The movement is based almost entirely on six motives surrounded by four more generic types of material. These are as follows.

1   The movement's most distinctive feature is a figure not yet heard in Nancarrow's work: an eleven-note octave chain outlining an additive acceleration from ten subdivisions to one (Example 8.54a). The inverted form of this figure is almost as common as the original, and at one point (3:41, p. 74) we hear it in retrograde, as a ritard. Whenever two of these figures coincide in the two voices, Nancarrow makes the interval between them a perfect fourth or fifth, creating a chaos of, say, Cs and Gs, a strikingly clean sonority in the context of his work.

2   A five-note circling motive with an opening grace-note (Example 8.54b).

3   A closely related five-note motive with a 3+3+2+2 rhythm (Example 8.54c). This and the previous motive, prominently audible, occur mostly in

Example 8.53 Study No. 48a, motives that signal tempo changes (renotated)

the first twenty-one pages (fifty-eight seconds), and they are not found between pp. 62 and 103. The first three motives fulfill basically the same function as the "clock" material of No. 48a: they tend to be the background, often *mp* or *mf*, over which louder and softer gestures are heard as interruptions. Unlike the background material of No. 48a, however, the motives are often repeated and their echoes are easy to pick out of the texture.

4   A quick, pitch-circling motive in the fastest note values (Example 8.54d).
5   Again, a related motive with an initial additive acceleration, usually slower, but sometimes doubled in tempo (Example 8.54e). Note that after

Example 8.54a   Study No. 48b, motive 1 (renotated)

Example 8.54b   Study No. 48b, motive 2 (renotated)

Example 8.54c   Study No. 48b, motive 3 (renotated)

Example 8.54d   Study No. 48b, motive 4 (renotated)

Example 8.54e   Study No. 48b, motive 5 (renotated)

Example 8.54f   Study No. 48b, motive 6 (renotated)

Example 8.54g   Study No. 48b, motive 7 (renotated)

Example 8.54h   Study No. 48b, motive 9 (renotated)

the acceleration, the central note (C) articulates every third eighth note, imposing a subtle triple rhythm. Each of these motives – 4 and 5 – is heard, fragmented or complete, about a dozen times in each voice.

6   In addition, one brief motive (Example 8.54f) occurs three times in each voice (two appearances and their upper-voice echoes begin at 1:37).

The remaining ideas are texturally more variable.

7   Open-position triads in the bass like those of No. 48a, usually stating either an accelerating rhythm or a 3+3+2+2+3+2+2 rhythmic motive, and often accompanied above by a repeated note or minor-third motive (Example 8.54g).

8   Fast major-triad arpeggios, always upward with a single exception.

9   Fast, quasi grace-note figures circling a single note (Example 8.54h), which, to the Nancarrow-accustomed ear, recall the Spanish-inspired Flamenco arabesques of Study No. 12. The arpeggios and arabesques (motives 8 and 9) fulfill a similar function here to the "Nancarrow licks" of No. 48a: at first they are *ff* interruptions in a *pp* texture, later they (with motives nos. 4 and 5) become the *pp* interruptions in a *ff* texture.

10   And, finally, in the last twenty pages, staccato octaves and triads in the bass accompanying the fast figures of motive 9.

It will be observed that motives 2, 3, 4, 5, and 9 all involve the circling of a single pitch. Motive 1, the octave-chain motive, consists of a single pitch, and a single pitch is often repeated above the bass open-position triads of motive 7. Nancarrow keeps all these closely-related motives distinct, but he fuses them increasingly as the movement progresses. The octave-chain motive is sometimes stated in repeated notes, not accelerating, but in the alternating three and two rhythm of the bass open-position triads (Example 8.55a, pp. 67–68 in the score, at 3:19). And, in a climactic moment at p. 116 (5:44), the octave chain's acceleration is made explicit by combining it with the note-circling arabesques, with an arpeggio tossed on at the beginning for good measure (Example 8.55b). Almost all the motives (including the major-triad arpeggios) are built around the repetition of a single pitch, and

Example 8.55a   Study No. 48b, octave-chain motive with 3 + 2 rhythm

Example 8.55b   Study No. 48b, octave-chain fused with arabesque

the remaining material consists mostly of bass accompaniment figures. Despite the number of motives, the movement is narrowly focused and lean-textured.

Nancarrow's contrapuntal procedure in No. 48b is intuitively simple, and quite different from that of No. 48a. In an opening ***pp*** texture, the first ***ff*** arabesque appears in the lower voice at p. 9 (0:14). When its upper-voice echo arrives at p. 11 (0:21), Nancarrow writes a brief ***ff*** octave chain to coincide in the lower voice. When *that* gesture appears in the upper voice at p. 13 (0:27), the third ***ff*** figure, a triadic arpeggio, occurs in the lower voice. And so on. There are breaks in the chain of coincidences, but in general, when a ***ff*** gesture recurs in the second voice, Nancarrow counters with a new one in the lower voice. By p. 39 (1:53), the background texture of ***pp*** motives has increased to ***p*** and Nancarrow begins to pair ***pp*** arpeggios in the same manner. Since the echo distance is ever decreasing, the intervals between these occurrences grow slowly shorter.

By p. 45 (2:12) the echo distance has decreased to the point that this method is less feasible, and such pairings appear only infrequently through the middle of the movement. Nancarrow resorts instead to more generic material such as the arabesques and bass-triad motives, which blur the distinction between the voices. Longer phrases begin to combine with their own immediate echoes in the later voice. At p. 101 (5:01) such pairings of ***pp*** and ***ff*** arpeggios between the voices begin again sporadically, separated by ***mf*** contrapuntal passages of the slower motives. Finally, at p. 116 (5:44), the echo distance is so small that even the arabesques and fastest motives echo in the second voice before they end in the first. From here to the end, ***ff*** and ***pp*** passages alternate, the ***ff*** passages usually ending

Example 8.56   Study No. 48b, in-and-out-of-focus technique

in an upward flash of arpeggios, and the voices so close that dynamic changes in the two almost coincide. In general, the entire movement illustrates a process of going out of and going back into focus, suggested in Example 8.56, in which correspondences between the two voices are clear at the beginning and end, muddier in the middle. The 60:61 tempo ratio, though imperceptible in itself, makes such a subtle form tempting, feasible, and effective.

By the time Nancarrow completed No. 48b, he had gone through the experience of recording the two-piano Studies Nos. 40 and 41 for 1750 Arch, and this may have made him aware of how much more easily two pianos could be synchronized on tape in the recording studio than live. Whatever the case, far more synchronization is built in to the combination of Nos. 48a and b to create No. 48c than was the case with either No. 40 or 41. The isomorphic relationship of dynamics between Nos. 48 a and b is remarkable. Both canons start off *pp* with occasional *ff* interruptions, then gradually crescendo until they are mostly *ff* with *pp* interruptions. Throughout the piece, most of those interruptions in one piano line up vertically with those in the other, intended to coincide in time. On the Wergo recording, though, No. 48b enters (0:10) over a page earlier than Nancarrow indicated in the score. For most of No. 48c the score is difficult to read because the two pianos are not in sync. Still, dynamic correspondences between the pianos are closest in the last twenty-eight pages where, given a synchronized ending, the voices would be most likely to be together, even if the tempo relationship is slightly off.

In No. 48a, the only *pp* figures in this final section are the arpeggio fragments drawn from the two twenty-eight-note "Nancarrow licks." Each time these occur after p. 101 Nancarrow matches them in No. 48b with *pp* fragments of motives 4 and 5, and sometimes the quasi grace-note arabesques. The final fourteen pages consist, in both pianos, of a *ff* texture interrupted by quick *pp* figures. In addition, at pp. 103–08 and 111–15, Nancarrow matches the *mf* ticking of the accelerating clock in No. 48a with *mf* returns of the slower motives of No. 48b. *Fortissimo* passages in both voices involve the fastest notes: stride-octave figures, tremolos, and trills in a, arabesques in b. From p. 101 on the pianos have come sufficiently well synchronized that the *pp* passages do overlap, and hearing the two pianos gradually slide into sync, if one is aware that it is supposed to happen, is an even more dramatic experience than it might have been had the relationship been "correct" all along. Even given a loose synchronization, the patterning of No. 48b's dynamic changes to match those of No. 48a creates an amazing set of

Example 8.57   Study No. 48c, page 126 of Nancarrow's score

isomorphically paired canons – surely one of the most incredible musical structures in the history of the art.

Perhaps more important: the third movement's final wall of sound (see Example 8.57, from the final score) created by four complex, *ff* high-speed voices, periodically evaporating for split seconds into a few tiny, *pp* gestures – like a series of roaring waves each dying just before the crash of the next – is a totally unprecedented noise complex which must be heard to be believed. If Studies Nos. 41 and 48 are to have their comparative merits weighed, it is this movement, I think, that gives No. 48 the edge. Study No. 41's first two movements, with their jazz tunes, fewer elements, and more audible acceleration (in No. 41b), have more personality, a more memorable progression of events, than the corresponding parts of No. 48. But the formal problem that Nancarrow had merely toyed with in No. 41c is solved in No. 48c in a thrilling and totally original manner. It may be the most exciting finale in an output generous with exciting finales.

9

Synthesizing a language

Studies Nos. 25, 35, 42, 45, 46, 47, 51, For Yoko, Contraption No. 1

Were Nancarrow a theorizing personality like so many other twentieth-century composers, he might have attempted to integrate his main ideas – ostinato, isorhythm, tempo contrast, acceleration, arpeggiated texture, and canon – into a consistent, all–encompassing system. Nothing could be further from his personality. Yet, in the late studies, we do find him synthesizing a heterogeneous language, reaping the benefits of decades of experimentation, and starting to combine structural ideas into new hybrids. None of the works in the present chapter *are* canons, but except for Nos. 45b and 46 all of them *contain* canons. In the late studies we find few new ideas – the irrational isorhythm of No. 45 is an exception – but we do find Nancarrow applying old ideas in new configurations, less concerned with what they sound like on the surface than with what they can offer him conceptually. By now he is so expert at his favorite devices that isorhythmic canons, accelerating canons, isorhythmic ostinatos, even isorhythmic canons of arpeggiated ostinatos, appear almost effortlessly. Devices merge and begin to resemble one another: what looks like ostinato in No. 45a turns out to be isorhythm, and what looks like isorhythm in No. 45b turns out to be something else altogether.

As Carlsen remarks, Study No. 35 already feels like an essay in compositional autobiography,[1] and this is true of No. 25 as well. In the pieces after No. 41 there is a new simplicity, a purity stemming from materials that have become generic. After such lush, generous music, the austerity can be difficult to adjust to. Glissandos, arpeggios, triads, minor-third motives, octave bass lines, ascending major/descending minor figures, are no longer differentiated: they are *markers* in a Nancarrovian syntax, articulation points of rhythmic processes. They are "Nancarrow licks." Everything that *can* be has been reduced to logic. But those gestures have taken on a life of their own, evolved over intense decades.

Study No. 25

Study No. 25 is one of Nancarrow's most spectacular works. It not only brings together all the techniques he had used previous to it – isorhythm, canon, acceleration – but discovers new ways to "orchestrate" the player piano effectively, foreshadowing all the great studies from No. 36 on. It was good salesmanship that led Peter Garland, in 1975, to publish Study No. 25 as the first Nancarrow work in his *Soundings* journal (the first Nancarrow publication in twenty-three years), for no other composition is such a treasure chest of every type of idea Nancarrow has worked with. Nor is any other of the studies so beautifully copied out, so accurate and clean.

This study is also the only one to make even slightly conventional use of a twelve-tone row – that is, in transposition, retrograde, and inversion. For Nancarrow to use a tone row is not unusual, but most of his rows are longer than twelve notes: twenty-eight in Study No. 48, for example, thirty in No. 1, fifty-one in No. 4, fifty-four in No. 21. As one might expect, his use of the twelve-tone row is a far cry from Schoenbergian practice. Study No. 25 is by no means twelve-tone in a global sense, and the row is limited sometimes to melody, other times to harmonic control: often it serves as a basis for triadic harmony, with pitches rotated (in the manner Stravinsky was developing at about the same time). Nancarrow professes little interest in dodecaphony, and he had forgotten that No. 25 contained a row. When I first told him, he protested: "It couldn't be. I never used any twelve-tone row. Maybe you found something that works out that way, but it couldn't have been intentional." After I had proved the row's existence to his satisfaction, he said,

> I remember, some time ago I read a very learned article proving that Bartók was a twelve-tone composer. You know, you can manipulate anything to prove almost anything. I just can't imagine myself doing that. But you found it, so I did. I had felt that this was one of my few pieces that was — not improvised, exactly, but free.[2]

Since the row appears in several forms, the matrix is given in Example 9.1.[3] The piece gets its distinctive and exciting sound, though, not from any inner system, but from Nancarrow's realization at this point that the player piano is more than just a rhythmically adept substitute for conventional instruments: it is capable of extreme speeds, lightning-fast glissandos, dozens of notes played all over the keyboard within a split second. This is the piece in which Nancarrow discovered what is *idiomatic* about the player piano, and in the studies that followed he made excellent use of his findings.

Study No. 25 divides into eight well-defined sections. All but the last are characterized by two to four simultaneous layers of activity. The piece is perceptually tied together by the extremely fast glissandos, arpeggios, and combinations of such figures that run throughout all but two sections. These two sections, 2 and 6, are characterized by quick triadic arpeggios, and are the only sections in

Example 9.1   Study No. 25, 12-tone row matrix

	I0	I10	I3	I6	I11	I1	I2	I4	I9	I8	I5	I7
P0	D#	C#	F#	A	D	E	F	G	C	B	G#	A#
P2	F	D#	G#	B	E	F#	G	A	D	C#	B♭	C
P9	C	B♭	D#	F#	B	C#	D	E	A	G#	F	G
P6	A	G	C	D#	G#	A#	B	C#	F#	F	D	E
P1	E	D	G	B♭	D#	F	F#	G#	C#	C	A	B
P11	D	C	F	A♭	C#	D#	E	F#	B	B♭	G	A
P10	C#	B	E	G	C	D	D#	F	A#	A	F#	G#
P8	B	A	D	F	B♭	C	C#	D#	G#	G	E	F#
P3	F#	E	A	C	F	G	A♭	B♭	D#	D	B	C#
P4	G	F	B♭	D♭	G♭	A♭	A	B	E	D#	C	D
P7	A#	G#	C#	E	A	B	C	D	G	F#	D#	F
P5	G#	F#	B	D	G	A	B♭	C	F	E	C#	D#

which the twelve-tone row does not appear. There are no fewer than three internal tempo canons, in sections 3, 4, and 6: the tempo ratios involved are 7:10, 21:25, and 9:10:12:15 respectively. Nothing distinguishes the sections more than the types of rhythm they juxtapose: seemingly random durations contrasted with a steady beat, a steady beat against isorhythm, isorhythm against itself, and so on. The chart in Example 9.2 gives an idea of the tremendous variety of qualities, methods, and sounds in this study, and also a hint of its unifying processes. Never before or since has Nancarrow used so many devices in a single movement, and yet the piece holds together like a rock through the audacity of its timbral gesture.

In section 1 (0:00–0:44, systems 1–13), the untransposed prime form of the row is stated in the bass three times (with varying octave placements) in sustained, seemingly random durations. Then, starting at system 7 (0:23), this now moves to the middle range of the piano for two statements, and two contrapuntal lines are added above it to form root-position major triads in open position. At system 10 the number of voices increases to four to make root-position dominant seventh chords for two more statements of P0, making seven in all. These chords gradually move upward in register until system 12, when they quickly plunge back toward the bass at the very end.

This entire chorale-like texture is sprinkled with sporadic timbral effects: diatonic glissandos, triadic and seventh-chord arpeggios, and a figure doing a glissando through the first sixteen harmonics of its bottom note. The notes of one remarkable eighty-five-note figure (Example 9.3) alternate between glissandos rippling in both directions at once (0:37); similar gestures recur in sections 4, 5,

Example 9.2   Study No. 25, sectional chart

Section:	1	2	3	4	5	6	7a	7b	8
Varied figures:	*		*	*	*		*		*
4-note arpeggios:		*				*			
Long arpeggios:						*		*	
Staccato chords:			*		*				
Sustained chords:	*						*	*	
Sustained arpeggios:		*							
Sustained single notes:	*			*					
Staccato single notes:		*							
Sustain pedal:					*				*
Tempo canon:			*	*		*			
12-tone row:	*	*	*	*	*		*	*	
Rhythm:									
Patternless:	*	*		*	*		*		
Isorhythmic:			*			*		*	
Regular Beat:		*			*	*			(*)
Acceleration:								*	

Example 9.3   Study No. 25, figure of simultaneous glissandos

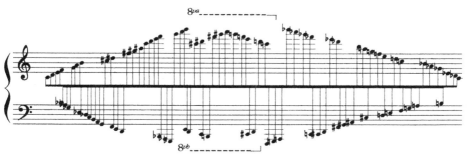

and 7. The timbral figures are spaced erratically as to rhythm, and tend to occupy the treble more when the twelve-tone chorale is in the bass, and vice versa. The tempo of the fast notes within each figure remains apparently constant, about 175 per second. So fast are these notes that Nancarrow has to insert them in the score with a kind of telescopic notation, drawing lines to show where they fit in (see Example 9.4, p. 23 from the score).

Section 2 (0:44–1:49, systems 14–34), subito **pp**, is in three layers. The first to appear is a feathery, four-note, staccato, major-triad arpeggio in the bass. It recurs every 34.5 millimeters in the score, marking a tempo of about 84, the root pitches of the triads moving in a chant-like line (unrelated to the twelve-tone row). Above this repeating arpeggio, sustained eight-note arpeggios in chains of thirds (for

Example 9.4   Study No. 25, page 23 from Nancarrow's score

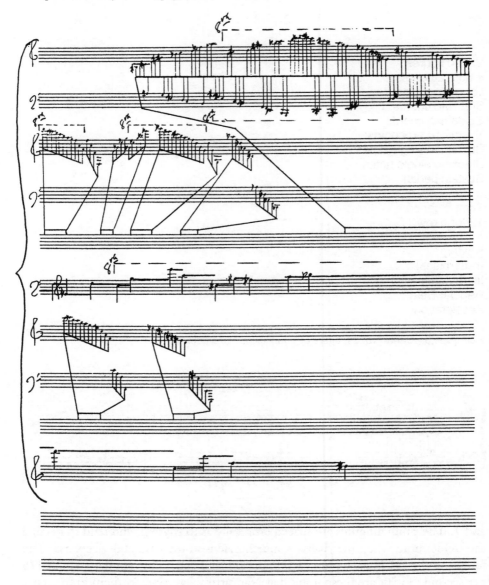

instance, A♭ C E♭ G B♭ D F A) float in the upper treble. These articulate a seem-ingly random duration series, from 16 to 182 millimeters. The roots of this arpeggio series spell out P5, RI5, R0, I10, and P5 of the row, each row inter-locking with the previous one by two notes (possible because the first and last intervals in the row are both whole steps). The other layer, in the lowest bass, is an unpatterned, staccato, non-twelve-tone line in separated octaves, a randomized version of Nancarrow's favorite jazz bass.

The texture remains static until about system 20, where the eight-note arpeggio line ascends, descending again by system 27. By system 24 the erratic stride bass has dropped out. At system 25, while the sustained eight-note arpeggios are still descending, the staccato four-note arpeggio drops out, returning a system later (1:22) at half tempo. At system 29 it drops out again, then is reincarnated (at 1:35) as a seven-note major triad marking a new tempo of about 67, four fifths of the previous tempo of 84.

Section 3 (1:49–2:21, systems 35–46) is a two-voice rhythmic canon, but the voices are not equivalent in texture. One voice consists of ten-note block chords, the other of twenty-note arpeggio patterns which descend through one major triad and ascend through another. The block chords are all identical in harmonic content: each contains every note of the chromatic scale except for those a minor third and a minor tenth above the bass. Nancarrow's harmonic control over these chords is curious. The first twelve chords state the P10 form of the row in the bass. The next twelve state P9 in the *second* lowest note, and the final twelve state P8 in the *third* lowest note. Since the chords are not parallel, however, this use of the row does not determine the other intervals, not even the bass line.

In the arpeggios, the roots of the falling triads spell out P7 and then P8, while the rising triads, rotating the last note to first in each case, spell out R11 and P0. The two voices state the same rhythm – 2+1+2+2+1+1+2+2+1+1+1+2+1+ 2+2 +1+1+2+1+1+1+1+2 and so on – at a rhythmic ratio of seven (arpeggios) to ten (chords). Because the slower voice starts just after the faster, there is no convergence point; though, given the dissimilarity between the voices, it would not be heard if there were. I find myself unable to hear the arpeggio patterns as a rhythm with an underlying steady beat, but similar phenomena return in sections 6 and 7, where they are more easily audible.

Section 4 (2:21–3:00, systems 46–59) pushes tempo canon to greater lengths: it is a complex double canon at a ratio of 21:25. One of the canonic themes is the untransposed retrograde form of the row stated seven times in unpatterned durations, sustained, and varying widely in register. The other canonic theme recycles the repertoire of timbral effects used in section 1. The complex amalgam of these two heterogeneous lines is imitated at the major second below at 25/21 tempo starting at system 48 (2:26). A convergence point passes unmarked in the middle of sustained pitches at system 58 (p. 32, 2:56), just before the end. One might possibly notice the CP in the parallel major seconds in the bass and the double glissandos, which closely parallel each other; more likely not.

"Ped." is the unfamiliar marking that begins section 5 (3:00–3:48, systems 59–76); as is often remarked, this is the only study in which Nancarrow uses the player piano's built-in sustaining pedal capacity. The section is a rough alternation of timbral figures and seven-note chords, contrasting *ff* with *pp*, and the pedal sustains the notes of most of the figures until they cut off abruptly with the arrival of the succeeding chord. Again, all of the chords have the same harmonic content: a Lydian scale built above the root, C–D–E–F♯–G–A–B. The chords, which cover the entire range of the keyboard, spell out P11 in the lowest notes of the first twelve, then P3 in the second-lowest notes of the next twelve.[4]

The glissando/arpeggio figures are much more varied and, in general, longer than they have been heretofore. One enormous 210-note figure at system 62 (one of the slower figures, it lasts 2.3 seconds) opens with a rising C major scale, jumps to an F-major arpeggio, slides down a B major scale, then down an Ab-major arpeggio, back up a G major scale, and so on. Another (system 66) consists of thirty-three major triads, ascending over and over in groups of three, caressing the keyboard *pianissimo*. Little consistency will be found in this passage of pure mechanical-keyboard fantasy. Once two chords occur without an intervening figure, then two figures (pedal held) without an intervening chord. Nor is the pedal always held. Nevertheless, beneath the figures the chords seem to imply an underlying beat of about 208, a duration of about 13.7 millimeters in the score. After system 71 (3:33), chords (not figures) become more frequent, and the implied beat becomes momentarily apparent.

Section 6 (3:48–4:23, systems 77–89) returns to the staccato arpeggio of section 2 and makes a tempo canon out of it. This four-voice canon of four-note, major/major seventh-chord arpeggios (played so fast they sound almost like block chords), uses imitation at the pitch interval of a perfect twelfth, and at tempo ratios of 9:10:12:15 (in terms of pitch analogues, a D–E–G–B chord). As usual, the slowest voice is the lowest and first to enter, the fastest is the highest and last to enter (at system 83). The canon ends without reaching its CP. Each voice stays within a small range: the melody outlined by the bottom notes of the arpeggios never exceeds the space of a tritone. The rhythm of each voice is *almost* repetitive, and very similar to that of section 3, an irregular grouping of "quarter-" and "eighth-" notes: 2+1+2+2+1+1+2+1+1+1+2+1+2+1+1+2+2+1+1+1+2+ 2+1+2+2+1+1+1+1+2+1+1+1+1+1+1. Given the elaborate texture of this canon, Nancarrow need use only the plainest of rhythms and pitch movements; the structure is sufficiently hidden as it is.

At system 85 a fifth voice enters, playing long, nineteen-note, major-triad arpeggios.[5] After its initial three arpeggios, the bass line of this voice follows the pitch canon of the others. The rhythm, however, is a regular beat articulating a pulse in between those of the 12 and 15 voices, forming a ratio to them of thirteen and a third. Therefore, in order to account for this fifth tempo as part of the total tempo structure, the ratios must be multiplied by 3, for a result of 27:30:36:40:45, with the top, thirteen-note arpeggios articulating the 40 tempo. Note that, high as these numbers are, every pair works down to a simpler ratio: 27:36 and 30:40 work down to two 3:4 ratios related to each other by 9:10, and so on.

Section 7 (4:23–5:31, systems 90–114) is once again in two layers: chords and glissando/arpeggio figures. The first twenty-five chords are taken verbatim from section 5, which contained only twenty-five chords. Thereafter, the chords continue the implied pattern: seven notes, comprising an entire Lydian scale over each bass note, and spelling out P0 in each third lowest note, then P8 in each

Example 9.5   Study No. 25, isorhythm of section 7

fourth lowest note. Figures like those from section 5 – various combinations of arpeggios and diatonic scales – are superimposed over the chords. The durations are without pattern until system 101 (4:53). Here, an acceleration canon begins, and both chords and figures fall into recognizable beats. Beginning with the sustained triad at system 101 (p. 60), the chords spell out a seven–note, eleven–beat isorhythm (Example 9.5). Beginning with the last arpeggio at system 101, the arpeggios are all twenty notes rising mostly by thirds, and they spell out the same rhythm as the chords. The chords, however, accelerate at a rate of 6.44 percent, while the arpeggios accelerate at exactly half that, 3.22 percent. The interval content of the arpeggios varies, but they all begin on $D\flat_2$, D_2, or $E\flat_2$.

The sustained chords no longer fill out a Lydian scale. Now they contain six notes, two major triads. The roots of the lower triads and the top note (either third or fifth) of the upper triad are determined by the twelve-tone row according to the following pattern:

system	upper triads	lower triads
101	P0: notes 9–11	P10: notes 10–15
103	R0	P10
108	P0: notes 10–12	P10
109	P0: notes 1–9	
111	R0: notes 5–12	R10: notes 10–12
111		R10
112	R0: notes 1–4	
113	P0: notes 2–12	
113		R10
113	P0: note 1	
113	R0: notes 1–8	
114		R10: notes 1–5

Since Nancarrow's row is not combinatorial, he does not use traditional Schoenbergian ways of combining rows. Instead he ensures harmonic variety by rotating the notes of the row in the upper triads, while essentially repeating the same row over and over in the lower triads. Note that the arrangement of the upper triads contains two palindromes: the last three notes of P0, first nine notes of P0, last eight notes of R0, and first four notes of R0 form a twenty-three-chord palindrome in systems 108–12 (upper triads only), and the last eight notes of P0, first note of P0, and first eight notes of R0 create a seventeen-chord palindrome at systems 113–14. Nancarrow voices these chords in a truly palindromic way in the upper triads only. He keeps the harmonies from repeating by having the lower triads repeat only in one direction. And yet, he does not aim for maximum dissonance, for the upper and lower triads occasionally duplicate each other.

The two-tiered accelerando explodes into the whirlwind of section 8 (5:31, systems 114–130). The final sixteen staves are a blur of continuous single notes sustained with the pedal. 1028 notes swirl by in less than twelve seconds, a rate of eighty-eight per second, half as fast as at the beginning, but still too fast for the ear to register as individual events: major triad arpeggios, scales, broken octaves, sudden leaps in register, twistings and turnings of key, every quick figuration used up until now (except the harmonic series figure) combined in one *Blitzkrieg* climax. There does not appear to be anything analyzable about this arpeggiated cacophony; indeed, many of the fragments are so short, so hidden by pivot-note overlappings, and so tonally ambiguous, that one quickly despairs of isolating meaningful units, nor, at this speed, would any conceivable system make a perceptible difference. Nancarrow describes it as a "negative pattern," which he devised to solve the logistical problem that at this speed he had to avoid repeating any notes too soon. The pedal is held down throughout to allow this glorious mess of sound to resonate.

Study No. 35

The overall tempo structure of Study No. 35 is clear, but it contains a daunting plethora of material and devices: canon, isorhythm, palindromes, proportional with metric notation, and the greatest wealth of melodic development of any of Nancarrow's works. No one can browse through this wildly inventive work and ever again believe Nancarrow's disingenuous comment, "I don't have much of a melodic imagination." Great works have been written on one fifth as many melodies.

There are two basic melodic patterns in this study, which I shall call A and B. Type A is based on an isorhythm, or rather a rhythmic motive, since it is rarely immediately repeated: 2+3+3+2+4+3+4+2. The opening melody uses this rhythm three times, the third time in retrograde (see Example 9.6). The type B melodic pattern is a jazzy melody in syncopated 6/8 meter, spelling out a triad in its opening notes (as the type A melody usually does as well), followed by a step in the opposite direction. The comparison in Example 9.7 shows its development through the second half of the piece. Type A has a hard, accented character, type B an easier, free-flowing lilt, and their alternation gives Study No. 35 a general ABABAB form. Nevertheless, there is no hard and fast line between the two types, and there is some merit to Carlsen's schema in which Study No. 35 only contains *one* theme, which evolves from the A melody into the B melody over the course of the work.[6]

For the sake of conveniently distinguishing the various compositional devices, I count eight sections in this work, even though some of them are brief and flow quickly into others. In particular, what I call sections 5 and 7 sound rather like loud interruptions in the softer texture of sections 4, 6, and 8, so that sections 4 – 8 could be considered a single section. Changes of tempo, however, delineate

Example 9.6   Study No. 35, type A melody

Example 9.7   Study No. 35, type B melody

eight sections. Every notated tempo in this study is a multiple of 5⅔. All told, eleven tempos are used: these are reducible to the following ratios.

tempos	ratios
79⅓	14
85	15
102	18
113⅓	20
119	21
141⅔	25
170	30
204	36
238	42
283⅓	50
340	60

The latter five of these are reducible to octave multiples of the first six, leaving only six real tempos: 14:15:18:20:21:25. (Converted to pitch ratios as overtones of C, these would represent B♭, B, D, E, F, and A♭.)

Section 1 (0:00–2:49, systems 1–23) has the feel of a canon – each of five voices enters at a faster tempo than the one before it, in a 21:30:36:50:60 ratio, while the others continue. However, the five melodies are different, though each moves to the same type of material as the others once the next voice enters. The first melody has already been given in Example 9.6. The four that follow are rhythmically similar in that they use mostly irregularly ordered durations of two, three, and four sixteenth notes, with occasional longer, sustained notes as cadences. Even so, each new melody is a little more regularized into 6/8 meter than the last, so that the last two begin to foreshadow the type B melody. All the melodies make prominent use of a motive involving a perfect fourth with an internal major second or minor third: D–C–F, or C–F–D, or E–B–D, and so on.

After each voice has finished its melody, it moves to a kind of irregular accompaniment pattern of minor thirds with single notes a major third below – in other words, a fragmented "boom-chick" major-triad pattern – and then to a line of single notes. Exceptions are the fastest voice, which skips the triad material, the 50 voice, which does not reach the single-note line, and the top 60 voice, whose initial melody brings the section to a close. Except for the first, each voice moves to the triads just before the next voice enters, and each moves to single notes when the succeeding one moves to triads, so that there is never more than one voice playing its melody or the triad material at a time. The structure of this section is outlined in Example 9.8. Nancarrow uses a few tricks within the accompaniment parts: there is a nine-note isorhythm (1+2+3+4+1+2+2+2+3) in the 36 voice from systems 18 to the end of the section, and Carlsen found a rhythmic (not pitch) palindrome in systems 6–7.[7] Otherwise, the material is free-composed. The counterpoint among the accompanying voices generally spells out a diatonic pitch collection at any given moment, though these moments never last long enough to establish a key.

The second section (2:49–4:37, systems 23–38) is similar to the first, except that it *begins* with the single-notes-and-thirds accompaniment and places three melodies above them: fewer expositions, but still five voices. Rather than moving to accompaniment material when subsequent voices enter, however, the voices continue in true counterpoint. Even more strongly than the first, this section falsely appears canonic, as though Nancarrow were trying to free himself from the discipline and still keep the canonic flavor. The first four phrases of each melody are almost identical except for the modality and inversion of the opening triads and the lengths of the sustained notes. The accompaniment (whose dyads include major seconds as well as minor thirds) plays with permutations of the type A rhythm, and the melodies all quote figures from the opening A melody, but the rhythm has moved even further into a syncopated 6/8 lilt.

Section 3 (4:37–5:36, systems 39–47) presents us with something new, or perhaps old: in fact, it looks like a quotation from Study No. 23, two lines in proportional notation against a middle, metered line full of motives made up of three-note chords slurred to single notes. The passage seems unrelated to the one preceding, but on closer examination the rhythms look familiar. The proportionally notated staccato lines use only a small repertoire of durations: mostly

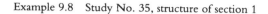
Example 9.8   Study No. 35, structure of section 1

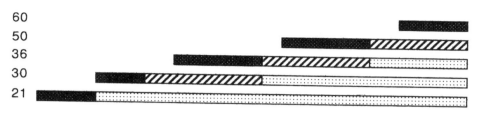

Melody
Thirds and triads
Single notes

9mm, 13, and 18, also 22, 26, and 35. The never-quite-repetitive deployment of 9s, 13s, and 18s matches that of the two, three, and four sixteenth note durations of the type A melody, and 9:13:18 and 2:3:4 are *almost* equivalent ratios, certainly for all rhythmic/perceptual purposes. The staccato notes, echoed three octaves and a fifth above in the first true canon of the piece, a 5:6 tempo canon, act as a continuation of the bass accompaniment of section 2. (The 13mm duration seems to be equal to a quarter note in the metered voice.) Even this voice quotes some A-like motives, and at system 44 we find our old isorhythmic friend 2+3+3+ 2+4+3+4+2. The entire section is a take-off on the type A melody "in the style of" Study No. 23. Oddly, the canon ends well before its convergence point.

Section 4 (5:36–6:00, systems 48–51) plunges us back into false canon. The two upper voices, contrasted at a 6:7 tempo ratio and each split into two contrapuntal lines, look as though they are going to form a double canon, and for the first eleven notes they do. These are jazz melodies in 6/16 metre, pure type B, and they are the prototype for those of the final four sections. Little points of imitation emerge and disappear. Each melody has its own walking bass, plus the staccato bass that continued from the metered voice at section 3. The tempo ratio of these three voices is 18:20:21, but since the staccato bass articulates quarter-notes and the melodies dotted eighth notes, the ratios are really 15:18:21, or 5:6:7.

Isorhythm is another device Nancarrow has hinted at without using much in this piece so far, and section 5 (6:00–6:12, systems 51–53) is a brief bridge on a real isorhythm – expressed in thirty-second notes, 7+5+7+9+4. This rhythm runs through the treble voice in octaves, in a line derived from the last few melodic notes of section 4, a cadential phrase of the B melody, another variation of which will recur again in section 8 (Example 9.9). Beneath it a line of staccato major triads and another of staccato octaves articulate ratios of 7:10 against the isorhythm's 9. The layers of section 6 (6:12–6:55, systems 53–59) seem similarly heterogeneous. A two-strand melodic voice picks up the type B melody from

Example 9.9   Study No. 35, cadential figure with isorhythm

Example 9.10   Study No. 35, section 7 melody

section 4 as though section 5 were merely an interruption. In the high treble, staccato dyads play with the type A melody's 2, 3, and 4 durations, while the bass punctuates with arpeggiated triads in open position. The three lines create a tempo ratio of 14:15:18.

The little bridge of section 7 (6:55–7:13, systems 60–62) is another interruption, a final burst of type A material before the B melody finale. The development that the A melody undergoes here is dazzling, showing Nancarrow's thought process in a microcosm. Over and over it begins again with the 2+3+3+2+ 4+3+4+2 isorhythm, extends it, goes back, repeats a fragment, in a clear, freely inventive way. Example 9.10 gives the melody in its entirety, separated to show the relation to the isorhythm, a rhythmic process analogous to the pitch-row process of Study No. 4. With one exception in each case there is always a four-note triad outlined at point A in the example, a perfect fourth followed by a repeated note at B, and a half-step at C. This melody, in the piano's middle range, is surrounded at great distance on each side by two versions of the 7+5+7+9+4 isorhythmic line from section 5, forming a 5:6 tempo canon. Together with the A melody the entire tempo resultant is 5:6:14. The isorhythmic canon ends at the convergence point at system 61, but the melody goes blithely on to lead to the final section.

Concluding section 8 (7:17–7:33, systems 62–65) is the piece's first totally canonic texture, and a double canon to boot. There are three tempos, at ratios of 18:21:25, and two contrapuntal strands in each tempo. The top line in each case is the B melody, derived from the melodies of sections 4 and 6, and imitated at two-octave intervals. The continuation of the line quotes patterns from the isorhythmic line of sections 5 and 7. For once the canon does not end at the CP; rather, the two lower voices switch to the fastest tempo and play their last thirteen octaves in unison. (The score indicates that all voices switch to the *slowest* tempo, but this seems to be a mistake.[8]) Carlsen has noted that this closing formula, curiously, is almost identical to that of Study No. 24.[9]

A diagram of the overall tempo structure (Example 9.11) cannot be quite faithful to the intricacies of the internal rhythms, but it shows a typical Nancarrow pattern, with fastest tempos at beginning and end, slower ones in the middle. Though the structure is elegant, this is one of Nancarrow's least rigid works. Its point seems to be evolution: from one melody into another, from melodic profusion to strict canon, from free rhythmic motive to isorhythm, from chaos to clarity. One can imagine it begun in a burst of inspiration, then finished with the hand of a skilled contrapuntalist.

Study No. 42

Like its remote predecessor No. 5, Study No. 42 is an experiment in cumulative acceleration, this time employing both isorhythm and canon. The piece's idea could hardly be simpler, but its arithmetical underpinnings are complicated. Seven

Example 9.11   Study No. 35, tempo structure

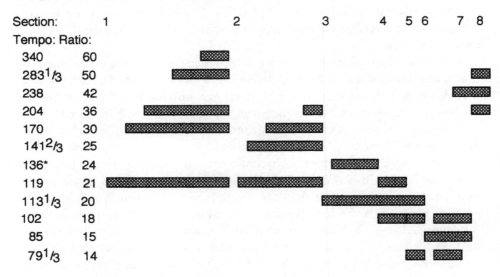

*The 24-tempo, 136, isn't notated as such, but results from the proportionally-notated 5:6 canon in section 3.

tempos run through the work at ratios of, in order from bottom of the score to top, 7:10:9:8:12:14:18 (the 14 and 18 tempos, of course, are octaves of the 7 and 9). In the manuscript score, Nancarrow places a pitch name next to each stave in the following order:

18 14 12 8 9 10 7
D B♭ G C D E B♭

These pitches correspond, of course, to the frequency ratios implied by the tempos, and to overtones of a basic tempo C=1. Six of the layers, including the staccato notes and triads, proceed systematically. Each of the lowest five voices (in the ratios 7:10:9:8:12) spells out the same 1+2+1+2+2 isorhythm in staccato notes, beginning with the lowest and increasing one by one. (The lowest voice follows an irregular pattern until the other voices have entered.) At system 16 these voices begin to accelerate by dropping one sixth of a beat's duration every few systems until, in the final three systems, each is moving eighteen times as fast as at the beginning. The acceleration of each voice, then, is arithmetical and by stages rather than continuous. An additional acceleration effect results from the fact that the voices are brought in one by one over the first thirty-four of sixty-five systems.

The original manuscript is marked off in beats, each with six subdivisions. The second sound heard, a major triad, initiates a series of triads which define an arithmetical acceleration from twenty-two $\frac{1}{3}$ beats (134 of the smallest subdivisions) of the 18 tempo to one beat, subtracting (with negligible discrepancies in the score) $\frac{1}{6}$ beat with each succeeding chord; in other words, an arithmetical

Example 9.12   Study No. 42, system 22, 7:9 canon

Example 9.13   Study No. 42, 6+6+4 isorhythm in 14 and 18 tempos

accelerando in relative durations of 134, 133, 132, 131, and so on. This super-imposed acceleration is reminiscent of the accelerating staccato octaves of Study No. 28 and the sustained octaves of No. 29. These triads are decorated with irregularly appearing grace-noted single notes; at first for about every third triad, then diminishing in frequency, but increasing at the end to almost every chord. The acceleration ends at system 62 (7:07), where all voices have reached, and continue at, maximum speed. The manuscript suggests that this hectic coda was added as an afterthought, and the piece needs it for fulfillment of the accelerando's excitement.

The remaining layers occupy the 14 and 18 tempos. These are, at first, little jazz riff fragments based on one of three rhythms: a repeating 5+3, a repeating 6+6+4, and 2+4+5+6+2+4+6+2+4+5. At six points, system 18 (2:09), 22 (2:38), 23 (2:45), 25 (3:02), 27 (3:14), and 43 (4:59), the same melodies appear in both voices at once to create brief 7:9 canons, ending each time at a convergence point (Example 9.12; while the score is proportionally notated, I have supplied the relative durations as they can be calculated from the manuscript). As one can see, the rhythm is based on a half-note beat divided interchangeably as 5+3 or 3+5. These canons give way to increasingly thick textures of more generic materials, either an F–G–A♭ motive (at any transposition) repeated over and over, or two notes alternating at a perfect fourth. Example 9.13 (2:51), using the 6+6+4 isorhythm in both 14 and 18 tempos at once, sounds like a music box out of whack. These repetitive figures and jazz riff fragments cluster in clouds of up to four lines at once, using two isorhythms in each of two tempos. In the three-system coda, the five lower voices play the 1+2+1+2+2 isorhythm on the fastest subdivision in five tempos at once, while the 14 and 18 tempos play off a 2+4+6 rhythm with triads.

Melodic aspects of the work are free and hard to pin down, but the harmonic aspects are simple. The study runs through four cycles of all twelve keys in an unvarying twelve-tone order: C A♭ E F D B♭ D♭ A G B E♭ F♯. The harmonic rhythm adds another level of acceleration: the first twelve systems are indeterminate as to key, then the first twelve-key cycle requires twenty-four systems, one key change about every fourteen seconds. The second cycle takes twenty systems, the third only six, then the coda zips through the final cycle in three systems. This kind of change is difficult to measure among clouds of staccato notes, some of which act as pivots between keys, but no acceleration seems to take place *within* each cycle, only in sudden steps from one to the next.

Aside from its acceleration, Study No. 42 is an exercise in moving from sparse chaos to a kind of frenetic order. It takes a long time for the acceleration to be felt (a quality of long arithmetical accelerations), and the exploded fragments that open the piece provide no hint of the underlying process. Over time, however, as the textural thickness increases, the materials become more regular and repetitive. If nothing else, the piece illustrates how statistical patterning becomes more obvious in conditions of greater density.

Study No. 45

Studies Nos. 45, 46, and 47 were written to fulfill a commission from Betty Freeman. Nancarrow felt that the commission deserved a truly major work, and, in all, wrote six movements, unified by use of a measure divided into 3, 4, and 5 as a rhythmic background, and by an irrational "spastic rhythm" (his own term) which runs thematically through five of the six movements (all except 45b). When a tape of the entire work was played as Study No. 45 at Los Angeles, Nancarrow felt that it was too long. He split it up, using three movements as No. 45, one each as Nos. 46 and 47, and discarding the brief, relaxed, remaining movement.[10]

Study No. 45 *looks* like an ostinato blues piece, and in fact it sounds like the *Boogie-woogie Suite* revisited, an updated version incorporating tricks that had occurred to Nancarrow in the intervening thirty-five years. However, Study No. 45 does not use true ostinatos, but rather blues–ostinato–like *colors* "screwed up" rhythmically by repeating *taleas*. The *talea* or isorhythm is a strange duration series Nancarrow concocted to use as a unifying motive throughout all five movements

Example 9.14   Study Nos. 45–47, approximation of "spastic rhythm"

Example 9.15a   Study No. 45a, section 3 rhythmic motive

octaves omitted; proportionally notated in the original

Example 9.15b   Study No. 45a, minor-third motive

of the original Study No. 45. The fifteen-note pattern of this "spastic rhythm" is not susceptible to rational notation, but was derived by combining notes from different tempos (actually, templates). As Nancarrow explains,

> I don't remember all the details, but I played around with tempo relations, taking a collage from all of them, parts of them. I remember I took a bunch of templates and started putting them together, purely intuitively, and finally came up with that proportion that I liked. If you wanted to notate that rhythm, you could only notate it as I did.[11]

In my Xerox score, at the point of greatest augmentation (No. 45c, systems 36ff.), the durations measure in millimeters approximately as follows (averages taken from several occurrences): 37.8, 35.7, 25, 22, 27, 13.2, 46, 12.8, 31.8, 35.7, 9.2, 17.1, 38.2, 22.4, 43.5. The near-equality of the first two durations added together to the following three suggests a duplet followed by a triplet, and the sixth, eighth, and eleventh notes are noticeably shorter than the others. One is tempted to transcribe this series in roughly approximate conventional notation, as in Example 9.14. However, this is still misleading; the final eighth and quarter should not really last as long as the opening dotted eighths, and the slight inequality between the three "even" eighth notes is carefully maintained through the score. Best to leave the rhythm as an irrational datum.

In No. 45a the *talea* flies by far too fast to hear this rhythm as such; all that reaches the ear is an unsettling, irregular, "spastic" line. The *color* in which Nancarrow expresses his isorhythm consists of 192 notes: twenty-seven octaves in a rising and descending sequence on C, twenty-three similar octaves on F, twenty-five on D, and twenty-one on G.[12] In each key the sequence follows a seven-note blues scale: G–A♯–B–C–E–E♯–F♯. (All glissandos in No. 45a follow this scale as well.) The smallest common multiple of 15 (notes in the *talea*) and 192 (notes in the *color*) is 960, so that *color* and *talea* catch up with each other 960 notes into the piece, after five repetitions of the *color*.

The C–F–D–G progression is stated eight times, forming the basis for as many sections. As in Study No. 3, the sections are most easily described in series.

Section 1 (0:00, systems 1–7): the bass blues ostinato (actually, *color*) is stated once by itself.

Section 2 (0:25, systems 7–13): melodic fragments based on a decelerating rhythmic motive alternate with glissandos (across the blues scale described above) which end in sustained triads.

Section 3 (0:50, systems 13–19): the "right hand" plays a staccato melody in octaves based on a three- or four-note rhythmic motive (Example 9.15a; this is renotated from the score's proportional notation). The melody will recur in section 7. At each pause in the melody, eight-note arpeggios are tossed in, alternating directions.

Section 4 (1:15, systems 20–26): subito *piano*. A melody in eighth notes and dotted eighth notes alternates between triads and a minor-third motive.

Section 5 (1:39, systems 26–32): blues-scale glissandos lead to repeated staccato triads and a form of the minor third motive that will recur prominently in No. 45b (Example 9.15b in Nancarrow's notation).

Section 6 (2:02, systems 32–38): subito *forte*. Over the ostinato lies a two-part canon based on a melody similar to that of section 4: that of minor-third motive punctuated with triads. The score is not drawn accurately enough to calculate the exact tempo ratio, but 5:7, 7:10, and 8:11 are close approximations. The canon ends just before the convergence point, a habit in this study.

Section 7 (2:24, systems 38–44): the melody from section 3 reappears in octaves in the middle register. Above it, repeated triads dot out a Morse code pattern of eighth notes, dotted eighth notes, and quarters.

Section 8 (2:48, systems 45–51): the octaves and triads of section 7 continue, but they are increasingly interrupted by fifteen-note glissandos, alternating up and down, culminating in a climax of almost continuous glissandos.

The perceptually simple second movement, a soft, leisurely blues, is built on the rhythmic framework found also in Studies 44, 46, and 47: a measure divided simultaneously into three, four, five, and fourteen equal divisions. The twenty-four-note quasi-ostinato, a blues pattern on I, IV, and V, sounds like a single line, but it skips freely back and forth between the 3-, 4-, and 5-tempos. The final score, which collapses the three tempos to one stave and contains no bar lines, makes the exact rhythm impossible to decipher in any meaningful way, but a look

Example 9.16   Study No. 45b, accompaniment renotated

Example 9.17   Study No. 45b, rhythmic motives

2 + 3 grouped into 5s:

2 + 3 + 3 grouped into 8s:

3 + 5 + 5 grouped into 13s:

at the original manuscript makes the pattern at least quantifiable (Example 9.16). At system 27 (out of forty-three systems, 2:55) this pattern accelerates abruptly via note-addition to about 160% of its initial average speed, where it remains until the end. At system 33 it also leaves its C–F–G key pattern and begins hopping around A♭, B, E, A, B, and so on in a quasi-random manner.

With that daunting analytical opacity behind us, the rest of the movement dissolves into a fairly straightforward melody in the 14-tempo. This melody's rhythm lopes along in suspiciously Fibonacci-like values of two, three, five, eight, and thirteen sixteenth notes. A line of thirds below the melody groups the 2+3 patterns into 5s, the 2+3+3 patterns into 8s, and the 3+5+5 patterns into 13s (Example 9.17a, b, and c, my notation based on Nancarrow's manuscript). These patterns create the effect of different tempos within one tempo, for Fibonacci numbers result in roughly identical ratios between adjacent pairs; the higher you go in the Fibonacci series, the closer the ratio between successive numbers approaches the Golden Ratio, .618 . . .:1. Thus, 3+5+5 is close proportionately to 2+3+3, only slowed down. (Nancarrow denies that he has ever used the Fibonacci series intentionally.)

Like No. 45a, 45b is loosely in variations form, though divisions are not clearcut. One could characterize the variations as follows:

1   (0:00, systems 1–3) "Spastic" ostinato only.

2   (0:20, systems 3–6) Single sustained notes approached via two grace notes, separated by a 2+3+3-rhythmed cadence played in counterpoint with its inversion.

3   (0:41, systems 6–12) A melody answered by its inversion, then a longer melody with similar contour, marked by thirds into 2+3+3. This phrase structure is repeated in expanded form.

4   (1:21, systems 12–16) A wide-ranging melody divided by thirds into a 3+5+5 pattern is then repeated with chords filled in.

5   (1:49, systems 16–20) sixteenth-note glissandos along a blues scale (diatonic with both flattened and natural thirds and sevenths) alternate up and down, with sustained triads in between.

6   (2:18, system 20–27) A beat five-sixteenths in duration appears, making clearer the syncopations of returned earlier figures. Against the random ostinato, this steady beat could be compared to the "ontological clock" of Study No. 27.

7   (3:04, systems 27–32)[13] The melody continues with minor-third motives (E–F–D repeated) accompanied by minor-third dyads articulating 3+2 patterns; this material is taken over from section 4 of No. 45a. As the five-sixteenth notes beat continues, the ostinato accelerates.

8   (3:37, systems 32–34) Staccato triads alternate with glissandos. This is where the ostinato leaves its C–F–G pattern and begins to jump randomly.

9   (3:50, systems 34–39) Sustained single notes (as at the beginning) alternate with twice-repeated triads.

10   (4:21, system 39) The five-sixteenths beat reemerges in treble octaves and descends, amid grace note runs, to a surprise cadence on D.

The contrast of regular rhythms in the melody against the drunkenly weaving bass has a particularly nice effect in this exposed context. Nancarrow times the wandering melodies of the upper layers to resolve back to the tonic at the same instant as the bass's move to the tonic, in delightful contradiction to the nonexpectations raised by the bass's random rhythm (Example 9.18 in Nancarrow's notation). This effect gives the movement a naive melodic charm not heard since Studies Nos. 3, 4, and 6.

Movement 45c is the climax of the set and longest movement, almost as long as the other two put together. Its basis is the "spastic rhythm" of No. 45a, couched

Example 9.18   Study No. 45b, cadence pattern (Nancarrow's proportional notation)

Example 9.19   Study No. 45c, "spastic rhythm" diffracted into four layers

once again in the same rising and falling octave bass. The movement's most obvious feature is the glissandos from which selected notes are sustained, a striking timbral device Nancarrow had discovered in Study No. 36. In the final section this device is used melodically, leading to triads, but at major structural points throughout, the glissandos leave huge, ringing polychords built of thirds. This is one of Nancarrow's least accurately drawn scores, and I assume no responsibility for arithmetical errors. Despite the mountains of notes here, the form is easily described: in terms of rhythmic structure, the movement consists entirely of the "spastic isorhythm," a new theme based on a 5+3 rhythm, and a few timbral effects. The movement's enormous (for Nancarrow) length results from the length of the main theme (fifty-three, sometimes fifty-four or fifty-five, notes) and the endless repetition of the spastic isorhythm.

In section 1 (0:00–0:29, systems 1–7) the introduction is set off by three long glissandos, some of whose notes are sustained to make huge chords of stacked thirds. In between, the "spastic rhythm" is introduced in blues octave bass patterns. This octave pattern is interrupted by passages in which the isorhythm is broken up among three different lines in a consistent pattern: the middle-register line (alternate notes of the isorhythm) expresses a minor-third motive in triads, the top (every fourth note) expresses a minor-third motive in single notes, and the bottom (every fourth note) alternates the notes of a perfect fourth (Example 9.19).

Section 2 (0:29–1:26, systems 8–20) is a long passage which appears to be based entirely on the "spastic isorhythm" (hereafter referred to as SI). It is again divided among three voices, but this time with no apparent pattern, and with octaves in treble and bass. The middle-voice triads outline a minor-third motive at first, then settle into a repeated C-major triad. At system 14 (0:56), after a brief bridge, this triad voice introduces the movement's fifty-three-note primary theme of the movement (see below), still embedded within the isorhythm.

The SI runs through the bass in section 3 (1:26–2:27, systems 20–35), leaping up an octave on alternate intervals. First, as introduction, five patterns of arpeggiated octaves based on the SI at a faster tempo zip up then down the keyboard, the first three running through sustained chords of stacked triads. Then, at system 27 (1:54) the main theme begins (Example 9.20, renotated from Nancarrow's proportional notation). Its rhythmic series, peculiar-looking without the bar lines – durations of 5 3 5 11 8 5 11 5 3 8 5 11 3 8 5 3 13 and so on – is easily analyzed as a 5+3 pattern with frequent rests. Five plus three, of course, is Nancarrow's standard jazz-nuanced division of the beat. This section simply contrasts the jazz swing of the theme with the unpredictability of the SI.

Now, in section 4 (2:27–3:54, systems 35–58), after another glissando as punctuation, the SI is stated in alternating bass notes and mid-range triads, like an oom-pah stride piano pattern. Again the theme is placed over it, this time expressed in arpeggios from which triads are sustained.

Section 5 (3:54–4:07, systems 58–61), a bridge, is a short pseudo-canon. Three SI voices plunge through an octave pattern outlining a tremendous dominant seventh chord, in tempo ratios of *approximately* 3½:7:10. This pseudo-canon ends slightly before its convergence point, as do the two real canons that follow.

In section 6 (4:07–4:46, systems 61–71) the SI runs through the bass in octaves, while the theme is stated in staccato triads in three canonic voices, at octave transpositions, and at tempo ratios that *seem* to equal 4:5:6.[14] (The second voice enters at 4:15, the third at 4:21.)

Section 7 (4:46–6:11, systems 71–94) is another tempo canon, following another brief bridge stating the SI in octaves. Over the SI bass, the theme is stated almost as it was in section 4, this time as glissandos, rather than arpeggios, from which triads are sustained. The effect sounds much like the strumming method Henry Cowell used in piano pieces such as *Aeolian Harp*. A top voice states the theme a perfect eleventh higher, in what *seems* to be a 4:5 canon. (The first canonic voice enters at 5:01, the second at 5:16.)

The massive finale, section 8 (6:11, systems 94–105), returns to the idea of section 2, dividing a single repeating SI into three voices – treble, middle, and bass. Now the top two voices are full four-note major triads, the bass is in octaves with the fifth filled in, and all three often sustain notes to create interlocking motives. After a pause a final flourish of octaves rises through the pitches C, E, G, and A in a final, very fast SI.

Nothing has yet been said about the tempo structure, for the SI and the theme do not recur at the same speeds throughout. In section 3 the SI is four times as slow as in section 1, and by the end it is twice as fast. The theme appears at five different tempos, in the ratios 4:5:8:10:12. There is no way to compare the SI

Example 9.20   Study No. 45c, main theme (renotated)

Example 9.21   Study No. 45c, tempo structure

Section:	1	2	3	4	5	6	7		8	
Spastic rhythm:	4	4	2	1	1.4	2	4	2	1.4	4	8
			8		2						
					4						
Theme:			10	4		8			4		
						10			5		
						12					

with the theme, for they have no durational common denominator, but Example 9.21 shows the comparative progression of tempos for each. Note that the SI is generally slowest in the middle of the piece, faster at each end. The theme compensates by having its fastest statement at section 6. Juxtaposing the same materials over and over in varying forms, Study No. 45 is not one of Nancarrow's most profound statements, but it is a relief for once to hear his ideas drawn out at length and given some breathing room. Studies Nos. 24, 25, and 35 express more ideas in four, five, and six minutes than No. 45 does in fifteen. Yet, by any other composer's standards, fifteen minutes would hardly be an unreasonable amount of time for grasping textures of such complexity. As a "Boogie-woogie Suite No. 2," the work deserves to become as popular as its distant sibling.

Study No. 46

The punching score gives evidence that Study No. 46 originally began with the entrance of the lowest ostinato at system 24 (1:17), one third of the way into the piece, and that the first ninety-five convergence periods were added afterward. Rhythmic analysis of the study requires knowledge of a notation not included in the final score: a measure divided by the various voices into three, four, five, fourteen, and sixteen units. In addition, several of the motives group those smaller units into odd-numbered durations. Altogether, the durations used include, in fractions of a measure: $\frac{1}{3}, \frac{1}{4}, \frac{1}{5}, \frac{1}{7}, \frac{1}{8}, \frac{1}{14}, \frac{9}{14}, \frac{13}{16}$ and $\frac{3}{16}$ or, in terms of tempo ratios, 144:182:351:468:585:624:819:936:1638. In addition, the "spastic isorhythm" from Study No. 45 reappears, introducing an irrational rhythmic element.

Nine different elements, playfully arranged, make up Study No. 46. Three of them are ostinatos, all based on Nancarrow's G–A–B–C–Bb–Ab pattern. The top two state that pattern in simplest form, a perfect eleventh away from each other.

263

Example 9.22a   Study No. 46, ostinatos (renotated)

Example 9.22b   Study No. 46, isorhythms

Ostinato 2:

Ostinato 1:

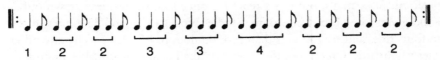

1   2   2   3   3   4   2   2   2

Example 9.23   Study No. 46, secondary melody

3   2 3   2 2 7   3   2 3   2 2 7

Example 9.24   Study No. 46, "spastic rhythm" lines (Nancarrow's notation)

system 20:

system 18:

The third fuses two such patterns into a bass of ascending and descending fourths. Nancarrow puts them together in such a way that they spell out tempos of 3:4:5, which, had he used bar lines, could have been notated as in Example 9.22a (bar lines and rests added). Note that these ostinatos are isorhythmic. The sixteen pitches of ostinato 3 recur in a three-note 2+2+1 rhythm, so that the whole ostinato – *color* plus *talea* – repeats only every forty-eight notes. The isorhythm of ostinato 2 (Example 9.22b) contains twenty-four notes, and ostinato 1 uses a thirty-note *talea*.[15] The piece originally began with the ostinatos introduced one by one and played off in pairs for forty-three such measures. The initial passage Nancarrow added introduces the ostinatos in fragmentary form, mixed with snatches of the other melodies. Once all three ostinatos have been heard together (system 35, 1:52), they continue uninterrupted for the remainder of the piece, as a constant background.

The study's focal point is a funereal melody in quadruple octaves, centering around D♯, and similar to the chant-like lines of No. 47 and the discarded movement of No. 45. (In the introduction this melody is doubled only two octaves below, and in systems 59–60 it is expressed in major triads.) The melody pounds out an unchanging beat wherever it appears, equal to $\frac{13}{16}$ of the prevailing measure; that is, in the 4/4 measure of ostinato 2, the D♯ melody could be notated in values thirteen sixteenth notes long. (A similar melody in Study No. 47 uses an 11/16 beat.) The emphasis on D♯ has a humorous off-center influence on the ostinatos, which create a feel for F major/minor. Also suggesting the key of F is a melody, usually in octaves, playing off of an F-major triad. Except for one occurrence, it takes place in the 16-tempo, with a rhythmic motive of 3+2+3+ 2+2 followed by a longer note. (Example 9.23 gives the 14-tempo occurrence, in my notation.) This alternates with a line of repeated-note octaves in the 14-tempo, grouped in durations of two, four, and six sixteenth notes, or $\frac{1}{7}$, $\frac{2}{7}$, and $\frac{3}{7}$ of a measure.

The "spastic rhythm" common also to Studies Nos. 45 and 47 runs throughout No. 46 in octaves. The points at which it occurs are separated by distances which are multiples of its length; that is, it is as though the "spastic rhythm" were running continually on a sequencer or tape loop, and each time it appears it enters where it would have done had the tape run continuously. (Nancarrow marked off lengths of the isorhythm, just over four times the measure length, on the top line of the manuscript even in systems where it does not appear.) This rhythm takes two forms, a chant-like line revolving around C or F the way the 13/16 melody does around D♯ and an ascending melody beginning with a perfect fourth, occasionally in the bass (Example 9.24a and b).

Another element is flurries of sixteenth-note octaves in the 14-tempo, usually circling F or C in the way the 13/16 melody circles D♯. In the introduction, these sixteenth notes fall in the 16-tempo. Twice (systems 11 and 45) a brief series of staccato triads appears, articulating a rhythm of nine sixteenths in the 14-tempo, or $\frac{9}{14}$ of the isorhythm measure. Example 9.24 shows the progression and

Example 9.25   Study No. 46, structural diagram

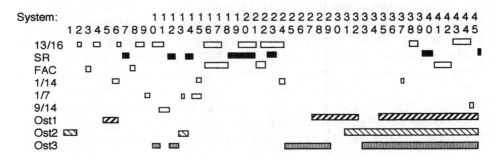

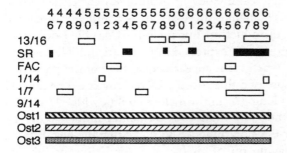

13/16 = octave melody around D#
SR = spastic rhythm
FAC = melody based on triads and minor-third motives
1/14 = 16th-note flurries in 14-tempo (16-tempo during introduction)
1/7 = repeated-note line using durations of 2, 4, and 6 16ths in the 14-tempo
9/14 = staccato triads articulating 9 16th-notes in the 14-tempo
Ost1 = highest ostinato
Ost2 = middle ostinato
Ost3 = lowest ostinato

combination of these elements. The 24-system introduction pairs these elements against each other to allow the ear to sample various combinations before they begin to accumulate. Once the ostinatos begin for good, the piece has the feel of a linear crescendo, the faster motives accumulating and beginning to overlap toward the end. With its stream-of-consciousness introduction, virtuoso octave runs, and unresolved tonal incongruities, this is a humorously enigmatic work.

Study No. 47

As of this writing, Nancarrow has lost the punching score to Study No. 47. The loss is a shame, for at six minutes forty seconds it is one of his longest single movements, and its variety of techniques, coupled with a rare melodic transparency, makes it one of his most delightful late works. However, he was kind enough to let me study the roll, and in his studio I found a punching score for six of the piece's eight sections. (They are labeled "#45e," since No. 47 was originally intended as a fifth movement of No. 45.) In its division into eight sections all using the same rhythmic and melodic materials in different configurations, and in its canon of arpeggios in section 6, Study No. 47 is reminiscent of Study No. 25, though more conventionally polyphonic and less given to pianistic fireworks.

Six of the sections are based on a measure divided at once into three, four and five. Over this the first two sections lay a 14 tempo, as in Studies Nos. 44 and 45b. In section 1 (0:00–0:50), a bass accompaniment of octaves and triads hops irregularly between these three tempos as single notes do in No. 45b, while the study's primary melody, a chromatic, chant-like line seventy-seven beats long in octaves (motivically related to the octave melody of Study No. 46), plows along in steady beats of $\frac{11}{14}$ of a measure. Reconstructed, the notation of the opening lines could be as in Example 9.26, though this gives little idea of the work's hectic speed.

Section 2 (0:50–1:50) continues the 14 tempo. What sounds like two melodies here, in treble and bass, is actually one line whose octaves leap back and forth across the entire keyboard (Example 9.27). The rhythm is an incredible, 99-note recurring isorhythm composed entirely of eighth notes and dotted eighths (twos and threes) that I cannot resist quoting in full:

3 3 3 3 2 3 2 3 3 3 3 3 3 2 3 2 3 3 2 3 3 3 3 3 2 3 2 3 3 3 3 3 2 3 2 3 2 3 2 3 2 3
2 3 3 3 3 3 2 3 2 3 3 2 3 3 3 3 3 3 2 3 3 3 3 3 3 3 2 3 2 3 2 3 3 3 2 3 3 3 3 3 3
3 3 3 2 3 3 3 2 3 2 2 2 2 2 2 2 2.

Next (at 1:05) this isorhythmic melody (call it melody B) is compressed into the bass, while triads above spell out a new melody (C) using the 3:4:5 rhythmic pattern duplicated from section 1. Melody C then switches to sustained octaves (at 1:20), with the isorhythmic melody (B) still in the bass. For the final statement of melody C (1:35) in triads, the isorhythmic melody spreads back out across the entire keyboard.

Section 3 (1:50–2:43) is a quasi-canon in staccato octaves at the ratios 3:4:5. Each line leaps around the entire range of the piano in a basic quarter-eighth note rhythm, though with some beats missing at first; the pattern is gradually filled in until steady beats are heard in each tempo. The second voice enters a fourth higher, the third a fourth lower, and both depart from canonic imitation after several measures. The convergence points for the different pairs among the three voices do not coincide.

Section 4 (2:43–3:26) is suddenly softer. The seventy-seven-beat melody of section 1 returns in the bass, while in the treble the irrational "spastic rhythm" is heard in octaves, in a melody that turns obsessively around minor thirds.

Example 9.26   Study No. 47, opening (renotated)

Section 5 (3:26–4:21) falls into four gestures. First, triads run through an additive deceleration pattern, then they accelerate back. Next, after a pause on a sustained chord (3:54), they accelerate while an octave bass line decelerates, then switch and ritard while the bass accelerates. Above this layer of activity, octaves on notes within a minor third (first F, G, and A♭, later B♭, C, and D♭) articulate a rhythm drawn by skipping around among the 3, 4, and 5 tempos, a melodic/rhythmic device reminiscent of Study No. 20; this rhythm is shown in Example 9.28 as notated on the piano roll. In the second half of this section, the 3:4:5 line in octaves is repeated in 3:5 canon with itself. Only five tempos are used, since the 3 division of the new, faster layer coincides with the 5 division of the original layer.

Section 6 (4:21–5:09), following another pause, is the arpeggio canon which brings Study No. 25 to mind. This is basically a restatement of section 5 in arpeggios and multiple octaves. The arpeggios restate the sustained–octave, minor-third melody from section 5, then repeat it $\frac{5}{3}$ as fast, then combine the five tempos in a sparser arpeggio line. During this process, multiple octaves twice spell out

Example 9.27   Study No. 47, isorhythmic melody of section 2

Example 9.28   Study No. 47, isorhythm derived from three tempos

as notated on piano roll:

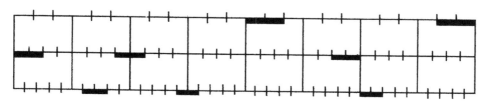

rewritten in musical notation:

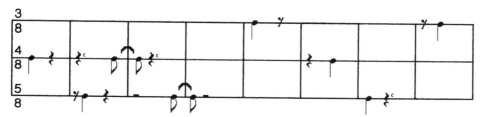

an acceleration and ritard, though the texture is so thick they can hardly be made out.

Brief but compelling section 7 (5:09–5:50) spells out the seventy-seven-beat opening melody in arpeggios, in counterpoint with quadruple octaves dotting out the spastic rhythm. (Sections 6 and 7 are missing from the "45e" punching score.)

Section 8 (5:50), calmer and finale-like, is an easily audible three-voice canon at the double octave on the opening melody in sustained octaves. Here Nancarrow uses the ratio 15:16:18, but he derives it from the 3:4:5 tempos by stating the first voice in four four-unit groupings of the 5 tempo, the second in three-unit groupings of the 4 tempo, and the last in two-unit groupings of the 3 tempo. Thus on the roll the *duration* ratios appear as $\frac{4}{5} : \frac{3}{4} : \frac{2}{3}$; invert those fractions to find the *tempo* ratio, multiply by 12, and you obtain 15:16:18.[16] The study ends at the canon's convergence point (or milliseconds before it) on a sextuple octave arpeggiated for a final flourish.

For Yoko

In January of 1990, Nancarrow caught pneumonia, and in the ensuing complications suffered the effects of a small stroke. The five pieces he has written since his recovery mark yet another new turn in his music. The new pieces (except for possibly the quintet for Parnassus, which was based on an older player-piano sketch and which I have not seen) are freer, more whimsical than his previous music. He has taken to writing pseudo-canons, or perhaps fugues – works that sound canonic but that depart from a strict rule. The ideas so crucial to his early work – canon, acceleration, isorhythm – appear here only ephemerally, touched upon in passing as though by now no more than a brief reference is necessary. Playful scale fragments echo from voice to voice. Sluggish as his memory and body have been in declining health, Nancarrow has found yet a new level of compositional freedom at the end of his eighth decade.

In particular, *For Yoko*, Study No. 51, and *Contraption No. 1* form a unified trio with similar strategies and characteristics. With *For Yoko* Nancarrow broke a 45-year habit of numbering his player piano works, titling this one with its dedication to his wife. (He also refers to the piece by its Spanish title, *Para Yoko*.) Of the three sections, the outer two sound canonic but are not strictly so. The three voices are related by tempo ratios of 4:5:6, the slower 4 voice beginning first, as usual. Exact imitation, however, is dropped in the 5 voice as soon as the 6 voice enters, and continued for a little longer in the 6 voice. The 5 and 6 voices drop out before even a theoretical convergence point would have been reached.

Contained within the canonic theme is an additive acceleration motive, which becomes the basis for the middle section. The latter is a brief interlude in which, at their respective tempos, the three voices articulate a subtractive accelerando from a note ten sixteenth notes in duration down to one that is one sixteenth note long. The final section is canonic only by rhythm and contour, climaxing in scales that sweep up and down the piano at once in the 4:5:6 tempos. They finally converge in a whimsical cadential flourish.

Study No. 51

When Carlos Sandoval asked Nancarrow what title he should put on the new player piano roll punched in 1992, Nancarrow replied, jokingly picking a number at random, "Oh, Study No. 3750." That is accordingly the number on the piano roll, and the joke fits well with Nancarrow's casual dismissal of his music's importance, but I hope to begin a trend by applying to the work its natural number in the series: Study No. 51.

Written soon after *For Yoko*, Study No. 51 is another pseudo-canon, beginning at a set of ratios Nancarrow had never used before: 12:16:21. Its first section, in wandering C major, is much like that of *For Yoko*: when each voice gets to the point at which the next voice enters, it abandons strict imitation, mostly to wander up and down the C-major scale. Then after a pause, a texture never before heard in Nancarrow's music begins: naive-sounding little scale fragments of three to five notes echo from voice to voice, 12-tempo to 16-tempo to 21-tempo, almost without overlap. A sustained chord is then followed by a weird, diatonic solo cadenza in the upper voice. Between this point and the end of the piece, three new tempos enter at ratios of 28, 38½, and 48 relative to the opening voices, for an ultimate tempo resultant of 24:32:42:56:77:96. Once the 56-tempo begins, isolated motives begin to echo through four tempos, followed by another lightning-fast treble flurry. At last a brief canon begins in the bass, involving all six tempos in a speedy yet calmly diatonic climax that cadences in a sustained major triad.

Contraption No. 1

Contraption No. 1, as its title suggests, was written for Trimpin's invention, the Contraption IPP: Instant Prepared Piano, a computer-run machine that lowers wedges, dampers, and dials on to the piano strings so that the preparations can change during the course of a piece. This is, then, Nancarrow's first work for prepared piano since Study No. 30. Choosing from possibilities Trimpin offered him, Nancarrow notated three basic types of piano sound: normal, bowed (Trimpin's machine includes little wheels with rubber loops which rotate, "bowing" the strings for a sustained tone), and "pizzicato," which here means damping the strings with rubber wedges, plastic foam, wood, or metal, depending on the register. Given Nancarrow's frenetically fast aesthetic (has any other composer written so little slow music?), some of the bowed tones did not have enough time to resonate, so Trimpin has experimented with having certain lines played on a computerized xylophone, to Nancarrow's satisfaction. *Contraption No. 1* was premiered on 4 November 1993 in San Francisco at the Other Minds festival with Nancarrow present, and presented again in Mexico City the following 22 November, but Nancarrow and Trimpin still consider it a work in progress.

The basic rhythmic unit of *Contraption No. 1* is a measure divided ultimately into seven different tempos at ratios of 8:10:12:14:17:20:24. For the first eighty-four (out of 180) measures, only the slowest three tempos are operative, at ratios of 4:5:6. The opening is a series of fragmentary gestures, alternating lines between different tempos with the non-overlapping, tempo-shifting melodicism character-istic of Nancarrow's most recent style. Soon a canon begins in the lowest voice, the imitation not too strictly observed, changing transposition level at the CP to initiate a series of decelerating triads in each voice. Scale fragments and staccato triads weave from tempo to tempo, much as in Study No. 51. At m. 85, the 14-tempo begins, initiating a 7:6:5 canon of scale fragments in the lower three voices, over which is placed a melody in minor-third dyads in the 4-tempo. Nancarrow alters the lines to reach a false CP at m. 101. Non-overlapping motives now echo among the four tempos, occasionally including long, bowed triads and eleventh chords.

Beginning at m. 129, the remaining three tempos enter one by one. From here motives simply echo from one tempo to another, without overlapping, from the fast 24-tempo in the bass through the 20-tempo, 17-tempo, and so on up to the 8-tempo in the treble, then back down again. Nancarrow has fun playing against canonic expectations: a motive will have three notes in one voice, four in the next, five in the next, and so on. At the very end the sustained triads and staccato lines begin to overlap, then suddenly pile together for a quick finish. Having followed Nancarrow's career from the ingenious devices of the early studies to the experimental structures of the middle ones to the massively intricate forms of the great canons, it is astounding to see him turn to these playful vignettes, so free, casual, formless, and naive, yet so entertaining and self-assured.

10

After the player piano

Tango?, Piece No. 2 for Small Orchestra, String Quartet No. 3, Two Canons for Ursula, Trio No. 2

In the late seventies, when Nancarrow's music became more easily available in Peter Garland's *Soundings* publications and the 1750 Arch records, his smoldering underground reputation was fanned into flame. Performers began to ask him for new, live-performable works. Not only were people willing to pay high commission fees for a Nancarrow première, he found that in the decades since his disastrous early performances musicians had come to accept far more in the way of rhythmic complexity. Naturally, in the works he has written for live instrumentalists the tempo ratios are generally less complex than in the late studies (though even in Study No. 49 he had returned to 4:5:6). But Nancarrow expends considerable ingenuity in wresting lively, unpredictable textures from the numbers 3, 4, 5, 6, and 7, and some of the star performers of contemporary music have realized his intentions with a fidelity and virtuosity which have delighted him.

The six nonmechanical works Nancarrow has written since 1983 are not merely an interesting appendage to his player piano studies. Taken together, they constitute a subtly new phase in his style. For one thing, the difficulties of tempo contrasts in live performance have forced him to find ingenious methods of getting complex ratios. In the works discussed in this chapter, once Nancarrow has set up a relatively simple contrast such as 5 against 3, he then uses a trick of articulating only every second, third, fourth, or fifth eighth note in order to build more complex ratios. (This approach is implied as early as Study No. 9.) Implicit here is the assumption that the group is either keeping a common one-measure beat in mind (in the case of a string quartet) or else following a conductor who beats once per measure. Nancarrow has also theorized about the possibility of synchronized video conductors, but he rejects mechanical substitutes because players have trouble switching tempos without being able to see the speed of a downbeat preparation. "I have an idea," he says, for a computerized conductor. There are plenty of things around, like click-tracks and other things, but they all have the disadvantage that whenever the tempo changes, there's no warning. It's just suddenly there. And I've got the idea of each performer having a small television screen, with something imitating a conductor that comes to the beat, so they can see it coming, whatever it is. I don't think it would be too complicated. It would probably be expensive, each one having his own screen.[1]

The furthest Nancarrow has ventured toward his ideal of live-performance complexity is the final acceleration canon of the String Quartet No. 3, written because he knew the Arditti Quartet could handle it.

Besides the technical innovations, these works show other, more general differences. Largely absent from them are the overpowering timbral effects of the late studies. In the late nonmechanical canons, convergence points tend to pass with little notice except as final flourishes. The emphasis is not on dramatic moments, but on smooth linearity of counterpoint. With a few exceptions (the first movement of the Orchestra Piece, the second *Canon for Ursula*) there is an under-stated restraint here, a contrapuntal introversion with which Nancarrow seems to return to the concerns of his early hero Bach. We are indebted to those who inspired these commissions, for they are among his finest works.

Tango?

The "tango" Nancarrow wrote in 1983 for pianist Yvar Mikhashoff (adding a question mark to the title perhaps to acknowledge that the piece would be difficult to dance to for two legs controlled by the same brain) is related in technique to the series of player piano studies he had recently written, Nos. 44, 45, 46, and 47, and also to the early No. 6. All of these pieces assume an ongoing polytempo of 3:4:5, with certain voices skipping back and forth between tempos.

Tango?'s eight sections are easily characterized. Generally speaking, this is a crescendo piece with a drop in intensity just before the end. Section 1 (0:00–0:19,[2] mm. 1–22) is melody-less, mostly staccato, with a recurring minor-third motive in the right hand, and, in the left, an accompaniment that contains a gloss on the upcoming main theme. Sections 2–8 state the main theme in the right hand seven times, changing in tempo at ratios of 3:4:5:6:4:2½:7. Dynamics increase by one level each section from *pp* to *ff* in sections 1 through 6, drop to *pp* again for section 7, then leap to *fff* in section 8. At the beginning, both hands play single notes. In section 2 minor-third dyads are added in the left hand, in section 3 variable dyads are added in the right, and in section 4 octaves are added in the left hand. In section 6 the texture, though *ff*, drops back to staccato single notes, with the right hand suddenly in a low register. In section 7 the minor-third dyads return in the highest range, then for a rousing finale the right hand plays full triads against the left hand's octaves. Except in the last section, the left hand switches continually between two different tempos, and the tempos change with each new section. Example 10.1 summarizes most of this information.

Example 10.1   *Tango?*, structural chart

Section:	1	2	3	4	5	6	7	8
Starting time:	0:00	0:19	0:49	1:12	1:32	1:48	2:03	2:30
Begins m.:	1	24	60	92	116	136	154	190
Length in mm.:	23	36	32	24	20	18	36	16
Dynamics:	*pp*	*p*	*mp*	*mf*	*f*	*ff*	*pp*	*fff*
Transposition:	C	F	C	G	C	D	G	C
RH tempo:	3	3	4	5	6	4	2.5	7
LH tempos:	4,5	4,5	6,5	6,4	5,4	6,5	6,4	5
RH dyads:			*	*	*			
RH articulation:	S	L	L	L	L	S	L	L
RH triads:								*
LH thirds:		*	*	*	*		*	*
LH octaves:				*	*			*

S = staccato
L = legato

Example 10.2   *Tango?*, comparison of section beginnings

The lengths of the seven melodic sections – proportionally 9, 8, 6, 5, 4½, 9, and 4 – are roughly related (in inverse proportion) to the tempos of the melody, but Nancarrow takes liberties with the rhythm, adding a rest here, lengthening a note there. Some of the slight variations can be seen in Example 10.2, which compares a few section beginnings. Furthermore, section 6 is interrupted when the melody is only half over. No two sections end the melody in quite the same manner, and the differences have to do primarily with moving from one range to another, since range is another varying factor. For instance, in section 1 the left hand stays primarily within the octave centered on middle C; in section 6 the right hand hovers in the lower part of the treble clef; in *pp* section 7 the G above middle C is a lower limit for the left hand, while the right moves into the highest octaves; and so on. The overall curve is pleasing, since section 6 foreshadows the

275

drop in intensity with its thinned out texture and lowered range, section 7 is long, soft, high, and gentle, and section 8 is a quick, whirlwind finish.

From time to time various derivative tempos are suggested in the left hand: in section 1, a beat equal to $\frac{3}{5}$ of a measure, then $\frac{2}{5}$, then $\frac{1}{2}$. Section 3 uses a playful alternation reminiscent of Study No. 6, switching between 5- and 6-tempos every three notes. For the pianist these rhythms demand a terrifically virtuosic ability to keep different divisions of the meter going at once. The aural effect, though, while subtle, is not really one of complexity, since each element of the texture – melody, third dyads, bass octaves – is kept fairly linear despite the left hand's skipping between parts. What one hears is a lively counterpoint in which the lines have a clear tonal relationship but seem completely independent as to rhythm: a vivacious and charming surface, well captured by Ursula Oppens on her recording.

Piece No. 2 For Small Orchestra

Nancarrow's second and most recent orchestra work was another Betty Freeman commission (the first being Study No. 45). It is scored for an orchestra of Classical period dimensions, with the substitution of piano for timpani: oboe, B♭ clarinet, bassoon, B♭ trumpet, French horn, piano (two performers), and strings. (This is two instruments fewer than the Orchestra Piece No. 1, which included trombone and an extra horn.) The piece's rhythmic premise is that the constant measure-long pulse is divided into five, six, and seven eighth notes by different instruments at different times.

In tonality and gesture, the ingratiating opening is more like the Franco-American school of the 1930s and 40s than anything more recent. The trumpet's five-note fanfare, quickly echoed in inversion by the French horn, plunges us *in medias res*, and sets up a pattern of triplet repeated notes, occasionally interrupted by hemiola, that continues throughout the first section. The woodwinds respond with expansive melodies of perfect fourths in the 6/8 meter. The strings, meanwhile, articulate a beat every four eighth notes in the 5-tempo in an aggressive series of seventh, eleventh, and thirteenth chords. Thus while the winds play dotted quarters and hemiolas in 6/8, the strings suggest a beat equal to $\frac{4}{5}$ of a measure, for a general, if inconsistent, 5:8 tempo ratio. From m. 40 on the piano punctuates the 6/8 meter with contrasting major triads in both hands. Such melodic momentum among unified instrumental groups in a texture devoid of common downbeats gives an invigorating feeling of unfettered rhythmic freedom.

As early as m. 35 (0:21 on Continuum's Musicmasters recording),[3] the horn further complicates matters by playing its repeated notes in a tempo of seven eighth notes to the measure, and the trumpet and horn compete in a Morse code rhythm of 6:7. This contrapuntal line glides smoothly into section 2 (0:31–2:03, mm. 49–138), a series of inversional quasi-canons based on the Morse code repeated note. Changing to a new pair every twelve measures, the winds play this

Example 10.3   Piece No. 2 for Small Orchestra, deceleration pattern

Measure:	67	79	91	103	115	127	139	151	163	175
Tempo:										
42	Trpt	Trpt								
36	Horn		Oboe							
30		Horn	Trpt	Clar	Oboe					
24				Horn		Trpt				
21					Bsn					
14							Horn	Clar		
10								Bsn	Trpt	
8									Horn	Oboe
5										Bsn	Clar
4										Bsn
Ratio:	6:7	5:7	5:6	4:5	7:10	7:12	5:7	4:5	5:8	4:5
Interval:	m2	M2	m3	M3	P4	A4	P5	m6	M6	m7

Example 10.4   Piece No. 2 for Small Orchestra, comparison of motives

Section 1:

Section 3:

motive with neighbor notes that become increasingly distant: half-step neighbor notes in the trumpet and horn, then minor third in the oboe and trumpet, major third in the clarinet and horn, and so on. With each new pairing the tempo of the repeated notes becomes slower in a ten-stage deceleration (shown in Example 10.3), while the tempo *ratios* become slightly more complex and then less so. The winds are not the only elements involved in the slowing-down process. Throughout this section the piano plays high-register six-note chords (pairs of major triads) at irregular intervals ranging from four to twenty-eight eighth notes and generally becoming less frequent. The pizzicato cello reinforces the 6/8 meter, with occasional patterns of 4+5+3 eighth notes interpolated, and finally slowing down to every ninth eighth note (by m. 163).

Section 3 (2:03–3:33, mm. 187–322) is dominated by a melody clearly conceived in 6/8, though played in other meters. As shown in Example 10.4, it seems intervallically derived from the first section's woodwind melody. It is first played at five eighth notes to the measure by the clarinet (mm. 187 ff.), then six eighths per measure by the oboe and French horn (mm. 229 ff.), and finally at seven eighths per measure by the trumpet and first violin (mm. 261 ff.). In the first instance it is accompanied pizzicato by the lower strings; the second statement is accompanied by the cellos articulating a half-note beat in 7/8; and the third statement is accompanied by the cellos playing on the downbeat while the piano articulates half and quarter notes at five eighths per measure. Between these statements of the melody are short bridges in which first the strings, then the brass and piano, articulate further conflicting beats. (These piano triads playing modal lines in an orchestral texture have a Bartókian sound, like a memory held over from the orchestral version of the Sonata for Two Pianos and Percussion.) After the final melody the opening repeated-note theme returns, alternating between strings and brass in 6/8, as the piano continues playing a quarter-note beat in 5/8. The passage ends with a flurry of upward diatonic scales in the strings, in 7/8 meter.

By now one expects canons in a Nancarrow instrumental work, and this first movement ends with two: the first for oboe, clarinet, and bassoon, the second for three-hand piano, both at tempo ratios of 5:6:7. The first canon, mm. 328–400 (3:33–4:25), keeps each player within an octave range, limited to two-note motives (mostly half-steps) and occasional single notes. Notationally, each line is written in virtual 6/8 meter: the first note of each motive is always divisible by a dotted quarter, and in the oboe's line, notated in 6/8, every note falls on the first or fourth eighth note. The second canon, mm. 406–536 (4:27–5:48), consists entirely of triads, almost all staccato, on the piano, a unique sound for an orchestral piece. (Nancarrow specifies two performers, which means that one player is expected to play either the 5:6 or the 6:7.) Toward the end (starting at m. 514), the players regularize into only half-note durations.

After its joyous opening burst of energy, the movement ends anticlimactically, but then segues without pause into the oboe solo and gradual crescendo of the second movement. As mentioned before, Nancarrow made a player piano version of the second movement and dubbed it Study No. 50. As such, the piece was analyzed in chapter 6 and need not be recapitulated here. One element of the orchestral version was omitted from Study No. 50, however: a trumpet part (joined by horn at the very end) consisting of small repeated-note motives involving half-steps and minor thirds, played in the 6-tempo. These motives are carried over from the first movement and form a thematic link in addition to the rhythmic links which unify the two movements.

String Quartet No. 3 – Canons 3/4/5/6

Two of Nancarrow's most recent live-instrumental works are entirely canonic. The Third String Quartet was written in 1987 for the Arditti String Quartet, who greatly impressed Nancarrow by the ease with which they sightread his First Quartet. "The Kronos [Quartet]," he says,

> were the ones who played my First Quartet for the first time, at the Cabrillo Festival. When I went there, they played it very well, but they said, "Look, we spent a lot of work on this, it's very difficult." Well, the First Quartet isn't simple, but it's not out of this world. And later, when I went to the Almeida Festival in

London, I took that quartet along to the Arditti. They said, "Come by, let's have sort of a reading, see how it goes." The reading – that was it! It was finished! Unbelievable. That's why I did this [Third] quartet. If anyone can do it, they can.[4]

The Arditti gave the new quartet its première in Cologne on 15 October 1988, and later its American première on 8 March 1989 in New York City.[5] (As mentioned earlier, the Second String Quartet is an unfinished torso from the forties, which will likely remain unfinished and unperformable.)

Each of the quartet's three movements is a canon at tempo ratios of 3:4:5:6. (See Example 1.11 on p. 27 for a diagram of each canon.) Measure lengths are the same for all four players (until the end of the finale). In the outer movements, the cello plays in 3/8 meter, the viola in 4/8, the second violin in 5/8, and the first violin in 6/8. In the second movement these meters are reversed, with the cello playing in 6/8, the viola in 5/8, and so on. The players are asked to keep a sense of one large, common beat per measure (Nancarrow marks the tempo as "measure = 72"), within which each plays his or her own subdivisions – a difficult task, but not, as the Arditti has shown, impossible. The effect is one of great freedom within cooperation: four players playing the same theme and disagreeing about tempo, each determined to stick to his or her own, and yet all somehow coming out right at the end.

The only remarkable feature of the first movement is that Nancarrow times the entrances of voices so that convergence points between pairs of instruments *do not* coincide for the entire group. The lengths of each instrument's part, and numbers of measures of rests before entrance and after cutting out, are as follows:

measures	of rest	playing	of rest
violin I (6-tempo)	$28\frac{1}{6}$	72^6	44
violin II (5-tempo)	21	$86\frac{3}{5}$	$36\frac{3}{5}$
viola (4-tempo)	12	$108\frac{1}{4}$	24
cello (3-tempo)	0	$144\frac{1}{3}$	0

Any two voices playing a tempo canon will eventually converge as long as the slower one begins first. However, given three or more voices, the pairs will converge at the same time only if their entrances are timed according to a given ratio dependent on the tempo ratios. With the tempo ratios at 3:4:5:6, the proportionate lengths of the players' lines will be 20:15:12:10 (divide each ratio term into the lowest common multiple, 60). If the cello begins 20x beats before a common convergence point, the viola would have to begin 15x beats beforehand, violin II 12x beats, and violin I 10x beats. Therefore, the viola's entrance would require a delay after the cello's entrance of 5x beats, violin II 8x beats, and violin I 10x beats. The ratio of measures of rest, moving from cello to violin I, would have to be 0:5:8:10.

Here, however, the measures-of-rest ratio is $0:12:21:28\frac{1}{6}$. The six convergence points all fall within a seventeen-measure passage. First the cello and viola converge at m. 48, then the cello and second violin at m. 53, cello and first violin at

Example 10.5   String Quartet No. 3, derived 3+3+2 rhythm

3   3   2   3   3   2   3   3   2   3   3

Example 10.6   String Quartet No. 3, second movement melody

Example 10.7   String Quartet No. 3, third movement convergence point

m. 57, viola and second violin at m. 58, viola and first violin at m. 61, and the two violins at m. 65. This intentional "mis"-timing precludes any climactic point at which all four strings create a collective effect; climaxes are saved for the second and third movements.

Structure aside, the first fourth of each part is primarily in eighth notes, with a recurring motive of a triple repeated note. At m. 39 (0:32; the timings refer to the Arditti's recording on Gramavision) the cello initiates a series of sixteenth-note runs, which spread up toward the first violin in a momentary flurry. The first CP at m. 48 (0:40) begins a section of double stops. At m. 68 (0:57), following the convergence points, violin I initiates a grace-noted minor-third motive, then at m. 85 (1:12) a little isorhythmic ostinato reminiscent of Study No. 2. By making alternate notes double stops, Nancarrow creates a half-concealed 3+3+2 rhythm (Example 10.5). Afterward each string goes through a brief series of trills, disappearing into a final glissando.

The unusual second movement, most of it in harmonics and much of it pizzicato, is extraordinarily delicate for Nancarrow. As mentioned, the voices enter from top (violin I) to bottom (cello), contrary to Nancarrovian habit. Measures of rest delay – 0, 18, 28⁴/₅, and 36 reading downward – fit the 0:5:8:10 ratio, and the four voices converge undramatically on a rest at m. 73 (1:32). With amazing

280

restraint, each voice restricts itself to only six diatonic pitches throughout the movement, organized into a homespun, American-sounding melody (Example 10.6). (So pure is that melody that the harmonic markers begin to look like little halos.) The second violin, viola, and cello enter on A, D, and D respectively, so that altogether eight pitches are present throughout the texture.

There are only two exceptions to this austerity. The first is an attention-grabbing minor-third double-stop, B–G♯ in violin I, which echoes from instrument to instrument at mm. 61–68 (1:15). The second is the canonic subject that enters just after the convergence point, in rising fourths unmistakably reminiscent of the closing fugue of Beethoven's Op. 110 Sonata; this subject briefly introduces two yet-unused pitches. The pitch F is banished from this movement. The convergence point comes unusually early – m. 73 out of a total of 249 – leaving the first violin a forty-four-measure closing solo in harmonics, all but the last few bars pizzicato. The gentle patter of pizzicatos and harmonics at different tempos is as quiet as falling snow, and the image is bolstered by the whiteness of the reduced pitch spectrum.

Nancarrow saves his dramatic effects for the finale. This movement is divided into three parts with measure proportions of 252, 77 and 43. Canon 1, accounting for over two-thirds of the movement, takes the final glissando, trills, grace-noted third motive, repeated notes, and scales hinted at in the first movement and whips them into a whirlwind canonic subject. The pitch line makes references to both Nancarrow's minor-third motive and the Beethovenian fourths – G C A D – of the second movement, but timbral and textural contrast are the real issue. A series of triple stops appears first in the cello at m. 213 (2:43), string counterparts to the triads Nancarrow uses for similar force in the player piano studies. Because the tempo ratios are proportionally so far apart, no phrases overlap until just before the convergence point at m. 251 (3:15), and the four voices end dramatically just a few beats before they would have converged.

Canon 2 is an unexpected reminiscence of the second movement, using pizzicato harmonics and the same diatonic pitch restrictions. A flurry of harmonic glissandos (Example 10.7) surrounds the CP at mm. 288–89 (3:55). This is the only real collective effect Nancarrow sets up in the entire piece. Like the second movement, canon 2 contains more measures after its CP than before it.

Canon 3 (4:39) is a virtuoso tour de force. Running through forty-three increasingly quick measures of trills, tremolos, and glissandos, the four players are asked to play, not at different tempos, but *at different rates of acceleration* – three, four, five, and six percent – as in Studies Nos. 22 and 27. To make this possible, Nancarrow has marked off an unchanging measure (tempo = 92) over each system, so that all four players can measure their accelerandos in reference to a consistent beat. The transposition levels are at the octave, so that the players all end together – if indeed they manage to do so – on a lightning quick A–B–C cadence. I have heard the Arditti achieve this unprecedented feat live, and the effect is electric.

Two Canons for Ursula

In response to a commission from Composers Forum in New York, Nancarrow originally intended to write three canons for pianist Ursula Oppens. The third would have required her to play no fewer than four tempos at once, at ratios of 6:9:10:15. Each hand was to keep up tempos of 3 against 5, and the two hands were related by a ratio of 2:3. When I visited Nancarrow in September 1988, he was struggling with this third canon, and soon after abandoned it as unsuitable for a single player. One can imagine Oppens' relief.

Nevertheless, the first canon retains a hint of that quadruple polytempo conception. Since each hand is often asked to play four in the space of five, the actual resultant tempos spell out a daunting framework of 20:25:28:35. This was a $15,000 commission, and the Two Canons are not tossed-off bagatelles, but a virtuosic showpiece of major proportions (for Nancarrow, anyway: twelve minutes). The first canon, at a difficult 5:7 tempo ratio, is 379 measures long. The left hand enters first and ends last; the right hand enters after sixty-nine measures and drops out thirty-nine measures before the left is through. Typically for Nancarrow's late, smoother style, the exact convergence point is not emphasized: it occurs at m. 242, in the middle of sustained chords in both hands, unarticulated by attack.

Determined to get maximum contrapuntal complexity from Oppens' willing fingers, Nancarrow outlines two voices in the opening single-note line, the lower of which suggests his favorite descending minor/ascending major motive (Example 10.8). The lines give the appearance of having been written with the 5-tempo in mind, not only because the four-in-the-space-of-five notations are awkwardly notated in 7/8, but because 3+2 and 2+1+2 isorhythms are common. The simple, quasi-symmetrical motives of the canon's first 168 measures suggest the Webern Op. 27 Variations, only transformed into consonance (Example 10.9). At m. 169, the right hand pauses for the first of several dissonant *sfz* five-note chords in the left hand. At m. 190, when that chord echoes in the right hand, it coincides with the left hand's second five-note chord, seven different pitches between them. Both are preceded by a string of alternating octaves, giving the moment the effect of a false convergence point (the real CP is still fifty-two measures away). This false CP (a device found elsewhere only in Study No. 41) is followed by a passage in which both hands play only major triads on the E, F♯, and G above middle C, arranged in such a way that they are heard over and over in that order although the hands alternate.

The CP passage, mm. 239–48, consists of seven five-note chords, each confined within a major seventh interval, in each hand. The first and last in the faster right hand coincide with the second and sixth in the left, outlining a slow, *ff* five-against-seven rhythm while the actual CP passes without articulation in the exact middle. Following the convergence point the canon restricts itself to tiny sets of pitches with near-minimalist obsession. In mm. 259–304 the right hand switches between two interval sets: one, a minor third plus major second, the other a minor third filled in. Between the two hands, they are staggered to create passages of

Example 10.8   *Two Canons for Ursula*, No. 1, opening line

Example 10.9   *Two Canons for Ursula*, No. 1, triad motive

Example 10.10   *Two Canons for Ursula*, No. 1 minimalist pointillism

pointillistic rhythm within a perfect fourth (Example 10.10). These passages, the live-performed reincarnation of Study No. 20's pitch bands, increase in length (from seven mm. to nine to thirteen to seventeen in the right hand) to keep pace with the increasing echo distance. In the middle such passage, the hands play the same pitches, E, F♯, and G, echoing the effect earlier achieved with triads. At m. 306 the triads and dyads of the opening return to fill out the canon, with one remaining *sfz* chord in each hand, after which the remainder of the material quotes from the opening page.

If the first canon draws tremendous variety and subtlety from a tiny amount of material, the second is an extravaganza of favorite tricks akin to Study No. 49c: glissandos, accelerating rhythms, octaves, isorhythms, and a grace-noted minor-third motive. (With one canon so introverted, the other so extroverted, it is small wonder Nancarrow failed in his search for a *tertium quid*.) The second canon's tempo ratio is a simplest-ever 2:3; out of 400 measures, the right hand begins at m. 134, and the final four-octave C is the only convergence point. The left hand opens with two two-octave glissandos, one up, a pause, then one down. Immediately, we hear in succession: a 7 6 5 4 3 2 1 rhythmic motive on a repeated D, a grace note to the minor third F, scales outlined in alternating octaves, a melody using staccato octaves, another gliss, and a 3+3+4+2+4 eighth note isorhythm using only the pitches A and E. These signal that this canon is about, not continuity, but contrast of timbral and rhythmic effects.

Nancarrow had never before used a tempo ratio as large as 3:2 without a mediating middle voice, and the echo distance does not become small enough to

Example 10.11   *Two Canons for Ursula*, No. 2, acceleration against isorhythm

Example 10.12   *Two Canons for Ursula*, No. 2, tempo canon within a tempo canon

be perceived until about the last twenty measures. Pacing, then, in this canon has mostly to do with bringing different types of effects together. At m. 146, soon after the right hand's entrance, we hear an acceleration 8 7 6 5 4 3 2 1 rhythm against the opening melody's steady quarter notes. Where glissandos fall in the new voice, Nancarrow inserts the minor-third motive in between. The jazzy melody that appeared unaccompanied in the left hand at mm. 52–81 returns at m. 168 in the right punctuated by the 3+3+4+2+4 isorhythm in quarter notes, and now appears to have been written to work with it in rhythmic counterpoint. One of the best effects is the same isorhythm pitted against the acceleration rhythm at mm. 189–96 (Example 10.11). It is as though Nancarrow cannot resist trying out the old ideas of the early studies for a live performer.

Tempo canon within a tempo canon must have been on Nancarrow's mind, and he tries again in this movement. At m. 198 he states a canonic voice in the left hand, based on alternations of a 5+3 rhythm and 4+4. At m. 206, still in the left hand, it is answered a perfect fifth above, in smaller rhythmic values: durations of three eighth notes are replaced by two, four (usually) by three, five by four, seven by five, eight by six, and nine by seven. Though arithmetically rather than geometrically derived, on the average, it is a 4:3 tempo canon (Example 10.12). (Remember, the right hand still has its own problems at this point.) At m. 231, where the left-hand convergence point would have occurred, Nancarrow quits and begins a new canonic subject, answered in the same manner at m. 240. The intricacy with which these canons are kept within the range of one hand is worthy of one of the fifteenth-century Netherlands masters, but Nancarrow refrains from asking miracles of his performer. The new canon ends, again, just shy of its CP, at m. 265, a fraction of a beat before the first canon is echoed in the right hand. Nancarrow spares his pianist a four-part tempo canon at ratios of 12:9:8:6.

As one would expect (and, by now, hope) the elements become simplified as the real convergence point nears. Staccato triads and the 3+3+4+2+4 isorhythm become more common, along with a series of wickedly irregular chromatic eighth-note figures drawn from player piano technique. In the closing twenty-one measures the texture reduces to sustained triads preceded by half-step grace notes before ending on a final flourish of glissandos.

Oppens premièred *Two Canons for Ursula* at Town Hall in New York City on 20 November 1989. (*Tango?* was her encore, and has been at other performances since.) Nancarrow may not acknowledge it, but her lithe, flexible performance, full of accents and dynamic nuance, demonstrated that even his music can benefit from that "human element" he has so often scoffed at.

Trio No. 2

With the single exception of Study No. 26, the Trio No. 2, written in 1991 for the Continuum ensemble, is the simplest piece rhythmically in Nancarrow's output. Consisting of one movement four minutes long, and scored like the 1930 Sarabande and Scherzo for oboe, bassoon, and piano, the piece is written in 3/4 meter with a 6/8 time signature, and contains not a single note that is not articulated on an eighth-note beat: there is no suggestion anywhere of conflicting tempos. The piano part throughout contains only single notes and close-position triads. The tonality is a pandiatonically firm C major, dotted (as in so much of Nancarrow's late work) with minor forays toward both the flat and sharp sides of the spectrum, and with no departure lasting more than two measures. Within this cheerful tonality the piece spins a charmingly idiosyncratic pointillism of isolated single notes and two- to four-note motives, passing from instrument to instrument in *Klangfarbenmelodie* manner.

The form is basically ABBCB, with a nine-measure extension in the latter two B sections which is not found in the first. The A section (mm. 1–30) is entirely in *Klangfarbenmelodie*, with no line containing more than three contiguous notes, and with no attacks in more than one instrument at a time. (This use of isolated,

Example 10.13   Trio 2, repeating timbral/rhythmic pattern

nonoverlapping motives links the piece with Nancarrow's late player piano works: *For Yoko, Contraption No. 1,* and Study No. 51.) The rhythmic process is smooth and consistent without being at all regular. For example, in the passage in Example 10.13 (mm. 12–18), the following figure is repeated: a few notes in the oboe, a triad in the piano right hand, an octave in the bassoon, a note or two in the piano left hand. But the triad sometimes precedes the bassoon by one eighth note, sometimes by two, sometimes by three. Expressed in eighth notes, the piano triads spell out a rhythm of 8+12+9+10, the bassoon octaves one of 11+10+8+10. Nancarrow's method here combines simplicity with asymmetry.

The B section, repeated three times (mm. 31–74, mm. 77–120, and mm. 152–195, with extensions at mm. 121–29 and mm. 196–205), is louder and more polyphonic, with scalar melodies running through all four lines (counting the right and left hand of the piano separately). The first B section decrescendos back into pointillism before repeating, and the three B sections differ in small melodic details, particularly with regard to octave register. The C section (mm. 130–51) begins even more pointillistically than the A section, with only single notes and triads at first, then expanding to three- and four-note motives. There are echoing rhythmic and timbral motives here, but no canons, isorhythms, or polytempo. The Trio No. 2 is an elegant, whimsical little piece, yet, without the piano's running triads, you might have never guessed the composer.

In 1977, when Nancarrow was sixty-five, he was virtually unknown outside the most serious underground new music circles. In 1994, New York's spring concert season alone included five separate performances of his music, including the Septet, *Tango?, Two Canons for Ursula,* and Yvar Mikhashoff's arrangements of Studies Nos. 3c, 6, and 7. Nancarrow is now internationally acclaimed, and his rare public appearances draw enthusiastic crowds. Continual presence in the music world, however, is still largely dependent on live performance, and his dozen-odd works for piano and chamber ensembles account for a disproportionate share of his public exposure. In addition to the five works described here, Nancarrow has also completed a quintet for New York's Parnassus Ensemble, based on an earlier abandoned sketch for player piano – a score I did not have access to in time to discuss. Mikhashoff's expert instrumental arrangements of Studies Nos. 1, 2, 3c, 5, 6, 7, 9, 12, 14, 18, and 19, just as charming as the originals when well played, are achieving new popularity for Nancarrow within European and American concert life. The increasing ease of performing the player piano studies "live" on MIDI-controlled pianos also helps bring Nancarrow to a larger concert audience.

Nancarrow's imagination has remained unself-repeatingly inventive into his eighties. When I last visited him in August of 1993, an unpunched piano roll lay across his working table, marked off at tempo ratios of 8:10:12:14:17:21:25:28. His most recent works suggest yet another new approach to tempo layerings, new scales of tempos covering several "octaves" of ratios; also new forms, whimsical and less structuralist than those of the preceding studies. It is unclear how much more music we can expect from him, but he has never ceased to offer promise of previously unimagined new directions. Wherever his music ends will seem like the middle of a brand new thought.

Notes

1 The music: general considerations

1 Henry Cowell, *New Musical Resources* (New York: Alfred A. Knopf, 1930), pp. 64–65.
2 Henry Cowell, "Music of and for Records," *Modern Music* 8/3 (March–April 1931), p. 34.
3 Letter to Charles Amirkhanian, 4 January 1981, Vienna.
4 *Works by Henry Cowell, Ruth Crawford Seeger, Wallingford Riegger, John J. Becker*, New World Records, NW 285.
5 I borrow the term "hypermeasure" from Jonathan Kramer's book *The Time of Music* (New York: Schirmer Books, 1988), to denote a group of measures that form a perceived unit within a larger rhythmic hierarchy.
6 Ibid., p.73.
7 Interview with the author, Mexico City, 14–16 September 1989.
8 Kramer, *The Time of Music*, p. 76.
9 "Conversations Around the Pacific Ring," program for the Pacific Ring Festival, Center for Music Experiment, University of California at San Diego, May 1986.
10 Assuming, that is, that there are no secondary tempo changes in between convergence points, as there have not yet been in Nancarrow's music. He has never written a canon in which one tempo changes to another via, say, a series of steps.
11 This statement assumes that the convergence period and echo distance are calculated using the same beat: quarter note, eighth note, whatever.
12 Gordon Numma, "Briefly about Nancarrow," in *Conlon Nancarrow: Selected Studies for Player Piano, Soundings* 4 (spring/summer, 1977), p. 4.
13 Interview with the author, 14–16 September 1989.
14 Ibid.
15 Quoted by James Tenney in "Conlon Nancarrow's Studies for Player Piano," *Soundings* 4, pp. 41–42.

2 A biographical sketch

1 Remembered by the composer's brother, Charles Nancarrow, in an interview with the author in Texarkana, Ark., July 1990. Conlon had remembered Gulf Oil.
2 Ibid.

3 Actually, neither the tree nor the stone is original. When a new street was built over the original site, Charles Nancarrow granted permission to plant a new tree rather than move the old one. During removal, the builders wrecked the monument, and that was replaced as well. The names of Samuel and Charles Nancarrow also appear on plaques on a bridge on Broad Street.

4 Cole Gagne and Tracy Caras, *Soundpieces: Interviews with American Composers* (Metuchen, N.J.: Scarecrow Press, 1982), p. 292.

5 Actually a widow, according to Charles Nancarrow (interview, July 1990).

6 William Duckworth, unpublished 1987 interview (for a projected book entitled *Talking Music: Interviews with Five Generations of American Composers*).

7 Ibid.

8 Interview with the author, Mexico City, 28–29 September 1988.

9 Charles Nancarrow, interview, July 1990.

10 Ibid.

11 Aaron Copland's review of Nancarrow ("Scores and Records," *Modern Music* 15/3 [March–April 1938], p. 180) quoted from Nancarrow's brief biography that he had gone there for two years, and Philip Carlsen identifies his studies there as lasting from 1929 to 1932. Nancarrow insisted to William Duckworth and myself that it was only a semester. Given his Vanderbilt experience, it's doubtful that even a check of Conservatory records would be much indication of his actual attendance.

12 Duckworth, unpublished 1987 interview.

13 Letter from Helen Zimbler to the author, October 1990.

14 Ibid.

15 Zimbler, in a 1990 interview, told me she remembered accompanying Nancarrow to a party at Schoenberg's apartment in Brookline, and claimed that Nancarrow had studied briefly with Schoenberg.

16 Interview with the author, 28–29 September 1988.

17 Ibid.

18 Nancarrow, telephone interview with the author, November 1990.

19 Interview with the author, 28–29 September 1988.

20 Interview with the author, 14–16 September 1989.

21 Peter Garland, *Americas: Essays on American Music and Culture* (Santa Fe: Soundings Press, 1982), p. 178.

22 Zimbler, interview, 1990.

23 Garland, *Americas*, p. 187, and Duckworth, unpublished 1987 interview.

24 Letter from Helen Zimbler to the author, October 1990.

25 Unpublished letter from Adeline Naiman, undated.

26 Interview with the author, 14–16 September 1989.

27 Zimbler, interview, 1990.

28 Letter from Zimbler to the author, October 1990.

29 "Scores and Records," p. 180.

30 Garland, *Americas*, p. 182.

31 Ibid., p. 163.

32 "Over the Air: Swing Jazz, Boogie-Woogie" in *Modern Music*, 17/4 (May 1940), p. 264.

33   Minna Lederman, *The Life and Death of a Small Magazine (Modern Music, 1926–1946)*, I.S.A.M. Monograph No. 18 (Brooklyn: Institute for Studies in American Music, 1983), p. 104.

34   Some confusion exists about an orchestral work Nancarrow supposedly wrote about this time. Apparently musicologist Otto Mayer gave the manuscript to conductor/composer Carlos Chavez (1899–1978), who never performed the work. Eva Soltes suggests that the score might be found in Chavez's library. But on the other hand this might be the same work that Carlos Sandoval found in Nancarrow's studio, which is an expansion of the Piece No. 1 for Small Orchestra (see p. 63 below).

35   Interview with the author, 14–16 September 1989.

36   Charles Nancarrow, interview, July 1990.

37   Interview with the author, 14–16 September 1989.

38   Amirkhanian, "Interview with Composer Conlon Nancarrow," *Soundings* 4, p. 8.

39   Interview with the author, 14–16 September 1989.

40   Interview with the author, 28–29 September 1988.

41   Garland, *Americas*, pp. 174–75.

42   Ibid., p. 166.

43   Liner notes, *Conlon Nancarrow: Studies for Player Piano*, Columbia MS 7222.

44   Garland, *Americas*, pp. 159–61.

45   Interview with the author, 28–29 September 1988.

46   I am grateful to Eva Soltes and her painstaking record-keeping for the chronology of Nancarrow's travels in the 1980s.

3 Foreshadowings: the early works

1   Gagne and Caras, *Soundpieces*, p. 285.

2   James Tenney points out an unusual pitch device in the Toccata. At mm. 107–12, the long sequence of pitches in the piano's left hand is derived by taking a five-interval row and increasing each interval a semitone with each repetition. Beginning with the pitches B♭–C–D♭–A–G♯, the intervals run as follows (in terms of semitones, with downward intervals indicated by minus signs):

2	1	−4	−1	3
3	2	−5	−2	4
4	3	−6	−3	5
5	4	−7	−4	6
6	5	−8	−5	7
7	6	−9	−6	8
8	7	−10	−7	9
9	7★	−11	−8	10

The anomalous 7 (★) in the last row occurs, Tenney theorizes, in order to end the sequence on A, the passage's apparent tonic.

3   The rhythm of this canon is complicated by the fact that the violin I and viola use dotted quarters for the notes that begin each phrase, while the violin II and cello use quarters. By the canon's end, eight eighth notes has become the rhythmic interval of imitation.

4 Blues years: the ostinato studies

1 Tenney's statement ("Conlon Nancarrow's Studies for Player Piano," p. 59) that Nos. 28 and 29 were also written for prepared player piano is in error.

2 Liner notes, *Sound Forms for Piano*, New World NW 203.

3 Roger Reynolds, "Conlon Nancarrow: Interviews in Mexico City and San Francisco," *American Music* 2/2 (Summer 1984). This is perhaps the most revealing of Nancarrow's interviews, but Reynolds' chronology is unreliable. For example, he dates the Cunningham choreography of Nancarrow's music from the late fifties (they were performed from 1960 to 1964).

4 Interview with the author, 28–29 September 1988.

5 To express a five-subdivision value, Nancarrow invents a notation that he later uses consistently, a wavy line with a stem: ♩. I haven't adopted it in this book because of its eventual ambiguity. First of all, intuitively, that symbol seems to indicate a quarter tied to a sixteenth, but in Study No. 1 Nancarrow uses it for an eighth note tied to a thirty-second. Secondly, the sign works up through a quarter-note value, but what about half and whole notes? I prefer the notation devised by George Crumb, which places a dot on either side of the note. In the examples, however, I have tried to avoid misunderstanding altogether by using conventional tied notes.

5 Isorhythm: the numbers game

1 Interview with the author, 14–16 September 1989.

2 In the published score, a G D F chord, audible on the recording, is missing at mm. 41 and 42; the sustained F minor triad appears to complicate the system, but it is a copying error.

3 Interview with the author, 14–16 September 1989.

4 For this study I will provide only the most common form of each rhythmic series, since there are discrepancies between occurrences; some of these are mistakes in the score, as a careful listening to the recording will attest. For example, the first statement of this first series contains the values 16 7 13 12 8, whereas in every other appearance they run 16 7 13 9 11, a difference that could have resulted merely from putting a note head one centimeter too far to the right.

6 Canon: phase I

1 Roger Reynolds, "Inexorable Continuities . . . A Commentary on the Music of Conlon Nancarrow," in *Soundings* 4, p. 26.

2 Charles Amirkhanian, "Interview with Conlon Nancarrow," in *Soundings* 4, p. 13.

3 Quoted from Archibald T. Davison and Willi Apel, *Historical Anthology of Music* (Cambridge, Mass.: Harvard University Press, 1976).

4 For example, the author, not surprisingly after all this analysis, has written a canon for piano and tape at a 23:24 tempo ratio, entitled *The Convent at Tepoztlan (Homage to Nancarrow)*.

5 This A♭ is omitted in the lowest voice.

6 Coincidentally, Ligeti wrote a two-piano piece in 1976, *Monument*, based on the superimposition of similar number series: e.g., 16 17 18 17 16 15 14 15. . . and 10 11 12 11 10 9 8 9. . . . Yet Ligeti knew nothing of Nancarrow's music until 1980. When the two became acquainted, both were surprised at how similar *Monument* sounded to Nancarrow's Study No. 20, but the rhythmic technique is even closer to that of these early canons.

7 Roger Reynolds, "Inexorable Continuities," p. 30.

8 Ibid.

9 Philip Carlsen, *The Player Piano Music of Conlon Nancarrow: An Analysis of Selected Studies*, I.S.A.M. Monograph No. 26 Brooklyn: Institute for Studies in American Music (1988). Carlsen is particularly complete in his analysis of Study No. 19, and the reader is referred to his monograph for further information.

10 Interview with the author, 28–29 September 1988.

11 Or it could be that he made a mistake. He cannot have lengthened the slower voices in order to bring them in earlier, for they enter in the score exactly where they would have had the 9:10:11 ratio been consistent. And, later, pauses between the different melodies are shortened out of proportion in the upper voices to make up for the discrepancy. Nancarrow *could* have accidentally put the 106⅔ tempo, which makes more arithmetical sense in the 10 tempo (it is $\frac{4}{3} \times 80$), into the 11 tempo, and put the 9-voice's 96 tempo in the gap left in the 10-voice. And so on. In any case, the important thing is that the score and recording match, so if the piece was calculated "wrong," it stayed wrong. And perhaps Nancarrow had something else in mind. As he would say, it doesn't matter much. Except to musicologists who lose sleep over it.

12 On the Wergo recording, that is. According to the faster, marked tempos, they should occur every thirty-three seconds.

13 An undated letter from Nancarrow states, "All that I remember about the rhythmic system of the lower 3 staves of No. 44 is that I tried to avoid exact repetition of any pattern. (There would be enough repetition in ten cycles.)"

14 The proportionate notation makes calculation of beats difficult, but the number 790 is borne out well by comparison of the three parts, and by the arithmetic of their vertical alignments.

15 There are minor divergences in pitch between the player piano and orchestral scores. Some of these are reflected in the recording of Study No. 50, others are not.

7 Stretching time: the acceleration studies

1 Carlsen, *The Player Piano Music of Conlon Nancarrow*, p. 35. I have no other source for the information on the original notation.

2 Ibid., p. 40. Carlsen derives these durations by adding consecutive durations, rather arbitrarily chosen, from the 19-series. The derivation I've given strikes me as looking more like Nancarrow's typical thought process, and the measurements seem to work out better.

3 Ibid., p. 42. Carlsen states that the repeated pattern is irregular; he seems either to have mismeasured, or not to have averaged out various appearances of the isorhythm in Nancarrow's imperfect notation.

4   The octave B at system 86 seems added out of nowhere to lengthen the line.

5   The first note in the lowest voice is notated as 75mm, that in the highest as 73mm, but the mathematics convinces me that identical opening tempos were intended.

6   Carlsen, *The Player Piano Music of Conlon Nancarrow*, p. 47.

7   Ibid., p. 49.

8   Ibid., pp. 52–54. Carlsen hypothesized, and proved to his own satisfaction, that Nancarrow had chosen pitches in this section by drawing lines through the beginnings and endpoints of previous notes and putting new notes where they converged. Nancarrow denies that he ever did such a thing, or that he ever let the visual appearance of the roll influence a musical decision. Indeed, it strikes me that such a non-musical strategy would be foreign to his thinking.

9   Reynolds, "Interviews in Mexico City and San Francisco," p. 9.

10 Tenney and Jan Jarvlepp both mistook this for an eight-voice canon in their respective Nancarrow articles: "Conlon Nancarrow's Studies for Player Piano," p. 58; "Conlon Nancarrow's *Study No. 27 for Player Piano* Viewed Analytically," *Perspectives of New Music* 23/1–2 [Fall–Winter 1983/Spring 1984], p. 221). Jarvlepp made many such mistakes from an apparent failure to look closely at the score. For instance, he assumed that the clock line in systems 99–104 used only its highest and lowest notes because Nancarrow left out the middle ones; in fact, the first few octaves contain all five notes followed by the marking "sim.," to show that they were to continue. And Jarvlepp's note that the clock line's pitches – D♯ E F G♭ – are a permutated transposition of the B A C H motive seems a trivial point.

11 Tempos in this study are calculated according to the marked tempo in the score, not according to the recordings, which are considerably faster. However, for ease of analytical listening, the length in seconds of each section is marked according to the recording. In general, measurements in this study necessarily consist more of approximations and averages than usual because of the score's imprecision.

12 Rather than 21:26:30, the triads, dyads, and single notes repeat at ratios close to 5:6:7, which may have been intended.

13 Interview with the author, 28–29 September 1988.

8 Beyond counterpoint: the sound-mass canons

1   Studies Nos. 15 and 17 contain short passages with two voices at the same tempo, but these result from overlapping passages in a simple canonic structure, not a rule-breaking shift to a 1:1 canon.

2   For a striking example, listen to Tatum's Capitol recording of *Willow Weep for Me*. I'm grateful to William Hogeland for drawing my attention to this connection.

3   Reynolds, "Interviews in Mexico City and San Francisco," p. 18.

4   *Die Reihe*, 3 (Vienna: Universal Edition, 1957).

5   Interview with the author, 14–16 September 1989.

6   Nancarrow occasionally drops a beat or two in duration from the final note, so that the number of notes times the beat length does not always equal the number of beats in each section.

7 One of Nancarrow's manuscripts is a complete version of No. 48a recopied a perfect fifth higher. Is it possible that Study No. 48 was originally intended to have a two-movement form more similar to No. 40 than to No. 41? The fifth-higher version is marked No. 39b (No. 48 was originally Study No. 39), and it appears as though Nancarrow intended No. 48a to be played through a second time against a transposed version of itself, as happens in No. 40 (except that No. 40b was untransposed). Perhaps the form was later recast to include a contrasting second movement. There is also, however, a final score numbered No. 39 which is identical to the final score of No. 48.

9 Synthesizing a language

1 Carlsen, *The Player-Piano Music of Conlon Nancarrow*, p. 55.
2 Interview with the author, 14–16 September 1989.
3 Some readers may not be conversant in twelve-tone terminology. The original form of the row is called P0, P standing for prime. P4 is the transposition of the row four semitones upward, P7 the transposition seven semitones upward, and so on. R denotes retrograde, the row read from right to left. I denotes inversion, the row upside-down, read on the matrix from top to bottom. RI means retrograde inversion, the row read on the matrix from bottom to top. I0 is the left-most column in the matrix. I5 is its transposition five semitones upward, and so on.
4 One exception: the fifth note of P3 is the *third* note from the bottom. These things happen.
5 The first arpeggio contains twenty notes, imposing a C in the E♭ triad, which I assume is a mistake.
6 Carlsen, *The Player-Piano Music of Conlon Nancarrow*, p. 63.
7 Ibid., p. 56.
8 The notated length of the final four 6/8 measures equals that of the 6/8 measures in the *fastest* voice, not the slowest one. It seems more likely that Nancarrow drew the score correctly and then absent-mindedly wrote the wrong tempo than that he misdrew the score in the first place. It isn't his style to slow down at a convergent ending.
9 Carlsen, *The Player-Piano Music of Conlon Nancarrow*, p. 55.
10 Nancarrow has no plans to record the discarded movement on the Wergo project, nor has he written out a final score, but he did play it for me. The slowest of the movements except for No. 45b, lasting about 3:20, it alternates two melodic voices over a quirky accompaniment of bass staccato notes, then falls into a chant-like melody similar to that of No. 47 and possibly related to it, over triads at a contrasting tempo. Markings on the piano roll reveal that it is the only movement to use the "spastic rhythm" (see analysis of No. 45a) in counterpoint with itself at different tempos. Its charm recommends it for ultimate inclusion in Nancarrow's complete works.
11 Interview with the author, 14–16 September 1989.
12 At the end of section 6 in the score three notes are dropped from the *color* (though not from the *talea*), presumably by mistake.

13 Warning for those able to obtain this score: in the final copy Nancarrow has inadvertently omitted system 23. I have numbered the systems as they would appear had that one been included.

14 The intended ratio could have been 10:12:15. Measurements conflict.

15 The score contains minor divergences from these patterns.

16 For his liner notes to the Wergo recording, Tenney correctly assessed this tempo ratio by ear. Good ear.

10 After the player piano

1 Interview with the author, 28–29 September 1988.

2 The timings given for *Tango?* are from Ursula Oppens' recording on the Music & Arts label. However, the player-piano version on Wergo is almost precisely the same length, the timings never varying from Oppens by more than two seconds. The Ensemble Modern's recording on RCA Victor (for which, unbelievably, the pianist is not identified), is $\frac{12}{11}$ as long, so about nine per cent should be added to each timing for that version.

3 The Ensemble Modern's recording on RCA Victor is only thirteen seconds longer than Continuum's, so the timings are pretty close.

4 Interview with the author, 28–29 September 1988.

5 The author was present at the American première, and reviewed it in the *Village Voice* of 4 April 1989.

6 The numbers fail to come out exactly proportionate because of an ambiguity in the length of the final glissando, which according to the score lasts a quarter note in the first violin and a dotted quarter in the other parts.

Discography

Complete Studies for Player Piano, Vols. 1 and 2 (Nos. 3, 4, 5, 6, 14, 20, 22, 26, 31, 32, 35, 37, 40, 41, 44, and *Tango?*). Wergo WER 60166/67–50 (released 1991)

Complete Studies for Player Piano, Vols. 3 and 4 (Nos. 1, 2a, 2b, 7, 8, 9, 10, 11, 12, 13, 15, 16, 17, 18, 19, 21, 23, 24, 25, 27, 28, 29, 33, 34, 36, 43, 46, 47, 50). Wergo WER 60166/67–50 (released 1990)

Complete Studies for Player Piano, Vol. 5 (Nos. 42, 45, 48, 49). Wergo WER 60165–50 (released 1989)

Complete Studies for Player Piano, Vol. 1 (Nos. 3, 20, 41). 1750 Arch S–1768 (released 1977)

Complete Studies for Player Piano, Vol. 2 (Nos. 4, 5, 6, 14, 22, 26, 31, 32, 35, 37, 40). 1750 Arch S–1777 (released 1979)

Complete Studies for Player Piano, Vol. 3 (Sonatina, Studies Nos. 1, 2, 7, 8, 10, 15, 21, 23, 24, 25, 33). 1750 Arch S–1786 (released 1981)

Complete Studies for Player Piano, Vol. 4 (Nos. 9, 11, 12, 13, 16, 17, 18, 19, 27, 28, 29, 34, 36). 1750 Arch S–1798 (released 1984)

Studies Nos. 1, 27, 36. (*Sound Forms for Piano: Experimental Music by Henry Cowell, John Cage, Ben Johnston, and Conlon Nancarrow.*) New World NW 203 (released 1976)

Studies for Player Piano (Nos. 2, 7, 8, 10, 12, 15, 19, 21, 23, 24, 25, 33). Columbia MS 7222 (released 1969; deleted 1973)

Studies (Studies for Player Piano Nos. 5, 2, 1, 6, 7, 3c, 9, 14, 12, 18, and 19 arranged by Yvar Mikhashoff; *Tango?*, Toccata, Piece No. 2 for Small Orchestra, Trio No. 1, Sarabande and Scherzo). Ensemble Modern, conducted by Ingo Metzmacher. RCA Victor 09026–61180–2 (released 1993)

String Quartet No. 1. Kronos Quartet. Nonesuch 79111–2 (released 1986)

Tango? (1983). Ursula Oppens, piano. Music & Arts CD–604 (released 1989)

String Quartet No. 3. Arditti Quartet. Gramavision R2 79440 (released 1990)

Piece for Small Orchestra No. 1; Toccata for Violin and Player Piano; Prelude and *Blues*; Study No. 15 (transcribed for piano four hands by Yvar Mikhashoff); *Tango?*; Sonatina; Trio for Clarinet, Bassoon, and Piano (first movement); String Quartet No. 1; Piece for Small Orchestra No. 2. Continuum Ensemble. Musicmasters 7068–2–C (released 1991)

Select Bibliography

Amirkhanian, Charles. "Interview with Composer Conlon Nancarrow," in *Conlon Nancarrow, Selected Studies for Player Piano, Soundings* 4, ed. Peter Garland, pp. 7–24. Berkeley: Soundings Press, 1977

Carlsen, Philip. "Nancarrow, Conlon," in *The New Grove Dictionary of American Music*, ed. H. Wiley Hitchcock and Stanley Sadie. London: Macmillan Press; New York: Grove's Dictionaries of Music, 1986

The Player-Piano Music of Conlon Nancarrow: an Analysis of Selected Studies. I.S.A.M. Monograph No. 26. Brooklyn: Institute for Studies in American Music, 1988

Carter, Elliott. "The Rhythmic Basis of American Music," *The Score and I.M.A. Magazine* 12 (June 1955), pp. 27–32

Commenday, Robert. "The Man Who Writes for Player Piano," *San Francisco Chronicle*, 30 June 1981

Furst-Heidtmann, Monika. "Conlon Nancarrow und die Emanzipation des Tempos," *Neue Zeitschrift für Musik* 7/8 (1989), pp. 32–38

"Conlon Nancarrow's 'Studies for Player Piano'/Time is the last frontier in music," *Melos* 4/1984, pp. 104–22.

"Ich bin beim Komponieren nur meinen Wunschen gefolgt" (interview with Conlon Nancarrow), *Musik Texte* 21 (October 1987), pp. 29–32.

Gagne, Cole, and Tracy Caras. "Conlon Nancarrow," in *Soundpieces: Interviews with American Composers*, pp. 281–303. Metuchen, NJ: Scarecrow Press, 1982

Gann, Kyle. "Conlon Nancarrow's Tempo Tornadoes," *Village Voice*, New York (5 October 1993), pp. 93 and 97

"A Feast of 16 Strings," *Village Voice*, New York (4 April 1989), p. 71

"Private Bells," *Village Voice*, New York (14 November 1989), p. 89

Garland, Peter. "Conlon Nancarrow: Chronicle of a Friendship," in *Americas: Essays on American Music and Culture (1973–80)*, pp. 157–85. Santa Fe: Soundings Press, 1982

Henck, Herbert, and Monika Furst-Heidtmann. "Neues von Nancarrow," *Neuland* 2 (1981/2), pp. 216–17

"Neues von Nancarrow," *Neuland* 3 (1983), pp. 247–50

"Neues von Nancarrow," *Neuland* 5 (1985), pp. 297–301

Jarvlepp, Jan. "Conlon Nancarrow's Study #27 for Player Piano Viewed Analytically," *Perspectives of New Music* 23/1–2 (Fall-Winter 1983/Spring-Summer 1984), pp. 218–22

LaBarbara, Joan. "The Remarkable Art of Conlon Nancarrow," *Musical America* (May 1984), pp. 12–13

Lederman, Minna. *The Life and Death of a Small Magazine* (Modern Music, 1926–1946). I.S.A.M. Monograph No. 18. Brooklyn: Institute for Studies in American Music, 1983

Mumma, Gordon. "Briefly About Nancarrow," in *Conlon Nancarrow, Selected Studies for Player Piano, Soundings* 4, ed. Peter Garland, pp. 1–5. Berkeley: Soundings Press, 1977

"Nancarrow Notes," in Walter Zimmermann, *Desert Plants*, pp. 247–51. Vancouver: A.R.C. Publications, 1976

Nancarrow, Conlon. "Mexican Music: a Developing Nationalism," *Modern Music* 19/1 (November/December 1941), pp. 67–69

"Over the Air," *Modern Music* 17/1 (November/December 1939), p. 55; 2 (January/February 1940), pp. 115–16; 3 (March/April 1940), pp. 191–93; 4 (May/June 1940), pp. 263–65.

"Unidentified Player-Piano-Roll Composition" (a facsimile of part of the roll to Study No. 23) in John Cage, *Notations*, unpaged. West Glover, Vt: Something Else Press, 1969

Reynolds, Roger. "Conlon Nancarrow: Interviews in Mexico City and San Francisco," *American Music* 2/2 (Summer 1984), pp. 1–24

"Inexorable Continuities . . . : A Commentary on the Music of Conlon Nancarrow," in *Conlon Nancarrow, Selected Studies for Player Piano, Soundings* 4, ed. Peter Garland, pp. 26–40. Berkeley: Soundings Press, 1977

Rockwell, John. "Conlon Nancarrow – Poet of the Player Piano," *The New York Times* (28 June 1981), pp. 17, 20

Rohter, Larry. "Conlon Nancarrow, On a Roll," *New York Times* (25 October 1987), section 2, p. 27

Slonimsky, Nicolas. "Complicated Problem – Drastic Solution," *The Christian Science Monitor*, Boston (10 November 1951), section B, p. 12.

Souster, Tim. "Conlon Nancarrow," *Neuland* 1/3 (1980), pp. 131–33

Tenney, James. "Conlon Nancarrow's Studies for Player Piano," in *Conlon Nancarrow, Selected Studies for Player Piano, Soundings* 4, ed. Peter Garland, pp. 41–64. Berkeley: Soundings Press, 1977

(unsigned), "Nancarrow Prize," *The New York Times* (1 January 1982)

Scores

Sarabande and Scherzo for oboe, bassoon, and piano (1930), Smith Publications

Blues for piano (1935), *New Music* 11/2 (January 1938)

Prelude for piano (1935), *New Music* 11/2 (January 1938)

Toccata for violin and piano (1935), *New Music* 11/2 (January 1938)

Sonatina for piano (1941), C.F. Peters Corporation

Sonatina for piano, four hands (arr. Yvar Mikhashoff), C.F. Peters Corporation

Trio for clarinet, bassoon, and piano (1942), Smith Publications

Piece No. 1 for Small Orchestra (1943), Smith Publications

String Quartet (1945), Smith Publications

Rhythm Study No. 1 for Player Piano, *New Music* 25/1 (October 1951)

Selected Studies for Player Piano (Nos. 8, 19, 23, 27, 31, 35, 36, 40), ed. Peter Garland. Berkeley: Soundings Press, 1977

Study No. 25 for Player Piano, *Soundings* 9 (Summer 1975)

Study No. 41 for Player Piano, Santa Fe: Soundings Press, 1981

Study No. 37 for Player Piano, Santa Fe: Soundings Press, 1982

Study No. 3 for Player Piano, Santa Fe: Soundings Press, 1983

Collected Studies for Player Piano, vol. 5 (Nos. 2, 6, 7, 14, 20, 21, 24, 26, 33), Santa Fe: Soundings Press, 1984

Collected Studies for Player Piano, vol. 6 (Nos. 4, 5, 9, 10, 11, 12, 15, 16, 17, 18), Santa Fe: Soundings Press, 1984

Tango? (1983), Smith Publications

Piece No. 2 for Small Orchestra (1985), Smith Publications

String Quartet No. 3 (1987), Smith Publications

Two Canons for Ursula (1988), Boosey and Hawkes

Index

Lightning Source UK Ltd.
Milton Keynes UK
UKHW030658091021
391542UK00015B/222